GERMAN-ENGLISH
DICTIONARY
OF
MATHEMATICAL SCIENCES

DICTIONARY
OF
MATHEMATICAL
SCIENCES

VOLUME I
GERMAN-ENGLISH

BY

LEO HERLAND, Ph.D.

FREDERICK UNGAR PUBLISHING CO.
NEW YORK

WÖRTERBUCH
DER
MATHEMATISCHEN
WISSENSCHAFTEN

BAND I
DEUTSCH-ENGLISCH

VON

LEO HERLAND, Ph.D.

FREDERICK UNGAR PUBLISHING CO.
NEW YORK

*The statistical entries
incorporated in this dictionary
are by*

GREGOR SEBBA, Ph.D.

*Professor of Economics, Chairman of Statistics,
College of Business Administration
University of Georgia*

The commercial entries are by

ROBERT GROSSBARD, LL.D.

PREFACE

Centering about the major subjects of mathematics and geometry, this volume, the first modern bilingual mathematics dictionary, also covers a number of fields of application, some of them in considerable detail, such as mathematical logic, statistics, and commercial arithmetic; others, such as physics and astronomy, in those concepts most readily accessible to mathematical treatment.

As far as the highly specialized terms of the various branches of mathematics and geometry are concerned, this concise dictionary does not claim completeness, although the aim has been to include all important terms. Nevertheless, any suggestions for additions to the present work, as well as any other suggestions from users of the dictionary, will be highly welcome.

It was necessary to include many words frequently used in daily life in a non-mathematical sense but which still have a technical meaning in mathematics, e.g., *innen, hoch, nach, und,* etc. Only meanings are given that bear reference to mathematics, e.g., *Kegel* cone, but not *Kegel* pin.

Some remarks about the general arrangement and most advantageous use of the volume may be in order.

The components of compound words, as well as prefixes and root words, are set off by dividing dots. Parts of speech and the relation of a verb to its object (as transitive, intransitive, reflexive, reciprocal verb) are given. Separable prefixes of verbs are indicated as such by the abbreviation (*sep.*). In some cases of ambiguity the syllabic stress is pointed out by putting an accent after the stressed syllable (e.g., *um'schreiben, umschrei'ben*).

The numerals from one to ten are treated elaborately and individually in many of their applications and compounds; numbers from ten to twenty only where deviating from the first ten; higher numbers only in special cases, e.g., *einundzwanzig, vierzig, hundert(und)eins,* etc.

Where there are several meanings of a key word, the entry is arranged in divisions with explanatory words in parentheses; often these are abbreviations qualifying the special field to which the meaning belongs. Wherever necessary, model usages showing the application and grammatical construction of the key word are supplied generously, far beyond the measure commonly allotted them in technical dictionaries. Special efforts have been made to put this work on a par with the standard expected from general bilingual dictionaries. The emphasis everywhere is on clarity and distinction.

The cross references, given in unusual completeness (virtually every passage containing the key word in question is listed in the cross references), form an essential constituent of the volume, and the user is invited to use them freely. These cross references often give indispensable model usages and are just as much a part of the entry as the model usages included immediately in the entry.

A bilingual dictionary does not carry encyclopedic definitions, translation being its main purpose. Nevertheless, the explanatory words given here in parentheses in both languages, in conjunction with the model usages accompanying the key words and those referred to in the cross references, will result in a fairly well-rounded picture of the key word.

A word of special appreciation is due several devoted collaborators. The commercial part, compiled by Dr. Robert Grossbard, and the statistical part, the work of Dr. Gregor Sebba, represent major contributions to the dictionary. My gratitude goes also to Dr. Imanuel Marx of the University of Michigan for checking the compiled material, and to Miss Hedy Kempny for the preparation of the final manuscript.

L.H.

VORWORT

Das vorliegende Werk, das erste zweisprachige Mathematische Wörterbuch, legt zwar das Schwergewicht auf die Hauptfächer der Mathematik und Geometrie, behandelt aber auch eine Anzahl von Anwendungsgebieten, und zwar einige, wie mathematische Logik, Statistik und kaufmännisches Rechnen, in größerer Ausführlichkeit, andere, wie Physik und Astronomie, nur in den wichtigsten Ausdrücken, die mathematischer Behandlung leicht zugänglich sind.

Soweit es sich um die hochspezialisierten Begriffe der einzelnen Zweige der Mathematik handelt, erhebt dieses Handwörterbuch nicht den Anspruch auf Vollständigkeit, obwohl es das Ziel war, doch alle wichtigen Ausdrücke einzubeziehen. Immerhin werden alle Vorschläge zur Bereicherung des Wortschatzes sowie auch sonstige Anregungen aus dem Kreise der Benützer des Wörterbuchs willkommen sein.

Es erwies sich als zweckmäßig, auch manche Ausdrücke aufzunehmen, die im täglichen Leben in einem nicht-mathematischen Sinne gebraucht werden, in der Mathematik aber eine fachtechnische Bedeutung haben, wie z.B. *innen*, *hoch*, *noch*, *und*, usw. Nicht angeführt sind Bedeutungen, die zur Mathematik keine Beziehung haben, so z.B. wohl *Kegel* cone, aber nicht *Kegel* pin.

Hier mögen noch einige Bemerkungen über die allgemeine Anwendung und vorteilhafte Benützung dieses Bandes Platz finden.

Bestandteile von zusammengesetzten Wörtern sowie Vorsilben und Wortstämme sind durch Zwischenpunkte abgetrennt. Redeteile sind angegeben, außerdem das Verhältnis des Zeitwortes zu seinem Objekt (als transitives, intransitives, reflexives oder reziprokes Verb). Trennbare Vorsilben von Zeitwörtern sind durch den Vermerk (*sep.*)

kenntlich gemacht. In zweideutigen Fällen wurde auch die Betonung durch einen Akzent nach der betonten Silbe angemerkt (z.B. *um'schreiben, umschrei'ben*).

Die Zahlwörter von eins bis zehn sind einzeln ausführlich in ihren Anwendungen und Zusammensetzungen behandelt, die von zehn bis zwanzig nur dort, wo sie von den ersten zehn abweichen, höhere Zahlen aber nur in speziellen Fällen, so z.B. einundzwanzig, vierzig, hundert-(und)eins usw.

Wo es mehrere Bedeutungen eines Stichworts gibt, ist der Artikel in Unterabteilungen gegliedert, die mit Klammererklärungen versehen sind. Oft bestehen diese in der Angabe des Fachgebiets, dem der betreffende Ausdruck angehört. Wo immer es sich als notwendig erwies, sind Musterbeispiele angeführt, die Anwendung und grammatikalische Konstruktion des Stichworts veranschaulichen, und zwar in einer Reichhaltigkeit, welche das ihnen sonst in Fachwörterbüchern eingeräumte Maß erheblich übersteigt. Überhaupt ist keine Mühe gescheut worden, dieses Buch auf ein solches Niveau zu bringen, wie es sonst wohl nur von allgemeinen Wörterbüchern erwartet werden darf. Überall wurde in erster Linie auf Klarheit und Deutlichkeit Nachdruck gelegt.

Die den Stichwörtern in ungewöhnlicher Vollständigkeit beigegebenen Hinweisvermerke (prinzipiell wird auf alle Stellen des Buches verwiesen, wo das betreffende Stichwort vorkommt) stellen einen wesentlichen Bestandteil des Bandes dar. Diese Hinweise, von denen der Benützer reichlichen Gebrauch machen möge und die ihm unentbehrliche Musterbeispiele an die Hand geben, bilden ebenso sehr einen Bestandteil des Stichwortartikels wie die in diesem unmittelbar enthaltenen Musterbeispiele.

Ein zweisprachiges Wörterbuch befaßt sich nicht mit Definitionen seiner Stichwörter nach Art eines Lexikons, da sein Hauptzweck das Übersetzen ist. Dennoch sollten die in beiden Sprachen gegebenen Klammererklärungen mit den im Artikel selbst enthaltenen und den in den Hinweisen erfaßten Musterbeispielen zusammen ein ziemlich abgerundetes Bild des Stichwortes ergeben.

Einigen eifrigen Mitarbeitern gebührt ein besonderes Dankeswort. Der von Dr. Gregor Sebba zusammengestellte statistische Teil und die von Dr. Robert Grossbard beigesteuerten Ausdrücke des kaufmännischen Rechnens stellen wesentliche Beiträge zu diesem Wörterbuch dar. Ich bin auch Dr. Imanuel Marx (Universität von Michigan) für die kritische Durchsicht des Materials und Frl. Hedy Kempny für die Fertigstellung des Manuskripts zu großem Dank verpflichtet.

L.H.

ABBREVIATIONS

abbr.	abbreviation	*It.*	Italian
acc.	accusative	*Lat.*	Latin
acoust.	acoustics	*log.*	logic
adj.	adjective	*m*	masculine
adv.	adverb	*mach.*	machinery
alg.	algebra	*mag.*	magnetism
Am.	American English	*math.*	mathematics
ant.	antonym	*meas.*	measure
arch.	architecture	*mech.*	mechanics.
astr.	astronomy	*meteor.*	meteorology
aux.	auxiliary	*mil.*	military
av.	aviation	*n*	neuter
ball.	ballistics	*N.*	proper name
Br.	British English	*nav.*	navigation
card.	cardinal	*num.*	numeral
cart.	cartography	*obj.*	object
cf.	confer	*opt.*	optics
chem.	chemistry	*ord.*	ordinal
cj.	conjunction	*pers.*	person
coll.	colloquial	*phys.*	physics
comm.	commerce	*pl.*	plural
comp.	comparitive	*p.p.*	past participle
cryst.	crystallography	*pref.*	prefix
cub.	cubic	*prep.*	preposition
dat.	dative	*pres.*	present
descr.	descriptive	*r.*	reflexive
dir.	direct	*rad.*	radio
elec.	electricity	*recip.*	reciprocal
engin.	engineering	*sep.*	separable
f	feminine	*sing.*	singular
fin.	finance	*sq.*	square
Fr.	French	*statist.*	statistics
gen.	genitive	*suf.*	suffix
geog.	geography	*sup.*	superlative
geol.	geology	*symb.*	symbol
geom.	geometry	*t.*	transitive
i.	intransitive	*usu.*	usually
ins.	insurance	*v.*	verb

A

A 1 (= *A eins*) *adj.* (*fin.*) (*Wertpapiere*) A1 (= A one), first grade, gilt-edged (securities)

ab *adv.* off, deduct(ed): *vier und fünf ist neun; drei ab, bleibt sechs* four and five is nine; deduct three, gives six; *ab an Regien* deduct expenses, expenses deducted; *zehn Mark auf oder ab* ten marks more or less

Abakus *m* (*pl. Abakus*) abacus [= RECHENBRETT; RECHENMASCHINE]

ab·ändern (*sep.*) *v.t.* change, alter, vary, modify

Ab·änderung *f* change, alteration, variation, modification

Ab·bild *n* image, map

ab·bilden (*sep.*) **1.** *v.t.* map; (*projizieren*) project: *eine Menge auf eine andere a.* map one set upon another. **2.** *v.r.*: *sich a.* be mapped; (*sich projizieren*) project

Ab·bildung *f* (*das Abbilden*) map, mapping; (*Abbild*) image; (*Projektion*) projection. [*cf.* EINDEUTIG; EINEINDEUTIG; ERHALTEN; FLÄCHENTREU; FLÄCHENTREUE; INVERS; LÄNGENTREUE; STETIG; ÜBERGEHEN; WINKELTREU; WINKELTREUE]

ab·brechen (*sep.*) *v.t.*, *v.i.* break off, stop short: *die Entwicklung bricht nach einer endlichen Anzahl von Schritten ab* the development breaks off after a finite number of steps; *wir können den Dezimalbruch an beliebiger Stelle a.* we can break off the decimal fraction at any point

Abel *m* N. [*cf.* ABELSCH]

abelsch *adj.* Abelian; (*kommutativ*) commutative: *abelsche Gruppe* Abelian (or commutative) group; *abelsche Identität* Abelian identity

Aberration *f* aberration

Ab·fall *m* (*der Neigung*) slant, dip; (*der Größe*) decrease

ab·fallen (*sep.*) *v.i.* **1.** (*sich neigen*) slant away, incline, decline, dip, slope down: *das Dach fällt steil ab* the roof inclines (or slopes down) sharply. **2.** (*abnehmen*) decrease: *die Geschwindigkeit fällt stark ab* the speed decreases sharply

ab·flachen 1. *v.t.* flatten, level off. **2.** *v.r.* *sich a.* level off, become level (or flat)

Ab·flachung *f* flattening; (*der Häufigkeitskurve*) platykurtosis (of the frequency curve)

Ab·gabe *f* (*comm., fin.*) duty, tax [*cf.* ZOLL]

ab·geflacht *adj.* flattened, oblate; (*Häufigkeitskurve*) platykurtic (frequency curve)

ab·gehen *v.i.* be deducted *davon gehen die Spesen ab* from this expenses have to be deducted

ab·gekürzt *adj.* abridged, short: *abgekürzte Division, Multiplika-*

tion short (or abridged) division, multiplication; *abgekürztes Verfahren* short method, shortcut [*cf.* SCHREIBUNG]

ab·geleitet *adj.* derived (by differentiation); *abgeleitete Funktion* derived function, derivative; *abgeleitete Menge* derived set [*cf.* ABLEITEN]

ab·geplattet *adj.* oblate, flattened; (*Häufigkeitskurve*) platykurtic (frequency curve)[*cf.* ROTATIONS-ELLIPSOID]

ab·geschlossen *adj.* closed: *eine abgeschlossene Menge enthält alle ihre Randpunkte* a closed set contains all its boundary points ; *abgeschlossene Hülle einer Menge* closure of a set [*cf.* ABSCHLIESSEN ; ALGEBRAISCH-ABGESCHLOSSEN; INTERVALL]

Ab·geschlossenheit *f* closure: *ganze A. eines Integritätsbereichs* integral closure of a domain of integrity (or: of an integral domain)

ab·gestumpft *adj.* truncated [*cf.* PYRAMIDE]

ab·gestutzt *adj.* truncated [*cf.* KEGEL; PYRAMIDE]

ab·grenzen *v.t.* **1.** (*begrenzen*) bound, delimit, demarcate, mark off. **2.** (*begrifflich* logically) define (the limits): *ein wohl abgegrenztes Gebiet* a well-defined region

Ab·grenzung *f* boundary, delimitation, demarkation

ab·hängig *adj.* dependent: *von einander abhängige Funktionen* dependent (or interdependent) functions [*cf.* LINEAR; VARIABLE]

Ab·hängigkeit *f* dependence; (*sta-*

tist.) association: *funktionale* (or *funktionelle*) *A.* functional dependence; *gegenseitige* (*oder wechselseitige*) *A.* interdependence, correlation; (*statist.*) *A. artmäßiger Merkmale* association of (qualitative) attributes; *A. zahlenmäßiger Merkmale* association of quantitative attributes, correlation [*cf.* AUSTAUSCHSATZ]

ab·heben (*sep.*) *v.t.* (*Geld*) draw (money): *ein Guthaben vom Konto a.* withdraw a deposit from one's account [*cf.* A CONTO]

Ab·hebung *f* (*von Geld im allg.*) drawing (of money); (*von Spareinlagen*) withdrawal (of savings deposits)

ab·kürzen (*sep.*) *v.t.* **1.** (*ein Verfahren*) abridge, shorten (a procedure). **2.** (*eine Bezeichnung*) abbreviate (a notation) [*cf.* ABGEKÜRZT]

Ab·kürzung *f* abridgment, shortening; abbreviation [*cf.* ABKÜRZEN]

Ab·lauf *m* course, sequence, passage [*cf.* GESETZLICH]

ab·laufen (*sep.*) *v.i.* pass, run

Ablebens·versicherung *f* straight life insurance [*cf.* VERSICHERUNG]

ableit·bar *adj.* deducible

Ableitbar·keit *f* deducibility

ab·leiten (*sep.*) *v.t.* **1.** (*eine Folgerung* a conclusion)deduce, derive: *eine Formel a.* derive a formula. **2.** (*differenzieren*) differentiate: *eine Funktion a.* differentiate a function [*cf.* ABGELEITET]

Ab·leitung *f* **1.** (*log.*) (*durch Schluß* by deduction) derivation [*cf.* STRENG]. **2.** (*Differentiation*) derrivation, differentiation: *durch A. erhalten wir* by derivation we obtain. **3.** (*Differentialquotient*) derivative, differential quotient: *erste, zweite A. einer Funktion* first, second derivative of a function; *partielle* (*totale*) *A.* partial (total) derivative; *A. nach x* derivative with respect to *x* [*cf.* ORDNUNG; STRICH; ZEITLICH]

ab·lenken (*sep.*) *v.t.* deflect, divert

Ab·lenkung *f* deflection, diversion

ab·lesen (*sep.*) *v.t.* read (off) [*cf.* FIGUR]

Ab·lesung *f* reading

ab·lösen (*sep.*) *v.t.* (*comm.*) **1.** (*rückkaufen, z.B.eine Polizze*) redeem, buy off (e.g. a policy). **2.** (*einen Anspruch im Vergleichswege*) settle (a claim) by compromise

Ab·lösung *f* (*comm.*) **1.** (*Rückkauf*) redemption. **2.** (*Vergleich*) composition [*cf.* ABLÖSEN]

Ablösungs·fonds *m.* (*fin.*) sinking fund; (*für Rückzahlungen*) redemption fund

Ablösungs·summe *f* (*comm.*) **1.** redemption amount. **2.** composition amount [*cf.* ABLÖSEN; ABLÖSUNG]

Ablösungs·zahlung *f* (*comm.*) **1.** redemption payment. **2.** composition payment [*cf.* ABLÖSEN; ABLÖSUNG]

ab·messen (*sep.*) *v.t.* measure (off)

Ab·messung *f* **1.** (*Messung*) measuring (off), measurement. **2.** (*Dimension*) dimension [*cf.* DIMENSION; LÄNGE]

Ab·nahme *f* decrease, decrement

ab·nehmen (*sep.*) *v.i.* decrease: *ab-*

nehmende Folge decreasing sequence [*cf.* MONOTON; ABFALLEN]

ab·pausen (*sep.*) *v.t.* trace

ab·platten (*sep.*) *v.t.* flatten [*cf.* ABGEPLATTET]

Ab·plattung *f* **1.** (*eines Sphäroids*) oblateness (of an ellipsoid), flattening (of an oblate spheroid); (*Betrag der A.* amount of flattening) ellipticity: *die A. der Erde beträgt ungefähr* $\frac{1}{300}$ the ellipticity of the earth is approximately $\frac{1}{300}$. **2.** (*statist.*) (*der Häufigkeitskurve*) platykurtosis (of the frequency curve)

ab·rechnen (*sep.*) **1.** *v.t.* (*abziehen*) deduct; (*comm.: Abzug gewähren*) allow, make allowance for. **2.** *v.i.* (*comm.*) settle (accounts) [*cf.* VERRECHNEN]

Ab·rechnung *f* (*Abzug*) deduction; (*comm.*, auch) allowance; (*zu bezahlende Rechnung*) bill, statement; (*Kontenausgleich*) settlement of accounts; (*im Bankenverkehr*) clearing

Abrechnungs·stelle *f* (*fin.*) clearing house

Abrechnungs·verfahren *n* (*zwischen Banken*) clearing (between banks)

ab·runden (*sep.*) *v.t.* **1.** (*eine Zahl*) round (off) (*a number*); *nach oben a.* [= AUFRUNDEN]. **2.** (*eine Kurve*) smooth (a curve)

Ab·rundung *f* (*einer Zahl*) rounding (off)(of)(a number); (*einer Kurve*) smoothing (of) (a curve) [*cf.* AUSGLEICHUNG; RECHENFEHLER]

Abrundungs·fehler *m.* rounding error, error in rounding off

ab·schätzen (*sep.*) *v.t.* estimate, appraise; (*genauer* more accurately) evaluate; (*nach dem Steuerwert*) assess (for taxable value)

Ab·schätzung *f* estimate, appraisal; evaluation; assessment [*cf.* AB-SCHÄTZEN]

Ab·schlag *m* (*comm.*, *fin.*) **1.** (*im Preis*) reduction, decline . (of price); (*Disagio*) disagio, loss (on exchange) [*ant.:* AUFSCHLAG]. **2.** (*Rate*) installment

ab·schlagen (*sep.*) (*comm.*) **1.** *v.t.* (*z.B.* 50 *Pfennig*) allow a reduction of (e.g. 50 pfennigs) [*ant.:* AUFSCHLAGEN]: *etwas vom Preis a.* allow a reduction from the price. **2.** *v.i.* decline: *die Kurse haben abgeschlagen* prices (or quotations) have declined

Abschlags·dividende *f* (*fin.*) interim dividend

ab·schließen (*sep.*) *v.t.* close, termihate: (*comm.*) *die Kosten* (*oder Bücher*) *a.* close (or balance) the accounts [*cf.* ABGESCHLOSSEN]

Ab·schließung *f* termination

Ab·schluß *m* (*comm.*) (*der Konten oder Bücher*) balancing (of accounts)

Abschluß·bilanz *f* (*comm.*) closing balance

Abschluß·kurs *m* (*fin.*) quotation (or rate, or price) agreed upon

ab·schneiden (*sep.*) *v.t.* cut off, intercept, subtend: *die Schenkel eines Zentriwinkels schneiden einen Bogen auf dem Kreisumfang ab* the sides of a central angle cut off (or intercept, or subtend) an arc on the circumference of a circle; *schief abgeschnittener Zylinder*(*stutz*), *Kegel*(*stutz*) ungula

of a cylinder, cone

Ab·schneidung *f* interception, cutting off

Ab·schnitt *m* section, segment, intercept: *A. auf der x-Achse* x-intercept; *A. der Zahlenreihe* segment of a set of integers; *A. eines Kreises* segment of a circle [*cf.* GOLDEN; GRAPHISCH]

ab·schreiben (*sep.*) *v.t.* (*comm.*) **1.** (*abziehen*) deduct: *5 Schilling von der Rechnung a.* deduct 5 schillings from the bill. **2.** (*streichen*) write off: *zweifelhafte Außenstände a.* write off a bad debt. **3.** (*den Wert heruntersetzen*) depreciate: *wir schreiben 10 % des Maschinenwertes ab* we depreciate the machinery by 10 % [*cf.* AMORTISIEREN]

Ab·schreibung *f* **1.** (*Abzug*) deduction. **2.** (*Streichung*) writing off. **3.** (*Wertverminderung*) depreciation [*cf.* AMORTISIERUNG]. [*cf.* ABSCHREIBEN]

Abschreibungs·reserve, *f* (*comm. fin.*) depreciation reserve (or fund)

Ab·sender *m* (*comm.*) sender; (*von Waren*) consignor (of goods) [*cf.* PORTOFREI; PORTOSPESEN]

ab·solut *adj.* absolute: *absolute Konstante* absolute constant; *absoluter Wert einer algebraischen Zahl* absolute value of an algebraic number [*cf.* KOMPLEX]; *absolute* (*oder unbenannte*) *Zahl* absolute (or abstract) number; *a. ganze algebraische Funktion* absolutely integral algebraic function [*cf.* BETRAG; FEHLER; MASSSYSTEM; NULLPUNKT]

Absolut·glied *n* absolute term

Absolut·striche *mpl.* absolute value sign

Absolut·wert *m* absolute value

Absorptions·linie *f* (*phys.*) absorption line

Absorptions·spektrum *n* absorption spectrum

Ab·stand *m* distance: *A. einer Geraden von einem Punkt* distance from a line to a point; *von gleichem A.* equidistant [*cf.* PUNKT ; SCHEINBAR]

ab·stecken (*sep.*) *v.t.* lay out, mark out, plot out, set out: *einen rechten Winkel a.* lay (or set) out a right angle

ab·stehen (*sep.*) *v.i.* (*von*) be distant (from), have a distance (from): *ein Punkt steht 5 cm von einer Geraden ab* a point has a distance of 5 cm. from a straight line; *gleich weit abstehend* equidistant, equally distant [*cf.* ORT]

ab·steigen (*sep.*) *v.i.* descend [*cf.* KNOTEN 3.; POTENZ; POTENZREIHE]

Ab·steigung *f:* (*astr.*) *gerade A.* right ascension [= *gerade* AUFSTEIGUNG]

ab·stoßen (*sep.*) *v.t.* repel

Ab·stoßung *f* repulsion

Abstoßungskraft *f* repulsive force

abstrakt *adj.* abstract: *abstrakte* (*oder unbenannte*) *Zahl* abstract number; *abstrakter Begriff* abstract concept

ab·streichen (*sep.*) *v.t.* **1.** (*wegstreichen*) discard, reject, strike out, cross out: *die letzten zwei Dezimalen a.* discard (or reject) the last two decimals. **2.** (*anstreichen*) check off: *Stichwörter*

im Register a. check off key words in the index

ab·stumpfen (*sep.*) *v.t.* truncate [*cf.* ABGESTUMPFT]

ab·stutzen *v.t* truncate [*cf.* ABGESTUTZT]

absurd *adj.* absurd

Absurdität *f* absurdity

absurdum [*cf.* FÜHREN]

Abszisse *f* abscissa

Abszissen·achse *f* axis of abscissas [*cf.* EINTEILUNG]

Abszissen·differenz *f* (*zweier Punkte*) run (between two points)

ab·teilen (*sep.*) *v.t.* (*teilen*) divide; (*absondern*) separate

Ab·teilung *f* division

ab·tragen (*sep.*) *v.t.* mark off, lay off, measure off: *auf einem Kreis gleiche Bogenlängen a.* mark off along a circle (intersecting) arcs with the same arc length

Ab·tragung *f* (*einer Strecke, eines Winkels*) marking off, laying off, measuring off (a distance, an angle)

abundant *adj.* (*Zahl*) redundant, abundant (number)

ab·wärts *adj.* downward(s), down [*cf.* NACH]

ab·wechseln (*sep.*) *v.i.* alternate

Ab·wechslung *f* alternation

ab·weichen (*sep.*) *v.i.* deviate, differ

Ab·weichung *f* deviation, variance; (*vom Meridian* from the meridian) bearing; (*statist.*) *mittlere A.* average deviation; *mittlere quadratische A.* standard (or mean square) deviation [*cf.* SCHWANKUNGSMASS ; VARIABILITÄTSINDEX] ; *Quadrat der mittleren*

quadratischen A. variance [*cf.*
STREUUNG]
ab·werten (*sep.*) *v.t.* (*fin.*) depreciate
Ab·wertung *f* depreciation
abwickel·bar *adj.* developable:
abwickelbare Fläche developable
(surface) [*cf.* SCHRAUBENFLÄCHE]
Abwickelbar·keit *f* developability
ab·wickeln (*sep.*) *v.t.* unroll, develop, unwind: *eine Fläche a.*
develop (or unroll) a surface; *die
Evolvente* (*von*) *einer Kurve a.*
unwind the involute of (or off) a
curve
Ab·wicklung *f* (*einer Fläche*) development (of a surface); (*einer
Kurve*) unwinding (a curve)
abzähl·bar *adj.* countable, denu-
merable, enumerable: *a. unendliche Menge* countably (or de-
numerably, or enumerably) infinite set; *nicht a.* non-denumer-
able, uncountable
Abzählbar·keit *f* (*einer Menge*)
countability, denumerability,
enumerability (of a set)
ab·zahlen (*sep.*) *v.t.* (*comm.*) pay off
ab·zählen *v.t.* count, denumerate
Ab·zahlung *f* (*comm.*) **1.** (*Tilgung*)
payment off. **2.** (*Teilzahlung*)
partial payment; (*Rate*) installment: *auf A. kaufen* buy on the
installment plan
Ab·zählung *f* count(ing), denumer-
ation
Abzahlungs·geschäft *n* (*Betriebs-
form*) installment business; (*abgeschlossenes Geschäft*) purchase
on the installment plan, hire
purchase; (*Kaufhaus*) (department) store selling on the install-

ment plan [= RATENGESCHÄFT]
Abzahlungs·system *n* (*comm.*) installment plan
ab·ziehen (*sep.*) *v.t.* deduct, subtract; (*comm., auch*) allow
Ab·zug *m.* deduction; (*comm.,
auch*) allowance [*cf.* ABRECHNEN;
ABRECHNUNG]
ab·züglich *prep.* (*gen.*) (*z.B.der
Spesen*) less, deducting (e.g. expenses)
a.c. (*abbr.*) [= A CONTO]
Achse *f* **1.** (*geom.*) (*Mittellinie*)
axis; (*Projektionsachse*) reference
line (of projection): *A. eines
Zylinders* axis of a cylinder;
imaginäre A. imaginary axis, axis
of imaginaries; *reelle A.* real axis,
axis of reals; *große* (*kleine*) *A.
einer Ellipse* major (minor) axis
of an ellipse; *reelle* (*imaginäre*) *A.
einer Hyperbel* transverse (conjugate) axis of a hyperbola. [*cf*
ACHSENSCHNITT; DREHEN; DRE-
HUNG; ELLIPSE; HALBACHSE;
HYPERBEL; LOGARITHMENPAPIER;
MITTEL; RECHTS-LINKS; SENK-
RECHT; SPIEGLUNG; TRÄGER;
UMKLAPPEN; VORN-HINTEN]. **2.**
(*engin.*) axle
Achsen·abschnitt *m* (*einer Geraden*)
intercept (of a straight line) on an
axis of coordinates [*cf.* ACHSEN-
SCHNITT]
Achsen·drehung *f* rotation, rota-
tory motion, revolution (about
an axis)
Achsen·dreibein *n* trihedral of the
coordinate axes
Achsen·kreuz *n* (graph formed by)
the two coordinate axes (in the
plane)

Achsen·schnitt *m* **1.** (*Schnitt durch die Achse*) section through the axis, meridional section. **2.** (*Achsenabschnitt*) intercept (of a straight line) on an axis of coordinates

Achsen·schnittform *f* (*der Gleichung einer Geraden, Ebene*) intercept form (of the equation of a straight line, plane)

Achsen·symmetrie *f* axial symmetry

achsen·symmetrisch *adj.* axially symmetric(al)

. . achsig *adj. suf.* . . axial [*cf.* DREIACHSIG; EINACHSIG; ZWEI-ACHSIG]

acht *card.num.* eight

acht. *ord.num.* eighth: *der achte Teil* the eighth part

Acht *f* (*Zahl, Ziffer*) (number, figure) eight: *eine A. schreiben* write a figure eight

Acht·eck *n* octagon

Achtel *n* eighth (part)

Achtel·kreis *m* octant (of a circle)

Achtel·kugel *f* octant (of a sphere)

Achtel·meile *f* furlong

achtens *adv.* eighthly, in the eighth place

Achter *m* (figure) eight

Achter·kurve *f* eight curve

acht·fach *adj.* eightfold

acht·fältig *adj.* eightfold

Acht·flach *n* octahedron [= OK-TAEDER]

acht·flächig *adj.* octahedral

Acht·flächner *m* octahedron [= OKTAEDER]

acht·hundert *card. num.* eight hundred

acht·mal *num.* eight times

acht·malig *adj.* (done) eight times [*cf.* DREIMALIG]

acht·seitig *adj.* eight-sided; (*Prisma, Pyramide*) octagonal (prism, pyramid)

acht·zählig *adj.* eightfold, octuple; (*Symmetrie, auch*) octagonal (symmetry)

acht·zehn *card.num.* eighteen

acht·zig *card.num.* eighty

acht·zigst *ord.num.* eightieth

Acker *m.* (*Flächenmaß* square measure) acre: *ein A. Landes* an acre of land

a conto (*comm.*) **1.** *n* part(ial) payment, down payment: *ich erlege ein a conto* I am making a partial (or down) payment. **2.** *adj.* partial: *eine Zahlung a conto, eine a conto Zahlung* a partial payment. **3.** *prep.* (*gen.*) (*zu Gunsten*) to the credit (of); (*zu Lasten*) to the debit (of): *ich erlege a conto meiner Schuld* I am making payment to the credit of my account; *a conto meines Guthabens hebe ich* 100 *Mark ab* I am drawing 100 marks to the debit of my account

ad absurdum *adv.* [*cf.* FÜHREN]

Addend *m* addend, summand [= SUMMAND]

addieren *v.t., v.i.* add [*cf.* FALSCH; ÜBERTRAGEN]

Addier·maschine *f* adding machine

Addierung *f* addition

Addition *f* addition [*cf.* ASSOZIATIV; AUSFÜHREN; KOMMUTATIV; PLUS; PLUSZEICHEN; UND]

Additions·fehler *m* mistake in adding (up)

Additions·formel *f* addition formula

Additions·maschine *f* adding machine

Additions·theoreme *npl* (*der Trigonometrie*) addition formulas (in trigonometry)

Additions·zeichen *n* addition (or plus) sign, sign of addition

additiv *adj.* additive

Adiabate *f* adiabatic (curve)

adiabatisch *adj.* adiabatic

ad infinitum ad infinitum

adjungieren *v.t.* adjoin

Adjunkte *f* (*eines Elements einer Determinante*) cofactor (of an element of a determinant)

Adjunktion *f* adjunction [*cf.* SYM-BOLISCH]

Adressat *m* addressee, consignee [*cf.* EMPFÄNGER]

affin *adj.* affine [*cf.* TRANSFOR-MATION]

Affinität *f* affinity

Affinitäts·achse *f* axis of affinity

A.G. (*abbr.*) *Aktiengesellschaft* (*Am.*) incorporated, (*abbr.*) Inc.; (*Br.*) limited, (*abbr.*) Ltd.: *Walzwerke A.G.* (*Am.*) Rolling Mills Inc., (*Br.*) Rolling Mills Ltd.

Aggregat·zustand *m* (*fester, flüssiger, gasförmiger*) (solid, liquid, gaseous) state of matter [*cf.* FESTHEIT; FESTIGKEIT]

Agio *n* (*fin.*) agio [*ant.:* DISAGIO] [*cf.* AUFSCHLAG]

Agio·gewinn *m* (*fin.*) speculative (or agio) profit

Agiotage *f* (*fin.*) agiotage, stock-jobbing

Agioteur *m* (*fin.*) stock exchange operator, stockjobber

agiotieren *v.i.* (*fin.*) speculate (in stocks)

Agnesi *m* *N.: Agnesische Kurve* witch of Agnesi, versiera [= VERSIERA]

ähnlich *adj.* similar: *ähnliche Dreiecke* similar triangles; *ä. liegend* (*oder gelegen*), *perspektivisch ä.* homothetic; *ähnliche und ä. gelegene Figuren* homothetic (or radially related) figures [*cf.* ÄHNLICH-GEORDNET; ÄHN-LICH-ISOMORPH]

ähnlich-geordnet *adj.* (*Menge*) similary ordered (set)

ähnlich-isomorph *adj.* (*Zahlenkörper*) order-isomorphic (number field)

Ähnlich·keit *f* similarity, similitude

Ähnlichkeits·punkt *m* (*zweier Konfigurationen*) center of similarity (or similitude) (of two configurations)

Ähnlichkeits·transformation *f* **1.** (*allgemeine*) general similarity transformation. **2.** (*perspektivische*) (perspective) transformation of similitude, homothetic transformation

Ähnlichkeits·verhältnis *n* ratio of similitude, ray ratio

Ähnlichkeits·zentrum *n* center of similarity (or similitude), ray center [*cf.* ÄHNLICHKEITSPUNKT]

Ähren·kurve *f* épi, Cotes's spiral

Aktie *f* (*comm., fin.*) share (of stock); *pl. Aktien* stock [*cf.* STÜCKELUNG; WERTPAPIERE; ZUSAMMENLEGUNG]

Aktien·gesellschaft *f* (*comm., fin.*) (stock) corporation [*cf.* A.G.]

Aktien·index *m* index of stocks

Aktien·kapital *n* (capital) stock [*cf.* STAMMKAPITAL]

Aktien·kurs *m* stock price

Aktien·notierung *f* stock quotation

Aktien·papiere *npl.* stock certificates

Aktien·stückelung *f* division into shares

Aktion *f* action: *Gesetz (oder Prinzip) der gleichen A. und Reaktion* law of action and reaction

Aktiv·posten *m* asset [*cf.* GUT-HABEN]

Aktivum *n* (*pl. Aktiva, Aktiven*) (*comm.*) asset; (*pl. auch*) resources: *flüssige (oder liquide) Aktiven (oder Aktiva)* liquid assets [*cf.* VERMÖGEN; VERMÖGENS-ANLAGE]

aktuell *adj.* actual [*cf.* ENERGIE]

Akustik *f* acoustics

akustisch *adj.* acoustic(al)

Akzept *n* (*comm.*) acceptance, accepted draft, note

Akzeptant *m* (*comm.*) accepter, acceptor: *A. im Konkurs* acceptor bankrupt

Akzept·bank *f* (*fin.*) *Am.* acceptance corporation, *Br.* accepting house

Akzept·buch *n* (*comm.*) acceptance ledger

Akzept·haus *n* (*fin.*) acceptance house

Akzept·höchstkredit *m* acceptance line

Akzept·kredit *m* (*comm.*) acceptance credit

Aleph *n* (*hebräischer Buchstabe* Hebrew letter א) aleph: *A.Null* aleph-null, aleph zero (*symb.*: א₀)

Algebra *f* **1.** (*Rechnung mit algebra-*

ischen Zahlen) (computation with algebraic numbers) algebra [*cf.* FUNDAMENTALSATZ; LOGIK; RICHTUNG]. **2.** (*hyperkomplexes System*) hypercomplex system, algebra

algebraisch *adj.* algebraic: *algebraische Gleichung* algebraic (or polynomial) equation [*cf.* DOP-PELWURZEL]; *algebraisches Vorzeichen* algebraic sign; *a. in bezug auf einen Zahlenkörper* algebraic with respect to a number field; *algebraische Zahl* a.) (*relative Zahl*) algebraic (or relative) number [*cf.* ZAHL]; b.) (*Wurzel einer algebraischen Gleichung*) algebraic number, (root of an algebraic equation) [*cf.* ABSOLUT; ALGEBRAISCH - ABGESCHLOSSEN; ALLGEMEIN; BASIS; FUNKTION; GROSS; ORDNUNG; SUMME; ZAHL]

algebraisch-abgeschlossen *adj.* algebraically closed

Algebren·klasse *f* class of algebras

Algebrenklassen·gruppe *f* group of classes of algebras

Algorithmus *m* algorithm [*cf.* EU-KLIDISCH]

aliquot *adj.* aliquot: *aliquoter Teil* aliquot part

allgemein *adj.* **1.** (*universell*) general, generic, universal: *allgemeine Gleichung n-ten Grades* general equation of degree *n*; *allgemeine Lösung einer Differentialgleichung* general solution of a differential equation; *allgemeines Glied einer Reihe* general term of a series; *allgemeiner Punkt einer algebraischen Mannigfaltigkeit* generic point of an algebraic manifold; *allgemeine Anziehung* universal attraction; *allgemeine* (*oder universelle*) *Konstante* universal constant; (*log.*) *allgemeines Urteil* universal judgment [*cf.* ÄHNLICHKEITSTRANSFORMATION; AUFLÖSUNG; AUSGLEICHUNGSRECHNUNG; NULLSTELLE; UNKOSTEN]. **2.** (*in Buchstaben*) literal: *allgemeine Zahl* literal number; *allgemeiner Ausdruck* literal expression

allgemein·giltig, allgemein·gültig *adj.* generally (or universally) valid [*cf.* IDENTISCH]

Allgemein·giltigkeit *f*, **Allgemeingültigkeit** *f* general (or universal) validity [*cf.* ENTSCHEIDEN]

Allgemeinheit *f* generality, universality

Allgemeinheits·zeichen *n*, **Allzeichen** *n* (*log.*) universal quantifier

Alpha *n* (*griechischer Buchstabe* Greek letter *A*, α) alpha

Alphabet *n* alphabet

alphabetisch *adj.* alphabetic(al)

Alpha·strahlen *mpl.* alpha rays

alternieren *v.i.* alternate: *alternierende Reihe, Gruppe* alternating series, group [*cf.* EINFACHHEIT]

Alters·gliederung *f* (*statist.*) age distribution

Alters·klasse *f* (*statist.*) age group

Alters·rente *f* old-age annuity (or: insurance benefit)

Alters·versicherung *f* old-age insurance

Amortisation *f* [=AMORTISIERUNG]

Amortisations·fonds *m* (*fin.*) sinking fund

Amortisations·rate *f* amortization rate

amortisieren *v.t.* (*tilgen*) amortize; (*abschreiben*) depreciate

Amortisierung *f* (*Tilgung*) amortization; (*Abschreibung*) depreciation

Ampère *n* (*elec.*) ampere

Ampère·meter *n* amperemeter, ammeter

Ampère·stunde *f* ampere-hour

Amplitude 1. (*Polarwinkel*) polar angle, amplitude, argument, anomaly, azimuth. **2.** (*Schwingungsweite* extreme departure in harmonic motion) amplitude

anallagmatisch *adj.* anallagmatic: *anallagmatische* (*oder unveränderliche*) *Kurve, Fläche* anallagmatic curve, surface

analog *adj.* analogous

Analogie *f* analogy: *Nepersche Analogien* Napier's analogies

Analyse *f* analysis [*cf.* ZERGLIEDERUNG]

analysieren *v.t.* analyze, analyse [*cf.* ZERGLIEDERN]

Analysis *f* analysis: (*höhere*) *A.* analysis, (infinitesimal) calculus; *A. situs* [*cf.* ANALYSIS SITUS]

Analysis situs *f* analysis situs, topology [=SITUATIONSKALKÜL; TOPOLOGIE] [*cf.* GEOMETRIE]

analytisch *adj.* analytic; (*adv.*) analytically: *analytischer Beweis* analytic proof, proof by analysis; *analytische Funktion* analytic function; *analytische Geometrie* analytic geometry [*cf.* FORTSETZUNG; MONOGEN; NEU; RESIDUUM]

Ana·morphose *f* anamorphosis

ander *adj.* other; *ein anderer, eine andere, ein anderes* another (one) [*cf.* ÜBERTRAGEN]

ändern *v.t., v.r.:* **sich ä.** change: *den Wert ä.* change the value; *das Vorzeichen ändert sich* the sign changes

andert·halb *adj.* one and a half

Änderung *f* change

Anfangs·bedingung *f* initial condition

Anfangs·geschwindigkeit *f* initial velocity

Anfangs·koeffizient *m* (*eines Polynoms*) leading (or highest) coefficient (of a polynomial)

Anfangs·lage *f* initial position

Anfangs·punkt *m* initial point, origin; (*einer Bewegung*) starting point (of a motion); *A. eines Halbstrahls* origin of a ray

Anfangs·richtung *f* (*des Radiusvektors*) initial (or prime) direction (of the radius vector)

Anfangs·wert *m* initial value

Anfangs·zustand *m* initial (or incipient) state (or condition)

An·gebot *n* (*comm.*) (*Einzelangebot*) offer; (*Marktangebot*) supply: *A. und Nachfrage* supply and demand

an·genähert *adj.* approximate: *angenähertes Resultat* approximate result [*cf.* ANNÄHERN; ANNÄHERND]

an·genommen *cj.* (*daß*) provided (that) [*cf.* ANNEHMEN 1.]

an·geordnet *adj.* ordered: *archimedisch angeordneter Zahlenkörper* ·number field with Archimedean ordering [*cf.* ANORDNEN; KÖRPER]

an·geschrieben *adj.* (*Kreis*) escribed (circle) [*cf.* ANSCHREIBEN]

an·gewandt *adj.* applied: [*cf.* ANWENDEN; MATHEMATIK]

an·gleichen 1. *v.t.* (*gleich machen*) equate; (*anpassen*) adjust, adapt, assimilate. **2.** *v.r.:* **sich a.** become adjusted (or adapted, or assimilated)

An·gleichung *f* equation; adjustment; adaptation [*cf.* ANGLEICHEN]

an·greifen (*sep.*) *v.i.* be applied: *die Kraft greift am längeren Hebelarm an* the force is applied to the longer lever arm

an·grenzen (*sep.*) *v.i.* (*an*) be adjacent (or adjoining, or contiguous) (to) [*cf.* ANSTOSSEN]

Angriffs·punkt *m* point of application

Ångström *n* (*meas.*) angstrom, Angström, Ångström

angular *adj.* angular [*cf.* MOMENT²]

an·hängen *v.t.* annex: *Nullen a.* annex zeros

an·häufen (*sep.*) *v.t., v.r.:* **sich a.** accumulate, cluster

An·häufung *f* accumulation, cluster

an·isometrisch *adj.* (*Projektion*) anisometric (projection)

an·isotrop *adj.* anisotropic(al)

An·isotropie *adj.* anisotropy

an·isotropisch *adj.* anisotropic(al)

An·kathete *f* side adjacent (to an oblique angle in a right triangle)

An·kreis *m* excircle, escribed circle; *Mittelpunkt des Ankreises* excenter

Ankreis·mittelpunkt *m.* excenter, center of escribed circle

21

Anlage *f* (*von Kapital*) investment (of capital)

Anlage·papier *n* (*fin.*) bond

Anlage·vermögen *n* (*fin.*) fixed capital (or resources)

Anlage·wert *m* (*fin.*) bond [*cf.* WERTPAPIERE]

an·lasten *v.t.* (*comm.*) charge against (or to) [*cf.* ANRECHNEN; AUFRECHNEN]

An·lastung *f* charging (against, to)

an·legen (*sep.*) *v.t.* **1.** (*legen an*) put to, set: *das Lineal a.* set the ruler; *das Dreieck an eine Linie a.* put the (drawing) triangle to a line. **2.** (*Kapital*) invest (capital)

An·leihe *f* (*fin.*) loan [*cf.* AUFNAHME; AUFNEHMEN; EMITTIEREN; EWIG; RÜCKZAHLUNG; ZURÜCKZAHLEN]

an·liegen (*sep.*) *v.i.* (*dat.*) be adjacent (or adjoining, or contiguous) (to)

an·liegend *adj.* adjacent, adjoining: *eine Seite und die anliegenden Winkel* (*im Dreieck*) a side and the adjacent (or adjoining) angles, two angles and the included side (in a triangle); *ein Winkel und die anliegenden Seiten* (*im Dreieck*) an angle and the adjacent sides, two sides and the included angle (in a triangle)

an·nähern (*sep.*) *v.t., v.r.:* **sich** *a.* approach, converge; (*in Genauigkeit*) approximate (in accuracy) [*cf.* ANGENÄHERT; NÄHERN]

an·nähernd *adj.* (*Wert*) approximate (value); *einem bestimmten Wert a. gleich sein* approximate a certain value [*cf.* ANGENÄHERT]

An·näherung *f* convergence; (*in Genauigkeit*) approximation (in accuracy): *A. an* (*oder gegen*) *einen Grenzwert* convergence to (or toward) a limit; *A. an den genauen Wert* approximation to the exact (or accurate) value; *rohe A.* rough (or crude) approximation; *gute* (*oder genaue*) *A.* good (or close) approximation

annäherungs·weise *adj.* approximately

An·nahme *f* **1.** (*Vermutung*) assumption, hypothesis: *nach der A.* by assumption. **2.** (*comm.*) (*einer Tratte*) acceptance (of a draft) [*cf.* EMPIRISCH; HEURISTISCH]

an·nehmen *v.t.* **1.** (*voraussetzen*) assume: *wir nehmen an* (*oder angenommen*), *daß* $x = y$ let us assume that $x = y$ [*cf.* ANGENOMMEN]. **2.** (*empfangen*) assume, accept: $f(x)$ *nimmt einen bestimmten Wert an* $f(x)$ assumes a definite value; (*comm.*) *eine Tratte a.* accept a draft

annullieren *v.t.* (*alg.*) annihilate: *annullierendes Ideal* annihilating ideal

Annullierung *f* (*alg.*) annihilation

Anomalie **1.** (*Polarwinkel*) polar angle, anomaly, amplitude, argument, azimuth. **2.** (*astr.*) (*wahre, mittlere, exzentrische*) (true, mean, eccentric) anomaly

an·ordnen (*sep.*) *v.t.* order, arrange [*cf.* EINTEILEN]

An·ordnung *f* (*einer Menge von Gegenständen*) arrangement, order(ing) of a set of things; (*in Reihen, Kolonnen*) array (of rows, columns); *umgekehrte A.* inverted (or inverse) order; *richtige* (*oder normale*) *A.* right (or normal) order [*cf.* EINTEILUNG]

an·passen (*sep.*) *v.t* fit, adapt, adjust: *eine Funktion an gegebene Daten a.* fit a function to given data [*cf.* EINPASSEN]

An·passung *f* fit, fitting: *A. einer Kurve an eine Reihe von gegebenen Punkten* fitting of a curve to a set of given points [*cf.* ANSCHMIE-GUNG; AUSGLEICHUNG; GÜTE]

an·rechnen (*sep.*) *v.t.* (*comm.*) **1.** (*anlasten*) charge against (or to). **2.** (*in Gegenrechnung stellen*) offset, balance, compensate. [= AUFRECHNEN 2, 3.]

An·rechnung *f* charging; balancing; compensation [*cf.* ANRECH-NEN]

An·satz *m* (*einer Gleichung*) set-up, arrangement (of an equation)

an·schaulich *adj.* graphic(al), clear by inspection: *ein anschauliches Beispiel* a graphic example (or illustration); *a. machen* illustrate; *a. darstellen* represent graphically

An·schauung *f* inspection: *der Beweis ergibt sich durch unmittelbare A.* the proof follows by inspection

an·schmiegen (*sep.*) **1.** *v.t.* (*an*) press closely (to), adapt (to), fit (to): *eine Kurve gegebenen Punkten a.* fit a (smooth) curve to a set of given points [*cf.* EINPASSEN]. **2.** *v.r.* sich *a.* (*an*) hug, osculate

An·schmiegung *f* **1.** (*Berührung*) osculation: *A. des Krümmungs-kreises an die Kurve* osculation of a curve by its circle of curvature. **2.** (*Anpassung*) adapta-

tion: *A. einer Kurve an gegebene Punkte* adaptation of a curve to given points

an·schreiben *v.t.* **1.** (*aufschreiben*) put down, write (on): *schreiben Sie die Gleichung an* put down the equation; *auf die Tafel a.* write on the blackboard [*cf.* BLEIBEN]. **2.** (*z.B. einem Dreieck einen Kreis*) escribe (e.g. a circle to a triangle); *angeschriebener Kreis eines Dreiecks* excircle (or escribed circle) of a triangle; *Mittelpunkt des angeschriebenen Kreises eines Dreiecks* excenter of a triangle [*cf.* ANGESCHRIEBEN]

an·setzen (*sep.*) *v.t.* (*eine Gleichung*) set up, arrange (an equation)

An·sicht *f* view [*cf.* SCHMALSEITEN-ANSICHT]

an·stoßen (*sep.*) *v.i.* **1.** (*angrenzen*) (*an*) be adjacent (or adjoining, or contiguous) (to) [*cf.* ANSTOSSEND]. **2.** (*auftreffen*) (*auf, gegen*) strike (or knock, or impinge) (against)

an·stoßend *adj.* adjacent, adjoining: *anstoßende Winkel* adjacent angles [*cf.* ANSTOSSEN]

an·streichen (*sep.*) *v.t.* check off, mark off [*cf.* ABSTREICHEN]

An·teil *m* share [*cf.* VERHÄLTNIS-MÄSSIG]

anti·klastisch *adj.* (*Krümmung*) anticlastic (curvature)

Anti·logarithmus *m* antilogarithm

Anti·nomie *f* (*log.*) antinomy

anti·parallel *adj.* antiparallel

Anti·parallelogramm *n* antiparallelogram, isosceles trapezoid

Anti·these *f* (*log.*) antithesis

an·wachsen (*sep.*) *v.i.* accrue, accumulate [*cf.* ZINS]

Anwartschafts·rente *f* deferred annuity

an·wenden (*sep.*) *v.t.* apply [*cf.* ANGEWANDT]

An·wendung *f* application [*cf.* AUSGLEICHUNGSRECHNUNG]

An·winkel *m* (*zweier Geraden und einer Transversalen*) one of a pair of either interior or exterior angles on different sides of two lines but on the same side of a transversal [*cf.* pairs of angles: A, D; B, C; A′, D′; B′, C′ in *Fig.* to TRANSVERSALE] [*cf.* ENTGEGEN-GESETZT; PARALLEL]

An·zahl *f* number [*cf.* ABBRECHEN; FREIHEITSGRAD; UNENDLICH]

Anzahl·begriff *m* concept of number

an·ziehen (*sep.*) **1.** *v.t.* (*Anziehungs-kraft ausüben*) attract. **2.** *v.i.* (*comm.*) (*steigen*) rise, run (or go, or move) up, advance: *die Preise zogen stark an* prices advanced sharply; *bei anziehenden Kursen* in a rising market

An·ziehung *f* attraction, pull: *A. der Schwere* (*oder Schwerkraft*) attraction (or pull) of gravity; *Mittelpunkt der A.* center of attraction [*cf.* ALLGEMEIN]

Anziehungs·kraft *f* attractive force, attraction, pull [*cf.* ANZIEHEN]

a·periodisch *adj.* aperiodic(al)

A·periodizität *f* aperiodicity

Aphel *n*, **Aphelium** *n* (*astr.*) aphelion [= SONNENFERNE]

apo·diktisch *adj.* (*log.*) apodic-tic(al)

Apo·gäum *n* (*astr.*) apogee [= ERDFERNE]

a·polar *adj.* apolar

A·polarität *f* apolarity

a posteriori a posteriori

a·posteriorisch *adj.* a posteriori

Apotheker·gewicht *n* apothecaries' weight

Applikate *f* z-coordinate [*cf.* KOTE]

Applikaten·achse *f* z-axis

Approximation *f* approximation; (*Exhaustion*) exhaustion [*cf.* GEOMETRISCH]

Approximations·methode *f* method of approximation; (*Exhaustions-methode*) method of exhaustion

approximativ *adj.* approximate

approximieren *v.t.* approximate

a priori *adj.* a priori

a·priorisch *adj.* a priori

Apsiden *f pl.* (*sing. Apsis*) (*astr.*) apsides (*sing.* apsis)

Apsiden·linie *f* (*astr.*) line of apsides

Apsis *f* [*cf.* APSIDEN]

Äquator *m* equator

Äquator·breite *f* equatorial latitude

Äquator·ebene *f* equator plane

äquatorial *adj.* equatorial

äqui·distant *adj.* equidistant

äqui·noktial *adj.* equinoctial

Äqui·noktium *n* (*astr.*) equinox [= NACHTGLEICHE; TAGUND-NACHTGLEICHE] [*cf.* VORRÜCKEN]

Äquipotential·fläche *f* equipotential surface

Äqui·valent *n* equivalent

äqui·valent *adj.* equivalent

Äqui·valenz *f* equivalence

Äquivalenz·relation *f* equivalence relation

Ar *n* (*Flächenmaß* square measure) are

Ära *f* era [*cf.* ZEITRECHNUNG]

arabisch *adj.* Arabic: [*cf.* ZAHL-
ZEICHEN]
Arbeit *f* work: *geleistete A.* work
done (or performed) [*cf.* LEISTEN;
LEISTUNG]
Arbeits·einheit *f* unit of work
Arbeits·fähigkeit *f* capacity for
performing work, energy, poten-
tial [*cf.* ENERGIE]
Arbeits·hypothese *f* working hypo-
thesis
Arbeits·leistung *f* (*phys.*) (rate of)
work done, power, output [*cf.*
EFFEKT]
arbiträr *adj.* arbitrary: *arbiträrer
Wert* arbitrary value
Archimedes *m N.* [*cf.* ARCHIME-
DISCH]
archimedisch *adj.* Archimedean:
archimedische Schraube Archimedean screw [*cf.* ANGEORDNET;
AXIOM; GEOMETRISCH; SPIRALE]
arcus *m* (*von* α) (symb.: arc α)
[= ARKUS]
arcus cosecans *m* (*von* α) [=
ARKUSKOSEKANS]
arcus cosecans hyperbolicus *m*
(*eines Winkels* α) (*symb.:* arc
cosec h α) inverse hyperbolic (or
antihyperbolic, or arc-hyperbolic) cosecant (of an angle α)
(*symb.:* cosech^{-1}α, csch^{-1}α)
arcus cosinus *m* (*von* α) [= ARKUS-
KOSINUS]
arcus cosinus hyperbolicus *m* (*eines
Winkels* α) (*symb.:* arc cos h α)
inverse hyperbolic (or antihyperbolic, or arc-hyperbolic) cosine
(of an angle α) (*symb.:* cosh^{-1}α)
arcus cotangens *m* (*von* α) (*symb.:*
arc cot α) [= ARKUSKOTANGENS]
arcus cotangens hyperbolicus *m*

(*eines Winkels* α) (*symb.:* arc
ctg h α, arc cot h α) inverse
hyperbolic (or antihyperbolic, or
arc-hyperbolic) cotangent (of an
angle α) (*symb.:* ctnh^{-1}α,
coth^{-1}α)
arcus secans *m* (*von* α) (*symb.:* arc
sec α) [= ARKUSSEKANS]
arcus secans hyperbolicus *m* (*eines
Winkels* α) (*symb.:* arc sec h α)
inverse hyperbolic (or antihyperbolic, or arc-hyperbolic) secant
(of an angle α) (*symb.:* sech $^{-1}$α)
arcus sinus *m* (*von* α) (*symb.:* arc
sin α) [= ARKUSSINUS]
arcus sinus hyperbolicus *m* (*eines
Winkels* α) (*symb.:* arc sin h α)
inverse hyperbolic (or antihyperbolic, or arc-hyperbolic) sine (of
an angle α) (*symb.:* sinh $^{-1}$α)
arcus tangens *m* (*von* α) (*symb.:*
arc tg α) [= ARKUSTANGENS]
arcus tangens hyperbolicus *m* (*eines
Winkels* α) (*symb.:* arc tg h α,
arc tang h α) inverse hyperbolic
(or antihyperbolic, or arc-hyperbolic) tangent (of an angle α)
(*symb.:* tanh $^{-1}$α)
Are *f* (in Switzerland = **Ar**) are
Argument 1. (*Polarwinkel*) polar
angle, argument, amplitude,
anomaly, azimuth. **2.** (*unabhängige Variable* independent variable) argument
Arithmetik *f* arithmetic [*cf.*
ELEMENT]
Arithmetiker *m* arithmetician
arithmetisch *adj.* arithmetic(al):
arithmetische Progression (*oder
Reihe*) arithmetic progression;
*Summe einer arithmetischen Reihe
(oder Progression)* arithmetic

series, sum of an arithmetic progression; (*statist.*) *arithmetische Kurve* arithmetic line chart

Arkus *m* (*eines Winkels* α) (*symb.:* arc α) arc (length) (through an angle α) in radians [*cf.* ARCUS; BOGEN]

Arkus·kosekans *m* (*eines Winkels* α) (*symb.: arc cosec* α) inverse cosecant, anticosecant, arc cosecant (of an angle α) (*symb.:* csc⁻¹α, arc csc α) [*cf.* ARCUS COSECANS]

Arkus·kosinus *m* (*eines Winkels* α) (*symb.:* arc cos α) inverse cosine, anticosine, arc cosine (of an angle α) (*symb.:* cos⁻¹α, arc cos α) [*cf.* ARCUS COSINUS]

Arkus·kotangens *m* (*eines Winkels* α) (*symb.:* arc ctg α, arc cot α) inverse cotangent, anticotangent, arc cotangent (of an angle α) (*symb.:* cot⁻¹α, ctn⁻¹α, arc cot α, arc ctn α) [*cf.* ARCUS COTANGENS]

Arkus·sekans *m* (*eines Winkels* α) (*symb.:* arc sec α) inverse secant, arc secant (of an angle α) (*symb.:* sec⁻¹α, arc sec α) [*cf.* ARCUS SECANS]

Arkus·sinus *m* (*eines Winkels* α) (*symb.:* arc sin α) inverse sine, antisine, arc sine (of an angle α) (*symb.:* sin⁻¹α, arc sin α) [*cf.* ARCUS SINUS]

Arkus·tangens *m* (*eines Winkels* α) (*symb.:* arc tg α, arc tang α) inverse tangent, antitangent, arc tangent (of an angle α) (*symb.:* tan⁻¹α, arc tan α) [*cf.* ARCUS TANGENS]

Art *f* kind, sort [*cf.* GEOMETRIE; SPITZE]

art·mäßig *adj.* (*statist.*) qualitative [*cf.* ABHÄNGIGKEIT; SACHLICH]

Aspekt *m* (*pl. Aspekte, Aspekten*) (*astr.*) aspect

assertorisch *adj.* (*log.*) (*Urteil*) assertorial (judgment)

assoziativ *adj.* associative: *assoziatives Gesetz der Addition* (*Multiplikation*) associative law for addition (multiplication)

Assoziativ·gesetz *n* associative law [*cf.* ASSOZIATIV]

Assoziativität *f* associativity

assoziiert *adj.* associate, associated [*cf.* GRÖSSE]

Ast *m* (*einer Kurve*) branch (of a curve)

Asteroid *m* (*astr.*) asteroid, planetoid [= PLANETOID]

Asteroide *f*, **Astroide** *f*, **Astrois** *f* astroid, tetracuspid [= *vierspitzige* HYPOZYKLOIDE; STERNKURVE]

Astrolabium *n* (*pl. Astrolabien*) (*astr.*) astrolabe

Astronomie *f* astronomy

astronomisch *adj.* astronomical

A·symmetrie *adj.* asymmetry, nonsymmetry; (*der Verteilung*) skewness (of distribution)

a·symmetrisch *adj.* asymmetric(al), (*statist.*) skew: *asymmetrische Verteilung* skew distribution; *linksseitig* (*rechtsseitig*) *asymmetrische Häufigkeitskurve* frequency curve skew to the left (right), positively (negatively) skew frequency curve

Asymptote *f* asymptote

Asymptoten·kegel *m* (*eines Hyper-*

boloids) asymptotic cone (of a hyperboloid)

asymptotisch *adj.* asymptotic(al): *asymptotischer Punkt* asymptotic point; *die logarithmische Spirale nähert sich dem Ursprung a.* the logarithmic spiral approaches the origin asymptotically

Aszensional·differenz *f* (*astr.*) ascensional difference

Äther *m* (*phys.*) ether

Atmo·sphäre *f* atmosphere

atmo·sphärisch *adj.* atmospheric: *atmosphärischer Druck* atmospheric pressure

Atom *n* atom [*cf.* KERN]

atomar *adj.* (*Energie*) atomic (energy)

Atom·batterie *f* atomic pile

Atom·bau *m* atom(ic) structure

Atom·energie *f* atomic energy

Atom·gewicht *n* atomic weight

atomistisch *adj.* atomistic

Atom·kern *m* atomic nucleus (or core)

Atom·modell *n* atom(ic) model

Atom·nummer *f* atomic number

Atom·säule *f* atomic pile

Atom·spektrum *n* atom(ic) spectrum

Atom·strahlen *m pl.* atomic rays

Atom·theorie *f* atomic theory

Atom·umwandlung *f* atomic transmutation

Atom·volumen *n* atomic volume

Atom·wärme *f* atomic heat

Atom·zahl *f* atomic number

Atom·zerfall *m* atomic decay (or disintegration)

Atom·zertrümmerung *f* atom smashing (or splitting)

auf·arbeiten (*sep.*) *v.t.* (*z.B. Daten*)

process (e.g. data); (*in Tafeln*) tabulate

Auf·arbeitung *f* processing; (*in Tafeln*) tabulation: *A.* (*oder Aufbereitung*) *statistischer Daten* processing (or tabulation) of statistical data

auf·bereiten (*sep.*) *v.t.* process [= AUFARBEITEN] [*cf.* AUFGLIEDERN]

Auf·bereitung *f* processing [= AUFARBEITUNG] [*cf.* AUFGLIEDERUNG]

Aufeinander·folge *f* succession, sequence [*cf.* FOLGE 1; ZEITLICH]

aufeinander·folgen (*sep.*) *v.i.* succeed (each other)

aufeinander·folgend *adj.* consecutive, successive [*cf.* VERHÄLTNIS]

aufeinander·legen (*sep.*) *v.t.* superpose, superimpose

Aufeinander·legung *f* superposition, superimposition

Auf·gabe *f* task, problem, exercise [*cf.* LÖSEN]

auf·geben (*sep.*) *v.t.* (*z.B. ein Problem*) set (or pose) (e.g. a problem)

auf·gehen (*sep.*) *v.i.* **1.** (*math.*) (*ohne Rest enthalten sein*) (be contained without remainder), (*in*) divide (*dir. obj.*): *6 geht in 24 auf* 6 divides 24, 24 is divided by 6; *die Division geht* (*ohne Rest*) *auf* the division is exact (or leaves no remainder) [*cf.* AUSGEHEN]. **2.** (*astr.*) rise

auf·gliedern (*sep.*) *v.t.* (*gliedern*) organize, classify; (*aufbereiten*) process: *statistisches Material a.* process statistical material

Auf·gliederung *f* (*Gliederung*) organization, classification; (*Aufbereitung*) processing

auf·hängen (*sep.*) *v.t.* suspend, hang (up) [*cf.* KARDANISCH]

Auf·hängung *f* suspension [*cf.* KARDANISCH]

auf·heben *v.r.:* **sich** *a.* cancel (out): *die beiden Klammerausdrücke heben sich auf* the two (expressions in) parentheses cancel (out) [*cf.* HERAUSHEBEN]

Auf·hebung *f* canceling (out), cancellation

auf·laufen (*sep.*) *v.i.* accrue, accumulate [*cf.* ZINS 1.]

auflös·bar *adj.* solvable, soluble: (*alg.*) *auflösbare Gruppe* solvable group

Auflösbar·keit *f* solvability

auf·lösen (*sep.*) *v.t.* solve, resolve: *eine Gleichung a.* solve (or resolve) an equation; *Klammern a.* remove parentheses [*cf.* KNOTEN]

Auf·lösung *f* **1.** (*einer Aufgabe*) solution (of a problem): *A. der allgemeinen Gleichung vierten Grades* solution of the general quartic. **2.** (*eines Knotens*) untying, disentanglement (of a knot)

Auf·nahme *f* (*von Geld*) borrowing (of money); (*einer Anleihe*) raising (of a loan)

auf·nehmen (*sep.*) *v.t.* (*Geld*) borrow (money); (*eine Anleihe*) raise (a loan)

auf·rechnen (*sep.*) *v.t.* **1.** (*hinzufügen*) add; (*comm.*) make additional charge for: *wir müssen die Wärmeausdehnung a.* we have to add the thermal expansion. **2.** (*comm.*) (*anlasten*) charge against (or to): *dem Käufer die*

Spesen a. charge the expenses against (or to) the buyer. **3.** (*comm.*) (*in Gegenrechnung stellen*) offset, balance, compensate: *einen Posten gegen einen anderen a.* balance one item against another

Auf·rechnung *f* addition; (additional) charge; charging; compensation, balancing [*cf.* AUFRECHNEN]

Auf·riß *m* front view, elevation, vertical projection [*cf.* DARSTELLEN; PROJEKTION]

Aufriß·ebene *f* vertical projection plane [*cf.* PROJEKTIONSEBENE]

auf·runden (*sep.*) *v.t.* **1.** (*eine ganze Zahl*) round off (a whole number) (to the next higher round number): *wir runden 998 zu 1000 auf* we round off 998 to 1000. **2.** (*eine Dezimalzahl*) round off (a decimal) (by dropping the remainder after a certain place and increasing the preceding digit by one): *wir runden π zu 3·1416 auf* we round off π to 3·1416 [*cf.* ABRUNDEN 1.]

Auf·rundung *f* rounding off to a higher number [*cf.* AUFRUNDEN]

Auf·schlag *m* (*comm.*) (*zum Preis*) addition (to price), additional price (or charge); (*zur Steuer*) surtax; (*Agio*) agio [*ant.:* ABSCHLAG]

auf·schlagen (*sep.*) *v.t.* (*comm.*) (*zusetzen*) add; (*erhöhen*) raise [*ant.:* ABSCHLAGEN]: *5% zum Preis* (*oder: auf den*) *Preis a.* add 5% to the price; *die Preise a.* raise the prices

auf·spannen *v.t.* span: *einen n-*

dimensionalen Raum a. span an n-dimensional space [*cf.* SPAN-NEN]

auf·speichern (*sep.*) *v.t.* accumulate

Auf·speicherung *f* accumulation

auf·steigen (*sep.*) *v.i.* ascend [*cf.* KNOTEN 3.; POTENZ; POTENZ-REIHE]

Auf·steigung *f* (*astr.*) ascension: *gerade* (*schiefe*) *A.* right (oblique) ascension [*cf.* ABSTEIGUNG]

auf·tragen (*sep.*) *v.t.* (*eine Strecke*) plot, lay off (a line segment); *die Distanz auf der x-Achse a.* plot the distance along the *x*-axis

Auf·tragung *f* plotting, laying off [*cf.* AUFTRAGEN]

auf·treffen *v.i.* (*auf, gegen*) strike (or knock, or impinge) (against) [*cf.* ANSTOSSEN]

Auf·trieb *m* (*phys.*) buoyancy

auf·wärts *adv.* upward(s), up [*cf.* NACH]

auf·zählen (*sep.*) *v.t.* enumerate

Auf·zählung *f* enumeration

auf·zeichnen (*sep.*) *v.t.* **1.** (*zeichnen*) draw, trace, plot, graph. **2.** (*registrieren*) register, record

Auf·zeichnung *f* **1.** (*Zeichnung*) drawing, tracing, plotting, graphing. **2.** (*Registrierung*) record

Auge *n* eye; (*des Würfels*) spot, point (of a die)

Augen·abstand *m* interocular (distance)

Augen·blick *m* moment, instant [*cf.* MOMENT [1]]

augen·blicklich *adj.* instantaneous, momentary: *augenblickliche Geschwindigkeit, Beschleunigung* instantaneous velocity, acceleration

Augen·maß *n* inspection: *zeichne nach dem A.* plot by inspection, sketch freehand [*cf.* AUSGLEICHUNG]

Augen·punkt *m* [= AUGPUNKT]

Augen·zahl *f* (*beim Würfeln*) number of spots (or points) (in casting dice)

Aug·punkt *m* point of sight, center of vision, principal point

aus·arbeiten (*sep.*) *v.t.* work out: *ein Beispiel a.* work out an example

Aus·arbeitung *f* working out [*cf.* AUSARBEITEN]

aus·borgen (*sep.*) *v.t.* borrow [*cf.* BORGEN]

aus·breiten 1. *v.t.* spread; (*auseinanderfalten*) fold out; (*fortpflanzen*) propagate. **2.** *v.r.:* **sich** *a.* spread; (*sich fortpflanzen*) be propagated [*cf.* NETZ]

Aus·breitung *f* spread; (*Fortpflanzung*) propagation

aus·dehnen (*sep.*) *v.t., v.r.:* **sich** *a.* extend, dilate, expand [*cf.* AUSGEDEHNT]

Aus·dehnung *f* **1.** (*Erweiterung*) extension, dilation, dilatation, expansion: *die A. der Formel auf andere Fälle* the extension of the formula to other cases [*cf.* KUBISCH; LINEAR; RÄUMLICH]. **2.** (*Dimension*) dimension, extension, extent [*cf.* DIMENSION; GRÖSSE; LINEAR; RÄUMLICH]

Ausdehnungs·koeffizient *m* coefficient of expansion [*cf.* LINEAR]

Aus·druck *m* expression; (*Glied*) term [*cf.* ALLGEMEIN; AUSWERTEN; DREIGLIEDRIGKEIT; EINGLIEDRIG; EINGLIEDRIGKEIT; EINSETZEN;

EINSETZUNG; ENTWICKELN; GLEICHSETZEN; GLIED; HAUPT-ZAHL; ISOBAR; MEHRFACH; MEHR-GLIEDRIG; RECHNERISCH; UM-GRUPPIEREN; VEREINFACHUNG; VIERT; WEGFALL; ZWEIGLIEDRIG-KEIT]

aus·drücken (*sep.*) *v.t.* express: *wir drücken die Gleichung durch die neue Variable aus* we express the equation in terms of the new variable

auseinander·falten *v.t.* unfold, fold out [*cf.* AUSBREITEN]

Auseinander·faltung *f* unfold(ing)

auseinander·laufen (*sep.*) *v.i.* diverge [*cf.* DIVERGENT]

Auseinander·laufen *n* divergence [*cf.* DIVERGENZ]

auseinander·laufend *adj.* divergent

ausführ·bar *adj.* that can be carried out, possible, feasible

Ausführbar·keit *f* possibility, feasibility

aus·führen (*sep.*) *v.t.* carry out, do, perform, execute: *eine Multiplikation a.* carry out (or perform) a multiplication; *eine Addition a.* do a sum; *eine Konstruktion a.* execute a construction [*cf.* KOPF]

Aus·führung *f* carrying out, execution, operation; (*einer Formel*) expansion (of a formula) [*cf.* RECHNEN]

aus·füllen (*sep.*) *v.t.* fill (up) (completely) [*cf.* ERFÜLLEN 2.]

Aus·füllung *f* filling (up) (completely) [*cf.* ERFÜLLUNG 2.]

Aus·gabe *f* (*fin.*) 1. (*z.B. von Obligationen*) issue (e.g. of bonds). 2. (*Kosten*) expense [*cf.* LAUFEN]

Ausgangs·punkt *m* starting point

Ausgangs·wahrscheinlichkeit *f* a priori (or initial) probability

aus·geben (*sep.*) *v.t.* (*fin.*) 1. (*Wertpapiere*) issue (securities). 2. (*verausgaben*) spend

ausgedehnt *adj.* extensive, extending: *der Raum ist nach drei Richtungen* (*oder Dimensionen*) *a.* space extends in three directions (or dimensions) [*cf.* AUSDEHNEN; GRÖSSE; HOCH]

Ausgedehnt·heit *f* extension, dimensionality

aus·gehen (*sep.*) I. *v.i.* 1. (*von*) start (from); (*von einem Punkt*) start, issue, radiate, emanate (*from a point*): *wir gehen von einem gegebenen Polynom aus* we start from a given polynomial [*cf.* AUSSTRAHLEN]. 2. (*aufgehen*) be exact, leave no remainder; *die Division geht aus* the division is exact (or leaves no remainder). II. *v.r.*: 3. sich *a.* check, add up, be correct; (*aufgehen*) be exact: *es geht sich* (*gerade*) *aus* it checks (or adds up) accurately

aus·gelöst *adj.* (*statist.*) (*Daten*) (data) collected by statistical agency [*cf.* NICHTAUSGELÖST]

aus·geschlossen *adj.* ruled out, excluded, impossible [*cf.* AUS-SCHLIESSEN; DRITT]

aus·gezeichnet *adj.* distinguished; (*Wert, Lösung*) singular (value, solution): (*log.*) *ausgezeichnete konjunktive Normalform* distinguished conjunctive normal form. [*cf.* UNTERGRUPPE]

aus·gezogen *adj.* (*Linie*) unbroken (line) [*cf.* AUSZIEHEN]

Aus·gleich *m* (counter)balance; (*comm.*, *fin.*) balance, offset; (*Abrechnung*) settlement; (*Kompromiß*) compromise [*cf.* Ausgleichung]

aus·gleichen (*comm.*) **1.** *v.t.* (*Posten*) (counter) balance, offset (an item); (*Konto*) settle (an account); (*buchmäßige Differenzen*) straighten out (differences on accounts). **2.** *v.t.:* **sich** *a.* (*sich aufheben*) (counter)balance oneself, be offset; (*Kompromiß schließen*) compromise

Ausgleichs·fonds *m* (*fin.*) equalization fund; (*für Währungen*) stabilization fund (for currencies)

Ausgleichs·kurve *f* fitted curve

Aus·gleichung *f* **1.** (*Abrundung*) smoothing, adjustment; (*Anpassung einer Kurve*) curve fitting; *zeichnerische A., A. nach dem Augenmaß* freehand smoothing, curve fitting by inspection [*cf.* Obergruppenbildung]. **2.** (*comm.*) [= Ausgleich]

Ausgleichungs·rechnung *f* (*allgemeines Verfahren* general method) calculus of observations; (*Anwendung auf statistisches Beobachtungsmaterial* application to statistical material) adjustment of observations

aus·gliedern (*sep.*) *v.t.* (*statist.*) classify

Aus·gliederung *f* (*statist.*) classification

aus·klammern (*sep.*) *v.t.* factor out: *einen Faktor a.* (*oder herausheben*) factor out a term

Aus·lage *f* (*fin.*) (*von Unkosten*) disbursement (of expenses)

Ausleger·balken *m* cantilever beam (or arm)

aus·machen *v.i.* total, amount to: *die Faktura macht* 100 *Mark aus* the invoice totals (or: amounts to) 100 marks

Aus·maß *n* amount, rate: *A. der Veränderung* rate of change

aus·messen (*sep.*) *v.t.* measure, take the dimensions of

aus·multiplizieren (*sep.*) *v.t.* multiply out

aus·quadrieren (*sep.*) *v.t.* square out

aus·rechnen (*sep.*) *v.t.* calculate, compute, figure (out), evaluate: *rechne* 2^3 *aus!* evaluate 2^3; *eine Determinante entwickeln und a.* evaluate (or expand) a determinant [*cf.* Kopf]

Aus·rechnung *f* calculation, computation, evaluation

aus·reduzieren (*sep.*) *v.t.* (*eine Darstellung*) reduce (a representation)

Aus·sage *f* sentence, statement, assertion, proposition [*cf.* Prädikatsbegriff; Richtig; Satz; Subjektsbegriff; Verknüpfen]

aus·sagen (*sep.*) *v.t.* state, assert

Aussagen·formel *f* (*log.*) sentential formula [*cf.* Präfix]

Aussagen·kalkül *m* propositional (or sentential) calculus [*cf.* Pränex]

Aussagen·variable *f* (*log.*) sentential variable

Aussagen·verbindung *f*, **Aussagenverknüpfung** *f* sentential combination (or connective), combination (or connective) of sentences: *eine schwächere* (*stärkere*) *A.* a weaker (stronger) sentential combination (or connective)

Aussage·zeichen *n* (*log.*) sentential symbol

aus·schalten (*sep.*) *v.t.* eliminate: *eine Fehlerquelle a.* eliminate a source of error

Aus·schaltung *f* elimination [*cf.* UMRECHNUNG]

Aus·schlag *m* (*eines Pendels, Zeigers*) amplitude, swing (of a pendulum, pointer); (*einer statistischen Reihe*) deviation (of a statistical series): *der volle A. ist 45°* the total amplitude (or swing) is 45°

aus·schlagen (*sep.*) *v.i.* swing; deviate [*cf.* AUSSCHLAG]

aus·schließen (*sep.*) *v.t.* exclude, rule out [*cf.* AUSGESCHLOSSEN]

aus·schließend *adj.* exclusive: *einander* (*gegenseitig*) *ausschließende Ereignisse* mutually exclusive events

aus·schließlich *adj.* exclusive

Aus·schließung *f* **Aus·schluß** *m* exclusion

aus·schneiden (*sep.*) *v.t.* (*aus*) cut (out) (from)

Aus·schnitt *m* sector: *A. eines Kreises* sector of a circle; *A. aus einer Fläche* piece of a surface, surface patch [*cf.* UMRANDET]

Ausschöpfungs·methode *f* method of exhaustion [*cf.* APPROXIMATIONSMETHODE]

aus·schreiben (*sep.*) *v.t.* write out (in full)

außen *adv.* externally, outside: *die beiden Kreise berühren sich*

von a. the two circles are externally tangent [*cf.* ÄUSSER; BERÜHREND]

aus·senden (*sep.*) *v.t.* (*z.B. Strahlung*) emit, send forth, give off (e.g. radiation)

Außendruck *m* external (or outward) pressure

Außen·fläche *f* outer (or exterior) surface

Außen·glied *n* (*einer Proportion*) extreme (term) (of a proportion)

Außenseite *f* outside, outer surface, exterior

Außen·stände *m pl.* (*comm.*) outstanding debts (or claims), accounts receivable [*cf.* ABSCHREIBEN; LANGFRISTIG]

Außen·winkel *m* exterior angle

äußer *adj.* outer, outside, exterior, external, extreme: *äußerer Punkt einer Menge* exterior point of a set, point exterior to a set; *Menge aller äußeren Punkte einer Punktmenge* exterior (complement) of a set of points; *der Punkt A teilt die Strecke BC im äußeren Verhältnis* 2 : 3 (*oder: von außen im Verhältnis* 2 : 3) the point *A* divides the line segment *BC* in the external ratio 2 : 3 (or: externally in the ratio 2 : 3); *äußeres Glied einer Proportion* extreme term of a proportion; (*astr.*) *äußerer Planet* superior (or outer) planet [*cf.* AUTOMORPHISMUS; PRODUKT; VERHÄLTNIS]

außer·halb *adv., prep.* (*gen.*) outside

außer·ordentlich *adj.* extraordinary [*cf.* STRAHL]

äußerst *adj.* outermost, extreme, ultimate

aus·springend *adj.* convex, salient: *ausspringender Winkel* convex angle; *Polygon mit lauter ausspringenden Winkeln* convex polygon

aus·strahlen (*sep.*) **1.** *v.t.* (*aussenden*) radiate, emit, send forth, give off. **2.** *v.i.* (*ausgehen*) radiate, emanate, issue, start

Aus·strahlung *f* radiation, emission

aus·streichen (*sep.*) *v.t.* cross out, strike out, cancel, delete [*cf.* STREICHEN]

Aus·streichung *f* cancellation, deletion [*cf.* STREICHUNG]

Aus·tausch *m* exchange, interchange; (*Ersetzung*) replacement

aus·tauschen (*sep.*) *v.t.* exchange, interchange; (*ersetzen*) replace

Austausch·satz *m* (*alg.*) (*der linearen Abhängigkeit*) replacement theorem (in linear dependence)

aus·üben (*sep.*) *v.t.* exert: *eine Kraft a.* exert a force

Aus·übung *f* (*z.B. einer Kraft*) exertion (e.g. of a force)

Aus·wahl *f* selection, choice; (*zwischen zwei Möglichkeiten* between two possibilities) alternative; (*statist.*) sampling: *bewußte A.* **a.** (*allgemein*) controlled sampling, deliberate selection; **b.** (*gruppenweise A.*) stratified sampling; *zufällige A.* random sampling [*cf.* GRUPPENWEISE]

Auswahl·axiom *n* (*der Mengenlehre*) axiom of choice (of set theory)

aus·wählen (*sep.*) *v.t.* select, choose

aus·weiten (*sep.*) *v.t., v.r.,* **sich** *a.* dilate, widen

Aus·weitung *f* dilatation, widening.

aus·wendig *adj.* (*Oberfläche*) outside (surface)

aus·werten (*sep.*) *v.t.* evaluate: *man werte den Ausdruck* $x^2 - y^2$ *für* $x = 2$, $y = 3$ *aus* evaluate the expression $x^2 - y^2$ for $x = 2$, $y = 3$

Aus·wertung *f* evaluation

aus·zahlen (*sep.*) *v.t.* pay out, disburse

aus·zählen (*sep.*) *v.t.* count; (*statist.*) sort; (*tabellarisch*) tabulate

Aus·zahlung *f* disbursement: *A. in bar* cash disbursement

Aus·zählung *f* count; (*statist.*) sorting; (*in Tabellen*) tabulation: (*statist.*) *elektrische A.* punch card sorting

aus·zeichnen (*sep.*) *v.t.* **1.** (*zeichnen* draw) fill in, trace: *von einer Kurve sind Punkte gegeben; zeichne die Kurve aus* points of a curve are given; fill in the curve. **2.** (*hervorheben*) distinguish, point out; (*vorziehen*) prefer: *kein Index ist vor dem anderen ausgezeichnet* no index is preferred to another. **3.** (*statist.: schlüsseln*) code [*cf.* AUSGEZEICHNET]

Aus·zeichnung *f* **1.** (*einer Kurve*) filling in (of a curve). **2.** (*Hervorhebung*) distinction; (*Vorzug*) preference. **3.** (*statist.: Schlüsselung*) coding

aus·ziehen (*sep.*) *v.t.* **1.** (*die Wurzel einer Zahl*) extract (the root of a number). **2.** (*eine gezeichnete Linie*) trace (out) (in full) (a drawn line), draw (in), mark by a full line: *dieser Teil der Figur ist stärker ausgezogen als das Übrige* this portion of the graph is drawn in heavier than the rest [*cf.* AUSGEZOGEN; SICHTBAR]

Aus·ziehung *f* (*einer Wurzel*) extraction (of a root)

Aus·zug *m* excerpt, abstract: (*comm.*) *A. aus dem Hauptbuch* ledger abstract

Auto·kaskoversicherung *f* automobile personal liability and property damage insurance

Auto·korrelation *f* (*statist.*) (*einer periodischen Reihe*) autocorrelation, lag correlation (of a periodical series) with itself

auto·morph *adj.* (*alg.*) automorphic

Automorphismen·gruppe *f* (*alg.*) automorphism group

Automorphismen·ring *m* (*alg.*) automorphism ring

Automorphismus *m* (*alg.*) automorphism: *äußerer* (*innerer*) *A.* outer (inner) automorphism

axial *adj.* axial

Axial·symmetrie *f* axial symmetry

Axiom *n* axiom: *archimedisches A.*

Archimedean axiom; *Axiome von Peano* Peano's axioms [*cf.* GRUNDSATZ; VERTRÄGLICHKEIT; WIDERSPRUCHSFREIHEIT]

Axiomatik *f* (*Axiomatisierung*) axiomatization; (*Axiomensystem*) (system of) axioms; (*Wissenschaft*) axiomatic theory

axiomatisch *adj.* axiomatic(al)

axiomatisieren *v.t.* axiomatize

Axiomatisierung *f* axiomatization [*cf.* AXIOMATIK]

Axiomen·system *n* system of axioms, axiom system [*cf.* AXIOMATIK]

Axonometrie *f* axonometry

axonometrisch *adj.* (*Projektion*) axonometric (projection)

Azimut *m* or *n* **1.** (*Polarwinkel*) polar angle, azimuth, anomaly, amplitude, argument. **2.** (*astr.*: *Winkel zwischen Höhenkreis und Meridian* angle between circle of altitude and meridian) azimuth, bearing

Azimutal·projektion *f* azimuthal projection

Azimut·kreis *m* (*astr.*) azimuth circle

azyklisch *adj.* acyclic

B

Bahn *f* path, orbit, track: *die jährliche B. der Sonne* the annual track (or orbit, or path) of the sun

Bahn·kurve *f* trajectory

Balken *m* beam; (*Träger*) girder [*cf.* FREITRAGEND; TRÄGER 3.]

Balken·darstellung *f*, **Balken·diagramm** *n* (*statist.*) bar graph (or chart)

Balken·wage *f* beam and scales, balance

Ballen *m* (*meas.*) bale

Ballistik *f* ballistics
ballistisch *adj.* ballistic: *ballistische Kurve* ballistic curve
Balmer·serie *f* (*phys.*) Balmer series
Band *n* band, strip: *Möbiussches B.* Möbius band (or strip)
Banden·spektrum *n* (*phys.*) band spectrum
Bänder·diagramm *n* (*statist.*) component (or broken) bar or line chart (or bar or line graph)
Bank *f* (*fin.*) bank [*cf.* ABRECHNUNGSVERFAHREN; DISKONTSATZ; GUTHABEN; ZUSAMMENLEGUNG]
Bank·abrechnung *f* (*fin.*) **1.** (*über Käufe und Verkäufe von Effekten*) contract note, bought or sold note (of a bank). **2.** (*Kontoauszug*) statement (of account) (of a bank) [*cf.* DISKONTTAGE]
Bank·akzept *n* bank acceptance
Bank·bilanz *f* balance sheet, statement of conditions (of a bank)
Bank·diskont *m* bank rate (or discount)
Bank·guthaben *n* bank deposit (or account)
Bank·konto *n* bank account
Bank·note *f* bank note [*cf.* BANKNOTENUMLAUF; FÜNFER; ZEHNER]
Banknoten·umlauf *m* (*Umlauf*) circulation of bank notes; (*Banknoten im Umlauf*) notes in circulation
Bank·tratte *f* bank draft
Bar·geld *n* cash (in hand), ready money [*cf.* BESTAND]
Bar·wert *m* (*einer Rente*) cash equivalent, present value (of an annuity)
Basis *f* **1.** (*einer ebenen Figur,*

eines Körpers) base (of a plane figure, a solid): *B. eines Dreiecks, eines Kegels* base of a triangle, a cone. **2.** (*eines Zahlensystems*) base (of a number system); (*einer Potenz, eines Logarithmus*) base, radix (of a power, a logarithmic system) [*cf.* GRUNDZAHL]. **3.** (*eines linearen Raums, Zahlenkörpers*) basis, (set of) fundamental points, simplex of reference (of a linear space, a number field): *algebraische B.* algebraic basis [*cf.* ORTHOGONAL]. **4.** (*cryst.: basisches Pinakoid*) basal pinacoid [*cf.* GERADENDFLÄCHE; SCHIEFENDFLÄCHE]
basisch *adj.* (*cryst.*) basal: *basisches Pinakoid* basal pinacoid [= BASIS 4.]
Basis·ebene *f* basal plane, plane of the base [*cf.* GRUNDEBENE]
Basis·element *n* (*in einem Vektorraum*) basis element (in a vector space)
Basis·fläche *f* (*eines Körpers*) base (of a solid) ˙
Basis·satz *m* (*alg.*) basis condition
Basis·vektor *m* basis vector
Basis·wert *m* (*statist.*) base (period) value
Basis·winkel *m* (*eines Dreiecks*) base angle (of a triangle)
Basis·zeitraum *m* (*statist.*) base period
be·anspruchen *v.t.* (*mech.*) stress
Be·anspruchung *f* (*mech.*) stress
be·deuten *v.t.* mean, signify, denote: *f(x) bedeute irgend eine Funktion* let *f(x)* denote any function
Be·deutung *f* significance, meaning

[*cf.* INHALTLICH; MITTEILEN; SINN; WERTGEBEND]

bedeutungs·los *adj.* (*unwichtig*) insignificant; (*sinnlos*) meaningless [*cf.* SINNLOS]

Bedeutungslosig·keit *f* (*Unwichtigkeit*) insignificance; (*Sinnlosigkeit*) meaninglessness [*cf.* SINNLOSIGKEIT]

be·dingt *adj.* conditional: *bedingte Konvergenz* conditional convergence; *b. konvergente Reihe* conditionally convergent series

Bedingt·heit *f* conditionality

Be·dingung *f* condition: *notwendige und hinreichende B.* necessary and sufficient condition [*cf.* GENÜGEN; ORT 2.]

be·freien *v.t.* clear: *eine Gleichung von Brüchen b.* clear an equation of fractions

Be·freiung *f* clearing [*cf.* BEFREIEN]

be·friedigen *v.t.* satisfy: *eine Gleichung b.* satisfy an equation [*cf.* ERFÜLLEN 1.]

Be·friedigung *f* satisfying, satisfaction [*cf.* ERFÜLLUNG]

begeb·bar *adj.* (*fin.*) (*Papier*) negotiable (paper)

Begebbar·keit *f* negotiability

be·gleiten *v.t.* accompany, move along with [*cf.* DREIBEIN]

Begleit·matrix *f* companion matrix

be·grenzen *v.t.* bound, intercept, limit: *begrenzt von Flächen* bounded by surfaces; *die Achsen b. vier Kreisquadranten* the axes intercept four quadrants of a circle [*cf.* ABGRENZEN]

Be·grenzung *f* boundary, delimitation [*cf.* ÜBERSCHREITEN]

Begrenzungs·fläche *f* (*eines Körpers*) periphery, (boundary) surface (of a solid); (*Seitenfläche eines Polyeders*) side, face (of a polyhedron) [*cf.* SEITE 2.]

Begrenzungs·linie *f* periphery, boundary (line)

Be·griff *m* concept, (abstract) idea, notion [*cf.* ABSTRAKT; BESTIMMUNG; ERWEITERUNG; INHALT; PRÄDIKATSBEGRIFF; SUBJEKTSBEGRIFF; UNENDLICHE(S); UMFANG]

begriff·lich *adj.* conceptual, abstract, logical [*cf.* ABGRENZEN]

Be·günstigte(r) *m* (*ins.*) beneficiary

be·haupten *v.t.* assert, state

Be·hauptung *f* assertion, statement

beheb·bar *adj.* removable [*cf.* NICHT]

Behebbar·keit *f* removability [*cf.* BEHEBBAR]

be·heben *v.t.* remove: *eine Unstetigkeit b.* remove a discontinuity

Be·hebung *f* removal [*cf.* BEHEBBAR; BEHEBEN] ·

beide *num.*, *pron.* both, the two [*cf.* FREMD; SENKRECHT]

bei·läufig *adj.* approximate: *beiläufiges Resultat* approximate result

bei·legen (*sep.*) *v.t.* assign: *wir legen dem gebrochenen Exponenten einen Sinn bei* we assign a meaning to the fractional exponent

Bei·legung *f* assignment [*cf.* BEILEGEN]

Bei·spiel *n* example [*cf.* ANSCHAULICH; AUSARBEITEN; DEZIMALRECHNUNG; KOPF]

Bei·wert *m* coefficient

be·jahen *v.t.* affirm, answer in the positive (or affirmative)

Be·jahung *f* affirmation, positive

Bel *n* (*meas.*) bel

be·lasten *v.t.* **1.** (*beladen*) load, charge; (*comm.*) (*mit Soll b.*) charge to: (*comm.*) *ein Konto mit einem Betrag b.* charge an amount to an account. **2.** (*comm.*) (*verpfänden, z.B. ein Wertpapier*) pledge (e.g. securities); *mit einer Hypothek b.* mortgage

Be·lastung *f* **1.** (*Last*) load, charge; (*comm.*) charging to. **2.** (*Verpfändung*) pledging; (*von unbeweglichem Besitz*) mortgaging [*cf.* BELASTEN]

be·lehnen *v.t.* (*z.B. Wertpapiere*) pledge (e.g. securities)

Be·lehnung *f* pledging [*cf.* BELEHNEN]

Belehnungs·wert *m* [= BELEIHUNGS-WERT]

be·leihen *v.t.* [= BELEHNEN]

Be·leihung *f* [= BELEHNUNG]

Beleihungs·grenze *f* (*comm.*) [= KREDITGRENZE]

Beleihungs·wert *m* (*comm.*) (*einer Polizze*) loan value (of a policy); (*von Realbesitz*) hypothecary value (of real estate) [= BELEH-NUNGSWERT]

be·liebig *adj.* arbitrary, any: *beliebige Zahl* arbitrary (or any) number; *b. kleine Zahl* arbitrarily small number

Beliebig·keit *f* arbitrariness

be·nannt *adj.* denominate, concrete: *benannte Zahl* denominate (or concrete) number [*cf.* UM-WANDLUNG; ZUSAMMENGESETZT]

be·nennen *v.t.* designate, denote [*cf.* BEZEICHNEN]

Be·nennung *f* designation, nomenclature, denomination: *B. einer Zahl durch Maß- oder Zähleinheit* denomination of a number by unit of measurement or counting [*cf.* BEZEICHNUNG]

be·obachten *v.t.* observe

Be·obachtung *f* observation [*cf.* REIHE]

Beobachtungs·fehler *m* error of observation

Beobachtungs·reihe *f* series (or sequence) of observations

Be·randung *f* boundary

berechen·bar *adj.* calculable, computable

Berechenbar·keit *f* calculability, computability

be·rechnen *v.t.* calculate, compute, figure (out): (*den Wert*) *b.* evaluate: *berechne* $5\frac{2}{3}$ *auf vier Dezimalstellen* evaluate $5\frac{2}{3}$ to four decimal places

Be·rechner *m* calculator, computer

Be·rechnung *f* calculation, computation: *falsche B.* miscalculation [*cf.* FALSCH; KALKULATION]

Be·reich *m* (*einer Funktion*) domain (of a function); (*einer Kurve, Fläche*) region, extent (of a curve, surface); (*einer Variablen*) range (of a variable) [*cf.* RAND; ZUSAMMENHÄNGEND]

be·reinigen *v.t.* (*statist.*) (*verbessern*) correct, adjust; (*verfeinern*) refine [*cf.* MITTELWERT]

Be·reinigung *f* (*statist.*) (*Verbesserung*) correction, adjustment; (*Verfeinerung*) refinement [*cf.* SAISONBEREINIGUNG]

be·richtigen *v.t.* correct

Be·richtigung *f* correction

Bernoulli *m* N.: *Bernoullische Zahlen* Bernoulli's numbers

Berufs·zählung *f* census of occupations

be·rühren *v.t.* be tangent (to), touch, osculate, meet (in contact of at least second order) [*cf.* AUSSEN]

be·rührend *adj.* tangent (to): *von außen (innen)* b. externally (internally) tangent

Berührende *f* tangent (line) [= TANGENTE 1.]

Berührung *f* contact, tangency, contingence; (*von wenigstens zweiter Ordnung* contact of at least second order, also) osculation: *Ordnung der B.* order of contact [*cf.* ANSCHMIEGUNG; INNER; ORDNUNG]

Berührungs·ebene *f* tangent plane

Berührungs·kegel *m* tangent cone

Berührungs·linie *f* tangent (line) [=TANGENTE 1.]

Berührungs·punkt *m* point of tangency (or contact) [*cf.* TANGENTE]

Berührungs·sehne *f* (*bezüglich eines Punktes außerhalb eines Kreises*) chord of contact (with reference to a point outside of a circle)

be·schleunigen 1. *v.t.* accelerate. 2. *v.r.:* sich b. be accelerated, gather speed

Be·schleunigung *f* acceleration: *gleichförmige B.* uniform acceleration [*cf.* AUGENBLICKLICH; KRAFT; UNGLEICHFÖRMIG]

Beschleunigungs·komponente *f* component of acceleration

Beschleunigungs·vektor *m* acceleration vector

be·schränkt *adj.* limited, bounded: *nach oben (unten)* b. bounded from above (below) [*cf.* GESELLSCHAFT]

Beschränkt·heit *f* (*einer Zahlenfolge*) boundedness (of a number sequence)

be·schreiben *v.t.* 1. (*zeichnen*) describe, trace: *einen Kreis b.* describe (or trace) a circle. 2. (*schreiben auf*) write upon [*cf.* EINSEITIG]. 3. (*bezeichnen*) label; (*mit Buchstaben versehen*) letter; (*beschriften*) supply with an inscription (or: a legend): *wir b. die Ecken des Dreiecks mit Großbuchstaben* we letter (or label) the vertices of the triangle with capitals

Be·schreibung *f* description; lettering; legend, inscription, label [*cf.* BESCHREIBEN]

be·schriften *v.t.* supply with a legend (or inscription) [*cf.* BESCHREIBEN]

Be·schriftung *f* legend, inscription

be·seitigen *v.t.* eliminate, remove [*cf.* ELIMINIEREN]

Be·seitigung *f* elimination, removal: *B. (oder Wegschaffung oder Eliminierung) einer Unbekannten aus einer Gleichung* elimination (or removal) of an unknown from an equation [*cf.* ENTFERNUNG]

Besetzungs·zahl *f* (*statist.*) class frequency.

Be·sitz *m* possession, property [*cf.* BELASTUNG; UNBEWEGLICH; VERMÖGEN]

be·sitzen *v.t.* possess

be·sonder *adj.* particular, special: *besondere Lösung* particular solution; (*log.*) *besonderes Urteil* particular judgment

Bessel *m N.: Besselsche Funktionen* Bessel (or cylindrical) functions [= ZYLINDERFUNKTIONEN]

Be·stand *m* (*comm.*) balance; (*an Effekten*) holdings *pl.*; (*an Geldmitteln*) funds *pl.*; (*an Bargeld*) cash in hand; (*an Waren*) goods in stock, inventory [*cf.* EFFEKTIV]

Bestandes·masse *f* (*statist.*) [= STRECKENMASSE]

be·ständig *adj.* constant, permanent, stable [*cf.* WERT]

Beständig·keit *f* constancy, permanence, stability

Bestands·masse *f* (*statist.*) [= STRECKENMASSE]

Bestand·teil *m* part, element, component, constituent

be·stätigen *v.t.* confirm, verify

Be·stätigung *f* confirmation, verification

Be·steck *n* (*nav.*) reckoning, ship's place on the chart; *das B. aufnehmen* prick the chart

Besteck·aufnahme *f* (*nav.*) reckoning: *B. auf Grund des zurückgelegten Wegs* dead reckoning

be·stehen *v.i.* **1.** (*existieren*) exist: *gleichzeitig b.* exist simultaneously, coexist [*cf.* GLEICHZEITIG]. **2.** (*aus, in*) consist (of, in)

be·stimmen *v.t.* determine; (*festlegen*) specify; (*einzeichnen*) plot; (*einen Begriff*) define: *eine Kurve punktweise b.* (*oder konstruieren*) plot a curve point by point [*cf.* FESTLEGEN]

be·stimmt *adj.* definite, determined, determinate, certain: *bestimmtes Integral* definite integral [*cf.* GRENZE]; *bestimmter Wert* definite value [*cf.* ANNÄHERND; ANNEHMEN]; *bestimmte Gleichung* determinate equation

Bestimmt·heit *f* definiteness

Bestimmtheits·axiom *n* (*der Mengenlehre*) identity condition (of set theory)

Be·stimmung *f* determination; (*eines Begriffs*) definition: *nähere B. zu einem Begriff* modifier to a concept

Bestimmungs·gleichung *f* conditional equation, equation of condition [*ant.:* IDENTITÄT, *identische Gleichung* (*cf.* IDENTISCH)]

Bestimmungs·relation *f* defining relation [*cf.* REKURSIV]

Bestimmungs·stück *n* datum, one of the data: *zu einem Kegelschnitt sind fünf Bestimmungsstücke notwendig* five data are required for (or: to determine) a conic

Beta *n* (*griechischer Buchstabe* Greek letter B, β) beta

Beta·funktion *f* beta function

Beta·strahlen *m pl.* beta rays

Be·trag *m* (*bestimmte Menge* definite quantity) amount; (*Größenverhältnis*) rate; (*absoluter Wert*) absolute value: *ein B. von hundert Dollar* an amount of one hundred dollars; *der B. der Geschwindigkeit* the rate of speed; (*alg.*) *der (absolute) B. einer Zahl, eines Körperelements* the absolute value of a number, a field element

[*cf.* ABPLATTUNG; BELASTEN; GRÖSSE]

be·tragen *v.t.* amount to, total [*cf.* ABPLATTUNG]

Betriebs·statistik *f* (*gewerbliche*) statistics (or census) of manufactures and trades; (*landwirtschaftliche*) census of agriculture

beugen *v.t.* (*opt.*) (*Strahlen*) diffract (rays)

Beugung *f* (*opt.*) diffraction

Beugungs·gitter *n* (*opt.*) diffraction grating

Beugungs·spektrum *n* (*opt.*) diffraction spectrum

Be·völkerung *f* population [*cf.* GESAMTHEIT ; GESAMTMASSE ; MASSE]

Bevölkerungs·statistik *f* vital (or population) statistics, demography

be·wegen *v.t.*, *v.r.*: sich *b.* move: *ein sich bewegender* (*oder: ein bewegter*) *Körper* a moving body [*cf.* SCHIEF]

beweg·lich *adj.* movable, moving, mobile; (*veränderlich*) changing: *bewegliche Rolle* moving pulley [*cf.* SAISONINDEX ; SAISONSCHWANKUNGEN ; SAISONVERÄNDERUNGSZAHLEN]

Beweglich·keit *f* movability, mobility

Be·wegung *f* motion, movement: *krummlinige B. um ein Kraftzentrum* curvilinear motion about a center of force [*cf.* BROWN; ENERGIE; FORTSCHREITEND; GERADLINIG; GLEICHFÖRMIG; HARMONISCH; KREISEN; KREISFÖRMIG; KREISLAUF; MITTEILEN; RECHT-

LÄUFIG; RECHTLÄUFIGKEIT; RÜCKLÄUFIGKEIT; UNGLEICHFÖRMIG]

Bewegungs·energie *f* kinetic energy, energy of motion

Bewegungs·gesetz *n* law of motion

Bewegungs·größe *f* (*phys.*) (linear) momentum, impulse

Bewegungs·lehre *f* theory of motion, kinematics

Bewegungs·masse *f* (*statist.*) [= PUNKTMASSE]

Be·weis *m* proof, demonstration, verification: *deduktiver* (*induktiver*) *B.* deductive (inductive) proof [*cf.* ANALYTISCH; ANSCHAUUNG; INDIREKT; NACH]

beweis·bar *adj.* provable, demonstrable

Beweisbar·keit *f* provability, demonstrability

be·weisen *v.t.* prove, demonstrate, verify [*cf.* Q.E.D.]

Beweis·führung *f* proof, argumentation, argument [*cf.* GEHEN]

Beweis·grund *m* argument

be·werten *v.t.* value, rate, estimate; (*für Steuerzwecke*) assess (for taxation)

be·wertet *adj.* (*alg.*) with valuation: *bewerteter Körper* field with valuation

Be·wertung *f* 1. (*alg.*) (*eines Zahlenkörpers*) valuation (of a number field). 2. (*comm.*) valuation, rating, estimate; (*für Steuerzwecke*) assessment (for taxation)

Bewertungs·ring *m* (*alg.*) valuation ring

be·zahlen *v.t.* pay [*cf.* ABRECHNUNG]

Be·zahlung *f* pay, payment

be·zeichnen *v.t.* **1.** (*benennen*) designate, denote, label [*cf.* BE-SCHREIBEN]. **2.** (*durch Zeichen*) notate, denote (by symbols)

be·zeichnet *adj.* (*Zahl*) signed (number)

Be·zeichnung *f* **1.** (*Benennung* name) designation, nomenclature, label. **2.** (*Schriftzeichen* symbol) notation [*cf.* ABKÜRZEN; BUCH-STABE]

Bezeichnungs·weise *f* [= BEZEICH-NUNG]

be·ziehen *v.t., v.r.:* **sich** *b.* (*auf*) relate, refer (to): *bezogen auf* referred to, relative to [*cf.* SEITE 4.]

Be·ziehung *f* relation, reference [*cf.* EINEINDEUTIG; EINMEHRDEUTIG; INTRANSITIV; NICHTTRANSITIV; PROJEKTIV; REFLEXIV; SYMMET-RISCH; TRANSITIV; UNVERBUNDEN]

Beziehungs·gerade *f* (*statist.*) line of regression

Beziehungs·gleichung *f* (*statist.*) regression equation

Beziehungs·linie *f* (*statist.*) line of regression

Be·zug *m* reference

Bezugs·reihe *f* (*statist.*) related time series used as trend

Bezugs·system *n* system (or frame) of reference, reference system (or frame)

bi·angular *adj.* biangular

Biege·festigkeit *f* bending strength

biegen *v.t., v.r.:* **sich** *b.* bend

bieg·sam *adj.* flexible [*cf.* SCHMIEG-SAM]

Biegsam·keit *f* flexibility [*cf.* SCHMIEGSAMKEIT]

Biegung *f* flexure, bend

Biegungs·festigkeit *f* bending strength

bi·konkav *adj.* biconcave

bi·konvex *adj.* biconvex

Bilanz *f* (*comm., fin.*) balance

Bild *n* (*Abbild*) image, picture, map; (*graphische Darstellung*) graph, line chart; (*statistisches*) picto-gram: *das B. eines Punktes ist wieder ein Punkt* the image of a point is another point; *das B. der Gleichung* $x = y$ the graph of the equation $x = y$ [*cf.* PERSPEKTI-VISCH; SPHÄRISCH; STATISTISCH; VIRTUELL]

Bild·ansicht *f* pictorial view

Bild·ebene *f* (*Perspektivbildebene*) picture (or perspective) plane; (*Projektionsebene*) projection plane

bil·den **1.** *v.t.* form, shape, make: *der Winkel, den die Gerade mit der x-Achse bildet* the angle the line makes with the x-axis; *a bildet mit b einen Winkel von* 45° a is at an angle of 45° from b. **2.** *v.r.:* **sich** *b.* form [*cf.* TRÄG-HEITSFORM]

bild·mäßig *adj.* pictorial

Bild·punkt *m* image point

bild·sam *adj.* plastic [*cf.* SCHMIEG-SAM]

Bildsam·keit *f* plasticity [*cf.* SCHMIEGSAMKEIT]

Bild·statistik *f* pictogram (or iso-type) method of statistical re-presentation, pictorial statistics [*cf.* METHODE]

Bildung *f* formation

bi·linear *adj.* bilinear: (*alg.*) *bili-neare Form* bilinear form

Bilinear·form f (*alg.*) bilinear form
Billion f ($=10^{12}$) *Am.* trillion, *Br.* billion: *tausend Billionen* ($=10^{15}$) *Am.* quadrillion; *Br.* a thousand billions
binär *adj.* binary [*cf.* FORM]
bin·okular *adj.* binocular
Bi·nom n binomial
Binomial·formel f binomial formula
Binomial·koeffizient m binomial coefficient
Binomial·reihe f binomial series
Binomial·satz m binomial theorem
bi·nomisch *adj.* binomial: *binomische Reihe* binomial series; *binomischer Satz* (*oder Lehrsatz*) binomial theorem; [*cf.* ENTWICKLUNG]
Bi·normale f binormal
bi·polar *adj.* bipolar
Bi·polarität f bipolarity
bi·quadratisch *adj.* biquadratic, of the fourth degree: *biquadratische Gleichung* biquadratic equation, equation of the fourth degree
birn·förmig *adj.* pear-shaped: *birnförmige Kurve* pear-shaped quartic
Blatt n **1.** (*Schleifenkurve* loop) folium, leaf: *Descartessches* (*oder Cartesisches*) *B.* folium of Descartes [*cf.* FOLIUM]. **2.** (*einer Riemannschen Fläche*) sheet (of a Riemann surface)
Blatt·kurve f folium, leaf: *doppelte B.* double folium [= ZWEIBLATT]
blei·ben *v.i.* remain, be left; *fünf und sieben ist zwölf, zwei angeschrieben, bleibt eins* five and seven is (or are, or equals) twelve,

put down two, (and) carry (the) one; 7 *weniger* 5, *bleibt* 2 5 from 7 leaves 2 [*cf.* AB; ENTHALTEN *adj.;* VON]
Bo·gen m **1.** (*einer Kurve*) arc (of a curve)[*cf.*ABSCHNEIDEN; GRAD]. **2.** (*Arkus*) arc (length) in radian measure [*cf.* EINHEITSKREIS]. **3.** (*Papiermaß* paper measure) sheet
Bogen·differential n differential of arc
Bogen·element n (*einer Kurve*) element of arc (or length), linear element (of a curve)
Bogen·grad m degree of arc
Bogen·länge f (*im Längenmaß*) arc length (in linear measure); (*einer Kurve*) curve length [*cf.* ABTRAGEN; KURVE]
Bogen·linie f curved (or sinuous) line
Bogen·maß n radian measure, circular measure (by radians): *Einheit im B.* radian (unit) $\left(=\dfrac{180°}{\pi} \right)$[*cf.* GRAD; UMRECHNEN]
Bogen·minute f minute of arc
Bogen·sekunde f second of arc
Bogen·zirkel m bow compass
Bonität f (*comm.*) credit, solvency
Bonus m (*comm. fin.*) **1.** (*Extradividende*) surplus (or extra) dividend. **2.** (*Gehaltszulage*) gratuity, remuneration, bonus, premium
bor·gen *v.t.* borrow: (*beim Subtrahieren*) *ich muß mir eins b.* (*oder ausborgen*) I have to borrow one (in subtraction)
Börse f (*comm., fin.*) stock exchange [*cf.* KURSSTREICHUNG; LAUFEN; NOTIERUNG; SCHLUSSKURS]

Börsen·auftrag *m* (*comm.*) buying order at the stock exchange [*cf.* EINSCHUSS; SICHERHEITSSUMME]

Börsen·drucker *m* (*comm.*) quotation ticker

Börsen·freiverkehr *m* (*comm.*) curb (market)

Börsen·index *m* (*comm.*) stock price average

Börsen·kurs *m* (*comm.*) stock exchange quotation

Börsen·notierung *f* (*comm.*) stock exchange quotation [*cf.* KURS]

Boyle - Mariottesches Gesetz *n* (*phys.*) Boyle's (and Mariotte's) law

Brachisto·chrone *f* brachistochrone

Brachy·achse *f* brachyaxis, brachydiagonal axis

brachy·diagonal *adj.* brachydiagonal

Brachy·diagonale *f* (*cryst.*) brachyaxis, brachydiagonal (axis) [= BRACHYACHSE]

Brachy·doma *n* (*pl. Brachydomen*) (*cryst.*) brachydome

Brachy·pinakoid *n* (*cryst.*) brachypinacoid, brachypinakoid

Brachy·prisma *n* brachyprism

Brachy·pyramide *f* (*cryst.*) brachypyramid

brechen 1. *v.t.* break; (*opt.*) refract. **2.** *v.r.:* sich *b.* be refracted

Brechung *f* (*opt.*) refraction

Brechungs·exponent *m*, **Brechungs-index** *m* index of refraction, refractive index, refraction coefficient

Brechungs·winkel *m* angle of refraction

breit *adj.* broad, wide [*cf.* WEIT]

Breite *f* **1.** (*Weite*) breadth, width [*cf.* WEITE]. **2.** (*geog.*) latitude: *geographische B.* (geographic) latitude [*cf.* GEOGRAPHISCH]

Breitengrad *m* (*geog.*) degree of latitude

Breiten·kreis *m* (*geog.*) circle (or parallel) of latitude

Brenn·fläche *f* caustic surface

Brenn·linie *f* caustic (curve)

Brenn·punkt *m* focus [= FOKUS]; *mit gemeinsamen Brennpunkten* confocal

Brennpunkt(s)·eigenschaft *f* (*der Kegelschnitte*) focal (or acoustical, or optical, or reflexion) property (of conics)

Brenn·strahl *m* (*eines Kegelschnittpunktes*) focal radius (or distance) (of a point of a conic)

Briggs *m* N. [*cf.* LOGARITHMUS]

brin·gen *v.t.* bring, put, reduce: *in Dezimalform b.* put into decimal form; *auf gemeinsamen Nenner b.* reduce to a common denominator; *einen Bruch auf die einfachste Form b.* (*oder zurückführen, oder reduzieren*) reduce a fraction to its lowest terms [*cf.* DECKUNG; TABELLE; TRANSPONIEREN]

Brown *n* N. *Brownsche Bewegung* Brownian movement (or motion)

Bruch *m* fraction: *echter* (*unechter*) *B.* proper (improper) fraction; *einfacher B.* simple fraction; *erweiterter B.* fraction in higher terms; *einen B. erweitern* reduce a fraction to higher terms [*cf.* BRINGEN; ERWEITERUNG; GEMEIN; GLEICH; IRREDUZIBEL; KLEINST; KÜRZEN; KÜRZUNG; UNGLEICH;

UNGLEICHNAMIG; UNKÜRZBAR;
VERWANDELN; WEGSCHAFFEN;
ZUSAMMENGESETZT, ZÄHLER]
Bruch·gleichung *f* fractional
equation
Bruch·strich *m* fraction bar (or
line)
Bruch·teil *m* fraction
brutto *adj.* (*comm.*) gross
Brutto·betrag *m* (*comm.*) gross
amount
Brutto·einnahme(n) *f pl.* (*comm.*)
gross receipts *pl.*
Brutto·ertrag *m*, **Brutto·gewinn** *m*,
Brutto·nutzen *m* (*comm.*) gross
profit
Brutto·preis *m* (*comm.*) gross
price
Brutto·tonnengehalt *m* (*comm.*)
gross tonnage
Buch *n* 1. (*comm.*) (*Konto*) (*oft pl.*)
accounts *pl.*: *B. führen* keep the
accounts. 2. (*Papiermaß* paper
measure) quire [*cf.* ABSCHLIESSEN;
ABSCHLUSS]
Bücher·abschluß *m* (*comm.*) balancing of accounts
Bücher·revisor *m* (*comm.*) (*einer
Firma*) (public) accountant (of a
firm); (*des Steueramts*) tax agent
(of the Internal Revenue Office)
Buch·forderungen *f pl.* (*comm.*)
accounts receivable
Buch·führung *f* (*comm.*) bookkeeping, keeping the accounts:
einfache (*doppelte*) *B.* (*oder Buch-*

haltung) bookkeeping by single
(double) entry
Buch·halter *m* (*comm.*) book-
keeper
Buch·haltung *f* (*comm.*) bookkeeping [*cf.* BUCHFÜHRUNG]
buch·mäßig *ad.* (*comm.*) according
to books (or records); *buch·
mäßige Schulden* accounts payable
Buch·schulden *f pl.* (*comm.*) ordinary debts, accounts payable
Buch·stabe *m* letter: *Bezeichnung
von Zahlen durch Buchstaben*
literal notation of numbers; *ein
Diagramm mit Buchstaben versehen* letter a diagram [*cf.* BE-
SCHREIBEN]
Buchstaben·bezeichnung *f* literal
notation
Buchstaben·formel *f* formula with
letters
Buchstaben·gleichung *f* literal
equation
Buchstaben·größe *f* literal number
Buchstaben·rechnung *f* operating
with letters, algebra
Buch·wert *m* (*comm.*) book value
Bündel *n* bundle, sheaf, star, two-
parameter family [*cf.* TRÄGER 2.]
bürgerlich *adj.* civil [*cf.* JAHR]
Bürg·schaft *f* (*comm.*) (*Unterpfand*)
pledge; (*Sicherheit*) security,
guarantee
Büschel *n* pencil, one-parameter
family [*cf.* TRÄGER 2.]

C

Cantor *m N.* [*cf.* FUNDAMENTAL-
REIHE; MENGE]
Cardanisch *adj.* [=KARDANISCH]
Cardanus *m N.* [*cf.* KARDANISCH]
Cartesisch *adj.* Cartesian [=KAR-
TESISCH]: *Cartesische Kurve* (*oder
Ovale pl.*) Cartesian (ovals);
Cartesische Parabel [*cf.* TRIDENS]
[*cf.* BLATT]
Cartesius *m N.* [=DESCARTES]
Cassini *m N.* [*cf.* CASSINISCH]
Cassinisch *adj.* Cassinian: *Cassini-
sche Kurve* (*oder Linie*) Cassinian
oval (or ellipse), oval of Cassini
Cassinoide *f* Cassinian oval, oval
of Cassini [=KASSINOIDE]
casus irreducibilis *m* (*Lat.*) irreducible case [*cf.* IRREDUZIBEL]
Celsius 1. *m N.* Celsius. 2. (*Thermo-
metergrad*) centigrade (degree):
100° *Celsius* 100° centigrade
Celsius·thermometer *n* centigrade
(or centesimal) thermometer
c.g.s.-System *n* (*abbr.*) *Zenti-
meter-Gramm -Sekunden - System*
centimeter-gram-second system
(of units), (*abbr.*) C.G.S. units
Charakter *m* (*alg.*) (*eines Gruppenelements*) character (of a group
element)
Charakteren·relation *f* (*alg.*) character relation
Charakteristik *f* 1. (*eines Logarithmus*) characteristic (of a
logarithm). 2. (*einer Fläche*)
characteristic (curve) (of a surface). 3. (*eines Primkörpers,
Schiefkörpers*) characteristic (of
a prime field, skew field)

Charakteristikum *n* (*pl. Charakte-
ristika*) characteristic, trait;
(*statist.*) parameter: *Charakte-
ristika einer Verteilung* parameters
of a distribution
charakteristisch *adj.* characteristic;
charakteristische Untergruppe
characteristic subgroup
Chemie *f* chemistry
Chemiker *m* (*Am.*) chemist, (*Br.*)
(scientific) chemist
chemisch *adj.* chemical
Chi *n* (*griechischer Buchstabe*
Greek letter X, χ) chi
Chordale *f* [=POTENZLINIE]
Chordal·punkt *m* [=POTENZPUNKT]
Christoffel *m N.* [*cf.* SYMBOL]
Chrono·meter *n* chronometer
chrono·metrisch *adj.* chronomet-
ric(al)
Clelia·kurve *f*, Clelie *f* clélie
cosecans *m* (*von* α) (*symb.*: cosec
α) [=KOSEKANS, KOSEKANTE]
cosecans hyperbolicus *m* (*eines
Winkels* α) (*symb.*: cosec h α)
hyperbolic cosecant (of an angle
α) (*symb.*: csch α, cosech α)
cosinus *m* (*von* α) (*symb.*: cos α)
[=KOSINUS] [*cf.* VERSUS]
cosinus hyperbolicus *m* (*eines
Winkels* α) (*symb.*: cos h α)
hyperbolic cosine (of an angle α)
(symb.: cosh α)
cosinus versus *m* (*von* α) (*symb.*:
covers α) [=KOSINUSVERSUS]
cotangens *m* (*von* α) (*symb.*: cot
α, ctg α) [=KOTANGENS, KO-
TANGENTE]
cotangens hyperbolicus *m* (*eines

Winkels α) (*symb.:* ctg h α, cot h α) hyperbolic cotangent (of an angle α) (*symb.:* ctnh α, coth α)

Coulomb *n* (*elec.*) coulomb

Curie *n* (*rad. meas.*) curie

D

Dach·gesellschaft *f* (*comm.*) [= HOLDINGGESELLSCHAFT]

dämpfen *v.t.* (*z.B. Schwingungen*) damp (out) (e.g. oscillations) [*cf.* GEDÄMPFT]

Dar·lehen *n* (*fin.*) loan [*cf.* VERZINSEN]

dar·stellen (*sep.*) *v.t.* **1.** (*in einer Form wiedergeben*) represent, render (in a form): *eine Kurve graphisch* (*oder zeichnerisch*) *d.* trace (or plot, or graph) a curve [*cf.* ANSCHAULICH; FIGUR]. **2.** (*alg.*) (*einen Ring*) represent (a ring). **3.** (*eine Projektion zeichnen von*) draw a view of, represent: *ein Prisma im Aufriß d.* draw the front view of a prism; *eine Ebene durch ihre Spuren d.* represent a plane by its traces [*cf.* DARSTELLEND; DARSTELLUNG 3.]

dar·stellend *adj.* descriptive: *darstellende Geometrie* descriptive geometry [*cf.* DARSTELLEN 2.; DARSTELLUNG 2.]

Dar·stellung *f* **1.** (*Wiedergabe in einer Form*) representation, rendering (in a form): *parametrische D.* parametric representation [*cf.* GRAPHISCH; KANONISCH]. **2.** (*alg.*) (*Homomorphismus* homomorphism) representation: *irreduzible D. einer Gruppe* irredu-cible representation of a group; *treue* (*untreue*) *D.* faithful (unfaithful) representation [*cf.* AUSREDUZIEREN; HAUPTCHARAKTER; REPRÄSENTATIV]. **3.** (*Projektion*) view, projection, representation: *D. im Grundriß* top view [*cf.* DARSTELLEN 2.; DARSTELLEND]

Darstellungs·modul *m* (*alg.*) representation module

Darstellungs·theorie *f* (*alg.*) representation theory

Datum *n* **1.** (*Gegebenheit*) (*pl. Daten, Data*) datum, one of the data, given fact [*cf.* ANPASSEN; AUFARBEITEN; AUFARBEITUNG; AUSGELÖST; ERHEBEN; NICHTAUSGELÖST; VERDICHTUNG]. **2.** (*pl. Daten*) (*des Kalenders*) date (of the calendar)

Datums·grenze *f* (*geog.*) (international) date line

Dauer *f* duration, period :*D. einer Schwingung* period of an oscillation

dauern *v.t., v.i.* last, continue, take (a time)

dauernd *adj.* permanent, continuous

decken 1. *v.t.* cover. **2.** *v.r.:* **sich d.** be superposable (or superimposable, or congruent, or coincident); *sich deckend* superposable, superimposable, congruent, coincident

Deck·fläche *f* (*eines Körpers*) upper (or covering) surface (or base) (of a solid) [*cf.* GRUNDFLÄCHE]

Deckung *f* superposition, superimposition, coincidence; *zur D. bringen* superpose, superimpose; *die beiden Figuren können zur D. gebracht werden* the two geometric figures are congruent

Deckungs·verhältnis *n* (*fin.*) (*einer Währung*) cover ratio (of a currency)

Dedekind *m* N. [*cf.* SCHNITT 3.]

De·duktion *f* (*log.*) deduction

de·duktiv *adj.* deductive: *deduktive Methode* deductive method [*cf.* BEWEIS]

deduzier·bar *adj.* deducible

Deduzierbar·keit *f* (*log.*) deducibility

de·duzieren *v.t.* deduce

definier·bar *adj.* definable

Definierbar·keit *f* definability

de·finieren *v.t.* define [*cf.* EINDEUTIG]

de·finit *adj.* (*alg.*) definite: *positiv* (*negativ*) *d.* positive (negative) definite

De·finition *f* definition

Definitions·bereich *m* domain of definition

de·fizient *adj.* deficient, defective [*cf.* ZAHL]

De·formation *f* deformation, strain

de·formieren *v.t.* deform, strain

De·formierung *f* deformation, strain

dehn·bar *adj.* tensile, ductile

Dehnbar·keit *adj.* tensility, ductility

dehnen *v.t.* stretch, elongate

Dehnung *f* stretch(ing), elongation [*cf.* LÄNGENAUSDEHNUNG]

Deka *n* dekagram [= DEKAGRAMM]

Dekade *f* decade

dekadisch *adj.* decadic, decimal: *dekadisches Zahlensystem* decadic number system, decimal system [*cf.* LOGARITHMUS; ZEHNERZAHL; ZEHNERLOGARITHMUS]

Dekagon *n* decagon [= ZEHNECK]

dekagonal *adj.* decagonal [= ZEHNECKIG]

Deka·gramm *n* (*abbr. dkg*) decagram, decagramme, dekagram, dekagramme (*abbr. dkg*.)

Deka·meter *n* decameter, dekameter

De·klination *f* (*astr., magn.*) declination

Deklinations·kreis *n* (*astr.*) circle of declination, declination circle

De·krement *n* decrement: (*bei gedämpften Schwingungen*) *logarithmisches D.* logarithmic decrement (in damped oscillations)

delisch *adj.* Delian: *delisches Problem* Delian problem

Delta *n* (*griechischer Buchstabe* Greek letter Δ, δ) delta

Deltoid *n* deltoid

De·monstration *f* demonstration

de·monstrieren *v.t.* demonstrate

De·positen *pl.* deposited valuables, deposits

De·pression *f* depression [*cf.* WIRTSCHAFTSZYKLUS]

Depressions·winkel *m* angle of depression

Derivation *f* derivation [= ABLEITUNG 2.]

Derivierte *f* derivative [=

DIFFERENTIALQUOTIENT, AB-
LEITUNG 3.]

Descartes *N.* [*cf.* BLATT; FOLIUM]

de·skriptiv *adj.* (*Geometrie*) descriptive (geometry)

Detail (verkaufs)preis *m* retail price

Determinante *f* determinant: *Entwicklung einer D., Schreibung
einer D. in entwickelter Form*
development (or expansion, or
evaluation) of a determinant;
Reihe (Kolonne) einer D. row
(column) of a determinant; *symmetrische (schiefsymmetrische) D.*
symmetric (skew-symmetric) determinant; *Jacobische D.* Jacobi-
an (determinant) [*cf.* ADJUNKTE;
AUSRECHNEN; DIAGONALGLIED;
ELEMENT; ENTHALTEN; FAKTOR;
HAUPTDIAGONALE; HAUPTGLIED;
MINOR; ORDNUNG; RÄNDERN;
SCHEMA; SUBDETERMINANTE;
UNTERDETERMINANTE; VER-
SCHWINDEN; ZWEIREIHIG]

Determinanten·teiler *m* (*einer
Matrix*) determinantal divisor
(of a matrix)

deuten *v.t.* interpret

Deutero·prisma *n* (*cryst.*) prism
of the second order, deuteroprism

Deutero·pyramide *f* (*cryst.*) pyramid of the second order, deutero-
pyramid

Deutung *f* interpretation [*cf.*
INHALTLICH]

de·veloppabel *adj.* developable

De·veloppable *f* developable (surface)

Devisen *f pl.* (*fin.*) foreign exchange
(*sing.*) [*cf.* MENGENNOTIERUNG]

Devisen·kurs *m* (*fin.*) rate of
foreign exchange

Devisen·reportgeschäft *n* [= KOST-
GESCHÄFT]

Dezi·bel *n* (*meas.*) decibel

Dezi·gramm *n* (*abbr. dg*) decigram,
decigramme, (*abbr. dg.*)

Dezil *n* (*statist.*) decile

Dezi·liter *n* deciliter, decilitre

Dezillion *f* (10^{60}) *Am.* novem-
decillion, *Br.* decillion

dezimal *adj.* decimal

Dezimal·bruch *m* decimal (fraction) [= DEZIMALZAHL]: *gemischter Dezimalbruch* mixed
decimal; *periodischer Dezimalbruch* periodic (or circulating, or
recurring, or repeating) decimal
[*cf.* ABBRECHEN; ENDLICH; FÜNF-
STELLIG; PERIODE; UNENDLICH;
VERWANDELN; VERWANDLUNG]

Dezimale *f* decimal (place) [*cf.*
ABSTREICHEN; GENAU]

Dezimal·form *f* decimal form [*cf.*
BRINGEN]

Dezimal·logarithmus *m* common
(or Briggs') logarithm

Dezimal·maß *n* decimal measure

Dezimal·punkt *m* decimal point
[*cf.* VERSCHIEBEN; WERTGEBEND]

Dezimal·rechnung *f* **1.** (*Verfahren*
method) decimal arithmetic (or
numeration). **2.** (*Beispiel* example) calculation (or computation, or sum) with decimals

Dezimal·schreibung *f*, **Dezimal-
schreibweise** *f* decimal notation

Dezimal·stelle *f* decimal (place)
[*cf.* BERECHNEN; GELTEN]

Dezimal·system *n* decimal (or
decadic) system

Dezimal·wage *f* decimal balance

Dezimal·zahl *f* decimal (number),
decimal fraction [= DEZIMAL-

BRUCH] [*cf.* AUFRUNDEN; DREI-
STELLIG; EINSTELLIG; FÜNF-
STELLIG; ..STELLIG; VIELSTELLIG;
ZWEISTELLIG]

Dezi·meter *n* (*abbr. dm*) decimeter,
decimetre (*abbr. dm.*)

dia·gonal *adj.* diagonal

Dia·gonale *f* diagonal

Diagonal·element *n* (*einer Determinante*) leading element (in a
determinant)

Diagonal·matrix *f* diagonal matrix

Diagonal·schnitt *m* diagonal section

Dia·gramm *n* diagram, graph,
schema [*cf.* BUCHSTABE; SCHEMA;
VERANSCHAULICHEN]

dia·grammatisch *adj.* diagram-
matic

Diagramm·karte *f* statistical map

Dia·kaustik *f* (*opt.*) diacaustic

Dia·meter *m* diameter

dia·metral *adj.* diametral, dia-
metric(al): *d. entgegengesetzt* dia-
metrically opposed (or opposite)

dicht *adj.* dense: *dichte Menge*
dense set; *überall d.* everywhere
dense [*cf.* WERT]

Dichte *f* density [*cf.* MITTEL]

Dicht·heit *f* (*einer Menge*) dense-
ness (of a set)

dick *adj.* thick, wide

Dicke *f* thickness, width

Di·ëder *n* dihedral

Differential *n* differential: *par-
tielles* (*totales*) *D.* partial (total)
differential [*cf.* TOTAL]

Differential·geometrie *f* differential
geometry [*cf.* GROSS]

Differential·gleichung *f* differential
equation [*cf.* ALLGEMEIN; SINGU-
LÄR; TOTAL]

Differential·quotient *m* differential
quotient (or coefficient): *partieller*
(*totaler*) *Differentialquotient* partial (total) differential quotient;
erster (*zweiter*) *Differentialquotient* first (second) differential
quotient [*cf.* ABLEITUNG; ZEIT]

Differential·rechnung *f* differential
calculus

Differentiation *f* differentiation

differentiieren *v.t., v.i.* differentiate
[= DIFFERENZIEREN]

Differenz *f* difference [*cf.* AUS-
GLEICHEN; ORDNUNG; RECH-
NUNGSMÄSSIG]

Differenzen·gleichung *f* difference
equation

Differenzen·methode *f* (*statist.*) **1.**
(*J.St. Mills D.*) John Stuart Mill's
method of difference; (*Methode
der konkurrierenden Variationen*)
method of concomitant variations. **2.** (*Untergruppenbildung*)
study of concealed classification
[*cf.* UNTERGRUPPENBILDUNG]. **3.**
(*Andersons D.*) variate-difference
method

Differenzen·quotient *m* difference
quotient

Differenzen·rechnung *f* calculus of
differences

Differenzen·schema *n* array of
differences

differenzier·bar *adj.* differentiable

Differenzierbar·keit *f* differenti-
ability

differenzieren *v.t., v.i.* differentiate
[*cf.* ABLEITEN 2.]

Differenzierung *f* differentiation

Differenz·methode *f* (*statist.*) [=
DIFFERENZENMETHODE]

diffundieren *v.t., v.i.* (*phys.*) diffuse

diffus *adj.* (*phys.*) diffuse
Diffusion *f* (*phys.*) diffusion
di·hexaedrisch *adj.* dihexahedral
di·hexagonal *adj.* (*cryst.*) dihexagonal

Di·mension *f* dimension: *der Raum hat drei Dimensionen* (*oder Ausdehnungen*) space has three dimensions; *die Dimensionen* (*oder Abmessungen*) *dieses Parallelepipeds sind:* the dimensions of this parallelepiped are: [*cf.* ABMESSUNG; AUSDEHNUNG; AUSGEDEHNT; FLÄCHENAUSDEHNUNG; LÄNGENAUSDEHNUNG; LINEAR; RAUMAUSDEHNUNG; RÄUMLICH]
..dimensional *suf. adj.* -dimensional: *n-dimensional* n-dimensional [*cf.* AUFSPANNEN]
Di·mensionalität *f* dimensionality
Dimensions·zahl *f* (*eines Ideals*) dimension (of an ideal)
di·metrisch *adj.* (*Projektion*) dimetric (projection)
diophantisch *adj.* diophantine: *diophantische Gleichung* diophantine equation
Di·pol *m* dipole, doublet
di·rekt *adj.* direct [*ant.:* INVERS]: *d. proportional* directly proportional; (*alg.*) *direktes Produkt zweier Untergruppen* direct product of two subgroups; (*alg.*) *d. zerlegbar* (*unzerlegbar*) directly decomposable (indecomposable) [*cf.* STEUER]
Di·rektrix *f* directrix
Dis·agio *n* (*fin.*) disagio, loss on exchange [*ant.:* AGIO] [*cf.* ABSCHLAG]
Dis·junktion *f* (*log.*) disjunction [*cf.* HINTERGLIED; VORDERGLIED]

Disjunktions·glied *n* (*log.*) partial (or: component of a) disjunction, disjunct [= TEILDISJUNKTION]
dis·junktiv *adj.* (*log.*) disjunctive
Dis·kont *m* (*comm.*) discount [*cf.* PREISNACHLASS]
Dis·konten *pl.* (*fin.*) discount bills
Diskonten·wechsel (*fin.*) [= DISKONT·WECHSEL]
Diskont·erlös *m* (*comm.*) (*eines Wechsels*) proceeds, net avails (of a bill of exchange)
diskont·fähig *adj.* (*fin.*) admitted to discount, discountable
dis·kontieren *v.t.* (*fin.*) discount, take on discount
dis·kontinuierlich *adj.* discontinuous, discrete [*cf.* FUNKTION]
Diskont·satz *m* (*comm.*) discount rate; (*einer Bank*) bank rate
Diskont·senkung *f* (*comm.*) lowering in the discount rate
Diskont·tage *m pl.* (*fin.*) (*in einer Bankabrechnung*) terms of discount, discount days
Diskont·wechsel *m* (*fin.*) discount bill
Diskont·wert *m* (*fin.*) discounted value
Dis·krepanz *f* discrepancy
dis·kret *adj.* discrete: *diskrete Punktmenge* discrete set of points: *diskrete Massen(teilchen)* discrete masses (particles) [*cf.* EINPASSEN]
Diskret·heit *f* discreteness
Dis·kriminante *f* discriminant
Dis·kussion *f* discussion
dis·kutieren *v.t.* discuss
Dispersion *f* (*opt.*) dispersion; (*statist.*) dispersion, variation, variance

Distanz *f* distance [*cf.* AUFTRAGEN; PUNKT]

dis·tributiv *adj.* distributive: *distributives Gesetz* distributive law

Distributiv·gesetz *n* distributive law

Dis·tributivität *f* distributivity

di·tetragonal *adj.* (*cryst.*) ditetragonal

di·trigonal *adj.* (*cryst.*) ditrigonal: *ditrigonales Prisma* ditrigonal prism, trigonal biprism

di·vergent *adj.* divergent: *divergente Reihe* divergent series; *divergente* (*oder auseinanderlaufende*) *Gerade* divergent lines [*cf.* UNBEDINGT]

Di·vergenz *f* divergence: *D. einer Folge, Reihe* divergence of a sequence, series; *D.* (*oder Auseinanderlaufen*) *zweier Linien* divergence of two lines; *D. einer Vektorfunktion F* (*symb.:* $\nabla \cdot F$ $\equiv div F$) divergence of a vector function *F* [*cf.* KRITERIUM]

Dividend *m* (*zu teilende Zahl* number to be divided) dividend

Dividende *f* (*comm., fin.*) (*Gewinnanteil*) dividend; (*eines Versicherten, auch*) bonus (of an insured person) [*cf.* GEWINNANTEIL; LAUFEN]

dividieren *v.t., v.i.* divide [*cf.* TEILEN]

Division *f* division [*cf.* ABGEKÜRZT; AUFGEHEN; AUSGEHEN; EINBEGREIFEN; TREIBEN; UNABGEKÜRZT]

Divisions·algebra *f* (*alg.*) division algebra

Divisions·algorithmus *m* (*alg.*) division algorithm

Divisions·zeichen *n* (*symb.:* :) division sign, (*symb.:* $\div$)

Divisor *m* divisor

Dodeka·eder *n* dodecahedron

Dodeka·gon *n* dodecagon

Doma *n* (*pl. Domen*) (*cryst.*) dome

doppel·brechend *adj.* (*opt.*) doubly refracting

Doppel·brechung *f* (*opt.*) double refraction

Doppel·bruch *m* compound fraction

Doppel·integral *n* double integral

Doppel·kegel *m* double cone; *eine Hälfte* (*oder: ein Teil*) *eines Doppelkegels* a nappe of a cone

Doppel·leihgeschäft *n* (*comm.*) [= KOSTGESCHÄFT]

Doppel·modul *m* (*alg.*) double module

Doppel·prämiengeschäft *n* (*comm.*) compound option

Doppel·punkt *m* **1.** (*einer Kurve*) double point, crunode (of a curve). **2.** (*einer Involution*) double point (of an involution)

Doppel·reihe *f* double series

Doppel·stern *m* (*astr.*) double star, binary

doppelt *adj.* double, duplicate [*cf.* BLATTKURVE; BUCHFÜHRUNG; INTEGRAL; GLIEDERUNG; KOMPOSITION; RAUMKURVE; SICHERSTELLUNG]

Doppel·tangente *f* double tangent, bitangent

doppelt·brechend *adj.* (*opt.*) doubly refracting

doppelt·logarithmisch *adj.* with logarithmic scale on both axes; *doppeltlogarithmische Kurve* logarithmic chart

Doppel·verhältnis *n* (*von vier Punkten auf einer Geraden*) double (or cross) ratio (of four collinear points); *nichtharmonisches D.* anharmonic ratio; *harmonisches D.* harmonic ratio; *mit demselben D.* equianharmonic

Doppel·winkel *m* double angle

Doppelwinkel·satz *m* double-angle formula

Doppel·wurzel *f* (*einer algebraischen Gleichung*) double root (of an algebraic equation)

Drall *m* **1.** (*mech.*) moment of momentum, angular momentum [= DREHIMPULS; IMPULSMOMENT] [*cf.* MOMENT²]. **2.** (*des Laufs einer Schußwaffe*) rifling, grooves (of the barrel of a firearm)

drehen *v.t.*, *v.r.*: sich *d.* turn; (*um eine Achse*) revolve, rotate (about an axis); *windschief* (*oder schraubig*) *gedreht* twisted, screwed

Dreh·impuls *m* (*phys.*) moment of momentum, angular momentum [= DRALL; IMPULSMOMENT] [*cf.* MOMENT²]

Dreh·körper *m* solid of revolution

Dreh·moment *n* (*einer Kraft*) turning moment, torque (of a force) [*cf.* MOMENT²]

Dreh·punkt *m* (*eines Hebels*) fulcrum (of a lever)

Dreh·schwingung *f* rotational oscillation

Dreh·sinn *m* direction of rotation (or revolution)

Drehung *f* **1.** (*Wendung*) turn. **2.** (*Umdrehung*) revolution, rotation: *D. um einen Punkt* rotation about a point; *D. um eine Achse* revolution (or rotation) about an axis; *D. der Koordinatenachsen um einen Winkel* α rotation of the coordinate axes through an angle α. **3.** (*Windung*) twist, torsion

Drehungs·achse *f* axis of revolution (or rotation)

drehungs·invariant *adj.* rotation-invariant

Drehungs·sinn *m* direction of rotation (or revolution)

Dreh·waage, Dreh·wage *f* torsion balance

drei *card. num.* three; *mit d. rechten Winkeln* trirectangular [*cf.* DREISTELLIG; HYPOZYKLOIDE]

Drei *f* (*Zahl, Ziffer*) (number, figure) three

drei·achsig *adj.* triaxial [*cf.* MITTEL]

Drei·bein *n* trihedral: *begleitendes D. einer Raumkurve* moving trihedral of a space curve

Drei·blatt *n* (*Kurve*) trifolium.

drei·dimensional *adj.* three-dimensional, tridimensional [*cf.* MANNIGFALTIGKEIT]

Drei·dimensionalität *f* tridimensionality

Drei·eck *n* triangle: *Pascalsches D.* Pascal's triangle [*cf.* ÄHNLICH; ANLEGEN; ANLIEGEND; ANSCHREIBEN; BASIS; BASISWINKEL; BESCHREIBEN; ECKE; ECKPUNKT; EINSCHREIBEN; FLÄCHE; FLÄCHENGLEICH; GEGENÜBERLIEGEN; GLEICHSCHENKLIG; GLEICHSEITIG; GRUNDLINIE; HÖHE; HÖHENSCHNITTPUNKT; KATHETE; KONGRUENT; MITTELLINIE; NEUNPUNKTEKREIS; RECHTWINKLIG;

SCHIEFWINKLIG; SPITZE; SPITZ-
WINKELIG; TREFFEN; UMFANG;
UMSCHREIBEN; UNGLEICHSEITIG]

drei·eckig *adj.* triangular

Dreiecks·koordinaten *f pl.* triangular (or trilinear) coordinates

Dreiecks·netz *n* triangulation network

Dreiecks·zahl *f* triangular number

Dreier *m* (figure) three

drei·fach *adj.* threefold, triple,
treble, triplicate: *d. orthogonales*
(*oder rechtwinkliges*) *Flächen-
system* triply orthogonal system
of surfaces [*cf.* INTEGRAL]

dreifach-rechtwinklig *adj.* (*System
von Linien, Flächen*) triply orthogonal (system of lines, surfaces);
(*sphärisches Dreieck*) trirectangular (spherical triangle)

drei·gliedrig *adj.* (*math.*) three-
termed, trinomial; (*log.*) three-
place, triadic:(*log.*) *dreigliedriges
Prädikat* triadic predicate [*cf.*
EINGLIEDRIG]

Dreigliedrig·keit *f* (*eines Ausdrucks*) (an expression) being (a)
trinomial; (*einer Operation*) (an
operation) being triadic [*cf.*
DREIGLIEDRIG]

Drei·heit *f* triad, triple

drei·hundert *card. num.* three
hundred

Drei·kant *n* trihedral (angle) [*cf.*
LINKSGERICHTET]

drei·mal *num.* three times,
thrice

drei·malig *adj.* (done) three times:
dreimaliges Integrieren integrating three times

Dreipunkt·perspektive *f* three-
point perspective

Drei·satz *m* rule of three [=
REGELDETRI]

Drei·seit *n* trilateral

drei·seitig *adj.* three-sided, triangular: *dreiseitiges Prisma* triangular prism

drei·spitzig *adj.* tricuspid [*cf.*
HYPOZYKLOIDE]

Dreispitz·zirkel *m* triangular compass

dreißig *card. num.* thirty

dreißigst *ord. num.* thirtieth

drei·stellig *adj.* (*ganze Zahl*) three-
figure, three-digit (integer);
(*Dezimalzahl*) three-figure, three-
place (decimal); (*log.: mit drei
Leerstellen*) three-place, triadic
[*cf.* FÜNFSTELLIG]

drei·strahlig *adj.* three-rayed, tri-
radiate

Dreitafel·projektion *f* projection
on three planes, three-plane projection

drei·teilen *v.t.* trisect

Drei·teilung *f* trisection

drei·wertig *adj.* (*math.*) three-
valued; (*chem.*) trivalent

Dreiwertig·keit *f* (*math.*) three-
valuedness, triplicity; (*chem.*) tri-
valence

drei·zählig *adj.* threefold, triple;
(*Symmetrie, auch*) trigonal (symmetry)

drei·zehn *card. num.* thirteen

drei·zehnt *ord. num.* thirteenth

dritt *ord. num.* third: *der dritte
Teil* the third part; *Kurve dritten
Grades* curve of third degree,
cubic (curve); *Gleichung dritten
Grades* equation of third degree,
cubic (equation); *Form dritten
Grades* form of third degree,

cubic (quantic); *Fläche dritter Ordnung* surface of third order; (*log.*) *Satz von ausgeschlossenen Dritten* law of the excluded middle [*cf.* Einheitswurzel; Erheben; Kubus; Potenz; Projektion; Projektionsebene; Proportionale; Tafelabstand; Wurzel]

Dritteil *n* [= Dritt·teil; Drittel]

Drittel *n* third (part)

drittens *adv.* thirdly, in the third place

dritt·halb *adj.* two and a half

dritt·letzt *adj.* last but two

Dritt·teil *n* [= Dritteil; Drittel]

Druck *m* (*phys.*) pressure [*cf.* kritisch]

drücken *v.t.* press

Druck·kraft *f* pressure, compressive force

Druden·fuß *m* pentagram, pentacle

dual *adj.* dual, reciprocal: *duale Sätze der projektiven Geometrie* dual (or reciprocal) theorems in projective geometry [*cf.* schneiden]

Dualität *f* duality

Dualitäts·prinzip *n* principle of duality

duo·dezimal *adj.* duodecimal

Duodezimal·system *n* duodecimal system

Dupin *m N.* [*cf.* Indikatrix]

du'rch·dividieren (*sep.*) *v.t.* divide through

durch·dri'ngen *v.t.*, *v.recip.:* **sich** (*oder* **einander**) *d.* penetrate (each other), cut into (each other), intersect: *zwei Kugeln d. sich in einem Kreis* two spheres pene-

trating each other intersect in a circle

Durch·dri'ngung *f* penetration, intersection

Durchdringungs·linie *f* (*zweier Flächen*) line of penetration (or intersection) (of two surfaces)

durch·ei'len *v.t.* traverse, travel, cover

du'rch·gehen (*sep.*) *v.i.* (*astr.*) transit, pass

durch·me'ssen *v.t.* traverse, travel

Du'rch·messer *m* **1.** (*eines Kreises, einer Kugel*) diameter, diametral line (of a circle, a sphere) [*cf.* inner; licht; konjugiert]. **2.** (*einer Punktmenge*) diameter (of a set of points)

du'rch·numerieren (*sep.*) *v.t.* number consecutively

du'rch·pausen (*sep.*) *v.t.* trace

durch·schnei'den *v.t.*, *v.recip.:* **sich** (*oder* **einander**) *d.* cut, intersect

Du'rch·schnitt *m* **1.** (*von Mengen, Klassen*) intersection, meet, product (of sets, classes) [*ant.:* Vereinigung] [*cf.* unverrückbar]. **2.** (*Querschnitt*) cross section. **3.** (*Mittelwert*) average: *im D.* on the (or: on an) average; *über* (*unter*) *dem D.* above (below) average; (*statist.*) *gleitende Durchschnitte* moving averages [*cf.* Mittelwert]

du'rch·schnittlich 1. *adj.* average: *durchschnittliche Leistung* average performance, **2.** (*adv.*) on the (or: on an) average: *wir machten d. 100 Meilen im Tag* we made 100 miles a day on the average

Durchschnitts·fälligkeit f (*fin.*) (*von Zahlungen*) equation (of payments), equated date (for a set of payments)
Durchschnitts·geschwindigkeit f average speed; average velocity [*cf.* GESCHWINDIGKEIT]
Durchschnitts·klasse f intersection of classes
Durchschnitts·laufzeit f (*fin.*) (*einer Serie von Zahlungen*) equated date (or period) (for a set of payments)
Durchschnitts·menge f 1. (*in der Mengenlehre*) intersection (or meet, or product) set (in theory of sets). **2.** (*durchschnittliche Menge*) average quantity
Durchschnitts·punkt m point of intersection
Durchschnitts·rechnung f (calculation of) averages (*pl.*)
Durchschnitts·wert m average value
Durchschnitts·zahl f average number

durch·se'tzen *v.t.* [=DURCHSTOSSEN]
durch·sto'ßen *v.t.* cut, pierce, pass through, intersect: *der Punkt, in welchem eine Gerade eine Ebene durchstößt* the point in which a line pierces a plane; *die Gerade durchstößt die Kugel in zwei Punkten* the straight line cuts (or passes through) the sphere at two points
Du'rchstoß·punkt m (*einer Geraden mit einer Ebene*) piercing (or intersection) point (of a line and a plane), foot (of a line intersecting a plane); *D. einer Geraden mit einer Koordinatenebene* trace of a line (in space)
Dutzend n dozen
Dyade f dyad
dyadisch *adj.* dyadic: *dyadisches Zahlensystem* dyadic number system
Dyn n (*phys.*) dyne
Dynamik f dynamics
dynamisch *adj.* dynamic
Dyne f (*phys.*) dyne

E

eben *adj.* (*flach*) plane; (*horizontal*) level: *ebener Schnitt* plane section; *ebene Fläche* plane surface; *auf ebenem Grund* on level ground [*cf.* BASIS; EBENFLÄCHIG; FIGUR; FLÄCHENELEMENT; GEOMETRIE; GRUNDLINIE; KURVE; PUNKTFELD; SEITE; STRAHLENFELD; WINKEL]
Ebene f plane; *in derselben Ebene* (*liegend*) coplanar; *von zwei Ebenen gebildet* dihedral [*cf.* ACHSENSCHNITTFORM; DARSTELLEN; DURCHSTOSSEN; DURCHSTOSSPUNKT; GEBILDE; HALBIERUNGSEBENE; LEGEN; NEIGUNGSWINKEL; OSKULIEREN; PROJIZIEREN; PUNKT; REKTIFIZIEREN; SENKRECHT; SPUR; UMKLAPPEN; UNEIGENTLICH; WINKEL]

Ebenen·bündel *n* bundle (or sheaf, or star) of planes

Ebenen·büschel *n* pencil of planes, axial pencil

eben·flächig *adj.* (*eben*) plane; (*mit ebenen Flächen*) with plane faces (or facets)

Echo·lot *n* sonic depth finder, fathometer

Echolot·messung *f* echo sounding

echt *adj.* proper: *echte Untermenge* proper subset; *A ist eine echte Obermenge von B A* includes *B* properly as a subset; *echter Teiler* proper divisor [*cf.* BRUCH]

..eck *n* polygon of ... sides, **..gon**: *Sechseck* hexagon [*cf.* ACHTECK; DREIECK; FÜNFECK; NEUNECK; SECHSECK; SIEBENECK; SIEBZEHNECK; VIERECK; ZEHNECK]

Ecke *f* (*eines Dreiecks, Vielecks, Polyeders*) vertex, corner (of a triangle, polygon, polyhedron) [*cf.* BESCHREIBEN; KÖRPERLICH]

Ecken·anzahl *f* [=ECKENZAHL]

Ecken·zahl *f* (*eines Polygons, Polyeders*) number of vertices (of a polygon, polyhedron)

eckig *adj.* angular [*cf.* EINKLAMMERN; GEBROCHEN; KLAMMER]

Eck·punkt *m* **1.** (*eines Dreiecks, Vielecks, Polyeders*) vertex, corner (of a triangle, polygon, polyhedron). **2.** (*einer Kurve*) salient (or corner) point (on a curve)

Efeu·linie *f* cissoid [=ZISSOIDE]

Effekt *m.* **1.** (*Wirkung*) effect **2.** (*phys.: Arbeitsleistung* rate of work done) action, power [*cf.* WIRKUNG]

Effekten *pl.* securities, bonds and

stocks [=WERTPAPIERE] [*cf.* BANKABRECHNUNG; BESTAND; EINLÖSBARKEIT; SCHALTERGESCHÄFT]

Effekten·börse *f* (*comm.*) stock exchange

Effekten·konto *n* (*comm.*) stock account

effektiv *adj.* (*wirksam*) effective; (*tatsächlich*) actual, real; (*comm. auch*) net: *effektive Verzinsung* net (or true) yield; *effektiver Bestand* actual balance; *effektiver Wert* actual (or real) value

Effektiv·bestand *m* (*comm.*) actual balance

Ehren·akzept *n* (*comm.*) acceptance for honor

eichen *v.t.* (*Maße und Gewichte*) calibrate, gauge, standardize (measures and weights)

Eichung *f* (*von Maßen und Gewichten*) calibration, gauging, standardization (of measures and weights)

Eigen·funktion *f* (*alg.*) eigenfunction, characteristic function

Eigen·gewicht *n* (*comm.*) dead weight [=LEERGEWICHT]

Eigen·schaft *f* property, quality, character [*cf.* GELTEN]

Eigen·schatten *m* shade [*ant.* SCHLAGSCHATTEN] [*cf.* SCHATTEN; SCHATTENGRENZE]

Eigenschatten·grenze *f* shade line

Eigen·tum *n* property, possession

Eigen·vektor *m* eigenvector, characteristic vector

Eigen·wechsel *m* (*comm.*) promissory note [*cf.* SOLAWECHSEL]

Eigen·wert *m* (*alg.*) eigenvalue, characteristic value

ein *card. num.* one [*cf.* EINSTELLIG]

ein·achsig *adj.* uniaxial, monaxial

ein·artig *adj.* (*alg.*) (*Ideal*) single-primed (ideal)

ein·begreifen (*sep.*) *v.t.* involve, imply, include : *die Gleichung begreift nicht die Division durch Null ein* (*oder: schließt nicht die Division durch Null in sich*) the equation does not involve division by zero

ein·betten (*sep.*) *v.t.* imbed, embed

Ein·blatt *n* simple folium [*cf.* FOLIUM]

Einbruchs·versicherung *f* burglary insurance

ein·deutig *adj.* unique, univocal, unambiguous; (*einwertig*) single-valued, one-valued: *eindeutige Abbildung* single-valued mapping (or image); *e. definiert* uniquely defined; *nicht e.* ambiguous

Eindeutig·keit *f* uniqueness

Eindeutigkeits·satz *m* (*alg.*) uniqueness theorem

ein·ebnen (*sep.*) *v.t.* level, plane (down)

Ein·ebnung *f* planation

ein·eindeutig *adj.* one-to-one, one-one, biunique: *eineindeutige Entsprechung, Beziehung, Abbildung* one-to-one correspondence, relation, mapping

ein·einhalb *num.* one and a half

ein·engen (*sep.*) *v.t.* narrow (down), constrict: *den Spielraum der Unsicherheit e.* narrow the margin of uncertainty

Ein·engung *f* striction, narrowing

Einer *m* (*Stellenwert* place value) unit [*cf.* ZEHNER]

Einer·kolonne *f* units column

Einer·stelle *f* unit's (or units) place

Einer·ziffer *f* digit in the units place

ein·fach *adj.* simple: *einfache Wurzel einer Gleichung* simple root of an equation; *einfaches totales Integral* simple integral; *einfache Gruppe* simple group; *einfache Zinsen* simple interest [*cf.* BRINGEN; BRUCH; BUCHFÜHRUNG; FOLIUM; GEBILDE; GEWÖHNLICH; GRUNDFORMEL; TYPENTHEORIE; VIERECK; VIERSEIT; ZUSAMMENHÄNGEND]

Einfach·heit *f* simplicity: (*alg.*) *E. der alternierenden Gruppe* simplicity of the alternating group

Ein·fall *m* (*von Strahlen*) incidence (of rays)

ein·fallen (*sep.*) *v.i.* fall in, be incident: *der einfallende Strahl* the incident ray

Einfalls·gruppe *f* (*statist.*) class containing the median

Einfalls·winkel *m* (*phys.*) angle of incidence

Einfuhr·zoll *m* (*comm.*) (import) duty

ein·geschlossen *p.p.* included

ein·geschrieben [*cf.* EINSCHREIBEN]

ein·gipfelig *adj.* (*Häufigkeitskurve*) unimodal (frequency curve)

ein·gliedrig *adj.* (*math.*) one-term(ed), monomial; (*log.*) one-place, monadic: *eingliedriger Ausdruck* monomial (expression); *eingliedrige Operation* one-place operation

Eingliedrig·keit *f* (*eines Ausdrucks*) (an expression) being (a) monomial; (*einer Operation*) (an oper-

ation) being monadic [*cf.* EIN-
GLIEDRIG]

Ein·heit *f* **1.** (*als Maß* as measure)
unit[*cf.*BOGENMASS; MASS; RAUM-
WINKELMASS; STATISTISCH; UM-
WANDLUNG]. **2.** (*als Zahl*) unity
(as number). **3.** (*Einzelstück*)
(single) item, unit [*cf.* STATI-
STISCH]

Einheits·element *n* (*einer Gruppe*)
identity (of a group)

Einheits·form *f* (*alg.*) **1.** (*primi-*
tives Polynom) primitive poly-
nomial. **2.** (*einer quadratischen*
Form) primitive form (of a quadratic form)

Einheits·ideal *n* (*alg.*) unit ideal

Einheits·kreis *m* unit circle; *Bogen*
im Einheitskreis von der Länge
eins (*oder Eins*) radian $\left(= \frac{180°}{\pi} \right)$

Einheits·kugel *f* unit sphere; *Fläche*
auf der E. vom Flächeninhalt eins
(*oder Eins*) steradian

Einheits·masse *f* (*phys.*) unit mass

Einheits·matrix *f* (*alg.*) unit (or
identity) matrix

Einheits·monat *m* (*statist.*) month
adjusted for calendar variation.
[*cf.* UMRECHNUNG]

Einheits·operator *m* (*alg.*) unity
operator

Einheits·punkt *m* (*alg.*) (*der Zahlen-*
linie, eines Vektorraums) unit
point (of the number scale, a
vector space)

Einheits·radius *m* unit radius

Einheits·strecke *f* unit of distance

Einheits·wurzel *f* (*alg.*) root of
unity: *dritte Einheitswurzel* third
(or cube) root of unity [*cf.*
PRIMITIV]

ein·hüllen (*sep.*) *v.t.* envelop [=
UMHÜLLEN]; *einhüllende Kurve*
(*Fläche*) envelope

Ein·hüllende *f* envelope [= UM-
HÜLLENDE]

ein·hundert *card. num.* one hundred

ein·kassieren (*sep.*) *v.t.* (*comm.*)
cash, collect

Einkaufs·preis *m* purchase price

ein·klammern (*sep.*) *v.t.* (*in runde*
Klammern) put (or collect) in
parentheses, parenthesize; (*in*
eckige Klammern) put (or collect)
in brackets

Ein·klammerung *f* aggregation,
collection (in parentheses, brackets) [*cf.* EINKLAMMERN]

Ein·kommen *n* (*comm.*) income

Einkommen·steuer *f* (*comm.*) income tax

Ein·künfte *pl.* (*comm., fin.*) [=
EINKOMMEN]

Ein·lage *f* (*fin.*) (*eines Guthabens*)
deposit; (*von Kapital*) investment
(of capital)

ein·legen *v.t.* (*fin.*) (*ein Guthaben*)
deposit (to an account); (*Kapital*)
invest (capital)

einlös·bar *adj.* (*comm., fin.*) (*durch*
Umtausch) convertible; (*durch*
Tilgung) redeemable [*cf.* EIN-
LÖSEN]

Einlösbar·keit *f* convertibility; re-
deemability [*cf.* EINLÖSBAR]

ein·lösen *v.t.* (*comm., fin.*) **1.** (*be-*
zahlen) pay; *einen Wechsel* (*nicht*)
e. honor (dishonor) (a bill of exchange). **2.** (*eintauschen*) (*gegen*
andere Wertpapiere) convert (to
other securities). **3.** (*durch Rück-*
zahlung tilgen) redeem. **4.** (*aus*

dem Verkehr ziehen) withdraw (from circulation). **5.** (*eine Verpflichtung*) discharge (an obligation) [*cf.* ZURÜCKZAHLEN]

Ein·lösung *f* payment; conversion; redemption; withdrawal; discharge [*cf.* EINLÖSEN; RÜCKZAHLUNG]

ein·mal *num.* once

Einmal·eins *n* multiplication table

ein·malig *adj.* (done) once

ein·mehrdeutig *adj.* (*Beziehung*) one-to-many (relation) [*cf.* EINEINDEUTIG]

Ein·nahme *f* (*comm.*) returns *pl.*

Einparameter·schar *f* one-parameter family, pencil

ein·passen (*sep.*) *v.t.* fit: *eine Kurve, eine Funktion in eine diskrete Menge von Punkten oder Werten e.* fit a smooth curve, a function to a discrete set of points or values [*cf.* ANSCHMIEGEN]

Ein·passung *f* fitting [*cf.* ANPASSUNG]

Einpunkt·perspektive *f* one-point perspective

ein·rechnen (*sep.*) *v.t.* count in, take into account, include

Ein·rechnung *f* counting in, taking into account, inclusion

eins *card. num.* one [*cf.* BORGEN; EINHEITSKREIS; EINHEITSKUGEL]

Eins *f* (*Zahl*) (number) one, unity; (*Ziffer*) (figure) one [*cf.* EINHEITSKREIS; EINHEITSKUGEL]

Ein·satz *m* (*des Zirkels*) **1.** (*Einsatzteil*) (exchangeable) point (of a compass). **2.** (*das Einsetzen*) setting in ([the needle point of] the compass)

Einsatz·teil *m* (*eines Zirkels*) (ex-

changeable) point (of a compass)

Einsatz·zirkel *m* compass, (pair of) compasses [*cf.* ZIRKEL]

ein·schalig *adj.* of one sheet, unparted [*cf.* HYPERBOLOID]

ein·schalten (*sep.*) *v.t.* (*einfügen*) insert, intercalate; (*interpolieren*) interpolate

Ein·schaltung *f* (*Einfügung*) insertion, intercalation; (*Interpolation*) interpolation

ein·scharig *adj.* (*Regelfläche*) singly ruled (surface)

ein·schließen (*sep.*) *v.t.* (*einhegen*) include, enclose; (*einbegreifen*) include, involve, comprise, imply: *zwei Seiten und der (von ihnen) eingeschlossene Winkel* two sides and the (or their) included angle; *zwei Radien, die einen Winkel von fünfzehn Grad e.* two radii enclosing an angle of fifteen degrees

ein·schließlich *adj.* including

ein·schreiben (*sep.*) *v.t.* inscribe: *eingeschriebener Kreis* inscribed circle, incircle; *der einem Dreieck eingeschriebene Kreis* the circle inscribed in a triangle; *Mittelpunkt des eingeschriebenen Kreises* incenter [*cf.* LIEGEN]

Ein·schuß *m* (*fin.*) (*bei Börsenaufträgen*) margin (for buying orders at the stock exchange) [*cf.* SICHERHEITSSUMME]

ein·seitig *adj.* **1.** (*mit nur einer Seite*) one-side(d), unilateral: *einseitige Fläche* one-side(d) (or unilateral) surface. **2.** (*verschieden auf einer Seite*) one-sided; (*schief auf einer Seite*) lop-sided, skew; (*adv.: nur auf einer Seite*) on one side (only):

e. beschrieben written upon on one side only

Eins·element *n* (*alg.*) identity (element), unity element

· **Einser** *m* (figure) one

ein·setzen (*sep.*) *v.t.* **1.** (*eine Zahl*) substitute (a number): *eine Größe in einen Ausdruck e.* substitute a quantity into an expression. **2.** (*den Zirkel*) set in (the compass) [*cf.* EINSATZ; ZIRKELEINSATZ]

Ein·setzung *f* (*einer Größe in einen Ausdruck*) substitution (of a quantity into an expression)

Einsetzungs·regel *f* (*log.*) rule of substitution

Eins·klasse *f* (*alg.*) unit class

ein·springend *adj.* (*Winkel*) reflex, reentrant (angle)

ein·stellig *adj.* **1.** (*math.*) (*ganze Zahl*) one-figure, one-digit (integer); (*Dezimalzahl*) one-figure, one-place (decimal); *einstellige Zahl* digit. **2.** (*log.: mit einer Leerstelle*) monadic, one-place: *einstelliges Prädikat* monadic (or one-place) predicate; *einstelliger Prädikatenkalkül* monadic predicate calculus

Einstell·werk *n* (*einer Rechenmaschine*) (calculator) keyboard

ein·stufig *adj.* (*alg.*) (*Isomorphismus*) simple (isomorphism) [*cf.* ISOMORPHISMUS]

Eins·und·eins *n* addition table

Eintafel·projektion *f* projection on one plane, one-plane projection

ein·tausend *card. num.* one (or a) thousand

ein·teilen (*sep.*) *v.t.* (*anordnen*) arrange; (*klassifizieren*) classify; (*unterteilen*) divide; (*mit Teil-*

strichen) graduate, calibrate (by marks) [*cf.* TEILEN]

Ein·teilung *f* (*Anordnung*) arrangement; (*Klassifikation*) classification; (*Unterteilung*) division; (*durch Teilstriche*) scale, graduation (by marks): *gleichbleibende E. auf der Abszissenachse, logarithmische E. auf der Ordinatenachse* uniform scale on the axis of abscissas, logarithmic scale on the axis of ordinates [*cf.* ZEIGER; KREISTEILUNG]

ein·tragen (*sep.*) *v.t.* (*einen Punkt*) plot (a point)

ein·und·einhalb *num.* one and a half

ein·und·zwanzig *card. num.* twenty-one

ein·und·zwanzigst *ord. num.* twenty-first

ein·wertig *adj.* (*math.*) one-valued, single-valued; (*chem.*) univalent, monovalent [*cf.* EINDEUTIG]

Ein·wertigkeit *f* (*math.*) one-valuedness, single-valuedness; (*chem.*) univalence, monovalence [*cf.* EINDEUTIGKEIT]

Ein·zahl *f* singular

ein·zeichnen (*sep.*) *v.t.* plot, fill in: *eine Kurve in eine Reihe von Punkten e.* fit a curve to (or fill in a curve in) a set of points [*cf.* BESTIMMEN]

Ein·zeichnung *f* plotting, filling in

Einzel·fall *m* individual case: (*statist.*) *Methode der typischen Einzelfälle* **a.** (*E. als Klassenrepräsentant*) representation of a statistical universe through selected individual cases; **b.** (*gruppenweise Auswahl*) stratified sampling

Einzel·gegenstand *m* single object, item [*cf.* POSTEN]
einzeln *adj.* single
Einzel·posten *m* item
Einzel·prämie *f* (*ins.*) single premium
Einzel·stück *n* (single) item [*cf.* EINHEIT; STATISTISCH]
Einzel·verkauf *m* retail (selling)
Einzel·verkäufer *m* retailer
einzig *adj.* unique, sole, single: *einziger Wert* single value [*cf.* SOLAWECHSEL]
ei·rund *adj.* oval
Ekliptik *f* (*astr.*) ecliptic [*cf.* SCHIEFE]
elastisch *adj.* elastic
Elastizität *f* elasticity
Elastizitäts·grenze *f* elastic limit (or strength)
Elastizitäts·modul *m* modulus of elasticity
elektrisch *adj.* electric(al) [*cf.* AUSZÄHLUNG; ZÄHLER]
Elektrizität *f* electricity
Elektrizitäts·menge *f* quantity of electricity
Elektro·dynamik *f* electrodynamics
elektro·dynamisch *adj.* electrodynamic
Elektro·magnet *m* electromagnet
elektro·magnetisch *adj.* electromagnetic [*cf.* FELD; LICHTTHEORIE]
Elektro·magnetismus *m* electromagnetism
Elektro·meter *n* electrometer
elektro·motorisch *adj.* electromotive: *elektromotorische Kraft* electromotive force
Elektron *n* (*phys.*) electron

Elektronen·lehre *f* electronics
Elektronen·schale *f* electron shell [*cf.* SCHALE]
Elektronen·spin *m* (*phys.*) electron spin
Elektronen·volt *n* (*elec.*) electron volt
Elektronik *f* (*phys.*) electronics
Elektro·statik *f* electrostatics
elektro·statisch *adj.* electrostatic
Element *n* element; (*Anfangsgründe*) (*pl.*) elements, rudiments: *E. einer Determinante, einer Menge* element of a determinant, of a set; *die Elemente der Arithmetik, Trigonometrie* the elements (or rudiments) of arithmetic, trigonometry [*cf.* ADJUNKTE; ENTGEGENGESETZT; ENTHALTEN; ERZEUGEN; FAKTOR; HALBWERTSZEIT; INEINANDERLIEGEN; INVERS; KOMMUTATOR; KOMPLEXION; KONJUGIERT; MENGE; MINOR; REZIPROK; SUBDETERMINANTE; TRANSPONIEREN; UNENDLICH; UNTERDETERMINANTE; VERSEHEN; ZUORDNEN; ZUSAMMENSETZUNG]
elementar *adj.* elementary: *elementare Operationen* elementary operations [*cf.* PLANCK]
elementar·symmetrisch *adj.* (*alg.*) (*Funktion*) elementary symmetric (function)
Elementar·teiler *m* (*alg.*) elementary divisor
Elevation *f* elevation
Elevations·winkel *m* angle of elevation
elf *card. num.* eleven
Elfer·probe *f* casting out elevens [*cf.* ELFERREST]
Elfer·rest *m* (*bei der Elferprobe*)

excess of elevens (in casting out elevens)

elft *ord. num.* eleventh

Elftel *n* eleventh (part)

Elimination *f* elimination

Eliminations·methode *f* method of elimination

Eliminations·problem *n* (*log.*) (*im erweiterten Prädikatenkalkül*) elimination problem (in extended predicate calculus)

Eliminations·theorie *f* (*der Gleichungen*) elimination theory (of equations)

eliminieren *v.t.* eliminate: *eine Unbekannte, eine Veränderliche e.* (*oder wegschaffen oder beseitigen*) eliminate an unknown, a variable

Eliminierung *f* elimination [*cf.* BESEITIGUNG]

Elle *f* (*meas.*) cubit

Ellipse *f* ellipse: *Kreis über der großen Achse der E.* auxiliary (or: major eccentric) circle of the ellipse; *Kreis über der kleinen Achse der E.* minor eccentric circle of the ellipse [*cf.* ACHSE; ENTARTEN; FADENKONSTRUK- TION; HALBACHSE; HAUPTACHSE; KUBISCH; LEITKREIS; NEBEN- ACHSE; NORMALFORM]

Ellipsen·gleichung *f* equation of an ellipse

Ellipsen·zirkel *m* ellipsograph, elliptic compass, trammel

Ellipso·graph *m* ellipsograph

Ellipsoid *n* ellipsoid [*cf.* HALB- ACHSE; MITTEL; VERLÄNGERT]

ellipsoidisch *adj.* ellipsoidal

elliptisch *adj.* elliptic(al): *ellip- tisches Paraboloid* elliptic para-

boloid; *elliptischer Kegel, Zy- linder* elliptic cone, cylinder; *elliptische Funktionen* elliptic functions [*cf.* MODUL]; *ellip- tisches Integral* elliptic integral [*cf.* MODUL]; *elliptischer Punkt auf einer Fläche* elliptic point on a surface [*cf.* GEOMETRIE; KO- ORDINATE]

Elliptizität *f* ellipticity

Elongation *f* (*astr.*) elongation

Emission *f* **1.** (*phys.*) emission. **2.** (*fin.*) issuance, issue [*cf.* EMIT- TIEREN]

Emissions·kurs *m* (*fin.*) issue price (or par), rate of issue

emittieren *v.t.* **1.** (*phys.*) (*Strahlen*) emit (rays). **2.** (*fin.*) (*z.B.eine Anleihe*) issue, float, launch (e.g. a loan)

Empfang *m* (*comm.*) receipt; (*rad.*) reception

empfangen *v.t.* receive [*cf.* AN- NEHMEN]

Empfänger *m* recipient; (*Adressat* addressee) consignee; (*rad.*) re- ceiver [*cf.* FRANKIEREN; PORTO- FREI]

Empfangs·bestätigung *f* (*comm.*) receipt

Empirie *f* empiricism; (*Erfahrung*) experience

empirisch *adj.* empirical, a pos- teriori: *empirische Formel, An- nahme, Regel, Wissenschaft* em- pirical formula, assumption, rule, science; *empirische Wahrschein- lichkeit* a posteriori prob- ability

empirisch-statistisch *adj.* nonsto- chastic

Ende *n* end, extremity: *die beiden*

Enden eines Intervalls the two ends (or extremities) of an interval; *ohne E.* nonterminating, never-ending, endless; *Schraube ohne E.* endless (or tangent) screw, worm [*cf.* SCHLUSS; SCHMALSEITE; SCHMALSEITENANSICHT]

en detail *adv.* (*comm.*) at retail

End·fläche *f* end, basis

End·geschwindigkeit *f* terminal velocity

end·gültig *adj.* definite, definitive

End·lage *f* terminal position

endlich *adj.* finite, terminating: *endliche Zahl, Größe, Menge* finite number, quantity, set; *e. viele Punkte* finitely many points; *e. viele Schritte* a finite number of steps; *endlicher Kettenbruch* terminating continued fraction; *endlicher Dezimalbruch* terminating decimal [*cf.* ABBRECHEN; GRUPPE; KOMMUTATIV]

Endliche(s) *n* finite, finitude; *Unstetigkeit im Endlichen* finite discontinuity

Endlich·keit *f* finitude, finiteness

endlich·viele *num.* a finite number of [*cf.* ENDLICH]

end·los *adj.* endless: *endlose Kette, Schraube* endless chain, screw

Endlosig·keit *f* endlessness

Endomorphismen·ring *m* (*alg.*) endomorphism ring

Endomorphismus *m* (*alg.*) endomorphism

End·punkt *m* end point [*cf.* FALLEN]

End·richtung *f* terminal direction

End·stellung *f* terminal position

End·wahrscheinlichkeit *f* proba-bility a posteriori, final probability

End·wert *m* (*einer Rente*) accumulation (or accumulated value) (of an annuity)

Energie *f* (*Arbeitsfähigkeit* capacity for performing work) energy; (*per Zeit*) (rate of energy) power: *kinetische* (*oder aktuelle*) *E., E.der Bewegung* kinetic (or actual) energy, energy of motion [*cf.* WUCHT]; *potentielle E., E. der Lage* potential energy [*cf.* ATOMAR; ERHALTUNG; KRAFT]

Energie·dichte *f* (*phys.*) energy density

Energie·gleichung *f* (*phys.*) energy equation

Energie·niveau *n* (*phys.*) energy level, quantum state

Energie·prinzip *n* (*phys.*) principle of energy

Energie·quant *n*, **Energie·quantum** *n* (*phys.*) quantum of energy

Energie·satz *m* (*phys.*) energy theorem

Energie·stufe *f* (*phys.*) energy level

Energie·übertragung *f* (*phys.*) transmission of energy

Energie·umwandlung *f* (*phys.*) transformation of energy

eng(e) *adj.* narrow, strict, restricted [*cf.* PRÄDIKATENKALKÜL]

Enge *f* narrowness, strictness

en gros *adv.* (*comm.*) wholesale

Engros·preis *m* (*comm.*) wholesale price

ent·arten *v.i.* degenerate: *die Ellipse entartet in zwei parallele Gerade* the ellipse degenerates into two parallel lines

ent·artet *adj.* degenerate [*cf.* KEGELSCHNITT]

Ent·artung *f* degeneration,
ent·behrlich *adj.* dispensable
Entbehrlich·keit *f* dispensability
ent·fernen *v.t.* remove
ent·fernt *adj.* distant, remote [*cf.*
WEIT]
Ent·fernung *f* **1.** (*zweier Objekte*)
distance (of two objects) [*cf.*
PUNKT]. **2.** (*Beseitigung*) removal
ent·gegengesetzt *adj.* opposite,
inverse, opposed: *entgegenge-*
setzter Winkel [= ANWINKEL];
(*alg.*) *entgegengesetztes Element*
eines Gruppenelements inverse
(element) of a group element
[*cf.* DIAMETRAL; UHRZEIGER]
entgegen·setzen (*sep.*) *v.t.* oppose
[*cf.* ENT́GEGENGESETZT]
Entgegen·setzung *f* (*log.*) opposition
ent·halten *v.t.* contain, involve:
jedes Glied einer Determinante
enthält ein und nur ein Element
aus jeder Zeile und eins aus jeder
Kolonne each term of a determinant involves one and only
one element from each row, and
one from each column; 5 *ist in*
32 *sechsmal e.* (*oder:* 5 *in* 32 *geht*
sechsmal), *bleibt* (*oder: Rest*) 2
5 is contained in 32 (or: 5 goes
into 32) six times (or: 5 into 32
is six), and 2 over (or left); 5 *ist*
in 30 *ohne Rest e.* 5 goes into 30
without a remainder [*cf.* AB-
GESCHLOSSEN; AUFGEHEN; IN-
HALT]
Entropie *f* (*phys.*) entropy
entscheid·bar *adj.* (*log.*) decid-
able
Entscheidbar·keit *f* (*log.*) decid-
ability

ent·scheiden *v.t.* (*log.*) decide:
(*log.*) *zwischen Allgemeingültig-*
keit und' Erfüllbarkeit e. decide
between universal validity and
satisfiability
Ent·scheidung *v.t.* (*log.*) decision
Entscheidungs·problem *n* (*log.*)
decision problem
ent·sprechen *v.i.* (*dat.*) correspond
(to); (*statist.*) be correlated (to):
(*einander*) *entsprechende Punkte*
corresponding points
ent·sprechend *adj.* corresponding;
(*in Gebilden* in geometric
elements) corresponding, homologous; (*statist.*) correlated; *sich*
selbst e. self-corresponding [*cf.*
INEINANDERLIEGEN]
Ent·sprechung *f* correspondence;
homology; (*statist.*) correlation
[*cf.* EINEINDEUTIG; ENTSPRE-
CHEND]
Entsprechungs·zahl *f* (*statist.*)
(*zweier Gesamtmassen*) statistical
ratio (between two universes)
Entsprechungs·ziffer *f* (*statist.*) coefficient of correlation
ent·stehen *v.i.* arise, be generated,
be produced: *so ist dieses Problem*
entstanden this is how the
problem arose; (*alg.*) *ein Zahlen-*
körper entsteht a number field is
generated
Ent·stehung *f* rise, origin
ent·werfen *v.t.* (*zeichnen*) trace,
plot, graph, design; (*skizzieren*)
sketch; (*planen*) design, plan
ent·werten *v.t.* (*comm.*) depreciate
Ent·wertung *f* depreciation
ent·wickeln *v.t.* develop, expand:
einen Ausdruck e. expand an expression [*cf.* AUSRECHNEN]

ent·wickelt *adj.* (*Funktion*) explicit (function): *Schreibung in entwickelter Form* development (in explicit form), expansion; *nicht entwickelte* (*oder implizite*) *Funktion* implicit function [*cf.* DETERMINANTE; ENTWICKLUNG]

Ent·wicklung *f* development; (*entwickelte Schreibweise*) explicit form, expansion; (*Tendenz*) trend: *binomische E., E. der binomischen Formel* binomial expansion; *E. einer Funktion in eine Reihe* expansion of a function in a series [*cf.* ABBRECHEN; DETERMINANTE; HAUPTRICHTUNG; TENDENZ]

Entwicklungs·richtung *f* trend

Enveloppe *f* envelope

Epheu·linie *f* cissoid [= ZISSOIDE]

Epi·trochoide *f* epitrochoid

Epi·zykel *m* epicycle

Epi·zykloide *f* epicycloid

Epsilon *n* (*griechischer Buchstabe* Greek letter E, ϵ) epsilon

Eratosthenes *m* N. [*cf.* SIEB]

Erd·achse *f* earth's (polar) axis, (polar) axis of the earth

Erd·äquator *m* geographic (or earth's) equator

Erd·bahn *f* orbit of the earth

Erdbeben·welle *f* seismic wave

Erd·drehung *f* earth rotation

Erd·durchmesser *m* earth's diameter, diameter of the earth

Erde *f* earth [*cf.* ABPLATTUNG]

Erden·jahr *n* terrestrial year

Erd·ferne *f* (*astr.*) apogee [*cf.* APOGÄUM]

Erd·jahr *n* terrestrial year

Erd·karte *f* map (or chart) of the world, terrestrial map

Erdkarten·projektion *f* map projection [*cf.* SINUSLINIG]

Erd·kugel *f* terrestrial globe (or sphere)

erd·magnetisch *adj.* geomagnetic

Erd·magnetismus *m* terrestrial magnetism

Erd·meridian *m* terrestrial meridian

Erd·messung *f* geodesy

Erd·mittelpunkt *n* earth('s) center, center of the earth

Erd·nähe *f* (*astr.*) perigee [*cf.* PERIGÄUM]

Erd·pol *m* earth's pole, pole of the earth

Erd·radius *m* earth's radius, radius of the earth

Erd·umdrehung *f* earth rotation

Erd·umfang *m* earth's circumference, circumference of the earth

Erd·umlauf *m* earth revolution

Er·eignis *n* event [*cf.* AUSSCHLIESSEND; VERKETTEN; ZUFÄLLIG]

Ereignis·masse *f* (*statist.*) [= PUNKTMASSE 2.]

Er·fahrung *f* experience, empirical knowledge; *vor aller E.* a priori; *nach der E.* a posteriori [*cf.* EMPIRIE]

Erfahrungs·wissenschaft *f* empirical science

er·fassen *v.t.* (*statist.*) (*sammeln*) collect, gather; (*erreichen*) reach: *Daten e.* collect (or gather) data; *einen Personenkreis e.* reach a group of people

Er·fassung *f* (*statist.*) (*Sammlung*) collection; (*Erreichung*) reach(ing) [*cf.* ERFASSEN; REPRÄSENTATIV]

erfüll·bar *adj.* satisfiable
Erfüllbar·keit *f* satisfiability [*cf.*
ENTSCHEIDEN]
er·füllen *v.t.* **1.** (*befriedigen*) fulfill,
satisfy: *eine Voraussetzung e.*
satisfy an assumption [*cf.* ORT].
2. (*ausfüllen*) fill (completely):
die Punkte e. die Ebene ganz
(*oder: füllen die Ebene ganz aus*)
the points fill the plane completely
Er·füllung *f* (*Befriedigung*) ful-
filling, satisfying; (*Ausfüllung*)
filling (completely)
Erfüllungs·system *n* (*log.*) truth-
value system
Erg *n* (*phys.*) erg
er·gänzen *v.t.* complete, supplement: *zu einem vollständigen*
Quadrat e. complete the square;
die beiden Winkel e. sich zu 90°
(180°, 360°) the two angles are
complementary (supplementary,
explementary)
Er·gänzung *f* (*z.B. zu einem voll-*
ständigen Quadrat) completion
(e.g. of the square); (*zu* 90°)
complement; (*zu* 180°) supplement ; (*zu* 360°) explement
er·geben 1. *v.t.* yield, produce,
result in. **2.** *v.r.:* *sich e.* result,
follow [*cf.* ANSCHAUUNG]
Er·gebnis *n* result
er·haben *adj.* **1.** (*Winkel*) reentrant, reflex (angle). **2.** (*Fläche*)
convex (surface)
er·halten *v.t.* **1.** (*bekommen, z.B.*
ein Resultat) get, obtain, (e.g. a
result) [*cf.* ABLEITUNG 2.]. **2.**
(*bewahren*) preserve, conserve:
die Winkel bleiben in der kon-
formen Abbildung e. angles are

preserved in conformal mapping
Er·haltung *f* preservation, con-
servation : *E. der Energie* con-
servation of energy
er·heben I. *v.t.* **1.** (*erhöhen*) raise:
zur dritten Potenz e. raise to the
third power, cube [*cf.* KUBIEREN].
2. (*sammeln*) collect: *Daten e.*
collect data. **II.** *v.r.:* *sich e.* rise,
arise [*cf.* HOCH; POTENZ]
Er·hebung *f* **1.** (*Höhe*) elevation
[*cf.* HÖHE]. **2.** (*zu einer Potenz*)
raising (to a power). **3.** (*Samm-*
lung, z.B. von statistischem
Material) collection (e.g. of
statistical material)
Erhebungs·formular *n* (*statist.*)
questionnaire, schedule
er·laubt *adj.* permissible
er·mitteln *v.t.* ascertain, determine;
(*errechnen*) compute
Er·mitt(e)lung *f* determination;
(*Errechnung*) computation
er·rechnen *v.t.* compute, determine
[*cf.* ERMITTELN]
Er·rechnung *f* computation, determination [*cf.* ERMITTLUNG]
er·richten *v.t.* erect, set up, put up:
eine Normale e. erect (or set up,
or put up) a perpendicular
Er·richtung *f* erection, setting up,
putting up
Er·satz *m* replacement, substitution
Ersatz·wert *m* (*ins.*) (*einer Polizze*)
full value (of a policy)
er·schließen *v.t.* (*log.*) infer, gather,
conclude
er·setzen *v.t.* replace, substitute
for: *x durch y ersetzen* replace *x*
by *y*, substitute *y* for *x* [*cf.*
AUSTAUSCHEN]

Er·setzung *f* replacement, substitution. [*cf* AUSTAUSCH]

Er·sparnisse *f pl.* (*fin.*) savings [*cf.* RÜCKLAGE]

erst *ord. num.* first: *das erste Glied* the first term; *die minus erste Potenz* the minus first power [*cf.* ABLEITUNG; DIFFERENTIALQUOTIENT; GEOMETRIE; GRÖSSE; PRÄDIKAT; PROJEKTION; PROJEKTIONSEBENE; QUADRAT; SPITZE; TAFELABSTAND; VIERTEL]

erstens *adv.* first(ly), in the first place

Er·trag *m* (*comm.*) proceeds, profit

Ertrags·rechnung *f* (*comm.*) profit and loss account

Ertrags·wert *m* (*comm.*) (*eines Unternehmens*) capitalized earning value (of an enterprise)

er·warten *v.t.* expect

Er·wartung *f* expectation [*cf.* MATHEMATISCH]

Erwartungs·wert *m* (*statist.*) (mathematical) expectation

er·weitern *v.t., v.r.:* **sich** *e.* dilate, widen, extend, expand: *einen Satz e.* extend a theorem (or law); *erweiterter Mittelwertsatz* extended mean value theorem [*cf.* BRUCH; PRÄDIKATENKALKÜL]

Er·weiterung *f* extension, expansion, dilatation, dilation: *E. eines Begriffs* extension of a concept; (*alg.*) *E. eines Zahlenkörpers* extension of a number field; *E. eines Bruchs* reduction of a fraction to higher terms [*cf.* AUSDEHNUNG; FLÄCHENAUSDEHNUNG; LINEAR; PERFEKT; RAUMAUSDEHNUNG; RÄUMLICH; REIN; TRANSZENDENT]

Erweiterungs·körper *m* (*alg.*) extension field [*cf.* ZUGEHÖRIG]

er·zeugen *v.t.* generate, produce; (*eine Fläche, auch*) sweep out (a surface): *die von den Elementen a, b . . . erzeugte Gruppe* the group generated by the elements *a, b . . .* [*cf.* GERADLINIG; GRÖSSE]

Er·zeugende *f* (*z.B. einer Regelfläche*) ruling, element, generator, generatrix, generating line (e.g. of a ruled surface): *E. eines Kegels, Zylinders* element (or ruling) of a cone, cylinder; *Länge der Erzeugenden eines Rotationskegels* slant hight of a cone of revolution [*cf.* SEITENHÖHE]; *geradlinige E. einer Regelfläche* rectilinear generator of a ruled surface; *Schar von Erzeugenden* **a.** (*allgemein*) family of generators, generation; **b.** (*einer windschiefen Fläche*) regulus (of a warped surface)[= REGELSCHAR]; *in einer zweischarigen Regelfläche schneidet jede E. einer Schar jede E. der anderen Schar* in a doubly ruled surface every element of either generation intersects every element of the other generation

Er·zeugung *f* generation, production

er·zwungen *adj.* forced: *erzwungene Schwingung* forced vibration (or oscillation)

Eta *n* (*griechischer Buchstabe* Greek letter H, η) eta

Eudoxus *m N.* [*cf.* KAMPYLA]

euklidisch *adj.* Euclidean: *euklidischer Algorithmus* Euclidean algorithm; *euklidische Geometrie* Euclidean geometry; *euklidischer*

Raum Euclidean space [*cf.* GEOMETRIE; RING]
Evolute *f* evolute
evolutorisch *adj.* (*statist.*) trend: *evolutorische Komponente* trend component
Evolvente *f* involute [= INVOLUTE] [*cf.* ABWICKELN]
ewig *adj.* eternal, perpetual: (*fin.*) *ewige Anleihe* perpetual bond [= RENTENANLEIHE]; *ewige Rente* perpetual annuity, perpetuity
exakt *adj.* exact: *exakte Wissenschaft* exact science
Exakt·heit *f* exactness, exactitude
Exempel *n* example
exemplifizieren *v.t.* exemplify
Exhaustion *f* exhaustion [*cf.* APPROXIMATION]
Exhaustions·methode *f* method of exhaustion [*cf.* APPROXIMATIONS-METHODE]
Existenz *f* existence
existieren *v.i.* exist [*cf.* BESTEHEN]
explizit *adj.* explicit: *explizite Funktion* explicit function; (*alg.*) *ein explizit gegebener Körper* a field given explicitly
explizite *adv.* explicitly
Exponent *m* exponent, index: *gebrochener E.* fractional exponent; *E. Null* zero exponent
Exponenten·bewertung *f* (*alg.*) exponential valuation
Exponential·funktion *f* exponential function
Exponential·gleichung *f* exponential equation
Exponential·größe *f* exponential
Exponential·kurve *f* exponential curve

Exponential·reihe *f* exponential series
Extensionalität *f* (*log.*) extensionality
Extensität *f* extensity
extensiv *adj.* extensive
Extra·dividende *f* (*comm., fin.*) surplus (or extra) dividend [*cf.* BONUS 1.]
Extra·polation *f* extrapolation [*cf.* WEITERFÜHRUNG]
extra·polieren *v.t.* extrapolate [*cf.* WEITERFÜHREN]
Extra·polierung *f* extrapolation
extrem *adj.* extreme: *extremer Wert einer Funktion* extremum, extreme (value) of a function
Extrem *n* extreme (value), extremum [= EXTREMUM]
Extremale *f* extremal, geodesic
Extrem·punkt *m* (*einer Kurve*) (*in kartesischen Koordinaten*) bend (or turning) point; (*in Polarkoordinaten*) apse (of a curve) [*cf.* SCHEITEL 1.]
Extremum *n* (*pl. Extrema*) (*einer Funktion*) extremum, extreme (value) (of a function)
ex·zentrisch *adj.* eccentric [*cf.* ANOMALIE]
Ex·zentrizität *f* (*eines Kegelschnitts*) 1. (*numerische E.*) eccentricity (of a conic). 2. (*lineare E.*) distance of focus from center (of a conic)
Exzeß *m* 1. (*Überschuß*) excess: *sphärischer E.* spherical excess. 2. (*statist.*: *Steilheit der Häufigkeitskurve*) kurtosis, excess (of a frequency curve)
exzessiv *adj.* excessive

F

Fabrikations·nummer *f* (*einer Maschine usw.*) serial number (of a machine, etc.)

. . fach *adj. suf.* . . fold: *n-fach* n-fold [*cf.* SYMMETRIE]

Fach·statistiker *m* professional statistician

Fach·werk *n* truss

Faden *m* (*meas.*) fathom

Faden·konstruktion *f* (*der Ellipse*) string construction (of an ellipse)

Faden·kreuz *n* cross hairs (or lines)

Fahrenheit·thermometer *n* Fahrenheit thermometer

Fahr·strahl *m* **1.** (*Ortsvektor*) radius vector. **2.** (*eines Kegelschnittpunkts*) focal radius (or distance) (of a point of a conic)

Faktor *m* **1.** (*eines Produkts*) factor (of a product): *in Faktoren zerlegen* factor, factorize, resolve into factors; *F. modulo p* factor modulo *p: integrierender F.* integrating factor [*cf.* AUSKLAMMERN; KÜRZEN; UNZERLEGBAR; WURZELAUSDRUCK; ZERLEGBAR; ZERLEGEN; ZERLEGUNG]. **2.** (*eines Elements einer Determinante*) cofactor (of an element of a determinant)

Faktoren·system *n* (*alg.*) factor set [*cf.* VERSCHRÄNKT]

Faktoren·zerlegung *f* factoring, factorization

Faktor·gruppe *f* (*alg.*) factor group

Faktorielle *f* factorial [= FAKULTÄT]: *Faktorielle r* factorial *r*, (*symb.: r !*) [*cf.* NULL]

Faktoriellen·reihe *f* factorial series

Faktor·zerlegung *f* factoring, factorization

Faktura *f* (*comm.*) invoice, bill [*cf.* AUSMACHEN]

fakturieren *v.t.* (*comm.*) invoice.

Fakultät *f* factorial [= FAKTORIELLE]: *r Fakultät* factorial *r* (*symb.: r!*)

Fall *m* **1.** (*Sinken*) fall, drop: *freier F.* free fall [*cf.* SENKUNG]. **2.** (*Einzelumstand*) case [*cf.* AUSDEHNUNG; GÜNSTIG; SPEZIELL; UNGÜNSTIG]

Fall·beschleunigung *f* acceleration of fall

fallen *v.i.* fall, drop; (*absteigen*) descend: *ein frei fallender Körper* a freely falling body; *der Endpunkt fällt auf die x-Achse* the end point falls on the *x*-axis [*cf,* ORDNEN; POTENZ; POTENZREIHE; PREIS; SENKEN; TENDENZ]

fällen *v.t.* drop: *von einem Punkt auf eine Gerade eine Normale* (*oder Senkrechte*) *f.* drop a normal (or perpendicular) to a line from a point

Fall·geschwindigkeit *f* velocity of fall

fällig *adj.* (*comm.*) due, payable [*cf.* VALUTA; ZAHLBAR]

Fällig·keit *f* (*z.B. eines Wechsels*) due date, maturity (e.g. of a bill of exchange)

Fälligkeits·datum *n* (*comm.*) due date

Fall·zeit *f* (*phys.*) time of fall

falsch *adj.* false; *den Dezimalpunkt f. setzen* misplace the decimal

point; *f. addieren. multiplizieren*
make a mistake in adding,
multiplying; *falsche Berechnung*
(*oder Kalkulation*) miscalculation
[*cf.* IMMER; ZIRKEL]
Falsch·heit *f* falsehood
falten *v.t* fold
. . . fältig *adj. suf.* . . . fold [*cf.*
ACHTFÄLTIG; ZWEIFÄLTIG; ZWIE-
FÄLTIG]
Faltung *f* convolution, fold(ing)
Farad *n* (*elec.*) farad
fassen *v.t.* hold: *der Tank faßt* 100
hl the tank holds 100 *hl.*
Fassungs·kraft *f* capacity [*cf.*
KAPAZITÄT; LADUNGSGEWICHT]
fast *adj.* nearly, almost: *die Funktion ist f. linear* the function is
nearly linear; *f. überall stetig*
continuous almost everywhere
fast-periodisch *adj.* (*Funktion*) almost periodic (function)
Feder *f* spring [*cf.* SPANNEN;
STRECKUNG]
Feder·zirkel *m* bow spring
compass, bow springs
Feder·wage *f* spring balance
Fehler *m* error, mistake, deviation:
absoluter (*relativer*) *F.* absolute
(relative) error; (*statist.*) *mittlerer
quadratischer F.* standard (or:
mean square) deviation; (*statist.*)
systematischer F. constant error,
bias [*cf.* GENAU; RECHENFEHLER]
Fehler·gesetz *n* law of errors:
Gaußsches F. Gaussian law of
errors
Fehler·glied *n* error term
Fehler·kurve *f* error curve [=
HÄUFIGKEITSKURVE, VERTEI-
LUNGSKURVE] [*cf.* NORMAL;
WAHRSCHEINLICHKEITSKURVE]

Fehler·quelle *f* source of error
[*cf.* AUSSCHALTEN]
Fehler·rechnung *f* theory of error
Fehler·spielraum *m* margin of
error, allowance, tolerance [*cf.*
SPIELRAUM]
fein *adj.* fine
Fein·gehalt *m* (*von Gold, Silber*)
fineness (of gold, silver); (*der
Prägung*) standard (of coinage)
Fein·struktur *f* fine structure
Feld *n* 1. (*Gebiet einer Funktion*)
field (of a function): *elektro-
magnetisches F.* electromagnetic
field; *skalares F.* scalar field.
2. (*statist.*) (*einer Korrelations-
tabelle*) cell (of a correlation
table)
feld·erzeugend *adj.* (*phys.*) field-
producing
feld·frei *adj.* (*Raum*) field-free,
zero-field (space)
Feld·gleichung *f* field equation
Feld·maß *n* land measure
Feld·stärke *f* field strength (or:
intensity)
Feld·theorie *f* field theory
Fermat *m N.* [*cf.* SATZ]
fern *adj.* distant, remote, far (away)
[*cf.* UNEIGENTLICH; UNENDLICH]
Ferne *f* (long) distance, remoteness
[*cf.* UNENDLICH; WEITE]
Fern·kraft *f* force at a distance,
distant (or long-range) force;
(*Fernwirkung*) action at a distance, distant (or long-range)
action
Fern·lenkung *f* remote control
Fern·rohr *n* telescope
Fern·wirkung *f* action at a distance,
distant (or long-range) action
[*cf.* FERNKRAFT]

fest *adj.* (*festgelegt*) fixed; (*konstant*) constant; (*starr*) solid; (*haltbar*) firm, strong: *feste Gerade* fixed line; *fester Punkt, Kreis* fixed point, circle; *fester Wert* fixed (or constant) value; (*phys.*) *fester Körper* solid (body) [*cf.* AGGREGATZUSTAND; FESTHEIT; INTERVALL; MERKMAL; VERMÖGENSANLAGE]

Fest·gelder *n pl.* (*fin.*) time deposits

Fest·heit *f* **1.** (*feste Lage*) fixed position. **2.** (*Aggregatzustand*) solidity, solid state (of matter). **3.** (*Haltbarkeit*) strength, firmness [*cf.* STARRE]

Festig·keit *f* (*mech.*) strength; (*Aggregatzustand*) solidity

fest·legen *v.t.* fix; (*bestimmen*) determine, specify: *der Neigungswinkel ist festgelegt bis auf Vielfache von* 2π the inclination is fixed, except for multiples of 2π [*cf.* BESTIMMEN; FEST]

fest·setzen *v.t.* posit, stipulate, fix

Fest·setzung *f* stipulation

fest·verzinslich *adj.* (*fin.*) bearing fixed interest

fiduziär *adj.* (*statist.*) fiduciary

Figur *f* figure, configuration, graph: *geometrische F.* geometric(al) figure; *ebene F.* plane figure; *in einer F. darstellen* represent by a graph (or figure); *die durch die Funktion* $f(x)$ *dargestellte F.* the graph of the function $f(x)$ [*cf.* BILD]; *lesen Sie die Werte aus der F. ab!* read off the values from the graph [*cf.* ÄHNLICH; AUSZIEHEN; BASIS; BESCHREIBEN; DECKUNG; FLÄCHENELEMENT; GERADLINIG; GRUND-

LINIE; HÖHE; KONGRUENT; KONGRUENZ; LISSAJOUS; SCHWERPUNKT; VERWANDELN; VERWANDLUNG].

figuriert *adj.* (*Zahl*) figurate, polygonal (number)

Finanz *f* finance

finanzieren *v.t.* finance

Finanz·jahr *n* (*fin.*) fiscal year

Finanz·periode *f* (*fin.*) fiscal period

Finanz·zoll(tarif) *m* (*comm., fin.*) tariff for revenue only

finden *v.t.* find

Finger·breite *f* (*meas.*) digit

Finsternis *f* (*astr.*) eclipse

Fiskal·jahr *n* (*fin.*) fiscal year

fix *adj.* fixed: *fixe Preise* fixed prices [*cf.* VERMÖGENSANLAGE]

Fix·punkt *m* fixed point

Fix·stern *m* (*astr.*) fixed star

flach *adj.* flat; (*Häufigkeitskurve*) platykurtic (frequency curve) [*cf.* EBEN]

Fläche *f* **1.** (*zweidimensionales Gebilde* two-dimensional geometrical element) surface: *krumme* (*oder gekrümmte*) *F.* curved surface; *verdrehte* (*oder geworfene*) *F.* twisted (or warped) surface; *F. zweiter Ordnung* quadric surface, conicoid; *Riemannsche F.* Riemann surface [*cf.* BLATT; VERZWEIGUNGSPUNKT]. [*cf.* ABWICKELBAR; ABWICKELN; ABWICKLUNG; ANALLAGMATISCH; AUSSCHNITT; BEGRENZEN; BEREICH; CHARAKTERISTIK; DREIFACHRECHTWINKLIG; DURCHDRINGUNGSLINIE; EBEN; EINHÜLLEN; EINSEITIG; ELLIPTISCH; ERHABEN; FLÄCHENINHALT; GERADLINIG; GESCHLECHT; INTEGRIERBAR;

KREISPUNKT; KRUMM; KRÜM-
MUNG; KRÜMMUNGSLINIE; MAN-
TEL; MASSENPUNKT; MATERIELL;
NABELPUNKT; OBERFLÄCHE;
ORDNUNG; PARABOLISCH; PARA-
METRISCH; PSEUDOSPHÄRISCH;
QUADRATUR; QUADRIEREN;
SCHALE; SCHNITT; SCHRAUBEN-
FÖRMIG; SECHST; SPHÄRISCH;
ÜBER; UMRANDEN; VERBIEGEN;
VERDREHEN; VERSCHNEIDEN; VER-
SCHNEIDUNG; VIERT; WINDUNG;
WÖLBEN; WÖLBUNG; ZWEIT]. **2.**
(*Flächeninhalt* content of a sur-
face) area; *F. eines Dreiecks* area
of a triangle [*cf.* EINHEITSKUGEL;
SCHRAFFIEREN]. **3.** (*Seitenfläche*)
face: *F. eines Polyeders* face of a
polyhedron [*cf.* EBENFLÄCHIG;
SEITENFLÄCHE]
Flächen·anzahl *f* [= FLÄCHENZAHL]
Flächen·ausdehnung *f* **1.** (*Erwei-
terung*) surface expansion. **2.** (*Di-
mension*) square dimension(s)(*pl.*)
Flächen·diagonale *f* plane diagonal
[*ant.:* KÖRPERDIAGONALE]
Flächen·einheit *f* unit (of) area,
square unit
Flächen·element *n* element of area:
F. einer ebenen Figur element of
plane area
Flächen·geschlecht *n* genus of a
surface
Flächen·gesetz *n* (*Keplers*) (Kep-
ler's) law of areas
flächen·gleich *adj.* equal, equiva-
lent (in area): *flächengleiche
Dreiecke* equal triangles [*cf.*
VERWANDELN; VERWANDLUNG]
Flächen·inhalt *m* area: *F. eines
Kreises* area of a circle; *F. einer
Fläche* surface area; *den F. einer*

.*Fläche bestimmen* square an area
[*cf.* EINHEITSKUGEL; FLÄCHE;
LIEGEN]
Flächen·integral *n* surface integral
Flächen·krümmung *f* curvature of
a surface
Flächen·maß *n* square (or surface)
measure
Flächen·raum *m* area [*cf.* VIEL]
Flächen·system *n* system of sur-
faces [*cf.* DREIFACH]
Flächen·theorie *f* theory of surfaces
flächen·treu *adj.* (*Abbildung*) equi-
areal, area-preserving, equivalent
(map) [*cf.* ZYLINDERPROJEKTION]
Flächen·treue *f* (*einer Abbildung*)
preservation of area (of a map)
Flächen·winkel *m* dihedral angle
Flächen·zahl *f* (*eines Polyeders*)
number of faces (of a polyhedron)
[*cf.* SEITENZAHL]
Flach·heit *f* flatness
Flasche *f* **1.** (*Gefäß* vessel) bottle:
Kleinsche F. Klein bottle. **2.**
(*Aufzugsvorrichtung* hoisting
device) block, pulley
Flaschen·zug *m* (*mech.*) block and
tackle
fliegen *v.i.* fly
Flieh·kraft *f* centrifugal force
fließen *v.i.* flow [*cf.* FLUSS]
Flucht·linie *f* vanishing line
Fluchtlinien·tafel *f* nomogram,
nomograph, alignment chart
Flucht·punkt *m* vanishing point
Flug *m* flight
Flug·bahn *f* trajectory
Flügel·gruppe *f* (*statist.*) end class:
offene F. open-end class
Fluidum *n* fluid
Fluktuation *f* fluctuation [*cf.*
SCHWANKUNG]

fluktuieren *v.i.* fluctuate [*cf.*
SCHWANKEN]
Fluß *m* (*Fließen*) flow, flux [*cf.*
AGGREGATZUSTAND; AKTIVUM]
Flüssig·keit *f* fluid, liquid
Flüssigkeits·druck *m* fluid pressure
Flüssigkeits·maß *n* liquid measure
Flüssigkeits·mechanik *f* mechanics
of fluids, hydrodynamics
Flüssigkeits·strömung *f* flow of a
fluid
Fluxion *f* fluxion
Fluxions·rechnung *f* (method of)
fluxions
fokal *adj.* focal
Fokal·distanz *f* (*opt.*) focal distance
Fokus *m* focus [= BRENNPUNKT]
Folge *f* 1. (*math.:Aufeinanderfolge*)
sequence [*cf.* ABNEHMEN; DIVER-
GENZ; GRENZWERT; INVERSION;
REIHE 1., 4.; UNENDLICH]. **2.**
(*log.: Folgerung*) consequence,
conclusion. **3.** (*Wirkung*) effect,
consequence [*cf.* WIRKUNG]
Folge·beziehung *f* (*log.*) relation
of implication
folgen *v.i.* (*dat.*) follow (*dir. obj.*)
folgend *adj.* following, subsequent
folgern *v.t.* deduce, infer, gather
Folgerung *f* 1. (*Schluß*) conclusion,
deduction, consequence. **2.** (*Fol-
gesatz*) corollary [*cf.* ABLEITEN;
FOLGE; SCHLUSS]
Folge·satz corollary [*cf.* FOL-
GERUNG]
Folium *n* folium: *Descartessches
F., F. des Descartes* folium of
Descartes [*cf.* BLATT: *Descartessches B.*]; *einfaches F.* simple
folium [= EINBLATT]
Fonds *m* (*fin.*) fund
fordern *v.t.* **1.** (*beanspruchen*)

claim. **2.** (*postulieren*) postulate
Forderung *f* 1. (*Anspruch*) claim
[*cf.* VERJÄHREN]. **2.** (*Postulat*)
postulate
Form *f* 1. (*Gestalt*) form, shape
[*cf.* BRINGEN; DARSTELLEN;
DARSTELLUNG; DETERMINANTE;
ENTWICKELT; UNBESTIMMT]. **2.**
(*alg.: homogene Funktion* homogeneous function) form, quantic:
kubische binäre F. cubic binary
form (or quantic); *quadratische
F.* quadratic form [*cf.* BILINEAR;
DRITT; EINHEITSFORM; HERMITE]
formal *adj.* formal [*cf.* GESTALT;
PERMANENZ]
formalisieren *v.t.* formalize
Formalisierung *f* formalization
Formalismus *m* formalism; (*Sym-
bolik*) symbolism
formal-reell *adj.* (*alg.*) (*Körper*)
formally real (field)
Form·änderung *f* change of form,
deformation
Formation *f* formation
Formel *f* formula: *Heronische,
Taylorsche F.* Hero(n)'s, Taylor's
formula [*cf.* ABLEITEN; AUS-
DEHNUNG; AUSFÜHRUNG; EMPI-
RISCH; ENTWICKLUNG; GRUND-
FORMEL; IDENTISCH; NACH]
Formel·sprache *f* language of
formulas, symbolic language
formen *v.t.* form
formieren *v.t.* form
Formierung *f* formation
formulieren *v.t.* formulate
Formulierung *f* formulation
Form·veränderung *f* change of
form, deformation
fort·laufend *adj.* continued, con-
tinuous: *fortlaufende Proportion*

continued proportion; *fortlaufende Numerierung* continuous numbering [*cf.* STETIG: *stetige Proportion*]

fort·pflanzen 1. *v.t.* propagate, transmit. **2.** *v.r.:* **sich** *f.* be propagated, be transmitted, travel [*cf.* AUSBREITEN]

Fort·pflanzung *f* propagation, transmission [*cf.* AUSBREITUNG]

Fortpflanzungs·medium *n*, **Fortpflanzungs·mittel** *n* medium of transmission

Fortpflanzungs·geschwindigkeit *f* speed, velocity of propagation (or transmission) [*cf.* GESCHWINDIGKEIT]

Fort·schreibung *f* (*statist.*) inter-census estimate

fort·schreiten *v.i.* proceed

Fort·schreiten *n* (*astr.*) (*der Tagundnachtgleichen*) precession (of the equinoxes)

fort·schreitend *adj.* translatory, progressive: *fortschreitende Bewegung* translatory motion, translation; *fortschreitende Welle* progressive (or traveling) wave

fort·setzen *v.t.* continue: (*alg.*) *einen Isomorphismus f.* continue an isomorphism [*cf.* WEITERFÜHREN]

Fort·setzung *f* continuation: (*alg.*) *F. eines Isomorphismus* continuation of an isomorphism; (*alg.*) *analytische F.* analytic continuation [*cf.* WEITERFÜHRUNG]

Fortsetzungs·punkte *m. pl.* continuation notation (*symb.:* . . .)

Foucault *m N.*[*cf.* PENDELVERSUCH]

Fourier *m N.* [*cf.* REIHE]

Frage *f* question, problem

Frage·bogen *m* (*statist.*) questionnaire

frankieren *v.t.* (*comm.*) (*einen Brief*) (*Postmarke aufkleben*) stamp (a letter); (*für den Empfänger freimachen*) prepay (a letter)

franko *adv.* (*comm.*) delivered free (of charge), free on board, (*abbr.*) F.O.B.: *f. Berlin* free delivered at Berlin, ex (warehouse) Berlin; *f. Zoll* free of duty

frei *adj.* free: *freie Schwingung* free oscillation (or vibration); *mit freier Hand zeichnen* draw (or plot) freehand, make a freehand sketch [*cf.* FALL; FALLEN; VARIABLE]

Frei·börse *f* (*comm.*) [= NACHBÖRSE]

Frei·hand *f* freehand: *mit F. zeichnen* draw freehand

frei·händig *adj.* **1.** (*zeichnen*) (draw) freehand, by inspection. **2.** (*comm.*) free, private: *f. verkaufen* **a.** (*privat*) sell privately; **b.** (*an der Freiverkehrsbörse*) sell on the curb exchange

Freihand·zeichnen *n* freehand drawing

Freiheits·grad *m* (*mech.*) degree of freedom: (*statist.*) *Anzahl der Freiheitsgrade einer Verteilung* number of degrees of freedom of a distribution

frei·machen *v.t.* (*comm.*) [= FRANKIEREN]

frei·tragend *adj.* cantilever: *freitragender Balken* cantilever beam (or arm)

Frei·verkehr *m* (*comm.*) [= NACHBÖRSE]

Freiverkehrs·börse *f* (*comm.*) [= NACHBÖRSE] [*cf.* FREIHÄNDIG]

fremd *adj.* exclusive, disjoint, extraneous: *zueinander f.* mutually exclusive (or disjoint); *durch Potenzieren beider Seiten kommen fremde Wurzeln in eine Gleichung* by raising both members to a higher power extraneous roots are brought into an equation

Frequenz *f* (*phys., statist.*) frequency

Frequenz·kurve *f* (*statist.*) frequency curve [= HÄUFIGKEITSKURVE]

Freundschafts·wechsel *m* (*comm.*) [= GEFÄLLIGKEITSAKZEPT]

Freundschafts·zahl *f* amicable number

Frist *f* (*comm., fin.*) (*Aufschub*) respite; (*Termin*) term, appointed day (or time)

Frist·verlängerung *f* (*comm., fin.*) (*bei Zahlungen*) extention of the terms (of payment)

frontal *adj.* frontal

Frontal·ansicht *f* front(al) view

Frontal·ebene *f* frontal plane

Frosch·perspektive *f* perspective from below (as if by a frog's eye), frog's-eye view (or perspective) [*ant.:* VOGELPERSPEKTIVE]

Frühlings·punkt *m* (*astr.*) vernal point (or equinox)

Frühlings-Tagundnachtgleiche *f* (*astr.*) vernal equinox

führen *v.t.* lead, guide, carry: *ad absurdum f.* show the absurdity of [*cf.* TREIBEN]

fundamental *adj.* fundamental

Fundamental·folge *f* (*alg.*) fundamental sequence

Fundamental·punkt *m* (*einer Punkt-* reihe) fundamental point (of a range of points)

Fundamental·reihe *f* fundamental sequence: *Cantorsche F.* Cantor fundamental sequence

Fundamental·satz *m* fundamental theorem (or law): *F. der Algebra* fundamental theorem of algebra

fünf *card. num.* five [*cf.* FÜNFSTELLIG]

Fünf *f* (*Zahl, Ziffer*) (number, figure) five

Fünf·eck *n* pentagon

fünf·eckig *adj.* pentagonal

Fünfecks·zahl *f* pentagonal number

Fünfer *m* **1.** (*Ziffer*) (figure) five. **2.** (*Banknote*) (bank note) five . . . note (or bill), (*coll.*) fiver, (*z.B. Fünfmarkschein* five-mark note)

fünf·fach *adj.* fivefold, quintuple

fünf·hundert *card. num.* five hundred

fünf·mal *num.* five times

fünf·malig *adj.* (done) five times [*cf.* DREIMALIG]

fünf·seitig *adj.* five-sided; (*Pyramide, Prisma*) pentagonal (pyramid, prism)

fünf·stellig *adj.* (*ganze Zahl*) five-figure, five-digit (integer); (*Dezimalzahl*) five-figure, five-place (decimal); (*log.: mit fünf Leerstellen*) five-place, pentadic: *fünfstellige Zahl* five-digit (or five-figure) number; *fünfstelliger Dezimalbruch, Logarithmus* five-place (or five-figure) decimal fraction, logarithm

Fünf·stern *m* five-pronged star, pentagram, pentacle

fünf·strahlig *adj.* five-rayed; (*Stern, auch*) five-pronged (star)

fünft *ord. num.* fifth: *fünften Grades, fünfter Ordnung* quintic [*cf.* VIERT]

Fünftel *n* fifth (part)

fünftens *adv.* fifthly, in the fifth place

fünf·zählig *adj.* fivefold, quintuple; (*Symmetrie, auch*) pentagonal (symmetry)

fünf·zehn *card. num.* fifteen

Fünfzehn·eck *n* pentadecagon

fünf·zig *card. num.* fifty

fünf·zigst *ord. num.* fiftieth

Funk·höhe *f* radio frequency

Funkmeß·gerät *n* radar

Funkmeß·ortung *f*, **Funkmeß-peilung** *f* (*nav., av.*) radio direction finding

Funkmeß·peiler *m* (*nav., av.*) radio direction finder

Funk·ortung (*nav., av.*) radio orientation

Funkortungs·gerät *n*, **Funk·peiler** *m* radio direction finder

Funk·strahl *m* radio beam

Funktion *f* function: *die F. ist unstetig* (*oder diskontinuierlich oder sprunghaft*) *in diesem Punkt* the function is discontinuous at this point; *F. einer F.* function of a function, functional; *algebraische, logarithmische F.* algebraic, logarithmic function; *F. zweier Variablen* function of two variables; *Veränderung* (*oder Variation oder Schwankung*) *einer F. in einem Intervall* change (or variation, or oscillation) of a function in an interval; *Lagrangesche F.* Lagrangian function; *Sturmsche Funktionen* Sturm's functions [*cf.* ABGELEITET; AB-HÄNGIG; ABLEITEN; ABSOLUT; AB-LEITUNG; ANALYTISCH; ANPASSEN; BEDEUTEN; BEREICH; BESSEL; EIN-PASSEN; ELEMENTARSYMMETRISCH; ELLIPTISCH; ENTWICKELT; ENT-WICKLUNG; EXPLIZIT; EXTREM; EXTREMUM; FAST; FAST-PERIO-DISCH; FELD; FIGUR; GANZ; GLEICHMÄSSIG; GLEICHGRADIG; GRADIENT; GRÖSST; HAUPTWERT; HOLOMORPH; HYPERBOLISCH; IM-PLIZIT; INVERS; INVERSHYPER-BOLISCH; INVERSTRIGONOMET-RISCH; KLEINST; LOGARITHMISCH; MEHRWERTIG; MEROMORPH; MESS-BAR; MONOGEN; NULL; NULL-STELLE; PARAMETER; POL; REIHEN-ENTWICKLUNG; RESIDUUM; STE-TIG; STETIGKEIT; SYMMETRISCH; TRANSZENDENT; TRIGONOMET-RISCH; UNIFORMISIEREN; UNI-FORMISIERUNG; UNSTETIG; VER-HALTEN; VERHALTEN; VERLAUF; VERLAUFEN; WERTEVORRAT; ZU-SAMMENGESETZT; ZYKLOMET-RISCH]

funktional, funktionell *adj.* functional [*cf.* ABHÄNGIGKEIT]

Funktionen·funktion *f* function of a function, functional

Funktionen·kalkül *m* (*log.*) functional calculus

Funktionen·körper *m* (*alg.*) function field

Funktionen·tafel *f* function table

Funktionen·theorie *f* function theory

Funktions·leiter *f*, **Funktions·skala** *f* (*statist.*) nomogram scale

Funktions·tafel *f* function table

Funktions·wert *m* function(al) value

Funktions·zeichen *n* functional symbol [*cf.* LEERSTELLE]

Fürsorge·statistik *f* welfare statistics [*cf.* SOZIALSTATISTIK]

Für·trag *m* (*comm.*) carry-over, continued account [= ÜBERTRAG; VORTRAG]

Fuß *m* (*meas.*) foot

Fuß·kerze *f* (*opt.*) foot-candle

Fuß·pfund *n* (*meas.*) foot-pound

Fuß·punkt *m* **1.** (*einer Normalen*) foot (of a perpendicular). **2.** (*des Horizonts*) nadir (of the horizon) [= NADIR]

Fußpunkt·kurve *f* pedal (curve)

Fußpunkt·fläche *f* pedal surface

G

Gallone *f* (*meas.*) gallon

Galois *m* N. [*cf.* GALOIS-FELD; GALOISSCH; GALOISSCH]

Galois-Feld *n* Galois field

galoissch *adj.* (*Gleichung, Körper*) normal (equation, field) [*cf.* GALOISSCH]

Galoissch *adj.* Galois: *Galoissche Resolvente, Gruppe, Theorie* Galois resolvent, group, theory [*cf.* VERSCHRÄNKT]

Galton *m* N.: *Galtonsche Kurve* Galtonian curve [*cf.* ZUFALLS-APPARAT; ZUFALLSKURVE]

Gamma *n* (*griechischer Buchstabe* Greek letter Γ, γ) gamma

Gamma·funktion *f* gamma function

Gamma·strahlen *m pl.* (*phys.*) gamma rays

Gang *m* (*einer Schraubenlinie, Schraube*) turn, thread (of a helix, screw)

Gang·höhe *f* (*einer Schraubenlinie, Schraube*) pitch, lead (of a helix, screw)

ganz *adj.* **1.** (*umfassend* comprehensive) whole, entire. **2.** (*ganz-zahlig*) integral, whole: *ganze Zahl* whole (or integral) number, integer [*cf.* AUFRUNDEN; DREI-STELLIG; EINSTELLIG; FÜNFSTEL-LIG; .. STELLIG; VIELSTELLIG; VIERSTELLIG; ZWEISTELLIG]; *ganze rationale Funktion* rational integral function; *ganze p-adische Zahl* p-adic integer [*cf.* ABGESCHLOSSENHEIT; ABSOLUT; GAUSSSCH; GRÖSSE]

ganz-abgeschlossen *adj.* (*alg.*) (*z.B. Ring*) integrally closed (e.g. ring)

Ganze(s) *n* whole [*cf.* VERHÄLTNIS; ZUSAMMENFASSEN]

Ganz·heit *f* **1.** (*Umfassendheit* comprehensiveness) wholeness, integrity. **2.** (*Ganzzahligkeit*) integralness, integrity

ganz·zahlig *adj.* integral: (*mit ganzen Koeffizienten*) with integral coefficients [*cf.* GANZ; UNZERLEGBAR]

Ganz·zahligkeit *f* integralness, integrity [*cf.* GANZHEIT]

Gas *n* (*phys.*) gas [*cf.* VERDÜNNEN; VERDÜNNUNG]

gas·förmig *adj.* (*phys.*) gaseous [*cf.* AGGREGATZUSTAND]

Gas·messer *m* (*phys.*) gas meter

Gauß *m N.* Gauss [*cf.* GAUSSSCH; GLEICHUNG; ZAHLENEBENE]

Gauß *n* (*mag.*) gauss

Gaußsch *adj.* Gaussian: *Gaußscher Zahlkörper* Gaussian number field; *Ring der ganzen Gaußschen Zahlen* ring of the Gaussian integers; *Gaußsche Summe* Gaussian sum [*cf.* FEHLERGESETZ]

geben *v.t.* give, render; *es gibt eine Größe* there is a quantity [*cf.* GEGEBEN; GLEICHES; IN]

Ge·biet *n* region, domain, field [*cf.* ABGRENZEN; FELD]

Ge·bilde *n* geometrical element, entity, construct: *Punkt, Gerade, Ebene sind die einfachsten geometrischen G.* point, line, plane are the simplest geometrical elements [*cf.* FLÄCHE; GROSS, GRÖSSE; ORT 2.]

ge·bogen *adj.* curved

ge·brochen *adj.* **1.** (*math.: Bruch . . .*) fractional [*cf.* EXPONENT]. **2.** (*geom.: eckig* angular) broken: *gebrochene Linie* broken line

ge·bunden *adj.* (*log.*) bound [*cf.* VARIABLE]

Geburten·tafel *f* (*statist.*) (actuarial) table of births

Geburten·ziffer *f* (*statist.*) birth rate

Gedächtnis·hilfe *f* mnemonic device

Gedächtnis·kunst *f* mnemonics

ge·dämpft *adj.* damped [*cf.* DEKREMENT; SCHWINGUNG]

Gedritt·schein *m* (*astr.*) trigon, trine

Ge·fälle *n* slope, grade, gradient

Gefälligkeits·akzept *n*, **Gefälligkeits·papier** *n* (*comm.*) accomodation bill (or note, or paper)

Gefrier·punkt *m* (*phys.*) freezing point

ge·geben *adj.* given [*cf.* ANPASSEN; ANPASSUNG; AUSGEHEN; AUSZEICHNEN; EXPLIZIT; GEBEN; GEHEN; MOMENT[1]; ORT 1.]

Gegeben·heit *f* datum, one of the data [*cf.* DATUM; REPRÄSENTATIV]

Gegen·drehung *f* counterrotation

Gegen·ecke *f* opposite vertex, vertex opposite

Gegen·forderung *f* (*comm.*) counterclaim; (*zur Ausgleichung*) offset [*cf.* GEGENRECHNUNG]

Gegen·gewicht *n* counterbalance, counterweight

Gegen·kante *f* opposite edge

Gegen·kathete *f* side opposite (oblique angle of a right triangle)

Gegen·kraft *f* opposing force, counterforce, reaction

Gegen·rechnung *f* (*comm.*) **1.** (*Gegenforderung*) counterclaim. **2.** (*Ausgleichung*) balancing, compensation; *in G. stellen* offset, balance, compensate [*cf.* ANRECHNEN 2.; AUFRECHNEN 3.]

Gegen·schein *m* (*astr.*) opposition [= OPPOSITION]

Gegensehnen·satz *m* Ptolemy's theorem [= *ptolemäischer Lehrsatz; cf.* PTOLEMÄISCH]

Gegen·seite *f* opposite side, side opposite [*cf.* TREFFEN]

gegen·seitig *adj.* mutual, reciprocal [*cf.* ABHÄNGIGKEIT; AUSSCHLIESSEND; VERSICHERUNG]

Gegenseitig·keit *f* mutuality, reci-

procity; *auf G.* mutual [*cf.*
SPARGENOSSENSCHAFT; VERSICHE-
RUNG]

Gegen·stand *m* object; (*log. auch*)
individual [*cf.* INDIVIDUELL;
SEITE 4.]

Gegenstands·variable *f* (*log.*) individual variable

Gegen·teil *n* opposite; (*Vernei-
nung*) negation; (*Widerspruch*)
contradictory, contradiction

gegenüber·liegen *v.i.* be opposite,
subtend (*dir. obj.*): *jede Seite eines
Dreiecks liegt einem Winkel ge-
genüber* each side of a triangle
subtends the opposite angle

gegenüber·liegend *adj.* opposite:
*einander gegenüberliegende Win-
kel* opposite angles; *zwei Seiten
und der der dritten gegenüberliegende Winkel* two sides and the
angle opposite to the third; *eine
Seite und der gegenüberliegende
Winkel* a side and the angle
opposite; *die dem Winkel α
gegenüberliegende Seite eines
Dreiecks* the side of a triangle
opposite to (or subtending) the
angle α

Gegen·versicherung *f* reinsurance

Gegen·wert *m* equivalent [*cf.*
VALUTA]

Gegen·winkel *m* (*zweier Geraden
und einer Transversalen*) one of a
pair of corresponding angles
(both on the same side of two
lines and on the same side of a
transversal) [*cf.* pairs of angles:
A, C; B, D; A′, C′; B′, D′ in *Fig.*
to TRANSVERSALE] [*cf.* KOR-
RESPONDIEREN; PARALLEL]

Gegen·wirkung *f* reaction

gehen *v.i.* go, run, pass: *ein Kreis,
der durch drei gegebene Punkte
geht* a circle which passes through
three given points; *die Beweisfüh-
rung geht folgendermaßen* the
argument runs like this; *die
Werte von y gehen von a bis b* the
values of *y* run from *a* to *b* [*cf.*
ENTHALTEN *adj.;* HINDURCH-
GEHEN; IN; PUNKT]

ge·hörig *adj.* (*zu*) belonging (to)
[*cf.* ZUGEHÖRIG]

ge·koppelt *adj.* coupled [*cf.*
SCHWINGUNG]

ge·krümmt *adj.* curved: *gekrümm-
ter Raum* curved space [*cf.*
FLÄCHE; GESCHWEIFT; KRÜMMEN;
RAUMKURVE]

Geld *n* money; (*pl.*) *Gelder* funds,
monies [*cf.* ABHEBEN; ABHEBUNG;
AUFNAHME; AUFNEHMEN]

Geld·abfindung *f* (*comm.*) monetary
indemnity

Geld·mittel *n pl.* (*fin.*) funds, resources [*cf.* BESTAND]

Geld·umlauf *m* (*fin.*) money circulation

ge·legen *adj.* situated, lying [*cf.*
ÄHNLICH; LIEGEN]

gelten *v.i.* hold, be (or hold) true,
be valid: *eine Eigenschaft gilt in
der Umgebung eines Punktes* a
property holds in the neighborhood of a point; *beide Gleichungen g. gleichzeitig* both
equations are true (or hold)
simultaneously; *geltende Dezimalstellen* significant figures

Geltung *f* validity, truth

ge·mein *adj.* common, vulgar,
ordinary: *gemeiner Bruch* common (or vulgar) fraction [*cf.*

VERWANDELN; VERWANDLUNG]
gemein·sam *adj.* common, joint:
größter gemeinsamer Teiler,
größtes gemeinsames Maß greatest common divisor (or measure)
[*cf.* G. G. T.]; *kleinstes gemein-*
sames Vielfaches smallest (or
least, or lowest) common multiple
[*cf.* K. G. V.]; *kleinster gemein-*
samer Nenner least (or lowest)
common denominator; *ohne ge-*
meinsames Maß incommensurable; (*comm.*) *gemeinsames Konto*
joint account [*cf.* BRENNPUNKT;
BRINGEN; MASS]
gemeinschaft·lich *adj.* common:
größtes gemeinschaftliches Maß
greatest çommon divisor
Gemeinschafts·konto *n* (*comm.*)
joint account
ge·mischt *adj.* mixed: *gemischte*
Zahl mixed number [*cf.* DEZIMAL-
BRUCH; MISCHEN; WURZELAUS-
DRUCK]
ge·mustert *adj.* patterned [*cf.*
SCHACHBRETTARTIG]
genau *adj.* exact, precise, accurate,
correct; (*Himmelsrichtung*) due
(a compass point); (*eingeschliffen,*
z.B. ein Werkstück) true (e.g. a
workpiece); (*comm.*) (*auf den*
Tag) *genaue Zinsen* exact interest;
auf Zehntel g. correct to the
nearest tenth; *auf fünf Dezimalen*
g. accurate (or correct) to five
decimal places; *auf Pfund g.*
(accurate) to the nearest pound;
ein Drahtzylinder g. innerhalb
eines Fehlers von einem Perzent
a wire cylinder true within an
error of one per cent; *g. westlich*
due west; *peinlich g.* minute [*cf.*

ABSCHÄTZEN; ANNÄHERUNG]
Genauig·keit *f* exactness, precision, accuracy, correctness:
peinliche G. minuteness, minute
accuracy [*cf.* ANNÄHERN; ANNÄ-
HERUNG]
Genauigkeits·grad *m* degree of
accuracy
Genauigkeits·schwelle *f* lower
limit of precision
General·indexziffer *f* (*statist.*) **1.**
(*einer Ware*) composite index
number (of a commodity).
2. (*Wirtschaftsindex*) index of
general business activity
Generalisation *f* generalization
generalisieren *v.t.* generalize
Generalisierung *f* generalization
General·nenner *m* common denominator
General·unkosten *pl.* (*comm.*) overhead expenses (or charges), overheads
generell *adj.* general, generic:
(*alg.*) *generelle lineare Gruppe*
full linear group
ge·nügen *v.i.* (*dat.*) satisfy (*dir.*
obj.): *einer Bedingung g.* satisfy
a condition
Geo·däsie *f* geodesy
Geo·däte *f* geodesic, extremal
geo·dätisch *adj.* geodesic: *geo-*
dätische Linie, Krümmung geodesic line, curvature
Geo·graphie *f* geography
geo·graphisch *adj.* geographic(al):
geographische Länge, Breite (geographic) longitude, latitude [*cf.*
LÄNGENUNTERSCHIED; MEILE]
Geoid *n* geoid
Geo·metrie *f* geometry: *ebene G.*
plane geometry, planimetry; *syn-*

thetische (*oder projektive*) *G.* projective geometry [*cf.* DUAL]; *hyperbolische* (*oder Lobatschewskijsche*) *G., nichteuklidische G. erster Art* hyperbolic (or Lobachevskian) geometry, non-Euclidean geometry of the first kind; *parabolische* (*oder euklidische*) *G.* parabolic (or Euclidean) geometry; *elliptische* (*oder Riemannsche*) *G., nichteuklidische G. zweiter Art* elliptic (or Riemannian) geometry, non-Euclidean geometry of the second kind; *G. der Lage* analysis situs, topology [= ANALYSIS SITUS; TOPOLOGIE] [*cf.* ANALYTISCH; DARSTELLEND; EUKLIDISCH; GROSS; NEU; TOPOLOGISCH]

geo·métrisch *adj.* geometric(al): *geometrischer Ort* (geometric) locus; *geometrische Reihe* (*oder Progression*) geometric progression [*cf.* VERHÄLTNIS]; *Summe einer geometrischen Reihe* geometric series; *geometrischer Körper* geometric solid; *Methode der geometrischen* (*oder archimedischen*) *Approximationen* method of geometric exhaustion (or of Archimedean approximations) [*cf.* FIGUR; GEBILDE; KURVE; LOGARITHMISCH; RICHTUNG; SCHNEIDEN]

ge·ordnet *adj.* ordered, arranged: *geordnete Menge* ordered set [*cf.* ÄHNLICH-GEORDNET; KÖRPER; ORDNEN; STEIGEN]

geo·thermisch *adj.* geothermal, geothermic: *geothermische Tiefenstufe* geothermic gradient

ge·rad(e) *adj.* **1.** (*durch zwei*

teilbar divisible by two) even: *gerade Zahl* even number [*cf.* PERMUTATION]. **2.** (*Linie*) straight, right (line) [*cf.* LINIE]. **3.** (*rechtwinklig*) right, right-angled [*cf.* ABSTEIGUNG; AUFSTEIGUNG; KEGEL; KREISKEGEL; KREISZYLINDER; PRISMA; SCHNITT; STROPHOIDE]

Ge·rade *f* (*pl.* Geraden, *nach num.* [after *num.*] *Gerade*) (straight) line: *drei Gerade* three (straight) lines; *mehrere Gerade* (*oder Geraden*) several (straight) lines; *alle Geraden* all (straight) lines; *lotrechte* (*oder senkrechte oder vertikale*) *G.* plumb (or perpendicular, or vertical) line; *senkrechte G.* **a.** (*normal*) normal (or perpendicular) line; **b.** (*lotrecht*) vertical (or perpendicular) line [*cf.* SENKRECHT]; *eine* (*mehrere*) *parallele G.* a (several) parallel line(s) [*cf.* ENTARTEN]; *Richtung einer Geraden* direction of a (straight) line; *Punkte, die auf derselben Geraden liegen* collinear points; *Ebenen, die durch dieselbe Gerade gehen* collinear planes [*cf.* ABSTAND; ABSTEHEN; ACHSENABSCHNITT; ACHSENSCHNITTFORM; ANWINKEL; BILDEN; DIVERGENT; DOPPELVERHÄLTNIS; DURCHSTOSSEN; DURCHSTOSSPUNKT; FÄLLEN; FEST; GEBILDE; GEGENWINKEL; GERADLINIG; INEINANDERLIEGEN; KONJUGIERT; KONVERGENT; NEIGUNGSWINKEL; NORMAL; NORMALFORM; RICHTUNGSKOEFFIZIENT; RICHTUNGSWINKEL; SCHIEF; SEIN; SEKANTE; SENKRECHT; SPURPUNKT; TRANS-

VERSALE; UNENDLICH; UNEIGENT-
LICH; WECHSELWINKEL; WIND-
SCHIEF; WINKEL]

Gerad·endfläche *f* (*cryst.: Basis im
tetragonalen und hexagonalen
System*) basal pinacoid (in
the tetragonal and hexagonal
systems)

Geraden·schar *f* family (or system)
of lines

Gerad·heit *f* (*einer Linie*) straight-
ness (of a line); (*einer Zahl*)
evenness (of a number)

gerad·linig *adj.* rectilinear,
straight-line; (*mit geradlinigen
Seiten*) straight-sided; (*von Geraden erzeugt*) ruled: *geradlinige
Bewegung* rectilinear (or translatory) motion; *geradlinige Figur*
rectilinear (or straight-sided)
figure; *geradlinige Fläche* ruled
surface [*cf.* ERZEUGENDE]

Geradlinig·keit *f* rectilinearity

gerad·zahlig *adj.* even-numbered

Geradzahlig·keit *f* (character of)
being even-numbered

Gerate·wohl *n* (*statist.*) random:
aufs G. at random

ge·richtet *adj.* directed, oriented:
gerichteter Winkel directed (or
oriented) angle. [*cf.* WINKEL];
gerichteter Strahl directed line;
gerichtete Strecke, Zahl directed
line segment, number [*cf.* GE-
SCHWINDIGKEIT; RELATIVGE-
SCHWINDIGKEIT; WINKELGE-
SCHWINDIGKEIT]

Gerichtet·heit *f* directedness,
orientation

Gesamt·betrag *m* total (or aggregate) amount

Gesamt·heit *f* totality; *statistische*

G. statistical universe (or
population)

Gesamt·impuls *m* (*phys.*) total
momentum

Gesamt·masse *f* 1. (*phys.*) total
mass. 2. (*statist.*) statistical uni-
.verse (or population) [*cf.* ENT-
SPRECHUNGSZAHL; STATISTISCH]

Gesamt·summe *f* (grand) total,
aggregate amount

Gesamt·versicherung *f* all-inclusive
(or all-in) insurance

Gesamt·wert *m* total value

Geschäfts·jahr *n* (*comm.*) fiscal (or
business, or commercial) year

Geschicklichkeits·spiel *n* (*statist.*)
game of skill

ge·schlängelt *adj.* sinuous, tortuous, winding

Ge·schlecht *n* (*einer Fläche*) genus
(of a surface)

Geschlechts·gliederung *f* (*statist.*)
sex distribution

Geschlechts·verhältnis *n* (*statist.*)
sex ratio

ge·schlossen *adj.* closed: *geschlos-
sene Kurve* closed curve [*cf.*
SCHLIESSEN]

ge·schlungen *adj.* curved, winding
[*cf.* KLAMMER]

ge·schweift *adj.* (*gekrümmt*) curved;
(*wellig*) sinuous [*cf.* KLAMMER;
TROCHOIDE; ZYKLOIDE]

Geschwindig·keit *f* (*gerichtete*
directed) velocity; (*ungerichtete*
scalar) speed, rate: *konstante*
(*oder gleichförmige*) *G.* constant
velocity (speed); (*skalare*) *G.*
speed; *eine G. von 3 km per
Stunde* a speed (or rate) of 3 *km.*
per hour [*cf.* ABFALLEN; AUGEN-

BLICKLICH; MOMENT; UNGLEICH-
FÖRMIG; RELATIV]
Geschwindigkeits·komponente   *f*
component of velocity
Geschwindigkeits·potential *n* velo-
city potential
Geschwindigkeits·vektor *m* velocity
vector
Gesechst·schein *m* (*astr.*) sextile
(aspect) [= SEXTILSCHEIN]
Gesell·schaft *f* (*comm.*) corpo-
ration, partnership, company:
G. mit beschränkter Haftung
(*abbr.*) *G.m.b.H.* limited liability
corporation
Gesellschafts·statistik *f* social
statistics [*cf.* SOZIALSTATISTIK]
Gesellschafts·steuer *f* (*fin.*) corporation tax
Ge·setz *n* law: *Keplersche Gesetze*
Kepler's laws; *Ohmsches Gesetz*
Ohm's law [*cf.* AKTION; ASSO-
ZIATIV; DISTRIBUTIV; KOMMU-
TATIV; SERIE; ZAHL]
gesetz·lich *adj.* according (or con-
formable) to law; (*regelmäßig*)
regular: *der gesetzliche* (*oder*
gesetzmäßige) *Ablauf der Natur-*
ereignisse the regular course (or
sequence) of natural events, the
passage (or sequence) of natural
events according to the laws of
nature
Gesetzlich·keit *f* conformity with
law; (*Regelmäßigkeit*) regularity
gesetz·mäßig *adj.* [= GESETZLICH]
Gesetzmäßigkeit *f* [= GESETZLICH-
KEIT]
Gesichts·kreis *m* horizon
Gesichts·punkt *m* (*der Perspektive*)
station point (of perspective)

Gesichts·winkel *m* visual angle
[*cf.* ISOPTISCH]
Ge·stalt *f* shape, form: *formale G.*
formal structure [*cf.* FORM;
VERLAUF; WAHR]
Gestehungs·kosten *pl.* (*comm.*) first
(or prime) cost
Gestehungs·preis *m* (*comm.*) purchase price
Ge·stirn *n* (*Stern*) star; (*Sternbild*)
constellation
ge·streckt *adj.* stretched; (*Winkel*)
flat, straight (angle) [*cf.* TRO-
CHOIDE; VERLÄNGERT; ZYKLOIDE]
ge·strichelt *adj.* broken, dotted:
gestrichelte Linie broken (or
dotted) line [*cf.* STRICHELN]
ge·sucht *adj.* required [*cf.* SUCHEN]
Gesundheits·statistik *f* health
statistics
Geviert·schein *m* (*astr.*) quadrate,
quartite (aspect), tetragon [=
QUADRATSCHEIN; QUADRATUR 2.]
Ge·wicht *n* weight: (*alg.*) *G. eines*
Polynoms, eines Gliedes weight of
a polynomial, a term [*cf.*
LADUNGSFÄHIGKEIT; LADUNGS-
GEWICHT; SPEZIFISCH]
Gewichts·einheit *f* unit of weight
Gewinn *m* (*comm.*) profit; (*eines*
Unternehmens) proceeds *pl.*, re-
turns *pl.* (of an enterprise); (*eines*
größeren) surplus; (*durch Speku-*
lation) gain (by speculation)
Gewinn·anteil *m* (*comm.*) share of
profits; (*Dividende*) dividend [*cf.*
DIVIDENDE]
Gewinn·beteiligung *f* (*comm.*) profit
sharing, participation in profits
Gewinn·spanne *f* (*comm.*) margin
of profit
ge·wiß *adj.* certain

Gewiß·heit *f* certainty [*cf.* SI-
CHERHEIT].

ge·wogen *adj., p.p.* (*of wägen,
wiegen*) weighted: (*statist.*) *ge-
wogenes Mittel* weighted mean
(or average)

gewöhn·lich *adj.* common, vulgar,
ordinary: *gewöhnlicher* (*oder einfacher*) *Punkt einer Kurve* ordinary (or simple) point on a curve
[*cf.* SCHRAUBENLINIE]

ge·wölbt *adj.* convex

ge·worfen *adj.* (*verdreht*) warped
[*cf.* FLÄCHE 1.; WERFEN 2.]

ge·wunden *adj.* winding, tortuous,
twisted [*cf.* VERSCHLUNGEN;
WINDEN]

Gewunden·heit *f* sinuosity, tortuousness [*cf.* VERSCHLUNGEN-
HEIT]

ge·würfelt *adj.* checkered [*cf.*
SCHACHBRETTARTIG]

Gezeiten *pl.* (*geog.*) tides

G.G.T. (*abbr.*) *größter gemeinsamer Teiler* greatest common
divisor, (*abbr.*) G.C.D.

giltig *adj.* [= GÜLTIG]

Giltig·keit *f* [= GÜLTIGKEIT]

girieren *v.t.* (*comm.*) (*einen
Wechsel*) indorse (a note)

Giro *n* (*comm.*) endorsement

Gitter *n* lattice; (*rad.*) grid

Gitter·theorie *f* lattice theory

glätten *v.t.* (*eine Kurve*) smooth
(a curve)

Glättung *f* (*einer Kurve*) smoothing
(of a curve)

Gläubiger *m* (*comm.*) creditor

gleich *adj.* equal, like, equivalent:
g. sein (+ *dat.*) be equal to, equal
[*cf.* ANNÄHERND]; (*Mengen*, sets,
also) coincide;(*symb.*: =); *Glieder*

mit gleicher Hauptzahl like terms
[*cf.* GLEICHNAMIG]; *gleiche Potenzen* like powers; *Brüche mit
gleichem Nenner* fractions with
equal denominators, similar fractions; *gleiche Mengen* coincident
(or equal) sets; *die beiden Mengen
sind g.* the two sets coincide (or:
are equal); *gleiche Winkel* equal
(or equivalent) angles; [*cf.* AB-
STAND; ABSTEHEN; AKTION;
ANGLEICHEN; GRÖSSER; HÖHE;
ISOPTISCH; IST; KETTENLINIE;
KLEINER; KREISTEILUNG; NIVEAU;
ORT; PAARWEISE; PARALLEL;
SETZEN; UMFANG; VIEL]

gleich·artig *adj.* (*ein Ding*) homogeneous (object); (*verschiedene
Dinge*) (objects) of the same
kind

Gleichartig·keit *f* (*eines Dinges*)
homogeneity (of an object);
(*verschiedener Dinge*) sameness
in kind (of different objects)

gleich·bedeutend *adj.* having the
same meaning (or significance),
equivalent, synonymous; (*mit*)
tantamount (to)

gleich·bleibend *adj.* uniform, constant [*cf.* EINTEILUNG]

Gleicher *m* (*geog.*) equator [=
ÄQUATOR]

Gleiche(s) *n* equal, equals *pl.*:
*Gleiches durch Gleiches dividiert,
gibt* (*wieder*) *Gleiches* if equals
are divided by equals, the results
are also equal (or: the quotients
and remainders are also equals)

gleich·förmig *adj.* **1.** (*konstant*)
constant, uniform: *gleichförmige
Bewegung* constant (or uniform)
motion [*cf.* BESCHLEUNIGUNG;

GESCHWINDIGKEIT]. **2.** (*homogen*)
homogeneous

Gleichförmig·keit *f* **1.** (*Konstanz*)
constancy, uniformity. **2.** (*Homogeneität*) homogeneity

Gleich·gewicht *n* equilibrium,
balance: *stabiles*, *labiles*, *indifferentes G.* stable, unstable,
neutral equilibrium [*cf.* IN-
DIFFERENT]

Gleichgewichts·bedingung *f* equilibrium condition

Gleichgewichts·lage *f* equilibrium
position

Gleichgewichts·lehre *f* statics

Gleichgewichts·zustand *m* state (or
condition) of equilibrium

gleich·gradig *adj.* uniform; *g.
stetige Funktionen* equicon-
tinuous functions

Gleich·heit *f* equality

Gleichheits·zeichen *n* equal sign,
sign of equality (*symb.:* =)

gleich·lang *adj.* equal, of equal
length

Gleich·lauf *m* **1.** (*von Linien*)
parallelism (of lines). **2.** (*von
Uhren*) synchronism (of clocks)

gleich·laufen *v.t.* **1.** (*Linien* lines)
be parallel. **2.** (*Uhren* clocks) be
synchronous

gleich·laufend *adj.* **1.** (*Linien*)
parallel (lines). **2.** (*Uhren*) synchronous (clocks)

gleich·liegend *adj.* homologous

gleich·mächtig *adj.* (cardinally)
equivalent, equinumerous, equipotent: *gleichmächtige Zahlen-
mengen* equipotent sets of numbers

Gleichmächtig·keit *f* (*zweier Zah-
lenmengen*) equal cardinality (or

power), equipotency (of two sets
of numbers)

gleich·mäßig *adj.* uniform, even:
*gleichmäßige Stetigkeit einer
Funktion* uniform continuity of
a function

gleich·möglich *adj.* (*statist.*) equally possible (or likely)

Gleichmöglich·keit *f* (*statist.*) (*von
Fällen*) equal possibility (or likelihood) of cases

gleich·namig *adj,* like, similar:
gleichnamige Glieder (*oder Zahlen*) like (or similar) terms (e.g.
2 a^2b, 5 a^2b) [*cf.* ZUSAMMEN-
FASSEN]

gleich·schenk(e)lig *adj.* (*Dreieck,
Trapez*) isosceles (triangle, trapezoid)

Gleichschenk(e)lig·keit *f* (*eines
Dreiecks*) isosceles character (of
a triangle)

gleich·seitig *adj.* equilateral: *gleich-
seitiges Dreieck* equilateral triangle; *gleichseitige Hyperbel*
equilateral (or equiangular, or
rectangular) hyperbola

Gleichseitig·keit (*einer Figur*)
equality of the sides, equilater-
ality (of a figure)

gleich·setzen *v.t.* equate, put equal
(to): *zwei Ausdrücke* (*einander*) *g.*
equate two expressions

Gleich·setzung *f* equating, equation, putting equal

Gleich·strom *m* (*elec.*) direct
current

Gleichung *f* equation: *Cartesische
G.* Cartesian equation [*cf.*
KARTESISCH]; *Gaußsche G.* Gauss'
equation [*cf.* ACHSENSCHNITT-
FORM; ALGEBRAISCH; ALLGEMEIN;

AUFLÖSEN; ·AUFLÖSUNG; AUS-
DRÜCKEN; BEFRIEDIGEN; BESEITI-
GUNG; BESTIMMT; BILD; BI-
QUADRATISCH; DIOPHANTISCH;
DRITT; EINBEGREIFEN; EINFACH;
ELIMINATIONSTHEORIE; FREMD;
GALOISSCH; GELTEN; GRAD;
GRAPHISCH; HOMOGEN; IDEN-
TISCH; IRREDUZIBEL; KARTESISCH;
KUBISCH; LINEAR; LOGARITH-
MISCH; LOGISCH; LÖSUNG; MAT-
RIX; METAZYKLISCH; MOLLWEIDE;
NORMALFORM; NUMERISCH; PARA-
METRISCH; PRIMZAHLGRAD;
PROBE; QUADRATISCH; REIN;
RESULTANTE; SEITE 3.; THEORIE;
TRANSPONIEREN; UNBESTIMMT;
VEREINFACHUNG; VERTRÄGLICH-
KEIT; VIERT; WIDERSPRUCHS-
FREIHEIT; WURZEL; ZURÜCK-
FÜHRUNG]

Gleichungs·system *n* system (or
set) of equations

gleich·verteilt *adj.* homogeneous,
evenly distributed

Gleich·verteilung *f* homogeneous
distribution

gleich·wahrscheinlich *adj.* (*statist.*)
equally likely (or probable)

gleich·wertig *adj.* equivalent

Gleich·wertigkeit *f* equivalence

gleich·wink(e)lig *adj.* isogonal,
equiangular

Gleichwink(e)lig·keit *f* isogonality,
equiangularity

gleich·zahlig *adj.* numerically
equivalent

Gleichzahlig·keit *f* numerical
equivalence

Gleichzeiten·kurve *f* [= ISOCHRONE]

gleich·zeitig *adj.* ṣimultaneous,
(existing) at the same time: *g.*

bestehend simultaneous [*cf.* BE-
STEHEN; GELTEN]

Gleichzeitig·keit *f* simultaneous-
ness, simultaneity

gleiten *v.i.* glide, slide: *gleitende
Skala* sliding scale [*cf.* DURCH-
SCHNITT; REIBUNG]

Gleit·kurve *f* glissette

Glied *n* **1.** (*eines mathematischen
Ausdrucks*) term (of a mathe-
matical expression): *höheres G.*
higher term; *G. einer Proportion*
term of a proportion [*cf.* ALL-
GEMEIN; ÄUSSER; GEWICHT;
GLEICH; GLEICHNAMIG; HÖHER;
REIHE; TRANSPONIEREN; UM-
GRUPPIEREN; VERHÄLTNIS; VER-
NACHLÄSSIGEN; WEGFALLEN; WEG-
HEBEN; WURZELAUSDRUCK; ZU-
SAMMENFASSEN]. **2.** (*einer logi-
schen Verknüpfung*) component
(of a logical connective) [*cf.*
AUSDRUCK; ENTHALTEN; INNER]

Gliedbildungs·verfahren *n* [=
GLIEDZIFFERNVERFAHREN]

gliedern 1. *v.t.* arrange (into
organized parts), organize. **2.**
v.r.: sich *g.* (*geordnet sein*) be
arranged (in organized parts), be
organized; (*sich verteilen*) be
distributed [*cf.* AUFGLIEDERN]

Gliederung *f* (*Ordnung*) arrangement (into organized parts),
organization; (*Klassifizierung*)
classification; (*Verteilung*) distribution: (*statist.*) *doppelte*
(*ṃehrfache*) *G.* double (manifold)
classification [*cf.* AUFGLIEDE-
RUNG]

Glied·korrelation *f* (*statist.*) serial
correlation

. . . gliedrig *suf.* *adj.* (*math.*)

-termed,   ... nomial;   (*log.*)
-place,   ... adic: *n-gliedrig* n-termed, n-adic [*cf.* DREIGLIEDRIG; EINGLIEDRIG; LINEARFORMEN-MODUL; ZWEIGLIEDRIG]
glied·weise *adj.* term by term
Glied·ziffer *f* (*statist.*) link relative [*cf.* KETTENINDEXZIFFER; KETTEN-ZAHL]
Gliedziffern·verfahren *n* (*statist.*) Person's method of link relatives
globular *adj.* globular
Globular·projektion *f* globular projection
Globus *m* (terrestrial) globe
Glocken·kurve *f* bell-shaped curve
Glücks·spiel *n* (*statist.*) game of chance, gamble
G.m.b.H. (*abbr.*) *Gesellschaft mit beschränkter Haftung* [*cf.* GE-SELLSCHAFT]
Gnomon *m* gnomon
gnomonisch *adj.* (*Projektion*) gno-monic (projection)
Gold·ausgleichsfonds *m* (*fin.*) (*einer Notenbank*) gold settlement fund (of an issuing bank)
Goldbarren·währung *f* [= GOLD-KERNWÄHRUNG]
golden *adj.* golden: *goldener Ab-schnitt* larger segment in golden section (or: in extreme and mean ratio) [*cf.* SCHNITT]
Goldkern·währung *f* (*fin.*) gold bullion standard
... gon *noun suf.* ... gon: *Poly-gon* polygon
... gonal *adj. suf.* ... gonal: *hex-agonal* hexagonal
Gonio·metrie *f* goniometry
gonio·metrisch *adj.* goniometric(al)
Grad *m* degree: *ein Bogen* (*Winkel*)

von dreißig Grad(*en*) (30°) an arc (angle) of thirty degrees; *sphäri-scher Winkel von einem G.* (1°) spherical degree; *G.* (*oder Winkel-maß*) *in Bogenmaß verwandeln* change degrees to radians; *Kurve n-ten Grades* curve of degree *n;* (*alg.*) *G. eines Polynoms* (*einer Gleichung*) degree of a polynomial (an equation); (*alg.*) *Polynom ersten Grades* (*oder: vom ersten Grade*) polynomial of the first degree, first-degree polynomial; *zehn G. Fahrenheit* (10° F) ten degrees Fahrenheit (10° F.) [*cf.* AUFLÖSUNG; DRITT; FÜNFT; HÖHER; MINUTE; REDUZIEREN; SECHST; VIERT; ZWEIT]
Grad·bogen *m* graduated arc, quadrant scale
grad(e) [= GERADE]
Grad·einteilung *f* graduation, scale (division); (*auf dem Kreisbogen*) graduated arc
Grad·heit *f* [= GERADHEIT]
Gradient *m* gradient: *G. einer Funktion* gradient of a function (*symb.: grad f*) [*cf.* NABLA]
grad·linig *adj.* [= GERADLINIG]
Gradlinig·keit *f* [= GERADLINIG-KEIT]
Grad·netz *n* (*geog.*) map grid, grid of parallels and meridians
graduieren *v.t.* graduate
Graduierung *f* graduation
Gramm *n* (*abbr.* g) gram, gramme (*abbr.* g.)
Gramm·atom *n* (*chem.*) gram atom
Grammatom·gewicht *n* (*chem.*) gram-atomic weight
Gramm·kalorie *f* gram calorie
Gramm·molekül *n* (*chem.*) gram

molecule   [= GRAMMOLEKÜL]
Gramm · molekular · gewicht   *n*
(*chem.*) gram-molecular weight
Grammolekül *n* [= GRAMM·MOLE-
KÜL]
Grammolekular·gewicht   *n*   [=
GRAMM·MOLEKULAR·GEWICHT]
Gran *n* (*Gewicht* weight) grain
graphisch *adj.* graphic(al): *graphische Methode* graphic method;
*in der Gleichung y = ax + b stellt
b graphisch den Abschnitt auf der
y-Achse dar* in the equation $y = ax
+ b$, *b* graphically represents the
y-intercept; *eine Gleichung g.*
(*oder: auf graphischem Wege*)
auflösen solve an equation graphically; *g. bestimmen* trace; *graphische Darstellung* graph [*cf.* DAR-
STELLEN]
Gratifikation *f* (*comm.*) bonus
Gravitation *f* (*phys.*) gravitation
Gravitations · beschleunigung   *f*
gravitational acceleration
Gravitations·gesetz *n* law of gravitation
Gravitations·konstante *f* constant
of gravity, gravitational constant
Grenz·bedingung *f* boundary condition
Grenze *f* border, boundary, bound,
limit: *obere G. einer Folge, Menge*
least upper bound of a sequence,
set; *untere G. einer Folge, Menge*
greatest lower bound of a sequence, set; *untere, obere G.
eines bestimmten Integrals* upper,
lower limit of a definite integral;
*das Verhältnis wächst über alle
Grenzen* the ratio grows beyond
all bounds [*cf.* ÜBERSCHREITEN]
grenzen·los *adj.* boundless, limit-

less, unlimited
Grenz·fall *m* limit(ing) (or border-
line) case
Grenz·fläche *f* boundary surface
Grenz·lage *f* limiting position
Grenz·linie *f* boundary line
Grenz·punkt *m* (*statist.*) (*einer
Gruppe*) class limit
Grenz·übergang *m* limiting process, passing to the limit
Grenz·wert *m* limit, limiting value:
G. einer Folge, Reihe limit of a
sequence, a series; *kleinster G.*
(*einer Folge*) inferior (or lower,
or minimum) limit, limit inferior
(of a sequence); *größter G.* (*einer
Folge*) superior (or upper, or
maximum) limit, limit superior
(of a sequence); *linksseitiger
(rechtsseitiger) G.* (*oder Limes*)
limit on the left (right); *dem G.
Null sich nähernd* approaching
the limit zero, infinitesimal, null
[*cf.* ANNÄHERUNG; NÄHERN;
NULL; ÜBERGANG; ÜBERGEHEN;
UNENDLICH; ZUSTREBEN]
Gros *n* gross (= 12 dozens)
groß *adj.* great, large: *die algebraische Geometrie betrachtet die
Gebilde im großen, die Differen-
tialgeometrie im kleinen* (*oder:
in der Nachbarschaft eines
Punktes*) algebraic geometry
studies geometric objects in the
large, differential geometry in the
small (or: in the neighborhood
of a point) [*cf.* ACHSE; ELLIPSE;
HALBACHSE; KALORIE; MASS-
STAB; UNENDLICH; ZAHL]
Größe *f* 1. (*Ausdehnung* extension)
magnitude, size: *ein Stern erster
G.* a star of first magnitude [*cf.*

MITTEL]. **2.** (*ausgedehntes Gebilde* extensive entity) quantity, magnitude, entity: *unbekannte G.* unknown quantity; (*alg.*) *ganze Größen eines Körpers* integral quantities of a field; (*alg.*) *assoziierte Größen erzeugen dasselbe Hauptideal* two associates generate the same principal ideal [*cf.* ABFALLEN; EINSETZEN; EINSETZUNG; ENDLICH; GEBEN; INFINITESIMAL; MASSGRÖSSE; MASSTAB; SKALAR; STETIG; ÜBERTRAGBAR; ÜBERTRAGBARKEIT; ÜBERTRAGEN; ÜBERTRAGUNG; UNENDLICH; VERHÄLTNIS; VERNACHLÄSSIGEN; VIEL]. **3.** (*Betrag*) rate, amount, value: *die G. der Geschwindigkeit* the rate of speed

Größen·lehre *f* theory of quantities; (*Mathematik*) mathematics

Größen·ordnung *f* (order of) magnitude: *von der G. Null* of zero magnitude [*cf.* ORDNUNG]

Größen·verhältnis *n* (*Verhältnis*) ratio, rate; (*Proportion*) proportion

größer *adj.* (*comp.* of **groß**) larger, greater, major: *a* (*ist*) *größer* (*als*) *oder gleich b a* is greater than or equal to *b*

Groß·handel *m* (*comm.*) wholesale

Großhandels·index *m* (*comm.*) index of wholesale prices

Großhandels·preis *m* (*comm.*) wholesale price

Groß·kreis *m* (*einer Kugel*) great circle (of a sphere)

größt *adj.* (*sup.* of **groß**) greatest, largest, maximal, maximum: *größter Wert einer Funktion in einem Intervall* greatest value of

a function in an interval [*cf.* GEMEINSAM; GEMEINSCHAFTLICH; GRENZWERT; MASS; WERT]

Großzahl·forschung *f* statistical method, statistics

Grund *m* ground; (*log.*) ground, reason; (*Voraussetzung*) premise [*cf.* EBEN]

Grund·aussage *f* (*log.*) (*elementare*) elementary sentence (or statement); (*grundlegende*) basic (or fundamental) sentence (or statement)

Grund·begriff *m* (*log.*) fundamental (or basic) concept

Grund·bewegung *f* (*statist.*) trend

Grund·ebene *f* ground plane; (*Basisebene*) basal plane, plane of the base; (*in der Kartenprojektion*) datum plane (in cartographic projection)

Grund·fläche *f* (*eines Prismas, Kegels, einer Pyramide*) base (of a prism, cone, pyramid): *Grund- und Deckfläche eines Zylinders* bases of a cylinder

Grund·form *f* basic form, fundamental form: (*alg.*) *wir wählen eine Hermitesche Form als G.* we choose a Hermitian form as fundamental form

Grund·formel *f* (*grundlegende Formel*) basic (or fundamental) formula; (*einfachste Formel*) primitive formula

Grund·gebilde *n* basic geometrical element [*cf.* SCHNEIDEN]

Grund·gesetz *n* basic law

Grund·kapital *n* [= GRÜNDUNGSKAPITAL]

Grund·körper *m* (*alg.*) ground field

Grund·lage *f* foundation

grund·legend *adj.* basic, fundamental [*cf.* GRUNDFORMEL]

Grund·linie *f* (*einer ebenen Figur*) base (of a plane figure): *G. eines Dreiecks, Trapezes* base of a triangle, trapezoid

Grund·operation *f* basic (or fundamental) operation

Grund·prisma *n* (*cryst.*) [= PROTO-PRISMA]

Grund·pyramide *f* (*cryst.*) [= PROTOPYRAMIDE]

Grund·rechenoperation *f* [= GRUND·RECHNUNGSART] [*cf.*VIER]

Grund·rechnungsart *f* fundamental (or basic) operation of arithmetic [*cf.* RECHNUNGSART; VIER]

Grund·riß *m* top view, (floor, or ground) plan [*cf.* DARSTELLUNG 2.; PROJEKTION]

Grundriß·ebene *f* horizontal projection plane, ground plane [*cf.* PROJEKTIONSEBENE]

Grund·satz *m* 1. (*Axiom*) axiom. 2. (*Prinzip*) principle

Grund·ton *m* (*acoust.*) 1. (*eines Klangs*) fundamental tone (of a sound). 2. (*einer Tonart*) key tone (of a key)

Gründungs·kapital *n* (*fin.*) nominal capital (or stock) [*cf.* STAMM-KAPITAL]

Grund·verknüpfung *f* (*log.*) fundamental connective (or combination)

Grund·zahl *f* 1. (*Kardinalzahl*) cardinal number. 2. (*Basis einer Potenz*) base (of a power)

Grund·züge *m pl.* fundamentals, principles

Gruppe *f* group; (*statist., auch*) class: *endliche* (*unendliche*) *G.* finite (infinite) group; *in einer G. zusammenfassen* group [*cf.* ABELSCH; ALTERNIEREN; AUFLÖS-BAR; DARSTELLUNG; ·EINFACH; EINFACHHEIT; EINHEITSELEMENT; ERZEUGEN; GALOISSCH; GENE-RELL; GRENZPUNKT; HAUPT-CHARAKTER; KOMMUTATOR; KON-JUGIERT; NORMALTEILER; NULL-ELEMENT; ORDNUNG; SYMME-TRISCH; VERSCHRÄNKT; ZENTRUM]

Gruppen·auswahl *f* (*statist.*) stratified sampling

Gruppen·bildung *f* grouping; (*statist.*) classification

Gruppen·charakter *m* group character

Gruppen·element *n* group element [*cf.* CHARAKTER; ENTGEGENGE-SETZT; INVERS; INVERSES; NOR-MALISATOR]

Gruppen·ring *m* (*alg.*) group ring

Gruppen·theorie *f* group theory

Gruppen·versicherung *f* collective insurance

gruppen·weise *adj.* by groups; (*statist.*) stratified: (*statist.*) *g. Auswahl* stratified sampling [*cf.* AUSWAHL; EINZELFALL]; (*statist.*) *g. Stichprobenerhebung* stratified random sampling

gruppieren *v.t.* group, arrange

Gruppierung *f* grouping, arrangement

Gruppierungs·prinzip *n* (*statist.*) principle of classification

gültig *adj.* valid, good, true: *g. sein* be (or hold) true, be valid (or good)

Gültig·keit *f* validity, truth

günstig *adj.* (*statist.*) successful, favorable; *günstiger Fall* success

gut *adj.* good [*cf.* ANNÄHERUNG; VALUTA]
Güte *f* goodness: (*statist.*) *G. der Anpassung* goodness of fit
Gut·haben *n* (*comm.*) **1.** (*Aktivposten*) asset; (*Saldo*) balance (due): *die amerikanischen G. im Ausland* American assets abroad;
Sie haben ein G. bei mir you have a balance with me; *es besteht ein G. zu seinen Gunsten* there is a balance due him. **2.** (*Konto*) account, deposit: *ein G. in der Bank* an account (or deposit) with the bank [*cf.* A CONTO; EINLAGE; EINLEGEN]

H

Haar·zirkel *m* hair compass
Haben *n* (*comm.*) credit (side), asset
Haft·pflicht *f* liability
Haftpflicht·versicherung *f* liability insurance
Haftung *f* (*comm., fin.*) liability [*cf.* GESELLSCHAFT]
halb *adj.* half, semi ... : *halber Umfang* semicircumference [*cf.* HALBACHSE; MITTEL; PARAMETER; SINUSVERSUS]
Halb·achse *f* semiaxis; *große (kleine) H.* (*oder: halbe große [kleine] Achse*) *einer Ellipse* (*eines Ellipsoids*) semimajor (semiminor) axis of an ·ellipse (an ellipsoid); *reelle (imaginäre) H. einer Hyperbel* semitransverse (semiconjugate) axis of a hyperbola
Halb·ebene *f* half-plane
halb·einfach *adj.* (*alg.*) semi-simple
Halb·einfachheit *f* (*alg.*) semisimplicity
halb·flächig *adj.* (*cryst.*) hemihedral
Halb·flächner *m* (*cryst.*) hemihedron
Halb·gruppe *f* (*alg.*) semigroup

halbieren *v.t.* divide in two (equal parts), divide in half, halve, bisect: *eine Strecke h.* bisect a line segment
Halbierung *f* bisection, division in half
Halbierungs·ebene *f* (*des Winkels zweier Ebenen*) bisector, bisecting plane (of the angle between two planes)
Halbierungs·linie *f* (*eines Winkels, einer Strecke*) bisector, bisecting line (of an angle, a line segment); (*einer Strecke, auch*) mid-perpendicular (of a line segment)
Halbierungs·punkt *m* (*einer Strecke*) bisecting point, midpoint (of a line segment)
Halb·jahres ... biannual
halb·jährlich *adj.* semiannual, biannual
halb·konvergent *adj.* semiconvergent
Halb·kreis *m* semicircle
halbkreis·förmig *adj.* semicircular
Halb·kugel *f* hemisphere
halbkugel·förmig *adj.* semispherical, hemispherical

halb·kugelig *adj.* hemispherical

halb·logarithmisch *adj.* semilogarithmic [*cf.* LOGARITHMEN-PAPIER]

Halb·messer *m* (*eines Kreises, einer Kugel*) radius (of a circle, a sphere)

halb·monatlich *adj.* biweekly

Halb·monats . . . biweekly

Halb·mond *m* half moon; (*Mondsichel*) crescent

halbmond·förmig *adj.* lunar, crescent-shaped

halb·rund *adj.* semicircular

Halb·rund *n* semicircle

Halb·schatten *m* half-shade, half-shadow; (*astr.*) penumbra, incomplete shadow

Halb·seite *f* half side

Halbseiten·sätze *m pl.* (*der sphärischen Trigonometrie*) half-side formulas (of spherical trigonometry)

Halb·strahl *m* half line, (half) ray [*cf.* ANFANGSPUNKT]

Halbwerts·zeit *f* (*eines radioaktiven Elements*) half life, half-life period (of a radioactive element)

Halb·winkel *m* half angle, semiangle

Halbwinkel·satz *m* half-angle formula

Hälfte *f* half [*cf.* TEILEN]

Handels·bank *f* (*comm.*) commercial bank

Handels·gesellschaft *f* (*comm.*) (trading) company, partnership: *offene H.* general partnership

Handels·gewicht *n* avoirdupois weight

Handels·index *m* (*comm.*) business index

Handels·schule *f* (*comm.*) commercial school, school of business

Handels·statistik *f* (*comm.*) commercial (or trade) statistics

Hand·zirkel *m* dividers

harmonisch *adj.* harmonic: *harmonische Bewegung* harmonic motion; *harmonische Teilung einer Strecke* harmonic division of a line (segment); *vier harmonische Punkte, zwei harmonische Punktpaare* harmonic range; *h. getrennt* separated harmonically; *harmonische Progression* (*oder Reihe*) harmonic progression; *harmonische Obertöne* harmonic overtones [*cf.* DOPPEL-VERHÄLTNIS; KONJUGIERT]

Hart·geld *n* (*fin.*) hard cash

häuf·bar *adj.* (*statist.*) cumulative

häufig *adj.* frequent [*cf.* WERT]

Häufig·keit *f* frequency [*cf.* HÄUFIGKEITSKOEFFIZIENT; RELATIV]

Häufigkeits·funktion *f* frequency function [*cf.* SCHEITELWERT]

Häufigkeits·gruppe *f*, **Häufigkeitsklasse** *f* (*statist.*) frequency class

Häufigkeits·koeffizient *m* (*statist.*) (*eines Merkmals*) **1.** (*allgemein: relative Häufigkeit*) relative frequency (of an attribute). **2.** (*relative Häufigkeit, im Unterschied von der Wahrscheinlichkeit des Merkmals*) rate (of an attribute) (as distinguished from its probability)

Häufigkeits·kurve *f* (*statist.*) frequency curve [=FEHLER-KURVE, VERTEILUNGSKURVE]; [*cf.* ABFLACHUNG; ABGEFLACHT; ABGEPLATTET; ABPLATTUNG; ASYM-

METRISCH; EINGIPFELIG; EXZESS; KURVENSCHIEFE; LINKSSCHIEF; MEHRGIPFELIG; NORMAL; NORMALFORM; RECHTSSCHIEF; SCHEITELPUNKT; SCHIEF; SCHIEFE; STATISTISCH; STEILHEIT; SYMMETRIE; SYMMETRISCH; ÜBERHÖHT; ÜBERHÖHUNG; WAHRSCHEINLICHKEITSKURVE; ZWEIGIPFELIG]

Häufigkeits·polygon *n* (*statist.*) frequency polygon

Häufigkeits·verteilung *f* (*statist.*) frequency distribution

Häufigkeits·vieleck *n* (*statist.*) frequency polygon

Häufigkeits·wert *m* (*statist.*) frequency value [*cf.* MODUS]

Häufigkeits·ziffer *f* [= HÄUFIGKEITSKOEFFIZIENT]

Häufung *f* accumulation

Häufungs·grenze *f* (*einer Menge*) limit (of a set): *untere H. einer Menge* inferior limit (or: limit inferior) of a set; *obere H. einer Menge* superior limit (or: limit superior) of a set

Häufungs·punkt *m* (*einer Punktmenge*) limit(ing) (or accumulation) point (of a set of points) [*cf.* PUNKTMENGE]

Häufungs·stelle *f* (*statist.*) cluster

Häufungs·wert *m* (*einer Funktion, einer Zahlenmenge*) limit(ing) value (or point) (of a function, a set of numbers)

Haupt·achse *f* principal axis; (*einer Ellipse*) major axis (of an ellipse); (*einer Hyperbel*) transverse axis (of a hyperbola)

Haupt·buch *n* (*comm.*) ledger [*cf.* AUSZUG]

Haupt·charakter *m* (*alg.*) (*einer*

Darstellung, Gruppe) principal character (of a representation, group)

Haupt·determinante *f* principal determinant

Haupt·diagonale *f* (*einer Determinante*) principal (or leading) diagonal (of a determinant)

Haupt·glied *n* (*z.B. einer Determinante*) principal term (e.g. of a determinant)

Haupt·ideal *n* (*alg.*) principal ideal [*cf.* GRÖSSE]

Hauptideal·ring *m* (*alg.*) principal ideal ring

Haupt·kreis *m* (*einer Kugel*) great circle (on a sphere)

Haupt·krümmung *f* (*einer Fläche*) principal curvature (of a surface)

Haupt·meßzahl *f* (*statist.*) composite index number

Haupt·nenner *m* (least) common denominator

Haupt·normale *f* (*einer Raumkurve in einem Punkt*) principal normal (to a space curve at a point)

Haupt·ordnung *f* (*alg.*) (*eines Körpers*) principal order (of a field)

Haupt·projektion *f* principal (or standard) view [*ant.:* NEBENPROJEKTION]

Haupt·punkt *m* principal point; *die vier Hauptpunkte der Windrose* the four cardinal points of the compass

Haupt·richtung *f* principal direction; (*der Windrose*) cardinal point (of the compass); (*statist.*) (*der Entwicklung*) trend

Haupt·satz *m* principal (or main) theorem [*cf.* THERMODYNAMIK]

Haupt·teil *m* principal part

Haupt·wert *m* principal value: *H. einer zyklometrischen Funktion* principal value of an inverse trigonometric function

Haupt·zahl *f* factor or power product qualified by a coefficient: *im Ausdruck* 9 x^3 *ist* 9 *der Koeffizient und* x^3 *die H.* in the term $9x^3$, x^3 is the factor qualified by the coefficient 9 [*cf.* GLEICH]

Hebel *m* (*mech.*) lever [*cf.* DREH-PUNKT; STÜTZPUNKT]

Hebel·arm *m* (*mech.*) lever arm [*cf.* ANGREIFEN]

heben 1. *v.t.* (*z.B. eine Last*) raise (e.g. a load); *aus der Klammer h.* factor out. 2. *v.r.*: *sich h.* cancel (out): 4 *y und* — 4 *y heben sich* 4 *y and* — 4 *y* cancel (out)

Hefner·kerze *f* (*opt. meas.*) Hefner candle

Heische·satz *m* postulate

Hekt·ar *n* (*Flächenmaß* square measure) hectare

Hekto·liter *n* (*abbr. hl*) hectoliter, hectolitre (*abbr. hl.*)

Hekto·meter *n* hectometer, hectometre

Hemi·brachydoma *n* (*pl. Hemibrachydomen*) (*cryst.*) hemibrachydome

Hemi·doma *n* (*pl. Hemidomen*) (*cryst.*) hemidome

Hemi·eder *n* (*cryst.*) hemihedron

Hemi·klinodoma *n* (*pl. Hemiklinodomen*) (*cryst.*) hemiclinodome

Hemi·makrodoma *n* (*pl. Hemimakrodomen*) (*cryst.*) hemimacrodomè

Hemi·orthodoma *n* (*pl. Hemi-orthodomen*) (*cryst.*) hemiorthodome

Hemi·prisma *n* (*pl. Hemiprismen*) (*cryst.*) hemiprism

hemi·prismatisch *adj.* hemiprismatic

Hemi·pyramide *f* (*cryst.*) hemipyramid

Hemi·sphäre *f* hemisphere

Hepta·gon *n* heptagon [= SIEBENECK]

hepta·gonal *adj.* heptagonal [= SIEBENECKIG]

herab·setzen (*sep.*) *v.t.* reduce; (*im Wert*) depreciate [*cf.* WERT]

Herab·setzung *f* reduction; (*im Wert*) depreciation

herab·sinken (*sep.*) *v.i.* drop [*cf.* PREIS]

heraus·fallen (*sep.*) *v.i.* cancel (out): *die ungeraden Potenzen fallen heraus* the odd powers cancel out

heraus·heben (*sep.*) 1. *v.t.* (*ausklammern*) factor out [*cf.* AUSKLAMMERN]. 2. *v.r.* sich *h.* (*sich aufheben*) cancel out

heraus·kommen (*sep.*) *v.i.* come out: *welcher Wert kommt heraus?* what value comes out?

Herbst·punkt *m* (*astr.*) autumnal point (or equinox)

Herbst-Tagundnachtgleiche *f* (*astr.*) autumnal equinox

Hermite *m N.:* (*alg.*) *Hermitesche Form* Hermitian form [*cf.* GRUNDFORM]; *Hermitesch symmetrisch* Hermitian symmetric

Hero(n) *m. N.* [*cf.* FORMEL]

Hertz *m N.: Hertzsche Wellen* Hertzian waves

Hertz *n* (*elec. meas.*) cycle (per second) [*cf.* SCHWINGUNG]

Herz·linie *f* cardioid [= KARDI-
OIDE]

hetero·grad *adj.* (*statist.*) hetero-
grade

heuristisch *adj.* heuristic, working:
heuristische Annahme working
hypothesis

Hex·ade *f* hexad

Hexa·eder *n* hexahedron: *reguläres H.* regular hexahedron, cube

hexa·edrisch *adj.* hexahedral

Hexa·gon *n* hexagon [= SECHSECK]

hexa·gonal *adj.* hexagonal [=
SECHSECKIG]: *hexagonales Kri-
stallsystem* hexagonal system of
crystallization [*cf.* GERADEND-
FLÄCHE; ... GONAL]

Hexa·gonalität *f* hexagonality

Hexagonal·zahl *f* hexagonal
number

Hexa·gramm *n* hexagram [*cf.*
SECHSSTERN]

Hexakis·oktaeder *n* (*cryst.*) hex-
octahedron, hexakisoctahedron

Hilfs·gleichung *f* auxiliary equation

Hilfs·größe *f* auxiliary (or subsidiary) quantity

Hilfs·linie *f* auxiliary line

Hilfs·satz *m* lemma

Hilfs·variable *f*, **Hilfs·veränder-
liche** *f* auxiliary (or subsidiary)
variable; (*Parameter*) parameter

Himmel *m* (*astr.*) sky [*cf.* HIMMELS-
GEGEND; STUNDENWINKEL]

Himmels·achse *f* celestial axis

Himmels·äquator *m* (*astr.*) celestial
equator, equinoctial (circle)

Himmels·gegend *f* **1.** (*astr.*) (*Ort
am Himmel*) region in the sky.
2. (*geog.*) (*Himmelsrichtung*)
compass point

Himmels·körper *m* (*astr.*) celestial
(or heavenly) body

Himmels·kugel *f* (*astr.*) celestial
sphere

Himmels·mechanik *f* (*astr., phys.*)
celestial mechanics

Himmels·meridian *m* (*astr.*) celestial meridian

Himmels·pol *n* (*astr.*) celestial pole,
pole of the celestial sphere

Himmels·punkt *m* (*astr.*) celestial
point [*cf.* POLDISTANZ; STUNDEN-
KREIS]

Himmels·richtung *f* (*geog.*) compass point [*cf.* GENAU; HIMMELS-
GEGEND]

hindurch·gehen (*sep.*) *v.i.* (*astr.*)
transit, pass: *durch den Meridian
(hindurch)gehen* pass (or transit)
(through) the meridian, cross the
meridian

hin·reichend *adj.* sufficient [*cf.*
BEDINGUNG]

hinter *adj.* back, rear, following

hinter *prep.* (*dat., acc.*) behind

Hinterbliebenen·versicherung *f* sur-
vivor's insurance

Hinter·ecke *f* rear corner

Hinter·fläche *f* rear face

Hinter·glied *n* (*ant.:* VORDERGLIED)
1. (*math.*) (*eines Verhältnisses*)
consequent (of a ratio). **2.** (*log.*)
(*einer Konjunktion, Disjunktion
usw.*) second component (of a
conjunction, disjunction, etc.)

Hinter·kante *f* rear edge

Hinter·seite *f* back (side), rear

hinüber·führen (*sep.*) *v.t.* carry
(over): *wir führen 5 in die Zehner-
kolonne hinüber (oder über)* we
carry 5 (over) to the column of
tens

hinüber·multiplizieren (*sep.*) *v.t.* cross-multiply

hinüber·schaffen (*sep.*) *v.t.* transpose, transfer, shift (to the other side) [*cf.* TRANSPONIEREN]

hinüber·transponieren (*sep.*) *v.t.* transpose, transfer, shift (to the other side)

Hin·weis *m* (cross) reference

hinzu·fügen (*sep.*) *v.t.* add [*cf.* AUFRECHNEN 1.]

Hinzu·fügung *f* addition

Hippo·pede *f* (*Kurve*) hippopede, horse fetter [= PFERDEFESSEL]

hoch *adj.* 1. (*nach oben ausgedehnt* extending upward) high, tall. 2. (*erhoben zur Potenz*) raised to the power: *fünf hoch ein Viertel* five raised to the power one-fourth (or: to the one-fourth power) (*symb.:* $5^{\frac{1}{4}}$)

Hoch·frequenz *f* (*phys.*) high frequency

hoch·gestellt *adj.* raised, superior: *hochgestellte Zahl, hochgestellter Index* superscript, superior (or raised) figure

höchst *adj.* (*sup.* of **hoch**) maximal, maximum [*cf.* KOEFFIZIENT; WERT]

Höchst·dimension *f* (*alg.*) (*eines Ideals*) highest dimension (of an ideal)

Höchst·kredit *m* (*comm.*) credit line, upper credit limit

Höchst·preis *m* (*comm.*) ceiling price

Höchst·stand *m* highest level

Höchst·wert *m* maximum (value), maximal value

Höchst·zahl *n* highest (or maximum) number (or figure)

Höchst·ziffer *f* highest (or maximum) figure (or number)

Hoch·zahl *f* exponent [= EXPONENT]

Hodo·graph *m* hodograph

Hoffnung *f* hope; (*statist.*) expectation [*cf.* MATHEMATISCH]

Höhe *f* 1. (*einer Figur, eines Körpers*) altitude, height (of a figure, a solid): *H. eines Kegels* altitude of a cone; *Schnittpunkt der drei Höhen eines Dreiecks* intersection point of the three altitudes of a triangle, orthocenter [*cf.* HÖHENSCHNITTPUNKT; TREFFEN]. 2. (*Erhebung*) elevation, altitude: *H. der Sonne über dem Horizont* altitude of the sun above the horizon [*cf.* ERHEBUNG]. 3. (*Niveau*) level: *auf gleicher Höhe* on the same level

Höhen·differenz *f* (*zweier Punkte*) rise (between two points)

Höhen·kote *f* (*auf einer Landkarte*) spot height (in a map) [= KOTE]

Höhen·kreis *m* (*astr.*) circle of altitude, vertical circle, almucantar

Höhen·linie *f* level (or contour) line [= ISOHYPSE; SCHICHTLINIE]

Höhenlinien·karte *f* contour map

Höhen·parallaxe *f* (*astr.*) altitude parallax

Höhen·schnittpunkt *m* (*eines Dreiecks*) orthocenter, intersection point of the three altitudes (of a triangle)

Höhe·punkt *m* culminating point, peak, climax

höher *adj.* (*comp. von* **hoch**) higher: *Glied höheren Grades* (*oder: von höherem Grade*) higher-degree term; *höhere Kurve, Kurve von höherem als zweitem Grad* higher curve, curve of degree higher than the second [*cf.* GLIED; ORDNUNG; PRIMIDEAL; UMWANDLUNG]

hohl *adj.* concave: *hohler Winkel* concave angle

Hohl·maß *n* measure of capacity

Hohl·spiegel *m* concave mirror [= KONKAVSPIEGEL]

Holding·gesellschaft *f* (*comm.*) holding (or controlling) company

Holo·eder *adj.* (*cryst.*) holohedron

holo·edrisch *adj.* (*cryst.*) holohedral

holo·morph *adj.* (*Funktion*) holomorphic (function)

Holz·maß *n* wood measure

homo·gen *adj.* homogeneous: (*alg.*) *homogenes algebraisches Polynom* homogeneous algebraic polynomial; *homogene Gleichung* homogeneous equation; *homogener Körper* (*geom.*) homogeneous solid, (*phys.*) homogeneous body; (*alg.*) *homogenes Ideal* homogeneous ideal; *homogene Koordinaten* homogeneous coordinates [*cf.* FORM; GLEICHFÖRMIG; TRANSFORMATION]

Homogeneität *f* homogeneity [*cf.* GLEICHFÖRMIGKEIT]

homo·grad *adj.* (*statist.*) homograde

homo·log *adj.* homologous

Homo·logie *f* homology

homo·morph *adj.* (*alg.*) homomorphic

Homo·morphie *f* (*alg.*) homomorphism

Homomorphie·satz *m* (*alg.*) law of homomorphism

Homo·morphismus *m* (*alg.*) homomorphism:

homöo·morph *adj.* homeomorphic

Homöo·morphie *f* homeomorphism

homo·topisch *adj.* homotopic

Horizont *m* horizon [*cf.* FUSSPUNKT; HÖHE; SCHEITELPUNKT]

horizontal *adj.* horizontal [*cf.* EBEN; PROJEKTION; PROJEKTIONSEBENE; SPUR]

Horizontal·ebene *f* horizontal plane

Horizontalität *f* horizontality

Horizontal·parallaxe *f* (*astr.*) horizontal parallax

Horizontal·projektion *f* horizontal projection

Horizontal·schnitt *m* horizontal section

Horner *m N.* [*cf.* METHODE]

Horopter *m*, **Horopter·kurve** *f* horopter

Huf *m* (*eines Rotationskörpers*) ungula (of a solid of revolution)

Hülle *f* (*alg.*) closure: *lineare H. eines Matrizensystems* linear closure of a system of matrices [*cf.* ABGESCHLOSSEN]

Hunde·kurve *f* curve of pursuit [= VERFOLGUNGSKURVE]

hundert *card. num.* (a) hundred, one hundred

Hundert *n* hundred: *Hunderte von Dollars* hundreds of dollars; *zwölf vom Hundert*, (*abbr.*) *zwölf v.H.* twelve per cent [*cf.* v.H.]

hundert·eins *card. num.* one hundred and one [= HUNDERTUNDEINS]

Hundertel *n* hundredth (part)

Hunderter *m* hundred: *die Stelle der H.* the place of hundreds, hundred's (or hundreds) place

hundert·erst *ord. num.* one hundred and first [=HUNDERTUNDERST]

Hunderter·stelle *f* hundred's (or hundreds) place

hundert·perzentig, hundert·prozentig *adj.* a (or one) hundred per cent

Hundert·satz *m* percentage

hundertst *ord. num.* hundredth: *der hundertste Teil* the one-hundredth part

Hundertstel *n* hundredth (part)

hundert·tausend *card. num.* a (or one) hundred thousand

hundert·teilig *adj.* (*Skala, Thermometer*) centesimal, centigrade (scale, thermometer)

hundert·und·eins *card. num.* one hundred and one

hundert·und·erst *ord. num.* one hundred and first

hundert·und·zehn, hundert·zehn *card. num.* one hundred and ten

Hydro·dynamik *f* (*phys.*) hydrodynamics, dynamics of fluids [*cf.* KONTINUITÄTSGLEICHUNG; WIRBEL]

hydro·dynamisch *adj.* (*phys.*) hydrodynamic(al)

Hydro·mechanik *f* (*phys.*) hydromechanics, mechanics of fluids

hydro·mechanisch *adj.* (*phys.*) hydromechanic(al)

Hydro·statik *f* (*phys.*) hydrostatics, statics of fluids

hydro·statisch *adj.* (*phys.*) hydrostatic(al)

Hyperbel *f* hyperbola: *Kreis über der reellen Achse der H.* auxiliary circle of the hyperbola [*cf.* ACHSE; GLEICHSEITIG ; HALBACHSE ;

HAUPTACHSE; KUBISCH; LEITKREIS; NEBENACHSE] .

Hyperbel·funktion *f* hyperbolic function: *inverse H.* antihyperbolic (or: inverse hyperbolic, or arc-hyperbolic) function

Hyperbel·gleichung *f* equation of a hyperbola

hyperbolicus *adj.* hyperbolic [*cf.* COSINUS HYPERBOLICUS; SINUS HYPERBOLICUS; COSECANS HYPERBOLICUS; SECANS HYPERBOLICUS; TANGENS HYPERBOLICUS; COTANGENS HYPERBOLICUS]

hyperbolisch *adj.* hyperbolic : *hyperbolischer Zylinder* hyperbolic cylinder; *hyperbolische Funktion* hyperbolic function; *hyperbolisches (oder windschiefes) Paraboloid* hyperbolic paraboloid [*cf.* SATTELFLÄCHE]; *hyperbolischer Punkt einer Fläche* hyperbolic point of a surface [*cf.* GEOMETRIE; LOGARITHMUS; SPIRALE]

Hyperboloid *n* hyperboloid: *einschaliges (zweischaliges) H.* hyperboloid of one sheet (of two sheets), unparted (parted) hyperboloid [*cf.* ASYMPTOTENKEGEL; SCHALE; STRIKTIONSLINIE]

Hyper·ebene *f* hyperplane: *uneigentliche H.* improper hyperplane

hyper·elliptisch *adj.* hyperelliptic

Hyper·fläche *f* hypersurface

hyper·geometrisch *adj.* hypergeometric: *. hypergeometrische Reihe* hypergeometric series

hyper·komplex *adj.* hypercomplex [*cf.* ALGEBRA]

Hyper·oskulation *f* superosculation

hyper·oskulieren *v.t.* superosculate

Hyper·raum *m* hyperspace
Hyper·sphäre *f* hypersphere
Hypotenuse *f* hypotenuse [*cf.*
RECHTWINKLIG]
Hypo·thek *f* (*fin.*) mortgage [*cf.*
BELASTEN 2.; RÜCKZAHLUNG;
ZURÜCKZAHLEN]
Hypotheken·brief *m* [= PFAND-
BRIEF]
Hypo·these *f* hypothesis

hypo·thetisch *adj.* hypothetic(al)
Hypo·trochoide *f* hypotrochoid
Hypo·zykloide *f* hypocycloid:
*dreispitzige H., H. mit drei
Rückkehrpunkten* tricuspid [=
Steinersche Kurve; cf. STEINER];
*vierspitzige H., H. mit vier
Rückkehrpunkten* tetracuspid,
astroid [= ASTEROIDE, ASTROIDE]
Hz (*abbr.*) *Hertz* cycle (per second)

I

ideal *adj.* (*alg.*) ideal: *ideale Zahl*
ideal number
Ideal *n* (*alg.*) ideal: *linksseitiges
(rechtsseitiges) I.* left (right) ideal;
zweiseitiges I. two-sided ideal
[*cf.* ANNULLIEREN; DIMENSIONS-
ZAHL; EINARTIG; HÖCHST-
DIMENSION; HOMOGEN; PRIMÄR;
TEILERLOS; TRÄGHEITSFORM; UN-
GEMISCHT]
Ideal·basis *f* (*alg.*) ideal basis
Ideal·quotient *m* (*alg.*) quotient
ideal
Ideal·theorie *f* (*alg.*) ideal theory
idem·potent *adj.* (*alg.*) idempotent
identisch *adj.* identical: *identische
Gleichung* identical equation;
identische Transformation identical transformation, identity;
(*log.*) *identische* (*oder allgemein-
gültige*) *Formeln des engeren
Prädikatenkalküls* universally
valid formulas of the restricted
predicate calculus
Identität *f* identity [*cf.* BESTIM-
MUNGSGLEICHUNG]

Ikosa·eder *n* icosahedron
ikosa·edrisch *adj.* icosahedral
Ikositetra·eder *n* (*cryst.*) icositet-
rahedron, trapezohedron, tet-
ragonal trisoctahedron
imaginär *adj.* imaginary: *rein
imaginäre Zahl* pure imaginary
number [*cf.* ACHSE; HALBACHSE]
immer *adv.* always; (*log.*) *i. richtig
(falsch)* logically true (false)
Im·mobilien *n pl.* (*comm.*) immovables, real estate [*cf.* VER-
PFÄNDEN; VERPFÄNDUNG]
Im·plikation *f* (*log.*) implication
im·plizieren *v.t.* (*log.*) imply
im·plizit *adj.* implicit: *implizite
Funktion* implicit function
im·plizite *adv.* implicitly
im·primitiv *adj.* (*alg.*) (*Gruppe*)
imprimitive (group)
Im·primitivität *f* (*alg.*) imprimitivity
Imprimitivitäts·gebiet *n* (*alg.*)
system of imprimitivity
Im·puls *m* (*mech.*) impulse, (linear)
momentum

Impuls·moment *n* moment of momentum, angular momentum, [=Drall; Drehimpuls]; [*cf.* Moment²]

Impuls·peilung *f* radar

in *prep.* (*dat., acc.*) in, into: 7 *in* 49 *ist* (*oder gibt*) 7 (*oder: geht sieben-mal*) 7 (divided) into 49 gives 7

in·äquivalent *adj.* inequivalent

In·äquivalenz *f* inequivalence

Index *m* index; (*unterer* inferior) *subscript;* (*oberer* superior) super-script: *kontravarianter* (*kovarianter*) *I.* contravariant (covariant) index; *I. einer Untergruppe* index of a subgroup [*cf.* auszeichnen; Kennziffer; reagibel; Strich; versehen; zweifach; Zeiger]

Index·zahl *f,* **Index·ziffer** *f* index number [*cf.* Kettenindexziffer]

in·different *adj.* indifferent; (*Gleichgewicht*) neutral (equilibrium) [*cf* Gleichgewicht]

In·dikator *m* indicator

Indikator·diagramm *n* indicator diagram

In·dikatrix *f* indicatrix: *Dupinsche I.* Dupin indicatrix

in·direkt *adj.* indirect: *indirekter Beweis* indirect (or: reductio ad absurdum) proof [*cf.* Steuer]

in·dividuell *adj.* individual: (*log.*) *individueller Gegenstand* individual constant; (*log.*) *individuelles Prädikat* predicate constant [*cf.* Prädikatenprädikat]

Individuen·bereich *m* (*log.*) domain of individuals

Individuen·prädikat *n* (*log.*) predicate of individuals: *prädikatives I.* predicative predicate of individuals

Individuen·variable *f* (*log.*) individual variable

In·dividuum *n* (*log.*) individual

In·dossament *n* (*comm.*) endorsement, indorsement [*cf.* übertragen 3.; Übertragung]

in·dossieren *v.t.* (*comm.*) endorse, indorse

In·duktanz *f* (*elec.*) inductance

In·duktion *f* induction: *vollständige I.* complete (or mathematical) induction

in·duktiv *adj.* inductive: *induktive Methode* inductive method [*cf.* Beweis]

ineinander·liegen (*sep.*) *v.i.* be incident: *je zwei entsprechende Elemente eines Strahlenbüschels und einer es in einer Punktreihe schneidenden Geraden liegen ineinander* any two corresponding (or homologous) elements of a pencil of lines and a line cutting it in a range of points are incident

Ineinander·liegen *n* incidence [*cf.* schneiden: *Schneiden und Verbinden*]

ineinander·schachteln (*sep.*) *v.t.* nest: *ineinandergeschachtelte Intervalle* nested intervals

in·ertial *ad.* inertial: *inertiales Koordinatensystem* inertial coordinate system

Inertial·system *n* inertial system

in·ferior *adj.* inferior [*cf.* Limes]

in·finitär *adj.* infinitary

in·finitesimal *adj.* infinitesimal: *infinitesimale Größe* infinitesimal (quantity)

Infinitesimal·größe *f* infinitesimal (quantity)

Infinitesimal·rechnung *f* infinitesimal calculus (or analysis)

Inflexions·punkt *m* [= WENDEPUNKT 1.]

Inflexions·tangente *f* [= WENDETANGENTE]

in·flexiv *adj.* (*log.*) inflexive, irreflexive [=IRREFLEXIV]

Inhaber·aktie *f* (*comm.*) bearer share

Inhaber·obligation *f* (*fin.*) bearer bond

Inhaber·papier *n* (*comm., fin.*) commercial (or negotiable) paper

In·halt *m* (*das Enthaltene*) content(s); (*Flächeninhalt*) area; (*Rauminhalt*) volume: (*alg.*) *I. eines Polynoms* content of a polynomial, greatest common divisor of the coefficients of a polynomial; *I. einer Menge* content of a set; (*log.*) *I. eines Begriffs* content of a concept; *I. eines Rechtecks* area of a rectangle; *I. eines Würfels* volume of a cube

inhalt·lich *adj.* as to the content(s); (*log.*) intuitive: (*log.*) *inhaltliche Bedeutung, Deutung* intuitive meaning, interpretation; (*log.*) *inhaltliches Schließen* intuitive conclusions

in·homogen *adj.* inhomogeneous [*cf.* UNGLEICHFÖRMIG]

In·homogeneität *f* inhomogeneity [*cf.* UNGLEICHFÖRMIGKEIT]

in·kommensurabel *adj.* incommensurable

In·kommensurabilität *f* incommensurability

in·korrekt *adj.* incorrect

Inkorrekt·heit *f* incorrectness

In·kreis *m* incircle, inscribed circle; *Mittelpunkt des Inkreises* incenter

Inkreis·mittelpunkt *m* incenter, center of inscribed circle

Inkreis·radius *m* radius of the inscribed circle; (*eines regelmäßigen Vielecks, auch*) short radius, apothem (of a regular polygon) [*cf.* POLYGON]

In·krement *n* increment

innen *adv.* internally, inside [*cf.* BERÜHREND]

Innen·fläche *f* interior surface

Innen·glied *n* (*einer Proportion*) mean (term) (of a proportion)

Innen·raum *m* interior (space)

Innen·seite *f* inside, inner surface, interior

Innen·winkel *m* interior angle

inner *adj.* inner, inside, interior, internal: *inneres Verhältnis* (*oder Teilungsverhältnis*) inner ratio (of division); *inneres Glied einer Proportion* mean term of a proportion; *innere Berührung* internal tangency; *innerer Punkt einer Menge* interior point of a set, point interior to a set; *Menge aller inneren Punkte einer Punktmenge* interior (complement) of a set of points; *innerer Durchmesser eines Zylinders* inside diameter of a cylinder; (*astr.*) *innerer Planet* inferior (or inner) planet [*cf.* AUTOMORPHISMUS; PRODUKT; VERANSCHAULICHUNG; VERHÄLTNIS]

Innere(s) *n* interior, inside: *Inneres* (*oder das Innere*) *einer Punktmenge* (the) interior of a set of points

inner·halb *adv.*, *prep.* (*gen.*) inside

innerst *adj.* (*sup.* of **inner**) innermost

in·separabel *adj.* inseparable

In·separabilität *f* inseparability

Integral *n* integral: *doppeltes* (*oder zweifaches*) *I.* double integral; *dreifaches* (*mehrfaches*) *I.* triple (multiple) integral; *unbestimmtes I.* (*einer Funktion*) indefinite (or primitive) integral, antiderivative (of a function); *I. nach x von a bis b* integral with respect to *x* from *a* to *b* [*cf.* BESTIMMT; EINFACH; ELLIPTISCH; GRENZE; ITERIERT; ÜBER, UNEIGENTLICH; UNENDLICH; ZWEIMALIG]

Integral·formel *f* integral formula

Integral·gleichung *f* integral equation [*cf.* KERN]

Integral·kosinus *m* integral cosine

Integral·logarithmus *m* integral logarithm

Integral·rechnung *f* integral calculus

Integral·satz *m* integral theorem

Integral·sinus *m* integral sine

Integral·zeichen *n* integral sign (*symb.:* $\int$)

Integrand *m* integrand

Integration *f* integration [*cf.* MECHANISCH; PARTIELL; REDUKTIONSFORMEL; TEILWEISE]

Integrations·formel *f* integration formula

Integrations·konstante *f* constant of integration

integrier·bar *adj.* integrable: *integrierbare* (*oder rektifizierbare*) *Kurve* integrable (or rectifiable) curve; *integrierbare* (*oder quadrierbare*) *Fläche* integrable (or squarable) surface; *integrierbarer* (*oder kubierbarer*) *Körper* integrable solid

integrieren *v.t.* integrate [*cf.* FAKTOR; NACH]

Integrierung *f* integration

Integritäts·bereich *m* (*alg.*) integral domain, domain of integrity [*cf.* ABGESCHLOSSENHEIT]

In·tensität *f* intensity

in·tensiv *adj.* intensive, intense

Inter·essen *n pl.* (*comm.*) interest [*cf.* ZINS]

Inter·ferenz *f* interference

Interferenz·bild *n* interference figure

Interferenz·streifen *m* interference fringe

inter·ferieren *v.i.* interfere

Inter·polation *f* interpolation [*cf.* EINSCHALTUNG]

Interpolations·formel *f* interpolation formula

Interpolations·rechnung *f* calculus of interpolation

inter·polieren *v.t.* interpolate [*cf.* EINSCHALTEN]

Inter·polierung *f* interpolation

Inter·vall *n* interval: *abgeschlossenes* (*offenes*) *I.* closed (open) interval; *festes I.* fixed interval [*cf.* ENDE; FUNKTION; GRÖSST; INEINANDERGESCHACHTELT; RANDPUNKT; RAUMARTIG; SPANNE; ZEITARTIG]

Intervall·schachtelung *f* nest of intervals

in·transitiv *adj.* intransitive: *intransitive Beziehung* intransitive relation

In·transitivität *f* intransitiveness, intransitivity

Invaliditäts·versicherung *f* disability insurance
in·variant *adj.* invariant [*cf.* UNTERGRUPPE]
In·variante *f* invariant
Invarianten·theorie *f* invariant theory
In·varianz *f* invariance
Inventar *n* (*comm.*) inventory [*cf.* KALKULATIONSAUFSCHLAG]
inventarisieren *v.t.* make (or take) an inventory
invers *adj.* inverse, reciprocal: *inverser Punkt, inverse Kurve in bezug auf einen Kreis* inverse of a point, a curve with respect to a circle; *inverse Funktion* inverse function; *inverse Transformation, Substitution, Abbildung* inverse (or reciprocal) transformation, substitution, mapping; *inverses Element eines Gruppenelements* inverse (element) of a group element [*cf.* DIREKT; HYPERBELFUNKTION; OPERATION; PROPORTIONAL; VERHÄLTNIS]
Inverse(s) *n* inverse: *Inverses eines Gruppenelements* inverse of a group element
invers·hyperbolisch *adj.* (*Funktion*) inverse hyperbolic, antihyperbolic, arc-hyperbolic (function)
In·version *f* inversion: *I.* (*oder Vertauschung*) *in einer Folge von Objekten* inversion in a sequence of objects; *I. eines Punktes in bezug auf einen Kreis* inversion of a point with respect to a circle
Inversions·zentrum *n* center of inversion
invers-isomorph *adj.* inverse-isomorphic

invers·trigonometrisch *adj.* (*Funktion*) inverse trigonometric, anti-trigonometric, arc-trigonometric (function)
invertier·bar *adj.* invertible
in·vestieren *v.t.* (*fin.*) invest
In·vestierung *f* (*fin.*) investment
In·volute *f* involute [= EVOLVENTE]
In·volution *f* involution
in·volutorisch *adj.* involutory
Iota *n* (*griechischer Buchstabe* Greek letter I, ι) iota
irdisch *adj.* terrestrial
ir·rational *adj.* irrational: *irrationale Zahl* irrational (number), surd [*cf.* WURZELAUSDRUCK]
Ir·rationalität *f* irrationality
Irrational·zahl *f* irrational (number)
ir·reduzibel *adj.* irreducible: *irreduzibler Fall* (*oder: casus irreducibilis*) *in der kardanischen Formel* irreducible case in Cardan's formula; *irreduzible Gleichung* irreducible equation; *irreduzibles Polynom* prime polynomial; *ein in einem gegebenen Körper irreduzibles Polynom* a polynomial irreducible in a given field; *irreduzibler Bruch* fraction in its lowest terms [*cf.* DARSTELLUNG]
Irreduzibilitäts·kriterium *n* irreducibility criterion
ir·reflexiv *adj.* (*log.*) irreflexive, inflexive [= INFLEXIV]
irren 1. *v.i.* err, be mistaken. **2.** *v.r.: sich i.* make a mistake, commit an error
ir·reversibel *adj.* irreversible
Ir·reversibilität *adj.* irreversibility
Irr·tum *m* error

iso·bar *adj.* (*Ausdruck*) isobaric (expression)

Iso·bare *f* (*meteor.*) isobar

iso·barisch *adj.* (*meteor.*) (*Linie*) isobaric (line)

Iso·chore *f* (*phys.*) isochor(e)

Iso·chron *adj.* isochronous, isochronal

Iso·chrone *f* isochrone, isochronous curve

iso·gonal *adj.* isogonal, equiangular

Iso·hypse *f* level (or contour) line [= HÖHENLINIE; SCHICHTLINIE]

isolieren *v.t.* isolate [*cf.* ISOLIERT]

isoliert *adj.* isolated: *isolierter Punkt einer Kurve* acnode, isolated (or conjugate) point of a curve; *isolierter Punkt einer Punktmenge* isolated point of a set of points; *isolierte Menge* isolated set [*cf.* PRIMÄRKOMPONENTE]

Iso·metrie *f* isometry

iso·metrisch *adj.* (*Projektion*) isometric (projection)

iso·morph *adj.* isomorphic [*cf.* ÄHNLICH-ISOMORPH; STETIG]

Iso·morphie *f* **1.** (*alg.*) isomorphism. **2.** (*cryst.*) isomorphism, homeomorphism

Isomorphie·satz *m* (*alg.*) law of isomorphism

Iso·morphismus *m* (*alg.*) iso-morphism: *einstufiger I.*, 1-*Isomorphismus* (simple) isomorphism, 1-isomorphism; *mehrstufiger I.* multiple (or general) isomorphism, homomorphism [*cf.* EINSTUFIG; FORTSETZEN; FORTSETZUNG; MEHRSTUFIG; RELATIV]

iso·perimetrisch *adj.* isoperimetric

Iso·phote *f* line of equal illumination

is·optisch *adj.* isoptic: *isoptische Kurve, Kurve gleichen Gesichtswinkels* isoptic curve

Iso·therme *f* isotherm

iso·thermisch *adj.* isothermal, isothermic(al)

Iso·top *n* (*phys., chem.*) isotope

iso·trop *adj.* (*cryst.*) isotropic

Iso·tropie *f* (*cryst.*) isotropy

iso·tropisch *adj.* (*cryst.*) isotropic(al)

ist (3*rd pers. sing. pres. of* **sein** be) is; (*ist gleich*) is (equal to), equals (*symb.:* =): *fünf mal fünf ist* (*gleich*) *fünfundzwanzig* five times five equals (or: is equal to) twenty-five (*symb.:* 5 × 5 = 25) [*cf.* AB; IN; UND]

Ist·bestand *m* (*comm.*) actual balance [*ant.:* SOLLBESTAND]

Iteration *f* iteration, repetition

iteriert *adj.* (*Integral, Operation*) iterated (integral, operation)

J

Jacobi *m N.* [*cf.* DETERMINANTE]

Jahr *n* year; *zweimal im J.* biannually; *alle zwei Jahre, jedes zweite J.* biennially; *bürgerliches, tropisches J.* civil, tropical year

Jahr·gang *m* (*statist.*) (*einer*

Bevölkerungsgruppe) age group, (age) year, (*coll.*) vintage (of a population)

Jahr·hundert *n* century

jährlich *adj.* annual [*cf.* BAHN]

Jahr·tausend *n* millennium

Jahr·zehnt *n* decade

je *adv.* each, by, in *sie kosten je*

5 *Mark* they cost 5 marks each; *je zehn und zehn* in (or by) tens [*cf.* ZU]

Jota *n* [= IOTA]

Joule *m* N.: *Joulesches* (*oder mechanisches*) *Wärmeäquivalent* Joule's equivalent (of heat)

Joule *n* (*meas.*) joule

K

Kalender *m* calendar

Kalender·jahr *n* calendar year: *K.* (*für Zinsenberechnung*) **a.** (*von 365 Tagen*) *nach amerikanischer Methode* civil year (of 365 days), **b.** (*von 360 Tagen*) *nach deutscher Methode* commercial year (of 360 days) (for the computation of interest)

Kalkül *m* calculus

Kalkulation *f* (*Berechnung*) calculation, computation; (*comm.*) (*der Kosten*) cost accounting [*cf.* FALSCH]

Kalkulations·aufschlag *m* (*comm.*) mark-up (figure): *K. auf das Inventar* inventory mark-up

Kalkulations·fehler *m* miscalculation

Kalkulations·tabelle *f* (*comm.*) pricing schedule

Kalkulations·zuschlag *m* [= KALKULATIONSAUFSCHLAG]

kalkulieren *v.t.* calculate

Kalorie *f* (*phys.*) calorie, calory: *große K.* large (or great) calorie; *kleine K.* small calorie

Kalotte *f* spherical cap

Kampf·preis *m* (*comm.*) competitive price

Kampf·tarif *m* (*comm.*) retaliatory tariff

Kampf·zoll *m* (*comm.*) retaliatory duty

Kampyla *f* (*Kurve*) (*des Eudoxus*) kàmpyle (or curve) of Eudoxus

kanonisch *adj.* canonical: (*alg.*) *kanonische Darstellung* canonical representation

Kante *f* edge: *von der K. aus gesehen* seen edgewise [*cf.* SCHMALSEITE; SICHTBAR]

Kanten·ansicht *f* edge view [*cf.* SCHMALSEITENANSICHT]

Kanten·anzahl *f*, **Kanten·zahl** *f* (*eines Polyeders*) number of edges (of a polyhedron)

Kapazität *f* (*Fassungskraft*) capacity; (*elec.*) capacity, capacitance

Kapital *n* (*comm., fin.*) capital, principal [*cf.* ANLAGE; ANLEGEN; EINLAGE; EINLEGEN; RÜCKZAHLUNG; VERMÖGEN; ZURÜCKZAHLEN]

Kapitals·anlage *f* (*comm., fin.*) investment (of capital)

Kappa *n* (*griechischer Buchstabe* Greek letter *K*, *κ*) kappa
Kappa·kurve *f* kappa curve
Karat *n* (*Gewicht* weight) carat
Karat·gewicht *n* troy weight
Kardan·gelenk *n* (*mech.*) Cardan (or universal) joint
kardanisch *adj.* Cardan('s), Cardanic: (*mach.*) *kardanischer Ring* gimbal (ring); (*phys., mach.*) *k. aufhängen* suspend on gimbals; (*phys., mach.*) *kardanische Aufhängung* Cardanic (or Cardan's, or gimbal) suspension [*cf.* IRREDUZIBEL; LÖSUNG]
Kardan·ring *m* (*mach.*) gimbal (ring)
Kardan·welle *f* (*mach.*) Cardan (or: universally jointed) shaft
Kardinal·zahl *f* cardinal number [*cf.* GRUNDZAHL]
Kardioide *f* cardioid [= HERZLINIE]
Kargo·versicherung *f* freight insurance
Karte *f* card; (*Landkarte*) map; (*Seekarte*) chart [*cf.* KOORDINATENNETZ; KOTE]
Kartei *f* (*statist., comm.*) card (index) file
Karten·entfernung *f* map range, cartographic distance
Karten·maßstab *m* map scale
Karten·netz map grid
Karten·projektion *f* cartographic (or map) projection [*cf.* GRUNDEBENE]
kartesianisch [= KARTESISCH]
kartesisch *adj.* Cartesian [= CARTESISCH]: *kartesische Koordinaten* Cartesian coordinates [*cf.* EXTREMPUNKT]; *kartesische Gleichung einer Kurve* Cartesian

(or rectangular) equation of a curve
Karto·gramm *n* statistical map, cartogram
Karto·graph *m* cartographer
Karto·graphie *f* cartography
karto·graphisch *adj.* cartographic
Karto·thek *f* (*statist., comm.*) card (index) file
Kasko·versicherung *f* insurance on the body (or: on hull and appurtenances)
Kassa·bestand *m* (*comm.*) cash in hand, cash holdings
Kassa·skonto *m* (*comm., fin.*) cash discount
Kassinoide *f* Cassinian oval [= CASSINOIDE]
Kata·kaustik *f* (*opt.*) catacaustic
Katalog·preis *m* (*comm.*) list price
Kategorie *f* category
kategorisch *adj.* (*log.*) categorical
Katenoid *n* catenoid [= KETTENFLÄCHE]
Kathete *f* (*eines rechtwinkligen Dreiecks*) leg, (other) side (of a right triangle); (*Basiskathete*) base (of a right triangle); (*senkrechte Kathete*) perpendicular (of a right triangle) [*cf.* RECHTWINKLIG]
Kauf *m* (*comm.*) buy, purchase [*cf.* BANKABRECHNUNG; TERMINKAUF]
kaufen *v.t.* (*comm.*) buy, purchase [*cf.* ABZAHLUNG; TERMIN]
Käufer *m* (*comm.*) buyer, purchaser [*cf.* AUFRECHNEN]
kauf·männisch *adj.* commercial, mercantile [*cf.* RECHNEN; SCHULD]
Kauf·preis *m* (*comm.*) purchase price

Kauf·schilling *m* [= KAUFPREIS]

kausal *adj.* causal

Kausal·gesetz *n* law of causality, causal law

Kausalität *f* causality

Kausal·nexus *m* causal connection (or nexus)

Kausalitäts·prinzip *n* principle of causality

Kaustik *f* (*opt.*) caustic

Kaution *f* (*comm.*) (*Sicherheit*) security, guarantee; (*beim Strafgericht*) bail (in court) [*cf.* SICHERHEIT; SICHERHEITSSUMME]

Kautions·versicherung *f* guarantee (or fidelity) insurance

Kavalier·perspektive *f* cavalier perspective · [= MILITÄRPERSPEKTIVE]

Kavalier·projektion *f* cavalier projection [= MILITÄRPROJEKTION]

Kegel *m* cone: *gerader* (*schiefer*) *K.* right (oblique) cone; *abgestutzter K.* frustum of a cone, truncated cone [*cf.* ABSCHNEIDEN; BASIS; ELLIPTISCH; ERZEUGENDE; GRUNDFLÄCHE; HÖHE; MANTEL; MANTELLINIE; SCHEITELPUNKT; SEITENLINIE; SPITZE; TANGENTIALEBENE; UMSCHREIBEN]

Kegel·achse *f* axis of a cone

Kegel·erzeugende *f* element (or ruling) of a cone [*cf.* MANTELLINIE]

Kegel·fläche *f* conic surface

kegel·förmig *adj.* conic(al)

kegelig *adj.* conic, cone-shaped, tapered

Kegel·mantel *m* lateral area of a cone

Kegel·projektion *f* conic(al) projection

Kegel·schnitt *m* conic (section): *entarteter K.* degenerate conic; *Pol und Polare eines Kegelschnitts* pole and polar of a conic [*cf.* BRENNPUNKTEIGENSCHAFT; BESTIMMUNGSSTÜCK; EXZENTRIZITÄT; PARAMETER; SCHEITEL; SEHNENSECHSECK; TANGENTENSECHSECK; ZWEIT]

Kegelschnitt·punkt point of a conic [*cf.* BRENNSTRAHL; FAHRSTRAHL; LEITSTRAHL; RADIUSVEKTOR]

Kegel·stumpf *m*, **Kegel·stutz** *m* frustum of a cone, conical frustum [*cf.* ABSCHNEIDEN]

Kehr·wert *m* reciprocal (value) [= REZIPROKE(S); *reziproker Wert, cf.* REZIPROK]

Keil *m* wedge

keil·förmig *adj.* wedge-shaped, cuneiform

Kenn·ziffer *f* 1. (*Index*) index. 2. (*Schlüsselzahl*) code number. 3. (*eines Logarithmus*) characteristic (of a logarithm)

Kepler *m* N. [*cf.* FLÄCHENGESETZ; GESETZ]

Kerb·holz *n* tally, score

Kern *m* 1. (*einer Integralgleichung*) kernel, nucleus (of an integral equation). 2. (*phys.*) (*eines Atoms*) nucleus, core (of an atom)

Kern·elektron *n* (*phys.*) nuclear electron

Kern·ladung *f* (*phys.*) nuclear charge

Kernladungs·zahl *f* (*phys.*) nuclear-charge number

Kern·physik *f* nuclear physics

Kern·reaktion *f* (*phys.*) nuclear reaction

Kern·schatten *m* umbra, full (or complete) shadow

Kerzen·stärke *f* (*opt. meas.*) candle power

Kette *f* chain: (*alg.*) *Sturmsche K.* Sturm's chain [*cf.* ENDLOS]

Ketten·bruch *m* continued fraction [*cf.* ENDLICH; NÄHERUNGSBRUCH; PERIODISCH]

Ketten·division *f* continued division

Ketten·fläche *f* catenoid [= KATENOID].

Ketten·indexziffer *f* (*statist.*) **1.** (*Indexzahl einer Gliedziffer*) link relative. **2.** (*Indexzahl einer Kettenzahl*) chain index number

Ketten·linie *f* catenary (curve), chainette: *K. gleichen Widerstands* catenary of uniform strength [= LONGITUDINALE]; *sphärische K.* spherical catenary; *Rotationsfläche der K.* catenoid

Ketten·rechnung *f* chain method

Ketten·regel *f* chain rule

Ketten·zahl *f* (*statist.*) **1.** (*Verkettung der Gliedziffern* chaining of link relatives) chain relative. **2.** (*Gliedziffer*) link relative [*cf.* KETTENINDEXZIFFER]

K.G.V. (*abbr.*) *kleinstes gemeinsames Vielfaches* least common multiple, (*abbr.*) L.C.M.

Kilo *n* (*Gewicht* weight) kilo

Kilo·gramm *n* (*abbr.* kg) kilogram, kilogramme (*abbr.* kg.) [*cf.* PRO]

Kilogrammeter *n* [= KILOGRAMM·METER]

Kilogramm·kalorie *f* (*phys.*) kilogram calorie

Kilogramm·meter *n* kilogram-meter, kilogramme-metre

Kilo·hertz *n* (*rad. meas.*) kilocycle

Kilo·meter *n* (*abbr.* km) kilometer, kilometre, (*abbr.* km.)

Kilo·watt *n* kilowatt

Kilowatt·stunde *f* kilowatt hour [*cf.* KWH; KWST]

Kinematik *f* kinematics

kinematisch *adj.* kinematic(al)

Kinetik *f* kinetics

kinetisch *adj.* kinetic [*cf.* ENERGIE]

Kissoide *f* cissoid [= ZISSOIDE]

Klafter *f* **1.** (*Längenmaß* linear measure) fathom. **2.** (*Holzmaß* wood measure) cord, line (of wood)

Klammer *f* sign of aggregation; *runde K.* parenthesis; *eckige K.* (square) bracket; *geschlungene* (*oder geschweifte*) *K.* brace [*cf.* EINKLAMMERN; HEBEN; SCHLIESSEN; SCHLUSS; ZUSAMMENFASSEN]

Klammer·ausdruck *m* expression (or aggregation) in parentheses, brackets, or braces [*cf.* KLAMMER]; *zu einem K. vereinigen* collect in parantheses, or brackets, or braces [*cf.* AUFHEBEN]

Klammer·zeichen *n* (*log.*) quantifier [*cf.* ALLZEICHEN; SEINSZEICHEN]

Klang *m* (*acoust.*) sound, tone [*cf.* GRUNDTON]

klappen *v.t.* [= UMKLAPPEN]

Klappung *f* [= UMKLAPPUNG]

Klasse class [*cf.* DURCHSCHNITT; REPRÄSENTANT; VEREINIGUNG; ZWEIT]

Klassen·breite *f* (*statist.*) class interval

Klassen·einheit *f* (*statist.*) class unit

Klassen·einteilung *f* partition into classes

Klassen·ende *n* (*statist.*) class limit

Klassen·funktion *f* (*log.*) class function

Klassen·größe *f* (*statist.*) class interval

Klassen·häufigkeit *f* (*statist.*) class frequency

Klassen·kalkül *m* (*log.*) class calculus, calculus of classes

Klassen·mitte *f*, **Klassen·punkt** *m* (*statist.*) class mid point (or mark)

Klassen·repräsentant *m* (*statist.*) representative of a class [*cf.* EINZELFALL]

Klassen·summe *f* (*alg.*) class sum

Klassi·fikation *f* classification [*cf.* EINTEILUNG]

klassi·fizieren *v.t.* classify [*cf.* EINTEILEN]

Klassi·fizierung *f* classification [*cf.* GLIEDERUNG]

klein *adj.* small: *im kleinen* in the small [*cf.* ACHSE; BELIEBIG; ELLIPSE; GROSS; HALBACHSE; KALORIE; MASSTAB; UNENDLICH; ZAHL]

Klein *m* N. [*cf.* FLASCHE; VIERERGRUPPE]

kleiner *adj.* (*comp.* of **klein**) minor; (*als*) smaller, less (than): *die Zahl a ist kleiner als b* the number *a* is less than *b* (*symb.:* a $<$ b); *x* (*ist*) *kleiner* (*als*) *oder gleich y x* is less than or equal to *y*

Klein·geld *n* (*fin.*) (small) change

Klein·kreis *m* (*einer Kugel*) small circle (on a sphere)

kleinst *adj.* (*sup.* of **klein**) smallest, least, minimum, minimal, lowest: *kleinster Wert einer Funktion* least (or smallest, or lowest, or

minimum) value of a function; *auf den kleinsten Zähler und Nenner gebrachter Bruch* fraction in its lowest terms; *Methode der kleinsten Quadrate* method of least squares [*cf.* GEMEINSAM; GRENZWERT]

Klein·struktur *f* structure in the small

Klino·achse *f* (*cryst.*) clinoaxis, clinodiagonal axis [= KLINODIAGONALE]

klino·diagonal *adj.* (*cryst.*) clinodiagonal

Klino·diagonale *f* (*cryst.*) clinoaxis, clinodiagonal (axis) [= KLINOACHSE]

Klino·doma *n* (*pl.* *Klinodomen*) (*cryst.*) clinodome

Klino·pinakoid *n* (*cryst.*) clinopinacoid, clinopinakoid

Klino·pyramide *f* (*cryst.*) clinopyramid

Klothoide *f* clothoid, Euler's (or Cornu's) spiral [= SPINNLINIE]

Knick *m* (*einer Kurve*) salient point (of a curve)

Knoten *m* **1.** (*Verschlingung* entanglement) knot: *einen K. binden, knüpfen* tie a knot; *einen K.* (*auf*)*lösen, aufknüpfen* untie (or disentangle) a knot [*cf.* LÖSEN]. **2.** (*Längenmaß* linear measure) (*nav.*) knot: *das Schiff macht zehn K. die Stunde* the ship makes ten knots per hour. **3.** (*astr.*) node: *aufsteigender* (*absteigender*) *K.* ascending (descending) node

Knoten·linie *f* (*astr.;* *stehende Wellen* stationary waves) nodal line

Knoten·punkt *m* (*einer Kurve*) node (of a curve)

ko·axial *adj.* coaxial

Kochleoide *f* cochleoid [= SCHNECKENHAUSLINIE, SCHRAUBENKURVE]

Koeffizient *m* coefficient: *höchster K.* leading (or highest) coefficient [*cf.* GANZZAHLIG; HAUPTZAHL; MATRIX; RATIONALZAHLIG; UNBESTIMMT]

Koeffizienten·bereich *m* (*alg.*) coefficient domain

Koeffizienten·determinante *f* determinant of the coefficients

Ko·funktion *f* (*eines Winkels*) cofunction, complementary trigonometric function (of an angle) [*cf.* TRIGONOMETRISCH]

ko·härent *adj.* coherent

Ko·härenz *adj.* coherence

Kohlenspitzen·kurve *f* bullet-nose curve

ko·inzident *adj.* coincident

Ko·inzidenz *f* coincidence

ko·inzidieren *v.i.* coincide

Kollektiv *n*, **Kollektiv·gegenstand** *m* (*statist.*) collective, statistical universe

Kollektiv·maßlehre *f* (*statist.*) theory of (statistical) variables

Kollektiv·reihe *f* (*statist.*) statistical series

kol·linear *adj.* collineatory [*cf.* TRANSFORMATION]

Kol·linearität *f* collinearity

Kol·lineation *f* collineation

Kolonne *f* column [*cf.* ANORDNUNG; DETERMINANTE; ENTHALTEN; REIHE; ÜBERFÜHREN; ÜBERTRAGEN; VERTAUSCHEN]

Kolonnen·index *m* column index

Kombination *f* combination: *K. mit Wiederholungen* combination with repetitions allowed

Kombinations·lehre *f* theory of combinations

Kombinatorik *f* theory of combinations

kombinatorisch *adj.* combinatorial

kombinieren *v.t.* combine

Kombinierung *f* combination

Kommandit·gesellschaft *f* (*comm.*) limited partnership

kom·mensurabel *adj.* commensurable

Kom·mensurabilität *f* commensurability

kom·mutativ *adj.* commutative: *kommutatives Gesetz der Addition* (*Multiplikation*) commutative law of addition (multiplication); (*alg.*) *endlicher kommutativer Körper* finite commutative field, Galois field [*cf.* VERTAUSCHBAR]

Kommutativ·gesetz *n* commutative law [*cf.* KOMMUTATIV]

Kom·mutativität *f* commutativity [*cf.* VERTAUSCHBARKEIT]

Kom·mutator *m* (*alg.*) (*von Elementen einer Gruppe*) commutator (of elements of a group)

Kommutator·gruppe *f* (*alg.*) commutator group

Kommutator·untergruppe *f* (*alg.*) commutator subgroup

Kom·paß *m* (mariner's) compass [*cf.* STRICH]

Kompaß·ablesung *f* compass reading

Kompaß·strich *m* (*nav.*) point of the compass

Kom·pensation *f* compensation, balancing

Kompensations·pendel *n* (*phys.*) compensation pendulum

kom·pensieren *v.t.* compensate, offset, balance

kom·planar *adj.* coplanar

Kom·planation *f* (*einer krummen Fläche*) complanation (of a curved surface)

Komplement *n* (*eines Winkels*) complement (of an angle)

komplementär *adj.* complementary

Komplementär·winkel *m* complementary angle

Kom·plex *m* complex

kom·plex *adj.* complex: *komplexe Zahl* complex number; *komplexe Zahlenebene* complex plane; *Modul* (*oder: absoluter Wert*) *einer komplexen Zahl* modulus (or absolute value) of a complex number [*cf.* KONJUGIERT]

Kom·plexion *f* (*von Elementen einer Menge*) arrangement (of elements of a set) [*cf.* TRANS-PONIEREN]

Kom·ponente *f* component [*cf.* EVOLUTORISCH; UNDULATORISCH]

Komponenten·ideal *n* (*alg.*) component ideal

kom·ponieren *v.t.* compose

Kom·position *f* composition: (*alg.*) *ein System mit doppelter K.* a system of double composition [*cf.* ZUSAMMENSETZUNG]

Kompositions·faktor *m* (*alg.*) composition factor

Kompositions·reihe *f* (*alg.*) composition series

Konchoide *f* conchoid [= MU-SCHELLINIE]

Kon·figuration *f* configuration [*cf.* ÄHNLICHEITSPUNKT]

kon·fokal *adj.* confocal

kon·form *adj.* conformal, equiangular [*cf.* ERHALTEN 2.; WIN-KELTREU]

kon·gruent *adj.* congruent, superposable, identical: *kongruente Figuren* congruent (or identical) figures; *die beiden Dreiecke sind kongruent* the two triangles are congruent; *a* (*ist*) *kongruent* (*mit*) *b modulo c a* is congruent to *b* modulo *c* [*cf.* TRANSFORMATION]

Kon·gruenz *f* (*von Figuren, Zahlen*) congruence (of geometric figures, numbers) [*cf.* MODUL]

Kongruenz·satz *m* congruence theorem

konisch *adj.* conic(al) [*cf.* SCHRAUBENLINIE]

kon·jugiert *adj.* conjugate: *konjugierte Durchmesser* conjugate diameters; *k. komplexe Zahlen* conjugate complex numbers, conjugate imaginaries; (*alg.*) *konjugierte Untergruppe* conjugate subgroup; (*alg.*) *konjugierte Elemente einer Gruppe, eines Körpers* conjugate elements of a group, a field; *harmonisch konjugierte Punkte in bezug auf zwei Punkte* harmonic conjugates with respect to two points; *konjugierte Winkel zweier Geraden mit einer Transversalen* angles on the same side of two lines but on different sides of a transversal [*cf.* pairs of angles: A, C′; C, A′; D, B′; B, D′ in *Fig.* to TRANSVERSALE]

Kon·jugierte *f* conjugate

Kon·junktion *f* (*log., astr.*) conjunction [*cf.* HINTERGLIED; VORDERGLIED]

111

Konjunktions·glied *n* (*log.*) partial (or: component of a) conjunction, conjunct [=TEILKONJUNKTION]

kon·junktiv *adj.* (*log.*) conjunctive [*cf.* AUSGEZEICHNET]

Kon·junktur *f* (*comm.*) business outlook

Konjunktur·bewegung *f* (*comm.*) business cycle, (cyclical) market fluctuation

Konjunktur·forschung *f* (*comm., statist.*) business cycle analysis

Konjunktur·index *m* (*comm., statist.*) index of general business activity, general business index

Konjunktur·institut *n* (*comm.*) institute for business cycle research

Konjunktur·schwankungen *f pl.* (*comm., statist.*) (cyclical) market fluctuations, business cycle

Konjunktur·statistik *f* (*comm.*) business cycle statistics

Konjunktur·zyklus *m* (*comm.*) business cycle

kon·kav *adj.* concave: *k. gegen einen Punkt* concave toward a point [*cf.* NACH]

Kon·kavität *f* concavity

konkav·konvex *adj.* (*Linse*) concavo-convex (lens)

Konkav·spiegel *m* concave mirror [=HOHLSPIEGEL]

kon·kurrieren *v.i.* compete

kon·kurrierend *adj* competitive; (*statist.*) *Methode der konkurrierenden Veränderungen* **a.** (*quantitativ*) correlation analysis; **b.** (*qualitativ*) method of concomitant variations

Konkurs *m* (*comm.*) bankruptcy, failure, mortality: *K. anmelden*

file a petition in bankruptcy; *die Zahl der Konkurse nimmt zu* the number of mortalities is increasing; *in K. geraten* (*oder gehen*) fail, become (or go) bankrupt [*cf.* AKZEPTANT]

Konoid *n* conoid

kon·servativ *adj.* conservative: (*phys.*) *konservative Kraft* conservative force

Konsortial·geschäft *n* (*comm.*) syndicate business

Konsortial·konto· *n* (*comm.*) [=GEMEINSCHAFTSKONTO]

kon·stant *adj.* constant [*cf.* GESCHWINDIGKEIT; GLEICHFÖRMIG; UMFANG; VERHÄLTNIS; WERT]

Kon·stante *f* constant [*cf.* ABSOLUT; ALLGEMEIN; WILLKÜR; WILLKÜRLICH]

Kon·stanz *f* constancy [*cf.* GLEICHFÖRMIGKEIT]

Kon·stituent *m* (*log.*) constituent

konstruier·bar *adj.* constructible

Konstruierbar·keit *f* constructibility

kon·struieren *v.t.* construct, plot [*cf.* BESTIMMEN]

Kon·struktion *f* construction: *K. mit Zirkel und Lineal* construction with compass and ruler, ruler and compass construction [*cf.* AUSFÜHREN]

Kon·takt *m* contact, contingence

Konten·ausgleich *m* (*fin.*) settlement of accounts [*cf.* ABRECHNUNG]

Kon·tingent *n* (*comm., fin.*) contingent, quota

Kontingenz·winkel *m* angle of contingence [=BERÜHRUNGSWINKEL]

kon·tinuierlich *adj.* continuous

Kon·tinuität *f* continuity

Kontinuitäts·axiom *n* axiom of continuity

Kontinuitäts·gleichung *f* (*in der Hydrodynamik*) equation of continuity (in hydrodynamics)

Kontinuitäts·prinzip *n* principle of continuity

Kon·tinuum *n* (*pl. Kontinua*) continuum

Konto *n* (*pl. Konten*) (*comm., fin.*) account [*cf.* ABHEBEN; ABSCHLIESSEN; ABSCHLUSS; AUSGLEICHEN; BELASTEN; BUCH; GEMEINSAM; GUTHABEN; RECHNUNGSMÄSSIG]

Konto·auszug *m* (*comm., fin.*) statement (of account), extract (or abstract) of account [*cf.* BANK-ABRECHNUNG]

Konto·korrent *n* (*comm.*) account current

Kontokorrent·konto *n* current (or continuing) account

Kontokorrent·kredit *m* (*comm.*) deposit loan

Konto·umsatz *m* (*comm.*) account turnover

kontra·diktorisch *adj.* (*log.*) contradictory

kontra·gredient *adj.* contragredient

Kontra·gredienz *f* contragredience

kontrār *adj* (*log.*) contrary

kontra·variant *adj.* contravariant [*cf.* INDEX; TENSOR]

Kontra·variante *f* contravariant

Kontra·varianz *f* contravariance

Kontrolle *f* check, checkup, control

Kontroll·frage *f* (*statist.*) check question

kontrollieren *v.t.* check, control [*cf.* STICHPROBENERHEBUNG]

Kontroll·methode *f* checking method

Konus *m* cone [= KEGEL]

Kon·vention *f* convention

kon·ventionell *adj* conventional

kon·vergent *adj.* convergent: *unbedingt konvergente Reihe* permanently convergent series; *unbedingt konvergente Potenzreihe* entire series; *konvergente* (*oder zusammenlaufende*) *Gerade* convergent lines [*cf.* BEDINGT]

Kon·vergenz *f* convergence [*cf.* BEDINGT; KRITERIUM; UNGLEICHMÄSSIG]

Konvergenz·intervall *n* interval of convergence

Konvergenz·kreis *m* (*einer Potenzreihe*) circle of convergence (of a power series)

Konvergenz·kriterium *n* (*für Reihen*) test of convergence (for series)

Konvergenz·radius *m* (*einer Potenzreihe*) radius of convergence (of a power series)

Konvergenz·satz *m* convergence theorem

kon·vergieren *v.i.* (*gegen*) converge (to, toward)

kon·vex *adj.* convex [*cf.* NACH]

Kon·vexität *f* convexity

konvex·konkav *adj.* (*Linse*) convexo-concave (lens)

Konvex·spiegel *m* convex mirror [= VOLLSPIEGEL]

Kon·zentration *f* concentration

kon·zentrieren *v.t.* concentrate

kon·zentrisch *adl.* concentric

Ko·ordinate *f* coordinate: *rechtwinklige kartesische Koordinaten* rectangular Cartesian coordinates; *elliptische Koordinaten* elliptic (or ellipsoidal) coordinates; *schiefwinklige Koordinaten* oblique coordinates [*cf.* HOMOGEN; KARTESISCH; KRUMMLINIG; LOGARITHMISCH; NATÜRLICH; SPHÄRISCH; ZUORDNEN; ZYLINDRISCH]

Koordinaten·achse *f* coordinate axis, axis of coordinates [*cf.* DREHUNG; RICHTUNGSWINKEL]

Koordinaten·dreibein *n*, **Koordinaten·dreikant** *n* coordinate trihedral

Koordinaten·ebene *f* coordinate plane [*cf.* DURCHSTOSSPUNKT]

Koordinaten·netz *n* coordinate frame; (*einer Karte*) map grid

Koordinaten·system *n* coordinate system [*cf.* INERTIAL; LINKSGERICHTET; POL; URSPRUNG]

Koordinaten·transformation *f* transformation of coordinates

Koordinaten·ursprung *m* origin of coordinates

Koordinaten·vektor *m* coordinate vector

Kopf *m* head: *K. oder Adler, Schrift oder Wappen* (*einer Münze*) head(s) or tail(s) (of a coin); *K. der Reißschiene* head of a T-square; *ein Beispiel im K. ausrechnen* (*oder ausführen*) do an example mentally

Kopf·quote *f* per capita ratio (or rate)

Kopf·rechnen *n* mental arithmetic

Kopf·steuer *f* poll tax

ko·planar *adj.* coplanar

Korollar *n* corollary

Körper *m* 1. (*phys.*) body, solid [*cf.* BEWEGEN; FALLEN; HOMOGEN;

RUHE; SCHWERPUNKT; STARR]. 2. (*geom.*) solid, body [*cf.* BASIS; BASISFLÄCHE; BEGRENZUNGSFLÄCHE: GEOMETRISCH; HÖHE; HOMOGEN; INTEGRIERBAR; NETZ; OBERFLÄCHE; UMFANG; VERSCHNEIDUNG; ZERRUNG]. 3. (*alg.*) (*Zahlenkörper*) (number) field, (number) domain: *geordneter* (*oder angeordneter*) *K.* ordered field; *vollkommener* (*unvollkommener*) *K.* perfect (imperfect) field [*cf.* BEWERTET; EXPLIZIT; FORMAL-REELL; GALOISSCH; GRÖSSE; HAUPTORDNUNG; IRREDUZIBEL; KOMMUTATIV; KONJUGIERT; METAZYKLISCH; MINIMALBASIS; NORMAL; PERFEKT; REDUZIEREN; REELL-ABGESCHLOSSEN; TRANSZENDENT; VERSCHRÄNKT]

Körper·adjunktion *f* (*alg.*) field adjunction

Körper·diagonale *f* body diagonal [*ant.*: FLÄCHENDIAGONALE]

Körper·diskriminante *f* (*alg.*) field discriminant

Körper·element *n* (*alg.*) field element [*cf.* BETRAG]

Körper·erweiterung *f* (*alg.*) field extension

Körper·grad *m* (*alg.*) field degree

körper·lich *adj.* solid: *körperlicher Winkel, körperliche Ecke* solid angle

Körper·netz *n* (*geom.*) development of a solid

Körper·schaft *f* (*comm., fin.*) corporation [*cf.* SCHULDBRIEF; SCHULDSCHEIN]

Körper·stumpf *m* (*geom.*) prismatoid, prismoid

kor·rekt *adj.* correct
Korrekt·heit *f* correctness
Kor·rektur *f* correction
Kor·relation *f* correlation [*cf.*
KORRELATIONSINDEX; PARALLE-
LISMUS; VERKETTUNG]
Korrelations·fläche *f* (*statist.*) cor-
relation (or frequency) surface
Korrelations·index *m* (*statist.*) **1.**
(*allgemein* in general) index of
correlation. **2.** (*für nichtlineare
Korrelation*) coefficient of nonlinear correlation [*ant.:* KOR-
RELATIONSZIFFER]
Korrelations·koeffizient *m* (*statist.*)
correlation coefficient
Korrelations·tabelle *f* (*statist.*) correlation table [*cf.* FELD]
Korrelations·verhältnis *n* (*statist.*)
correlation ratio
Korrelations·ziffer *f* (*statist.*) coefficient of linear correlation
[*ant.:* KORRELATIONSINDEX]
kor·relativ *adj.* (*statist.*) correlative
kor·relieren *v.t.* (*statist.*) correlate
[*cf.* VERKETTEN]
korreliert *adj.* (*statist.*) correlated
Kor·respondenz *f* correspondence
kor·respondieren *v.i.* (*mit*) correspond (to): (*mit einander*) *kor-
respondierende Punkte* corresponding points; *korrespondie-
rende Winkel zweier Geraden
und einer Transversalen* corresponding angles of two lines and
a transversal [= GEGENWINKEL]
kor·rigieren *v.t.* correct
Ko·sekans *m* (*von* α) (*symb.:*
cosec α) [*cf.* KOSEKANTE, CO-
SECANS]
Ko·sekante *f* (*eines Winkels* α)
(*symb.:* cosec α) cosecant (of an

angle α) (symb.: csc α, cosec α)
[*cf.* COSECANS; KOSEKANS]
Kosekanten·linie *f* cosecant curve
Ko·sinus *m* (*eines Winkels* α)
cosine (of an angle α) (*symb.:*
cos α) [*cf.* COSINUS]
Kosinus·linie *f* cosine curve,
cosinusoid
Kosinusoide *f* [= KOSINUSLINIE]
Kosinus·satz *m* cosine law
Kosinus·tafel *f* table of (natural)
cosines
Kosinus·versus *m* (*eines Winkels*
α) versed cosine, coversed sine,
coversine (of an angle α) (*symb.:*
covers α ≡ 1 − sin α) [*cf.*COSINUS
VERSUS; VERSUS]
Kosten *pl.* (*comm.*) cost, expenses
[*cf.* KALKULATION]
Kosten·preis *m* (*comm.*) cost price
Kost·geschäft *n* (*fin.*) (*in Devisen*)
swap (of foreign exchange)
Ko·tangens *m* (*von* α) (*symb.:*
cot α, ctg α) [*cf.* COTANGENS;
KOTANGENTE]
Kotangens·linie *f* [= KOTANGEN-
TENLINIE]
Ko·tangente *f* (eines Winkels α)
(*symb.:* ctg α, cot α) cotangent
(of an angle α) (*symb.:* ctn α,
cot α) [*cf.* COTANGENS;
KOTANGENS]
Kotangenten·kurve *f*, **Kotangenten-
linie** *f* cotangent curve
Kote *f* (*auf der Karte*) spot height,
index number of altitude (on a
map); (*Applikate*) z-coordinate
kotieren *v.t.* (*eine Karte*) index (a
map) with spot hight (or
altitude) numbers; *kotierte Projektion* horizontal projection
(with index numbers of altitudes)

115

ko·variant *adj.* covàriant [*cf.*
INDEX; TENSOR]
Ko·variante *f* covariant
Ko·varianz *f* covariance
Ko·variation *f* covariation
Kraft *f* (*phys.*) **1.** (*Ursache der
Beschleunigung* cause of accelera-
tion) force. **2.** (*Energie*) energy,
power: *lebendige K.* kinetic
energy. [*cf.* ANGREIFEN; AUSÜBEN;
AUSÜBUNG; DREHMOMENT;
ELEKTROMOTORISCH; KONSERVA-
TIV; MOMENT²; RESULTANTE;
ÜBERTRAGBAR; ÜBERTRAGBAR-
KEIT; ÜBERTRAGEN; ZUSAMMEN-
SETZUNG]
Kraft·arm *m* (*phys.*) (*eines Hebels*)
lever arm to which the force is
applied [*ant.:* LASTARM]
Kräfte·funktion *f* (*phys.*) force
function
Kraft·einheit *f* (*phys.*) unit of force
Kräfte·paar *n* (*mech.*) (force)
couple
Kräfte·parallelogramm *n* (*mech.*)
parallelogram of forces
Kräfte·polygon *n* (*mech.*] polygon
of forces, force polygon
Kräfte·zerlegung *f* (*mech.*) de-
composition of forces
Kräfte·zusammensetzung *f* (*mech.*)
composition of forces
Kraft·feld *n* (*phys.*) field of force
Kraft·komponente *f* (*mech.*) com-
ponent (of) force
Kraft·lehre *f* (*phys.*) dynamics
Kraft·linie *f* (*phys*) line of force
Kraft·moment *n* (*mech.*) (*in bezug
auf einen Punkt*) moment of
force, turning moment (about
a point)
Kraft·polygon *n* (*mech.*) [=

KRÄFTEPOLYGON]
Kraft·röhre *f* (*phys.*) tube of force
Kraft·übertragung *f* (*phys.*, *mach.*)
power transmission
Kraft·vektor *m* (*mech.*) force
vector
Kraft·zentrum *n* (*phys.*) center of
force [*cf.* BEWEGUNG]
Kranken·versicherung *f* health
insurance
Kredit *m* (*comm.*, *fin.*) credit
[*cf.* TERMINKAUF]
Kredit·genossenschaft *f* (*comm.*)
mutual loan society
Kredit·grenze *f* (*comm.*) credit
line, line of credit
Kredit·würdigkeit *f* (*comm.*) credit,
solvency
Kreis *m* circle: *größter K. auf
einer Kugel* great circle on a
sphere [*cf.* ABSCHNITT; ABTRA-
GEN; ANGESCHRIEBEN; ANSCHREI-
BEN; AUSSCHNITT; AUSSEN;
BERÜHRUNGSSEHNE; BESCHREI-
BEN; DURCHDRINGEN; DURCH-
MESSER; EINSCHREIBEN; FEST;
FLÄCHENINHALT; GEHEN; HALB-
MESSER; INVERS; LIEGEN; OSKU-
LIEREN; POTENZ; POTENZLINIE;
POTENZPUNKT; POTENZZENTRUM;
QUADRATUR; RADIUS; SCHLA-
GEN; SCHMIEGEN; SEHNENVIER-
ECK; TANGENTENVIERECK; UM-
SCHREIBEN; ZENTRALE; ZENTRUM;
ZIRKEL]
Kreis·abschnitt *m* segment of a
circle
Kreis·ausschnitt *m* sector of a
circle
Kreis·bahn *f* circular orbit (or
track, or path)
Kreis·bewegung *f* circular motion

Kreis·bogen *m* arc of a circle, circular arc [*cf.* GRADEINTEILUNG]

Kreis·bündel *n* bundle (or sheaf) of circles

Kreis·büschel *n* pencil of circles

Kreis·diagramm *n* (*statist.*) circular graph (or chart), pie chart

Kreis·einteilung *f* circular graduation

Kreisel *m* (spinning) top, gyroscope

kreisen *v.i.* circle, circulate, revolve rotate; *kreisende Bewegung* circulatory (or circular) motion

Kreis·evolvente *f* involute of a circle

Kreis·fläche *f* circular area

kreis·förmig *adj.* circular: *kreisförmige Bewegung* circular motion [*cf.* KREISLAUF]

Kreis·funktion *f* circular (or trigonometric) function

Kreis·gleichung *f* equation of a circle

Kreis·inversion *f* circular inversion

Kreis·kegel *m* circular cone: *gerader, schiefer K.* right, oblique circular cone

Kreis·konchoide *f* conchoid of a circle, Pascal's limaçon [*cf.* SCHNECKE: *Pascalsche Sch.*]

Kreis·körper *m* (*alg.*) cyclotomic field

Kreis·lauf *m* **1.** (*kreisförmige Bewegung*) circular course, circulation [*cf.* UMLAUF; UMLAUFEN]. **2.** (*zyklische Bewegung*) cycle

Kreis·linie *f* circular line, circle

Kreis·messung *f* cyclometry

Kreis·polarisation *f* (*phys.*) circular polarization

Kreis·prozeß *m* cyclic process

Kreis·punkt *m* **1.** (*Punkt eines Kreises*) point of a circle. **2.** (*K. einer Fläche*) circular point (on a surface)

Kreis·rechenschieber *m* circular slide rule

Kreis·ring *m* circular ring, annulus [*cf.* RING]

kreis·rund *adj.* circular

Kreis·schnitt *m* circular section

Kreis·segment *n* segment of a circle

Kreis·sektor *m* sector of a circle

Kreis·teilung *f* **1.** (*in gleiche Teile* division into equal parts) cyclotomy. **2.** (*Einteilung*) circular graduation

Kreisteilungs·gleichung *f* cyclotomic equation

Kreisteilungs·körper *m* (*alg.*) cyclotomic field

Kreisteilungs·polynom *n* (*alg.*) cyclotomic polynomial

Kreis·umfang *m* periphery (or perimeter, or circumference) of a circle [*cf.* ABSCHNEIDEN]

Kreis·verwandtschaft *f* correspondence mapping circles into circles, and straight lines into straight lines

Kreis·viereck *n* [=SEHNENVIERECK]

Kreis·zweieck *n* lune, crescent [*cf.* MÖNDCHEN]

Kreis·zylinder *m* circular cylinder: *gerader (schiefer) K.* right (oblique) circular cylinder

Kreuz *n* cross [*cf.* MULTIPLIZIEREN]

kreuzen *v.t. v.recip.:* **sich** (*oder einander*) *k.* cross, intersect

kreuz·förmig *adj.* cruciform

Kreuz·kurve *f* cross curve

Kreuz·riß *m* [=SEITENRISS]

Kreuzriß·ebene *f* [=SEITENRISS-

EBENE] [*cf.* PROJEKTIONSEBENE]
kreuz·weise *adj.* crosswise [*cf.*
MULTIPLIZIEREN]
Kristall *m* crystal
Kristall·fläche *f* face (or facet) of
a crystal
Kristallo·graphie *f* crystallography
kristallo·graphisch *adj.* crystallo-
graphic(al)
Kristallo·metrie *f* crystallometry
kristallo·metrisch *adj.* crystallo-
metric
Kristall·system *n* system of crystallization, crystal (or crystallo-
graphic) system [*cf.* HEXAGO-
NAL]
Kriterium *n* (*pl. Kriteria*) criterion,
test: *K. für die Konvergenz oder
Divergenz einer Reihe* test of the
convergence or divergence of a
series
kritisch *adj.* critical: (*phys.*) *kritischer Punkt einer Substanz*
critical point of a substance;
kritischer Druck critical pressure;
kritische Temperatur critical temperature
krumm *adj.* curved; (*verdreht*)
twisted; (*Fläche, auch*) warped
(surface) [*cf.* FLÄCHE; LINIE;
MANTEL]
krümmen *v.t., v.r.:* **sich** *k.* bend,
wind [*cf.* GEKRÜMMT]
krumm·flächig *adj.* (with) curved
(surface)
krumm·linig *adj.* curvilinear:
krummlinige Koordinaten curvilinear coordinates [*cf.* BE-
WEGUNG]
Krumm·stab *m* (*Kurve*) lituus
[=LITUUS]
Krümmung *f* curvature: (*erste*) *K.*

einer Raumkurve first curvature
of a space curve; *Torsion* (*oder
Windung oder zweite K.*) *einer
Raumkurve* torsion (or second
curvature) of a space curve;
Gaußsche K. einer Fläche Gaussian (or total) curvature of a
surface; *Riemannsche K.* Rie-
mannian curvature [*cf.* ANTIKLA-
STISCH; GEODÄTISCH; SYNKLA-
STISCH]
Krümmungs·achse *f* (*einer Raumkurve*) axis of curvature (of a
space curve) [=POLARE 2.]
Krümmungs·kreis *m* (*einer Kurve*)
circle of curvature, osculating
circle (of a curve) [*cf.* AN-
SCHMIEGUNG]
Krümmungs·linie *f* (*einer Fläche*)
line of curvature (of a surface)
Krümmungs·mittelpunkt *m* center
of curvature
Krümmungsmittelpunkts·kurve *f*,
Krümmungsmittelpunkts·linie *f*
evolute [=EVOLUTE]
Krümmungs·radius *m* radius of
curvature
Kubatur *f* cubature
kubier·bar *adj.* 1. (*geom.: Körper*)
(solid) whose volume can be
determined; (*integrierbar*) integrable (solid). 2. (*math.: Zahl,
Ausdruck*) (number, expression)
whose cube can be determined
[*cf.* INTEGRIERBAR]
kubieren *v.t.* 1. (*math.: zur dritten
Potenz erheben*) cube, raise to
the third power. 2. (*geom.:
einen Körper*) cube, determine
the volume of (a solid)
Kubierung *f* 1. (*math.: einer Zahl*)
cubing (of a number), raising (a

number) to the third power.
2. (*geom.: eines Körpers*) cubature, cubage

Kubik·dezimeter *n* (*abbr.* cdm, dm³) cubic decimeter (or decimetre), (*abbr.* cub. dm.)

Kubik·fuß *m* (*meas.*) cubic foot, (*abbr.* cub. ft.)

Kubik·inhalt *m* cubic contents, volume

Kubik·kilometer *n* (*abbr.* ckm. km³) cubic kilometer (or kilometre), (*abbr.* cub. km.)

Kubik·maß *n* cubic measure

Kubik·meter *n* (*abbr.* cbm, m³) cubic meter (or metre), (*abbr.* cub. m.)

Kubik·millimeter *n* (*abbr.* cmm, mm³) cubic millimeter (or millimetre), (*abbr.* cub. mm.)

Kubik·myriameter *n* (*abbr.* cbμm, μm³) cubic myriameter

Kubik·wurzel *f* cube root

Kubik·yard *n* cubic yard, (*abbr.* cub. yd.)

Kubik·zahl *f* cube, cubic number

Kubik·zentimeter *n* (*abbr.* ccm, cm³) cubic centimeter (or centimetre), (*abbr.* cub. cm.)

Kubik·zoll *m* cubic inch, (*abbr.* cub. inch)

kubisch *adj.* cubic, cubical: *kubische Gleichung* cubic (equation); (*alg.*) *kubische Resolvente* cubic resolvent; *kubischer Kegelschnitt* cubic conic (section); *kubische Ellipse, Hyperbel, Parabel* cubical ellipse, hyperbola, parabola; (*phys.*) *kubische Ausdehnung* cubical expansion; [*cf.* FORM; LÖSUNG; PARABEL]

Kubus *m* (*Würfel* hexahedron;

dritte Potenz third power) cube

Kubus·verdopp(e)lung *f* duplication of the cube

Kugel *f* sphere, globe [*cf.* DURCH-DRINGEN; DURCHMESSER; GROSS-KREIS; HALBMESSER; HAUPT-KREIS; KLEINKREIS; KREIS; POTENZ; POTENZEBENE; POTENZ-PUNKT; POTENZZENTRUM; RADIUS; ZENTRALE; ZWICKEL]

Kugel·abschnitt *m* spherical segment

Kugel·ausschnitt *m* spherical sector

Kugel·bündel *n* bundle (or sheaf) of spheres

Kugel·büschel *n* pencil of spheres

Kugel·dreieck *n* spherical triangle

Kugel·fläche *f* spherical surface [*cf.* KUGELOBERFLÄCHE]

kugel·förmig *adj.* spherical, globular

Kugel·funktion *f* spherical function

Kugel·geometrie *f* spherical geometry

Kugel·haube *f* spherical cap

kugelig *adj.* spherical, globular

Kugel·inversion *f* spherical inversion

Kugel·kalotte *f* spherical cap

Kugel·kappe *f* spherical cap

Kugel·keil *m* spherical wedge (or ungula)

Kugel·koordinate *f* spherical coordinate

Kugel·mütze *f* spherical cap

Kugel·oberfläche *f* (*Kugelfläche*) spherical surface, surface of a sphere; (*Oberflächeninhalt*) surface (area) of a sphere

Kugel·pendel *n* spherical pendulum

Kugel·schale *f* spherical shell

Kugel·schar *f* family of spheres

Kugel·schicht *f* spherical segment (of two bases)
Kugel·segment *n* spherical segment (of one base)
Kugel·sektor *m* spherical sector
Kugel·welle *f* spherical wave
Kugel·zone *f* spherical zone
Kugel·zweieck *n* spherical lune
Kulmination *f* (*astr.*) culmination
Kulminations·punkt *m* culminating point
kulminieren *v.i.* (*astr.*) culminate
Kulminierung *f* culmination
Kunden·akzept *n* (*comm.*) trade acceptance
Kupon *m* (*comm.*) coupon
Kurs *m* 1. (*Lauf*) course. 2. (*fin.*: *Börsennotierung*) quotation, rate, price (at the stock exchange) [*cf.* ABSCHLAGEN; ANZIEHEN]
Kurs·entwicklung *f* (*comm.*) trend of quotations (or prices)
Kurs·schwankung *f* (*comm., fin.*) price fluctuation, variation in price (or rate, or quotation)
Kurs·streichung *f* (*comm.*) (*an der Börse*) non-quotation (at the stock exchange)
Kurve *f* curve: *ebene K.* plane curve [*cf.* SCHMIEGUNGSKREIS; WINDUNG]; *Bogenlänge einer K.* curve length; *linksgängige* (*oder linksgewundene oder linkswendige*) *Kurve* left-handed (or sinistrorse) curve, sinistrorsum; *rechtsgewundene* (*oder rechtsgängige oder rechtswendige*) *Kurve* dextrorse curve, dextrorsum [*cf.* ABRUNDEN; ABRUNDUNG; ABWICKELN; ABWICKLUNG; ANALLAGMATISCH; ANPASSUNG; ANSCHMIEGEN; ANSCHMIEGUNG;

ARITHMETISCH; AST; AUSGLEICHUNG; AUSZEICHNEN; BALLISTISCH; BEREICH; BERÜHRENDE; BESTIMMEN; BIRNFÖRMIG; BOGENELEMENT; CARTESISCH; CASSINISCH; DARSTELLEN; DOPPELPUNKT; DOPPELTLOGARITHMISCH; DRITT; ECKPUNKT; EINHÜLLEN; EINPASSEN; EINZEICHNEN; EXTREMPUNKT; GALTON; GESCHLOSSEN; GEWÖHNLICH; GLÄTTEN; GLÄTTUNG; GRAD; HÖHER; INTEGRIERBAR; INVERS; ISOLIERT; ISOPTISCH; KARTESISCH; KNICK; KNOTENPUNKT; KRÜMMUNGSKREIS; LISSAJOUS; LOGARITHMISCH; NORMALE; PARABOLISCH; PARAMETRISCH; RATIONAL; REKTIFIZIEREN; SCHEITEL; SCHLEIFE; SCHLINGE; SCHMIEGEN; SCHNABEL; SELBSTBERÜHRUNGSPUNKT; SINGULÄR; SPITZE; STEINER; SYMMETRIEACHSE; TANGENTE; VERLAUF; VERLAUFEN; VIERT; VIVIANI; WENDETANGENTE; WENDUNG; ZEICHNEN; ZWEIG; ZWEIT]
Kurven·anpassung *f* curve fitting
Kurven·bogen *m* arc of a curve [*cf.* LÄNGE]
Kurven·bündel *n* bundle (or sheaf) of curves
Kurven·büschel *n* pencil of curves
Kurven·darstellung *f* curve plotting
Kurven·glättung *f* curve smoothing
Kurven·gleichung *f* equation of a curve [*cf.* NATÜRLICH]
Kurven·lineal *n* curved ruler, curve
Kurven·linie *f* curved line, curve
Kurven·messer *m* curvometer
Kurven·papier *n* graph (or scale) paper

Kurven·punkt *m* point of a curve [*cf.* NORMALENLÄNGE; TANGENTENLÄNGE]
Kurven·schar *f* family of curves
Kurven·schiefe *f* (*statist.*) (*der Häufigkeitskurve*) curve skewness, allokurtosis (of the frequency curve)
Kurven·stück *n* segment of a curve
Kurven·zerlegung *f* (*statist.*) analysis (or decomposition) of a time series
kurz *adj.* short
kürzen *v.t.* reduce, cancel: *einen Bruch* (*durch einen Faktor*) *k.* reduce a fraction (by a factor); *wir kürzen diesen Bruch* (*oder: Zähler und Nenner dieses Bruches*) *durch zwei* we cancel two out of (the numerator and denominator

of) this fraction; *einen Bruch k.* (*oder vereinfachen*) reduce a fraction to its lowest terms.
kurz·fristig *adj.* short-term [*ant.:* LANGFRISTIG]
Kürzung *f* reduction, cancellation: *K. eines Bruches* reduction of a fraction to lower terms; *K.* (*des Zählers und Nenners*) *eines Bruches durch eine Zahl* cancellation of a number out of (numerator and denominator of) a fraction; *nach* (*der*) *K. lautet der Bruch* after cancellation the fraction reads
Kurz·welle *f* (*phys.*) shortwave
kurz·wellig *adj.* (*phys.*) shortwave
kW (*abbr.*) *Kilowatt* kilowatt, (*abbr.*) kw
kWh, kWst (*abbr.*) *Kilowattstunde* kilowatt hour, (*abbr.*) kwh

L

labil *adj.* unstable, instable, labile [*cf.* GLEICHGEWICHT]
Labilität *f* instability, unstability, lability
laden *v.t.* charge, load
Laden·preis *m* selling (or retail) price
Ladung *f* charge [*cf.* LADUNGSGEWICHT]
Ladungs·dichte *f* (*phys.*) density of charge
Ladungs·fähigkeit *f* (*nach Volumen*) cubic capacity; (*nach Gewicht*) tonnage
Ladungs·gewicht *n* 1. (*Gewicht der Ladung*) useful (or paying) load

[*ant.:* EIGENGEWICHT]. 2. (*Fassungskraft*) freight capacity, tonnage
Lage *f* 1. (*Stellung*) (*z.B. eines Punktes*) position, location (e.g. of a point) [*cf.* ENERGIE; FESTHEIT; GEOMETRIE; MITTELWERT; ORT; PERSPEKTIV]. 2. (*Papiermaß* paper measure) (=5 *Bogen*) gathering (of 5 sheets)
Lage(n)beziehung *f* topological relation
Lager·bestand *m* (*comm.*) [= INVENTAR]; *den L. aufnehmen* [=INVENTARISIEREN]
Lage·regel *f* (*statist.*) (*der Mit-*

telwerte) position rule (of averages)

Lagrange *m. N.* [*cf.* FUNKTION]

Lambda *n* (*griechischer Buchstabe* Greek letter *Λ λ*) lambda

Land·karte *f* map; (*Seekarte*) chart [*cf.* HÖHENKOTE; VERMITTELND]

Land·maß *n* (land) surveyor's measure

lang *adj.* long [*cf.* ANGREIFEN]

Länge *f* **1.** (*lineare Abmessung* linear dimension) length: *L. einer Strecke, eines Rechtecks* length of a line segment, of a rectangle; *L. eines Kurvenbogens* length of arc (or arc length) of a curve [*cf.* REKTIFIZIEREN]; (*alg.*) *L. einer Normalreihe* length of a normal series [*cf.* WAHR]. **2.** (*geog.*) longitude: *geographische L.* (geographic) longitude [*cf.* EINHEITSKREIS; ERZEUGENDE; GEOGRAPHISCH; LÄNGENUNTERSCHIED; TANGENTE; VERLÄNGERN]

Längen·ausdehnung *f* **1.** (*Dimension*) linear dimension. **2.** (*Dehnung*) elongation

Längen·dimension *f* linear dimension

Längen·einheit *f* unit (of) length, standard of length

Längen·grad *m* (*geog.*) degree of longitude

Längen·kreis *m* circle (or meridian) of longitude

Längen·maß *n* linear measure [*cf.* BOGENLÄNGE]

längen·treu *adj.* length-preserving, equidistant

Längen·treue *f* (*einer Abbildung*) preservation of length (of a map)

Längen·unterschied *m* **1.** (*linearer Unterschied*) difference in length. **2.** (*Unterschied der geographischen Länge*) difference in longitude; *L. zweier Meridiane* departure between two meridians

lang·fristig *adj.* (*fin.*) long-term [*ant.:* KURZFRISTIG]: *langfristige Außenstände* long-term accounts receivable

länglich *adj.* elongated, oblong

länglich·rund *adj.* oval

Längs·achse *f* longitudinal axis

Längs·doma *n* (*pl. Längsdomen*) (*cryst.*) brachydome

Längs·profil *n* longitudinal profile

Längs·schnitt *m* longitudinal section

Längs·schwingung *f* (*phys.*) longitudinal oscillation (or vibration)

Längs·welle *f* (*phys.*) longitudinal wave

Lang·welle *f* (*phys.*) long wave

lang·wellig *adj.* (*phys.*) longwave

Last *f* (*mech.*) load [*cf.* BELASTUNG; HEBEN]

Last·arm *m* (*mech.*) (*eines Hebels*) lever arm to which the load is applied [*ant.:* KRAFTARM]

lasten·frei *adj.* (*comm.*) unencumbered [*cf.* SCHULDENFREI]

latent *adj.* latent

Latenz *f* latency

Lauf *m* course, run: *L. der Planeten um die Sonne* course of the planets around the sun [*cf.* KURS 1.]

laufen *v.i.* run: (*um ein Zentrum*) revolve (about a center): (*comm.*) *laufende Ausgaben* running (or current) expenses; *laufende Rechnung, laufendes Konto* current account; (*bei einem Kaufhaus*) charge account (with a department store); *laufende Notierung an der Börse* consecutive quotation (at the stock exchange); *laufende Dividende, Zinsen* accrued dividend, interest; *laufende Wechsel* notes in circulation; *das laufende Quartal* the present quarter; *laufende Nummer* serial number [*cf.* PARALLEL]

Läufer *m* (*des Rechenschiebers*) cursor (of slide rule)

Lauf·zeit *f* (*comm.*) (*eines Wechsels*) term (or time) of a draft

Lebens·dauer *f* (*statist.*) duration of life, life span; *mutmaßliche L.* life expectancy

Lebenshaltungs·index *m* (*statist.*) cost-of-living index

lebens·länglich *adj.* life(long): (*ins.*) *lebenslängliche Rente* life annuity, perpetuity

Lebens·rente *f* (*ins.*) life annuity [= LEIBRENTE]

Lebens·versicherung *f* life insurance, *Br.* life assurance [*cf.* VERSICHERUNG]

Lebensversicherung·polizze *f* life insurance policy, (whole) life policy

Lebens·wahrscheinlichkeit *f* (*ins.*) life expectancy

leer *adj.* empty, null, vacant, void: *leere Menge* empty (or null) set; *leerer Raum* empty space, vacuum

Leere *f* emptiness, void

Leer·gewicht *n* (*comm.*) dead weight

Leer·heit *f* emptiness

Leer·stelle *f* (*log.*) (*eines Funktionszeichens*) argument place (of

a functional symbol):*Funktionszeichen mit n Leerstellen* functional symbol with *n* argument places, *n*-place (or *n*-adic) functional symbol [*cf.* DREISTELLIG; EINSTELLIG; FÜNFSTELLIG; . . . STELLIG; VIELSTELLIG; VIERSTELLIG; ZWEISTELLIG]

legen *v.t.* lay, put, place, pass: *eine Ebene durch einen Punkt l.* pass a plane through a point

Lege·verfahren *n* (*statist.*) hand sorting

Lehre[1] *f* (*Theorie*) teachings, theory, doctrine [*c.f* LICHT; SCHALL]

Lehre[2] *f* (*Maß*) gauge

Lehr·satz *m* proposition, theorem, thesis, law, lemma [*cf.* BINOMISCH; GEGENSEHNENSATZ; PTOLEMÄISCH; PYTHAGORÄISCH; SATZ]

Leib·rente *f* (*ins.*) life annuity [= LEBENSRENTE]

leihen *v.t.* (*fin.*) loan

Leih·kapital *n* (*fin.*) loaned capital, loan

leisten *v.t.* (*Arbeit*) perform, do, put out (work); (*eine Zahlung*) make, render (a payment) [*cf.* ARBEIT; LEISTUNG; RÜCKZAHLUNG; ZURÜCKZAHLEN]

Leistung *f* **1.** (*von Arbeit*) achievement, performance, output (of work); (*phys.: geleistete Arbeit*) power, rate of work done. **2.** (*einer Zahlung*) making, rendering (of a payment). **3.** (*eines Dienstes*) service [*cf.* VALUTA 4.]

leistungs·fähig *adj.* efficient

Leistungs·fähigkeit *f* efficiency

Leit·ebene *f* (*einer windschiefen*

Regelfläche) director plane, plane
director (óf a warped surface)
leiten *v.t.* (*phys.*) (*z.B. Wärme*)
conduct (e.g, heat)
Leiter *m* (*phys.*) conductor
Leiter *f* (*Skala*) scale; (*Steigleiter*)
ladder
Leiter·tafel *f* alignment chart,
nomogram, nomograph
leit·fähig *adj.* (*phys.*) conductive,
conducting
Leitfähig·keit *f* conductivity
Leit·kegel *m* (*einer windschiefen
Regelfläche*) director cone, cone
director (of a warped surface)
Leit·kreis *m* **1.** (*einer Ellipse*)
circle around one focus with
radius equal to the major axis.
2. (*einer Hyperbel*) circle around
one focus with radius equal to
the transverse axis
Leit·linie *f* directrix
Leit·strahl *m* **1.** (*eines Kegelschnittpunktes*) focal radius (or
distance) (of a point of a conic).
2. (*Ortsvektor*) radius vector
Lemniskate *f* lemniscate
letzt *adj.* last [*cf.* VIERTEL; WEG-
FALLEN]
lexiko·graphisch *adj.* lexico-
graphic(al): *lexikographische
Ordnung* lexicographic order
Libelle *f* level
Libration *f* (*astr.*) libration
Licht *n* (*opt.*) light: *Lehre vom L.*
theory of light, optics
licht *adj.* **1.** (*hell*) bright. **2.**
(*inner*) inside: *lichter Durchmesser, lichte Weite* inside diameter (or width)
Licht·äther *m* (*opt.*) luminiferous
ether

Licht·druck *m* (*phys.*) light pressure
licht·elektrisch *adj.* (*phys.*) photoelectric
Licht·elektrizität *f* (*phys.*) photoelectricity
Licht·fortpflanzung *f* (*opt.*) light
transmission
Licht·geschwindigkeit *f* (*phys.*)
velocity of light
Licht·intensität *f* (*opt.*) intensity
of light
Licht·quantum *n* (*phys.*) light
quantum, photon
Licht·quelle *f* (*opt.*) light source
Licht·stärke *f* (*opt.*) intensity of
light
Licht·strahl *m* (*opt.*) light ray
Licht·theorie *f* (*phys.*) theory of
light: *elektromagnetische L.* electromagnetic theory of light
Licht·welle *f* (*phys.*) light wave
liegen *v.i.* lie, be situated: *der
Flächeninhalt eines Kreises liegt
zwischen den Flächeninhalten der
ein- und umgeschriebenen Vielecke*
the area of a circle lies between
the areas of inscribed and circumscribed polygons [*cf.*
ÄHNLICH; EBENE; GELEGEN]
Limes *m* limit: *unterer L., L.
inferior* (*einer Menge*) inferior
limit, limit inferior (of a set);
oberer L., L. superior (*einer
Menge*) superior limit, limit
superior (of a set) [*cf.* GRENZ-
WERT]
Lineal *n* ruler, rule, straightedge
[*cf.* ANLEGEN; KONSTRUKTION]
linear *adj.* linear, line: (*alg.*)
l. abhängig (*unabhängig*) linearly
dependent (independent); *lineare
Gleichung* linear (or simple) equa-

tion; *lineare Ausdehnung* a. (*Erweiterung*) linear expansion, b. (*Dimension*) linear dimension; *linearer Ausdehnungskoeffizient* coefficient of linear expansion; *linearer Wert* linear (or line) value; (*alg.*) *linearer Raum* linear space [*cf.* BASIS 3.]; [*cf.* AUSDEHNUNG; AUSTAUSCHSATZ; EXZENTRIZITÄT; FAST; GENERELL; HÜLLE; LÄNGE; LÄNGENUNTERSCHIED; MATRIX; MOMENT²; TRANSFORMATION]

Linear·form *f* (*alg.*) linear form

Linearformen·modul *m* (*alg.*) module of linear forms: *n-gliedriger L.* n-termed module of linear forms, n-dimensional vector space

Linear·funktion *f* (*alg.*) linear function

Linear·gleichung *f* linear equation

Linearität *f* linearity

Linear·kombination *f* (*alg.*) linear combination

Linear·perspektive *f* linear perspective

Linie *f* 1. (*Kurve*) line, curve; *gerade L.* (straight) line; (*gezeichnete* drawn line, also) rule; *mit geraden Linien versehen* rule(d); *krumme L.* curved line, curve; *in einer L. mit* in a line with, in alignment with, flush with [*cf.* AUSGEZOGEN; AUSZIEHEN; CASSINISCH; DIVERGENZ; DREIFACH-RECHTWINKLIG; GEBROCHEN; GEODÄTISCH; GERADE; GERADHEIT; GESTRICHELT; GLEICHLAUF; GLEICHLAUFEN; GLEICHLAUFEND; ISOBARISCH; LOGARITHMISCH;

LOXODROMISCH; MATERIELL; PUNKT; PUNKTIEREN; SCHLEIFSCHNITT; SCHRAUBENFÖRMIG; STRICH; STRICHPUNKTIERT; SYSTEM; UNGERADE; UNGERADHEIT; VERLÄNGERN; VOLLAUSGEZOGEN; WÖLBEN; WÖLBUNG; ZIEHEN; ZIEHUNG; ZUSAMMENSTELLUNG]. 2. (*Längenmaß* measure of length) ($= \frac{1}{12} Zoll$) line ($= \frac{1}{12}$ inch)

Linien·diagramm *n* (*statist.*) (broken) line chart (or graph)

Linien·geometrie *f* line geometry

Linien·integral *n* line integral

Linien·koordinate *f* line coordinate

Linien·perspektive *f* linear perspective

Linien·spektrum *n* (*phys.*) line spectrum

linieren, liniieren *v.t.* rule

link *adj.* left, left-hand: *linke Seite* left side [*cf.* SEITE]

links *adv.* on (or to) the left

Links·ansicht *f* left-side view

Links·drall *m* left-handed twist

links·drehend *adj.* (*phys*) levorotatory

Links·drehung *f* left-handed rotation, levorotation

links·gängig *adj.* left-handed, sinistrorse [*cf.* KURVE]

links·gelegen *adj.* left, left-hand

links·gerichtet *adj.* left-handed: *linksgerichtetes Koordinatensystem, Dreikant* left-handed coordinate system, trihedral

Links·gewinde *n* (*einer Schraube*) left-handed thread (of a screw)

links·gewunden *adj.* left-handed, sinistrorse [*cf.* KURVE]

Links·ideal *n* (*alg.*) left ideal
Links·inverse *f,* **Links·inverse(s)** *n* left inverse
links·schief *adj.* (*statist.*) (*Häufig-keïtskurve*) skew to the right, positively skew (frequency curve) [*cf.* LINKSSTEIL]
links·seitig *adj.* left, left-hand, on the left [*cf.* ASYMMETRISCH; GRENZWERT; IDEAL; STETIG]
links·steil *adj.* [= LINKSSCHIEF]
links·wendig *adj.* left-handed, sinistrorse [*cf.* KURVE]
Linse *f* (*opt.*) lens [*cf.* KONKAV-KONVEX; KONVEXKONKAV]
liquid *adj.* (*comm.*) liquid [*cf.* AKTIVUM]
Lissajous *m N. Lissajoussche Kurven* (*oder Figuren*) Lissajous (or Bowditch) curves (or figures)
Listen·preis *m* (*comm.*) list price
Liter *n* or *m* (*abbr.* l) liter, litre (*abbr.* l.)
Lituus *m* (*Kurve*) lituus [= KRUMM-STAB]
Lobatschewskij *m N.* Lobachevski [*cf.* GEOMETRIE]
Loch *n* hole
Loch·karte *f* punch card [*cf.* ZÄHLBLATT]
Logarithmen·papier *n* (full-)log-arithmic coordinate paper; *L. mit halblogarithmischer Teilung* (*oder: mit logarithmischer Teilung auf nur einer Achse*) semi-logarithmic (coordinate) paper, ratio paper
Logarithmen·system *n* system of logarithms, logarithmic system [*cf.* MODUL]
Logarithmen·tafel *f* logarithm (or logarithmic) table [*cf.* NACH-SCHLAGEN; TAFELDIFFERENZ]
logarithmieren *v.t.* (*eine Zahl*) take the logarithm of (a number)
logarithmisch *adj.* logarithmic: *logarithmische Gleichung* logarith-mic equation; *logarithmische Linie* logarithmic curve; *logarith-mische Funktion, Reihe* logarith-mic function, series; *logarith-mische Koordinaten* logarithmic coordinates; *logarithmische Skala* (*oder Teilung*) logarithmic scale; (*statist.*) *logarithmische* (*oder geometrische*) *Kurve* semilogarithmic chart (or graph) [*cf.* DEKREMENT; EINTEILUNG; FUNKTION; LOGARITHMENPAPIER; SPIRALE]
Logarithmus *m* (*einer Zahl m*) logarithm (of a number *m*): *L.* (*von*) *m* logarithm (of) *m* (*symb.:* log *m*); *Briggsscher* (*oder dekadischer*) *L.* Briggs' (or Brigg-sian, or common) logarithm; *Nepersche* (*oder Napiersche*) *Lo-garithmen* Naperian logarithms; *L. des reziproken Werts einer Zahl* cologarithm of a number [= MITLOGARITHMUS]; *natürlicher* (*oder hyperbolischer*) *L.* natural (or hyperbolic) logarithm; *L. sinus von* α logarithmic sine of α (*symb.:* log sin α) [*cf.* BASIS; CHARAKTERISTIK; FÜNFSTELLIG; MANTISSE; ZEHNERLOGARITHMUS]
Logik *f* logic: *symbolische* (*oder theoretische oder mathematische*) *L., Algebra der L.* [= LOGIK-KALKÜL; LOGISTIK] symbolic (or mathematical) logic, logistic, algebra of logic, logical calculus
Logiker *m* logician

Logik·kalkül *m* logical calculus, symbolic (or mathematical) logic, logistic, algebra of logic [= LOGISTIK]; [*cf.* LOGIK]

logisch *adj.* logical: *logische Summe* logical sum, conjunction; *logisches Produkt* logical product, disjunction; *logische Gleichung* logical equation [*cf.* GLIED; MITTELBEGRIFF; RECHNERISCH; WIRKUNGSBEREICH; ZIRKEL]

Logistik *f* logistic, symbolic (or mathematical) logic, algebra of logic, logical calculus [= LOGIK-KALKÜL]; [*cf.* LOGIK]

Lohn·satz *m* (*comm.*) rate of wages

lombardieren *v.t.* (*comm.*) pledge, pawn

Lombardierung *f* (*comm.*) pledging, pawning

longitudinal *adj.* longitudinal

Longitudinale *f* (*Kurve*) catenary of uniform strength [*cf.* KETTENLINIE]

Longitudinalität *f* longitudinality

Longitudinal·schwingung *f* (*phys.*) longitudinal oscillation (or vibration)

Longitudinal·welle *f* (*phys.*) longitudinal wave

lös·bar *adj.* solvable, soluble

Lösbar·keit *f* solvability

lösen *v.t.* **1.** (*eine Aufgabe*) solve (a problem). **2.** (*einen Knoten*) untie, disentangle (a knot) [*cf.* KNOTEN]

Lösung *f* solution: *kardanische L. der kubischen Gleichung* Cardan's solution of the cubic [*cf.* ALLGEMEIN; BESONDER; PROBE; NICHTTRIVIAL; SINGULÄR; TRIVIAL; VERDÜNNEN; VERDÜNNUNG]

Lot *n* **1.** (*Bleilot*) plumb. **2.** (*Normale*) normal, perpendicular

lot·recht *adj.* vertical, perpendicular, plumb [*cf.* GERADE; SENKRECHT]

Loxo·drome *f* loxodrome, rhumb (line), spherical helix

loxo·dromisch *adj.* loxodromic(al), rhumb: *loxodromische Linie* loxodromic line (or spiral, or curve), rhumb line

Ludolph *m* N.: *Ludolphische Zahl* Ludolphian (or Ludolph's) number (= π)

Lumen *n* (*opt. meas.*) lumen

Lux *n* (*opt. meas.*) lux, meter candle [= METERKERZE]

M

Mäander *m* meander, Greek fret (or key pattern)

Mächtigkeit *f* (*einer Zahlenmenge*) cardinality, cardinal number, manyness, potency, power (of a set of numbers)

Maclaurin *m* N. [*cf.* REIHE]

magisch *adj.* magic [*cf.* QUADRAT]

Magnet *m* (*phys.*) magnet

Magnetismus *m* (*phys.*) magnetism

Majorante *f* (*einer Punktmenge*)

majorant, upper bound (of a set of points)

Majorität *f* majority

Makler *m* (*comm.*) broker

Makler·gebühr *f* (*comm.*) brokerage

Makro·achse *f* (*cryst.*) macroaxis, macrodiagonal axis

makro·diagonal *adj.* (*cryst.*) macrodiagonal

Makro·diagonale *f* (*cryst.*) macrodiagonal (axis) [= MAKROACHSE]

Makro·doma *n* (*pl. Makrodomen*) (*cryst.*) macrodome

Makro·pinakoid *n* (*cryst.*) macropinacoid, macropinakoid

Makro·prisma *n* (*cryst.*) macroprism

Makro·pyramide *f* (*cryst.*) macropyramid

mal, Mal *n* times, (multiplied) by: *minus m. minus gibt plus* minus (multiplied) by minus gives plus [*cf.* IST]

... mal *num. suf.* times [*cf.* ACHTMAL; DREIMAL; EINMAL; FÜNFMAL; NEUNMAL; SECHSMAL; SIEBENMAL; VIERMAL; ZEHNMAL; ZWEIMAL]

... malig *adj.suf.* done ... times [*cf.* ACHTMALIG; DREIMALIG; EINMALIG; FÜNFMALIG; NEUNMALIG; SECHSMALIG; SIEBENMALIG; VIERMALIG; ZEHNMALIG; ZWEIMALIG]

Mal·zeichen *n* sign of multiplication

mangel·haft *adj.* defective, deficient [*cf.* ZAHL]

mannig·faltig *adj.* (*vielfach*) manifold; (*vielfältig*) varied [*cf.* VIELFÄLTIG]

Mannigfaltig·keit *f* (*Vielfachheit*) manifold: (*Vielfältigkeit*)

variety: *dreidimensionale M.* three-dimensional manifold [*cf.* ALLGEMEIN]

Mantel *m* **1.** (*eines Zylinders, Kegels, einer Pyramide*) lateral area (of a cylinder, cone, pyramid). **2.** (*Schale einer krummen Fläche*) sheet (of a curved surface)

Mantel·fläche *f* [= MANTEL]

Mantel·linie *f* (*eines Zylinders, Kegels*) element (or ruling) of a cylinder, cone [= ZYLINDERERZEUGENDE; KEGELERZEUGENDE]

Mantisse *f* (*eines Logarithmus*) mantissa (of a logarithm)

Marken·klebeverfahren *n* (*statist.*) code stamp method of tabulation

Markt *m* (*comm.*) market

Markt·wert *m* (*comm.*) market value

Maschine *f* machine [*cf.* FABRIKATIONSNUMMER]

Maß *n* **1.** (*Maßgröße*) measure; (*Teiler, auch*) divisor; (*Einheit*) unit: *größtes gemeinsames M.* greatest common measure (or divisor) [= *größter gemeinsamer* TEILER]; *mit einen gemeinsamen M., mit demselben M. meßbar* commensurable; *M. einer Punktmenge* measure of a point set [*cf.* EINHEIT; GEMEINSAM; GEMEINSCHAFTLICH; STATISTISCH]. **2.** (*Verhältnis*) rate, ratio; (*Grenzmaß*) limit: *M. der Veränderung* rate of change [*cf.* ÜBERSCHREITEN]. **3.** (*Meßgerät*) measure, gauge [*cf.* LEHRE²]

Maß·analyse *f* (*chem.*) volumetric analysis

maß·analytisch *adj.* (*chem.*) volumetric

Maß·bestimmung *f* mensuration, metric determination

Maß·blatt *n* dimensional specifications

Masse *f* (*phys.*, *statist.*) mass: *statistische M.* statistical universe (or population) [*cf.* DISKRET; TRÄG]

masse·frei *adj.* [= MASSENFREI]

Maß·einheit *f* unit of measure (-ment) [*cf.* BENENNUNG]

masse·los *adj.* (*phys.*) massless

Massen·anziehung *f* (*phys.*) mass attraction, gravitation

Massen·beschleunigung *f* (*phys.*) mass acceleration

Massen·einheit *f* (*phys.*) mass unit

Massen·defekt *m* (*phys.*) mass defect

Massen·erscheinung *f* (*statist.*) mass phenomenon

massen·frei *adj.* (*phys.*) **1.** (*frei von Massenpartikeln*) free of mass (particles). **2.** (*ohne Masse*) massless

Massen·mittelpunkt *m* (*phys.*) (*eines Systems von materiellen Punkten*) mass center (or centroid) of particles [*cf.* MASSENSCHWERPUNKT; SCHWERPUNKT]

Massen·punkt *m* (*phys.*) mass point, point mass, differential mass, element of mass, particle; *Fläche aus Massenpunkten* material surface [*cf.* PUNKTMASSE]

Massen·schrumpfung *f* (*phys.*) mass reduction (or shrinkage)

Massen·schwerpunkt *m* [= MASSENMITTELPUNKT]

Massen·spektroskop *n* (*phys.*) mass spectroscope

Massen·spektroskopie *f* (*phys.*) mass spectroscopy

Massen·teilchen *n* (*phys.*) mass particle, element of mass [*cf.* DISKRET]

maß·gleich *adj.* isometric

Maß·gleichheit *f* isometry

Maß·größe *f* **1.** (*messende Größe*) measuring quantity, measurement: *die Maßgrößen auf der y-Achse* the measurements along the *y*-axis. **2.** (*meßbare Größe*) dimensional (or measurable) quantity

Maß·stab *m* **1.** (*Meßgerät*) measuring device; (*Stab*) measuring stick (or rod), yardstick; (*Band*) measuring tape; *mit demselben M. meßbar* commensurable. **2.** (*Vergleichsmaß*) yardstick (of comparison). **3.** (*relative Größe* relative size) scale (of measurement): *in großem* (*kleinem*) *Maßstab* on a large (small) scale; *in vergrößertem* (*verkleinertem*) *M.* at an enlarged (a reduced) scale; *im M.* 100 : 1 in scale of 100 : 1; *eine Zeichnung in großem M.* a large-scale drawing [*cf.* VERJÜNGEN; VERJÜNGUNG; VERKLEINERN; VERKLEINERUNG]

Maßstab·fehler *m* scale error

maßstab·getreu *adj.* (in) scale, (true) to scale: *maßstabgetreue Zeichnung* scale diagram [*cf.* ZEICHNEN]

Maßstab·karte *f* scale map (or chart)

maßstäblich *adj.* (in) scale, (true) to scale; *m. verkleinern* scale down

Maßstabs·verhältnis *n* scale ratio
Maß·system *n* system of measurement (or: of units): *absolutes M.* absolute (system of) units [= ZENTIMETER-GRAMM-SEKUNDEN-SYSTEM]
Maß·zahl *f* coefficient of measure
Material *n* material [*cf.* ERHEBUNG]
Materie *f* (*phys.*) matter
materie·frei *adj.* (*phys.*) free of matter
materiell *adj.* (*phys.*) material: *materieller Punkt* material point, particle; *Linie* (*Fläche*) *von materiellen Punkten* material line (surface) [*cf.* MASSENMITTEL-PUNKT]
Materie·welle *f* (*phys.*) matter wave
Mathematik *f* mathematics: *angewandte* (*reine*) *M.* applied (pure) mathematics [*cf.* GRÖSSENLEHRE]
Mathematiker *m* mathematician
mathematisch *adj.* mathematical: *mathematische Erwartung* (*oder Hoffnung*) mathematical expectation [*cf.* GLIED; LOGIK; PENDEL; WAHRSCHEINLICHKEIT]
Matrix *f* (*pl. Matrizes oder Matrizen*) (*alg.*) matrix: *M. der Koeffizienten eines Systems simultaner linearer Gleichungen* matrix of the coefficients of a system of simultaneous linear equations; *quadratische M.* square matrix; *symmetrische M.* symmetric matrix [*cf.* RANG; SCHIEFSYMMETRISCH; SPUR; TRANSPONIEREN; UNIMODULAR; VERTAUSCHEN]
Matrix·produkt *n* (*alg.*) matrix product
Matrizen·ring *m* (*alg.*) matrix ring [*cf.* VOLL]

Matrizen·system *n* (*alg.*) system of matrices [*cf.* HÜLLE]
maximal *adj.* maximal, maximum [*cf.* POSSIBILITÄT; WERT]
Maximum *n* (*pl. Maxima*) maximum
Mechanik *f* (*phys.*) mechanics
mechanisch *adj.* (*phys.*) mechanical: *mechanische Integration, Quadratur* mechanical integration, quadrature [*cf.* JOULE]
median *adj.* median
Mediane *f* median, mid-line, line of centers
Medium *n* medium [*cf.* MITTEL]
Meeres·spiegel *m* sea level
Mega·hertz *n* (*rad. meas.*) megacycle
mehr·deutig *adj.* ambiguous
mehr·eindeutig *adj.* many-to-one [*cf* EINEINDEUTIG]
mehr·fach *adj.* repeated, multiple; (*adv., auch*) several times; (*mannigfach*) manifold: *mehrfacher Punkt* multiple point; *mehrfache Tangente* multiple tangent; *mehrfache Wurzel einer Gleichung* multiple (or repeated) root of an equation; *dieser Ausdruck kommt m. vor* this expression appears several times [*cf* GLIEDERUNG; INTEGRAL; RAUMKURVE; ZUSAMMENHÄNGEND]
Mehrfach·heit *f* multiplicity
Mehrfach·korrelation *f* multiple correlation
mehr·gipfelig *adj.* (*Häufigkeitskurve*) multimodal (frequency curve)
mehr·gliedrig *adj.* polynomial (expression)
mehr·malig *adj.* repeated
mehr·mals *adv.* several times

mehr·mehrdeutig *adj.* many-to-many [*cf.* EINEINDEUTIG]

mehr·stufig *adj.* (*alg.*) (*Isomorphismus*) multiple (*isomorphism*) [*cf.* ISOMORPHISMUS]

mehr·wertig *adj.* many-valued, multiple-valued: *mehrwertige Funktion* multiple-valued function

Mehrwertig·keit *f* multiplicity, multiple-valuedness

Mehr·zahl *f* plurality; (*ant.: Einzahl*) plural; (*ant.: Minderzahl*) majority

Meile *f* (*meas.*) mile: *geographische M.* geographical mile

Menge *f* **1.** (*Quantität*) quantity, multitude. **2.** (*von Elementen*) set, aggregate, assemblage, complex (of elements): *Cantorsche M.* Cantor set [*cf.* ABBILDEN; ABGELEITET; ABGESCHLOSSEN; ABZÄHLBAR; ABZÄHLBARKEIT; ÄHNLICH-GEORDNET; ANORDNUNG; DICHT; DURCHSCHNITT; ELEMENT; ENDLICH; GEORDNET; GLEICH; HÄUFUNGSGRENZE; INNER; INHALT; KOMPLEXION; LEER; LIMES; MESSBAR; NICHTDICHT; OBERMENGE; RAND; RANDPUNKT; REIHE; UMFASSEND; UNENDLICH; VEREINIGUNG; WOHLGEORDNET; ZUORDNEN; ZUSAMMENSETZUNG]

Mengen·lehre *f* theory of sets, set theory [*cf.* AUSWAHLAXIOM; BESTIMMTHEITSAXIOM]

mengen·mäßig *adj.* quantitative

Mengen·notierung *f* (*fin.*) (*bei Devisen*) indirect rate of (foreign) exchange

Mengen·rabatt *m* (*comm.*) quantity discount

mengen·theoretisch *adj.* set-theoretical

Mengen·verhältnis *n* quantitative (or quantity) ratio; (*statist.*) quantity relative (number); (*chem.*) volumetric ratio

Meniskus *m* meniscus [*cf.* MÖNDCHEN]

Mercator·projektion *f* (*cart.*) Mercator projection

Meridian *m* meridian [ABWEICHUNG; HINDURCHGEHEN; LÄNGENUNTERSCHIED; PASSIEREN; VERBINDEN]

Meridian·durchgang (*astr.*) (*eines Sterns*) meridian transit (of a star)

Meridian·ebene *f* meridian plane [*cf* ZWICKEL]

Meridian·kreis *m* (*astr.*) meridian (circle)

Meridian·schnitt *m* meridian (section)

meridional *adj.* meridional

Merkator·projektion *f* (*cart.*) Mercator projection

Merkmal *n* attribute, characteristic, trait: (*statist.*) *festes M.* (statistical) attribute; (*statist.*) *veränderliches M.* (statistical) variable [*cf.* ABHÄNGIGKEIT; HÄUFIGKEITSKOEFFIZIENT]

Merkmals·betrag *m* (*statist.*) (statistical) value

Merk·tafel *f* tally, score

meromorph *adj* (*Funktion*) meromorphic (function)

Meson *n*, **Mesotron** *n* (*phys.*) meson, mesotron

Meß·band *n* measuring tape

meß·bar *adj.* (*Menge, Funktion*) measurable (set, function) [*cf.*

MASS; MASSGRÖSSE; MASSSTAB]
Meßbar·keit *f* measurability
messen *v.t., v.i.* measure [*cf.*
MASSGRÖSSE; UMKREIS]
Messer *m* meter, measuring device
(or instrument) [*cf.* ZÄHLER]
Meß·gerät *n* measuring device
[*cf.* MASS; MASSSTAB; NORMEN;
NORMUNG]
Meß·instrument *n* measuring
instrument
Meß·kette *f* (*meas.*) (surveyor's)
chain (=66 feet)
Meßketten·glied *n* (*meas.*)
(surveyor's) link (=7·92 inch.)
Meß·kunst *f* mensuration
Messung *f* measurement, mensura-
tion [*cf.* ABMESSUNG]
Meß·zahl *f*, **Meß·ziffer** *f* (*statist.*)
index number
Meta·konto *n* [= GEMEINSCHAFTS-
KONTO]
meta·zyklisch *adj.* (*alg.*) (*Körper,
Gleichung*)metacyclic(field, equa-
tion)
Meter *n* (oder *m*) (*abbr.* m) meter,
metre (*abbr.* m.) [*cf.* PER]
Meter·kerze *f* (*opt. meas.*) meter
candle, lux [= LUX] .
Meter·zentner *m* (*Gewicht* weight)
metric (or double) centner
Methode *f* method, procedure:
Hornersche M. Horner's method;
Wiener M. der Bildstatistik [=
BILDSTATISTIK]; [*cf.* EINZELFALL;
GEOMETRISCH; GRAPHISCH; IN-
DUKTIV; KLEINST; KONKURRIE-
REND; UNBESTIMMT]
Metrik *f* (*z.B. des Raums*)
metric(s) (e.g. of space)
metrisch *adj.* metric(al), metriz-
able: *metrischer Raum* metric (or

metrizable) space; *metrisches
System* metric system [*cf.* TONNE]
Metro·logie *f* metrology
Metro·nom *n* (*acoust.*) metro-
nome
Mieder·fläche *f* hyperboloid of
one sheet [=EINSCHALIGES
HYPERBOLOID]
Miete *f*, **Miet·zins** *m* (*comm.*)
rent [*cf.* ZINS]
Mikro·bewegung *f* micromotion
Mikro·coulomb *n* (*elec.*) micro-
coulomb
Mikro·erg *n* (*phys.*) microerg
Mikr·ohm *n* (*elec.*) microhm
Mikro·meter *n* micrometer
Mikron *n* (*meas.*) micron (*abbr.*:μ)
Mikro·sekunde *f* microsecond
Mikro·skop *n* microscope
mikro·skopisch *adj.* microscopic(al)
Mikro·volt *n* (*elec.*) microvolt
Mikro·welle *f* microwave
Mikro·zoll *n* microinch
Militär·perspektive *f* [= KAVALIER-
PERSPEKTIVE]
Militär·projektion *f* [= KAVALIER-
PROJEKTION]
Milli·ampère *n* (*elec.*) milliampere
Milliarde *f* (=10^9) *Am.* billion;
Br. milliard
Milli·curie *n* (*phys.*) millicurie
Milli·gramm *n* (*abbr.*:mg) milli-
gram, milligramme (*abbr.*: mg.)
Milli·meter *n* (*abbr.*: mm) milli-
meter, millimetre (*abbr.*:mm.)
Millimeter·papier *n* graph (or co-
ordinate) paper ruled in milli-
meter squares [*cf.* QUADRILLIERT]
Milli·mikron *n* millimicron (*abbr.*:
mμ)
Million *f* million
Milli·sekunde *f* millisecond

Milli·volt *n* (*elec.*) millivolt
minder *adj.* (*comp.* of **wenig**) less
Minder·zahl *f* minority
mindest *adj.* (*sup.* of **wenig**) least
Mindest·wert *m* minimum (value), minimal value
minimal *adj.* minimal, minimum
Minimal·basis *f* (*alg.*) (*eines Körpers*) minimal (or linearly independent) basis (of a field)
Minimal·fläche *f* minimal surface
Minor *f* (*pl. Minoren*) (*eines Elements einer Determinante*) minor (determinant), subdeterminant (of an element in a determinant) [= UNTERDETERMINANTE; SUBDETERMINANTE]
Minorante *f* (*einer Punktmenge*) minorant, lower bound (of a set of points)
Minorität *f* minority
Minuend *m* minuend
minus *adj.* minus; (*in einer Subtraktion* in a subtraction) minus, less: *minus x* minus *x* (*symb.: − x*); *fünf m. drei* five minus (or less) three [*cf.* ERST; MAL; WENIGER]
Minus·zeichen *n* minus (or negative) sign
Minute *f* (*sechzigster Teil einer Stunde, eines Grads* sixtieth part of an hour, a degree) minute [*cf.* TOURENZAHL]
Minuten·zeiger *m* minute hand
mischen *v.t.* mix [*cf.* GEMISCHT]
Mischungs·rechnung *f* (rule of) alligation
Mise *f* [= BARWERT]
Mit·logarithmus *m* cologarithm [*cf.* LOGARITHMUS]
mit·schwingen (*sep.*) *v.i.* covibrate, resonate
Mit·schwingen *n* resonance
mit·schwingend *adj.* resonant
Mittags·kreis *m* (*geog.*) meridian
Mitte *f* middle, midst; *in der M. zwischen* midway between
mit·teilen (*sep.*) *v.t.* **1.** (*eine Bedeutung*) communicate (a meaning). **2.** (*eine Bewegung*) impart (a motion)
mittel *adj.* middle, mean, medium: *mittlere Dichte, Größe* mean density, size; *mittlere Proportionale* mean proportional; *halbe mittlere Achse eines* (*dreiachsigen*) *Ellipsoids* semimean axis of an ellipsoid; *mittlerer Wert* median [*cf.* ABWEICHUNG; ANOMALIE; FEHLER; QUARTILSABSTAND; SONNENZEIT]
Mittel *n* **1.** (*Mittelwert*) mean (value): *arithmetisches, geometrisches, harmonisches M.* arithmetic, geometric, harmonic mean; (*statist.*) *quadratisches M.* quadratic mean. **2.** (*Medium*) medium: *optisches M.* optical medium
Mittel·begriff *m* (*im logischen Schluß*) middle term (of a syllogism)
Mittel·ebene *f* medium plane
Mittel·größe *f* medium size
Mittel·linie *f* **1.** (*Halbierungslinie*) bisector, bisecting line, median: *M. einer Strecke* bisector of a line segment. **2.** (*Ort der Mittelpunkte*) line of centers, mid-line, median: *M. eines Zylinders* line of centers of a cylinder; *M. eines Dreiecks, Trapezes* mid-line (or median) of a triangle, trapezoid;

Schnittpunkt der Mittellinien eines Dreiecks median point of a triangle [*cf.* ACHSE]

Mittel·punkt *m* center, midpoint, central point: *M. einer Strecke* midpoint of a line segment [*cf.* ANKREIS; ANSCHREIBEN; ANZIEHUNG; EINSCHREIBEN; INKREIS; MITTELLINIE; TRÄGER 2.; UMKREIS; UMSCHREIBEN; ZENTRUM]

Mittelpunkts·kegelschnitt *m* central conic

Mittelpunkts·winkel *m* (*eines Kreises*) central angle (in a circle) [= ZENTRIWINKEL]

Mittel·schnitt *m* (*z.B. eines Prismatoids*) median section (e.g. of a prismatoid)

Mittel·senkrechte *f* (*einer Strecke*) mid-perpendicular (of a line segment)

Mittel·wert *m* mean (value); (*Durchschnitt*) average: (*statist.*) *bereinigter M.* corrected (or modified) mean; (*statist.*) *provisorischer M.* auxiliary (or assumed) mean; (*statist.*) *Mittelwerte der Lage* positional averages; [*cf.* DURCHSCHNITT; MITTEL]

Mittelwert·satz *m* mean value theorem, law (or theorem) of the mean [*cf* ERWEITERN; VERALLGEMEINERN]

mittler *adj.* (*comp.* of mittel) **1.** [= MITTEL]. **2.** (*näher zur Mitte*) nearer the middle

Mnemonik *f* mnemonics

Möbius *m N.* [*cf.* BAND]

Modell *n* model

Modul *m* modulus, module:

M. eines Logarithmensystems modulus of a logarithmic system; *M. einer Kongruenz* modulus of a congruence; *M. eines elliptischen Integrals, einer elliptischen Funktion* modulus of an elliptic integral, an elliptic function [*cf.* KOMPLEX]

Modul·basis *m* (*alg.*) module basis

Modul·homomorphismus *m* (*alg.*) module homomorphism

modulo *adv.* (*alg.*) modulo [*cf.* FAKTOR; KONGRUENT; RESTCHARAKTER]

Modus *m* (*der Häufigkeitswerte*) mode (of frequency values)

Moebius [*cf.* MÖBIUS]

möglich *adj.* possible, potential

Möglichkeit *f* possibility, potentiality; (*einer von zwei Wegen* one of two ways) alternative [*cf.* AUSWAHL; WAHL]

Moivre *m N.* de Moivre: *Moivrescher Satz* de Moivre's theorem

Mol *n* (*chem.*) mole

molar *adj.* (*chem.*) molar

Molekül *n* molecule

molekular *adj.* molecular

Molekular·gewicht *n* (*chem.*) molecular weight

Mollweide *m N. Mollweidesche Gleichungen* Mollweide equations

Moment¹ *m* (*Augenblick*) moment, instant: *Geschwindigkeit in einem gegebenen M.* (*oder Augenblick*) velocity at a given moment (or instant)

Moment² *n* (*phys.*) moment, momentum: (*statisches*) *M.* (*oder Drehmoment*) *einer Kraft* (*in bezug auf einen Punkt, eine Achse*) static (or turning)

moment, moment of force, torque
(about a point, an axis); *lineares
M.* (linear) momentum, impulse
[= BEWEGUNGSGRÖSSE; IMPULS];
angulares M. angular momentum,
moment of momentum [= DRALL;
DREHIMPULS; IMPULSMOMENT]
momentan *adj.* instantaneous
Momentan·beschleunigung *f* in-
stantaneous acceleration
Momentan·geschwindigkeit *f* in-
stantaneous velocity
Momenten·satz *m* momentum
theorem
Monat *m* month; *alle zwei Monate,
jeden zweiten M.* bimonthly
monatlich *adj.* monthly [*cf.*
SAISONVERÄNDERUNGSZAHLEN]
Monats·durchschnitt *m* monthly
average
Monatsdurchschnitts·verfahren *n*
(*statist.*) averages method of com-
puting stable seasonal index
Mond *m* moon [*cf.* VERFINSTERN;
VERFINSTERUNG; VIERTEL; WIE-
DERKEHREN]
Mond·bahn *f* orbit (or track, or
path) of the moon
Möndchen *n* (*Kreiszweieck*) lune,
crescent; (*Meniskus*) meniscus
Mond·finsternis *f* (*astr.*) lunar
eclipse
Mond·jahr *n* lunar year
Mond·monat *m* lunar month
Mond·phase *f* (*astr.*) phase of the
moon
Mond·sichel *f* crescent (moon)
Mond·viertel *n* quarter of the moon
mono·dimetrisch *adj.* (*cryst.*)
monodimetric
monogen *adj.* monogenic: *mono-
gene analytische Funktion* mono-

genic analytic function
monoklin, monoklinisch *adj.* (*cryst.*)
monoclinic [*cf.* SCHIEFEND-
FLÄCHE]
mon·okular *adj.* (*opt.*) monocular
Monom *n* monomial
mono·ton *adj* monotone, mono-
tonic; *m. abnehmende* (*zunehmende*) *Reihe* monotone decreasing (increasing) series
Mono·tonie *f* monotony
Morgen *m* (*Flächenmaß* square
measure) acre
multipel *adj.* multiple
Multiplikand *m* multiplicand
Multiplikation *f* multiplication:
skalare (*vektorielle*) *M. zweier
Vektoren* scalar (vector) multiplication of two vectors [*cf.*
ABGEKÜRZT; ASSOZIATIV; KOM-
MUTATIV; UNABGEKÜRZT]
Multiplikations·zeichen *n* sign of
multiplication
multiplikativ *adj.* multiplicative
Multiplikator *m* multiplier
Multiplikatoren·bereich *m* (*alg.*)
domain of multipliers
multiplizieren *v.t., v.i.* (*mit*) multi-
ply (by): *kreuzweise* (*oder: übers
Kreuz*) *m.* multiply crisscross,
cross-multiply (e.g. $\frac{2}{8} = \frac{x}{y}$, $2y = 5x$)
[*cf.* FALSCH; UNABGEKÜRZT]
mündel·sicher *adj.* (*fin.*) (*Wert-
papiere*) gilt-edged, *Am.* legal
investment (securities)
Muschel·linie *f* conchoid [=
KONCHOIDE]
Muster *n* pattern [*cf.* SCHEMA]
My *n* (*griechischer Buchstabe*
Greek letter M, μ) mu
Myriameter *n* (*abbr.*) μm (*abbr.
μm*) myriameter, myriametre

N

Nabel·punkt *m* (*einerFläche*) umbilic, umbilical point (of a surface)
Nabla *n* del, nabla (symb.: ∇): *der Operator N.* the operator del (or nabla); *der Gradient Nabla f* the gradient del *f*, (*symb.:* grad $f = \nabla f$)
nach *prep.* (*dat.*) (*Reihenfolge* sequence) after; (*Richtung* direction) to, toward; (*gemäß*) according to, by, after; (*in bezug auf*) with respect to: *Beweis n. Formel* (6) proof by formula (6); *konkav* (*konvex*) *n.* aufwärts (*abwärts*) concave (convex) up (down); *nach x integrieren* integrate with respect to *x* [*cf.* ABLEITUNG; ABRUNDEN; INTEGRAL]
Nachbar·schaft *f* neighborhood, vicinity; (*Nähe*) nearness, closeness, proximity: *in der N. eines Punktes* in the neighborhood of a point; *N. im Raum* nearness (or closeness) in space [*cf.* GROSS; NÄHE]
Nach·börse *f* (*fin.*) curb (exchange), curb (or open, or outside) market
nach·eilen (*sep.*) *v.i.* lag, be retarded: *die Phase eilt nach* the phase lags
Nach·eilung *f* lag, retardation
nach·einander *adv.* successively
Nach·folger *m* successor, consequent [*cf.* ZAHLENREIHE]
Nach·frage *f* (*comm.*) demand [*cf.* ANGEBOT]
nach·prüfen (*sep.*) *v.t.* check (up)
Nach·prüfung *f* check, checkup
Nach·satz *m* (*log.*) consequent

(sentence)
nach·schlagen (*sep.*) *v.t., v.i.* (*z.B. in der Logarithmentafel*) look up (e.g. in the logarithm table)
Nachschlage·tabelle *f* reference table
nächst *adj.* (*sup. von* **nah**) (*am nächsten*) nearest, closest; (*nächstfolgend*) next
nächst·folgend *adj.* next, consecutive, following [*cf.* NÄCHST]
Nacht·bogen *m* (*astr.*) (*der Sonne*) nocturnal arc (of the sun)
Nacht·gleiche *f* equinox [= ÄQUINOKTIUM, TAGUNDNACHTGLEICHE]
Nach·weisung *f* record, datum, verification: *statistische Nachweisungen* statistical records (or data)
Nach·zahl *f* (*statist.*) cumulative frequency of classes following median class
Nadir *m* (*geog., astr.*) nadir [*cf.* FUSSPUNKT 2.]
nah(e) *adj.* near, close [*cf.* NÄCHST; NÄHER]
Nähe *f* nearness, closeness, proximity; (*Nachbarschaft*) neighborhood, vicinity [*cf.* VERHALTEN; NACHBARSCHAFT]
näher *adj* (*comp. von* **nah**) nearer, closer [*cf.* BESTIMMUNG]
nähern *v.t., v.r.:* **sich n.** approach, converge to (or toward): *sich einem Grenzwert n.* approach a limit, converge to (or toward) a limit [*cf.* ASYMPTOTISCH; GRENZWERT; NULL; UNENDLICH]

Näherung *f* approximation, approximate value

Näherungs·bruch *m* (*eines Kettenbruchs*) convergent (of a continued fraction)

Näherungs·formel *f* approximate formula

Näherungs·rechnung *f* approximation calculus

Näherungs·verfahren *n* approximation method

näherungs·weise *adj.* approximate

Näherungs·wert *m* approximate value

Nah·kraft *f* close-range force; (*Nahwirkung*) close-range action

Nah·wirkung *f* close-range action [*cf.* NAHKRAFT]

Napier *m* N. [*cf.* LOGARITHMUS; NEPER]

Natur *f* nature

Natur·ereignis *n* natural event [*cf.* GESETZLICH]

Natur·gesetz *n* law of nature, natural law

Natur·lehre *f* physics

natürlich *adj.* natural: *natürliche Zahl* natural number; *natürliche Koordinaten, Kurvengleichungen* natural (or intrinsic) coordinates, equations of a curve; *natürliche Größe* actual size [*cf.* LOGARITHMUS; ZAHLENLINIE; ZAHLENREIHE]

Navigation *f* navigation

navigieren *v.t.* navigate

Navigierung *f* navigation

Nebel·kammer *f* (*phys.*) cloud chamber

Neben·achse *f* secondary axis; (*einer Ellipse*) minor axis (of an ellipse); (*einer Hyperbel*) conjugate axis (of a hyperbola)

Neben·bestandteil *m* secondary part

Neben·bürgschaft *f* (*comm.*) collateral (security)

Neben·diagonale *f* secondary diagonal

Neben·ecke *f* (*eines vollständigen Vierecks*) diagonal point (of a complete quadrangle)

Neben·einkommen *n*, **Neben·einkünfte** *pl.* (*fin.*) additional income

Neben·faktor *m* secondary factor

Neben·gruppe *f*, **Neben·klasse** *f*, **Neben·komplex** *m* (*alg.*) coset: *rechtsseitige N.* right coset

Neben·projektion *f* (*descr.*) auxiliary view [*ant.:* HAUPTPROJEKTION]

Neben·seite *f* (*eines vollständigen Vierseits*) diagonal (of a complete quadrilateral)

Neben·veränderliche *f* auxiliary variable, parameter

Neben·winkel *m* adjacent supplementary angle [*cf.* pairs of angles: A, A′; A, B; A′, B′; B, B′; C, C′; C, D; C′, D′; D, D′ in *Fig.* to TRANSVERSALE]

n-eck *n* n-gon

Negation *f* negation

Negations·strich *n* (*log.*) negation bar (or sign)

Negations·zeichen *n* (*log.*) negation sign

negativ *adj.* negative: *negative Zahl* negative number [*cf.* DEFINIT; ORIENTIEREN; VORZEICHEN; WINKEL]

negieren *v.t.* deny, answer in the negative, negate

neigen 1. *v.t.* tilt, incline. **2.** *v.r.:* sich *n.* slope, slant (away), be inclined [*cf.* ABFALLEN; SENKEN]

Neigung *f* inclination, grade gradient, slope, dip: *die stärkste (schwächste) N.* the maximum (minimum) inclination [*cf.* SENKUNG]

Neigungs·winkel *m* angle of inclination (or slope): *N. einer Geraden in der Ebene mit der positiven x-Achse* (angle of) inclination of a line in the plane; *N. einer Geraden mit einer Ebene* angle between a line and a plane; *N. zweier Ebenen* angle between two planes, dihedral angle [*cf.* FESTLEGEN; SEIN]

Nenn·betrag *m* (*comm., fin.*) nominal amount

Nenner *m* denominator [*cf.* BRINGEN; GEMEINSAM; GLEICH; KLEINST; KÜRZEN]

Nenner·determinante *f* denominator determinant

Nenn·wert (*comm., fin.*) face (or nominal) value [= NOMINALWERT]

Neper *m* N. [= NAPIER] [*cf.* ANALOGIE; LOGARITHMUS; NAPIER]

Nephroide *f* nephroid [= NIERENKURVE]

netto *adj.* (*comm.*) net: *n. Kassa im voraus* net cash in advance

Netto·betrag *m* (*comm.*) net amount

Netto·einnahme(n) *f* (*pl.*), **Netto· erlös** *m*, **Netto·ertrag** *m* (*comm.*) net proceeds *pl.* (or returns *pl.*)

Netto·gewicht *n* net weight

Netz *n* **1.** (*Linienwerk* configuration of lines) net, network. **2.** (*ausgebreitete Oberfläche eines Körpers*) development (of the surface of a solid): *N. eines Würfels, einer Pyramide* development of a cube, a pyramid

Netz·tafel *f* (*statist.*) net·chart (or graph)

neu *adj.* new; (*modern*) modern: *neuere (analytische) Geometrie* modern analytic geometry, projective geometry (treated by analytic methods)

Neu·mond *m* (*astr.*) new moon

neun *card. num.* nine

Neun *f* (*Zahl, Ziffer*) (number, figure) nine

Neun·eck *n* nonagon

Neuner *m* (figure) nine

Neuner·probe *f* casting out nines [*cf.* NEUNERREST]

Neuner·rest *m* (*bei der Neunerprobe*) excess of nines (in casting out nines)

neun·hundert *card.num.* nine hundred

neun·mal *num.* nine times

neun·malig *adj.* (done) nine times [*cf.* DREIMALIG]

Neunpunkte·kreis *m* (*eines Dreiecks*) nine-point circle (of a triangle)

neunt *ord.num.* ninth

Neuntel *n* ninth (part)

neuntens *adv.* ninthly, in the ninth place

neun·zehn *card.num.* nineteen

neun·zig *card.num.* ninety

neun·zigst *ord.num.* ninetieth

Neu·ries *n* (*Papiermaß* paper measure) 1000 sheets [*cf.* RIES]

Newton *m* N. [*cf.* TRIDENS]

nicht *adv.* not, non . . . : *n. behebbare Unstetigkeit* nonremovable discontinuity [*cf.* ABZÄHLBAR;

ENTWICKELT; UMKEHRBAR]
nicht·archimedisch *adj.* non-Archimedean

nicht·ausgelöst *adj.* (*statist.*) (*Daten*) (data) collected by administrative agency [*cf.* AUSGELÖST]

nicht·dicht *adj.* (*Menge*) nondense (set)

nicht·diskret *adj.* nondiscrete

nicht·euklidisch *adj.* non-Euclidean [*cf.* GEOMETRIE]

Nicht·existenz *f* nonexistence

nicht·harmonisch *adj.* anharmonic [*cf.* DOPPELVERHÄLTNIS]

nicht·häufbar *adj.* (*statist.*) noncumulative

nicht·homogen *adj.* nonhomogeneous

nicht·konvergent *adj.* nonconvergent

nicht·leitend *adj.* (*phys.*) nonconducting, nonconductive

Nicht·leiter *m* (*phys.*) nonconductor

nicht·linear *adj.* nonlinear [*cf.* KORRELATIONSINDEX]

Nicht·linearität *f* nonlinearity

nicht·orientierbar *adj.* nonorientable

nicht·parallel *adj.* nonparallel

nicht·periodisch *adj.* nonperiodic

nicht·reflexiv *adj.* (*Beziehung*) nonreflexive (relation)

nicht·singulär *adj.* nonsingular

nicht·symmetrisch *adj.* nonsymmetric(al)

nicht·transitiv *adj.* (*Beziehung*) nontransitive (relation)

nicht·trivial *adj.* (*Lösung*) nontrivial (solution)

nicht·umkehrbar *adj.* irreversible, nonreversible

Nicht·umkehrbarkeit *f* irreversibility, nonreversibility

nicht·zusammenfallend *adj.* noncoincident

nieder *adj.* low, lower [*cf.* PRIMIDEAL]

niedrig *adj* low: *die niedrigste Zahl* the lowest number; *niedrigster Wert* lowest (or minimum) value [*cf.* UMWANDLUNG]

Nieren·kurve *f* nephroid [= NEPHROIDE]

Niete *f* (*statist.*) failure

nil·potent *adj.* (*alg.*) nilpotent

Niveau *n* level: *auf gleichem N.* on the same level [*cf.* HÖHE; STUFE]

Niveau·fläche *f* equipotential surface

Niveau·linie *f* equipotential line

Nomen·klatur *f* nomenclature

Nominal·betrag *m* (*fin.*) nominal amount

Nominal·wert *m* (*fin*) face (or nominal) value [= NENNWERT]

Nomogramm *n* nomograph, nomogram, alignment chart [*cf.* RECHENTAFEL]

Nomographie *f* nomography

Nonagon *n* nonagon [= NEUNECK]

nonagonal *adj.* nonagonal [= NEUNECKIG]

Nonillion *f* (10^{54}) *Am.* septendecillion, *Br.* nonillion

Nonius *m* nonius

Nord *m*, **Norden** *m* north [*cf.* WEISEN]

nördlich *adj.* northern, northerly

Nord·pol *m* north pole [*cf.* VERBINDEN]

Nord·punkt *m* north point

Nordsüd·abweichung f (*der Magnetnadel*) declination (of the magnetic needle); (*eines Schiffes*) (magnetic, or compass) bearing (of a ship)

Nordsüd·meridian m north-south meridian

Norm f norm [*cf.* REDUZIEREN]

normal *adj.* **1.** (*regelrecht*) normal, standard: *normale Fehlerkurve* (*oder Häufigkeitskurve oder Verteilungskurve*] normal error (or frequency, or distribution) curve [= NORMALKURVE; WAHRSCHEINLICHKEITSKURVE]; [*cf.* ANORDNUNG; REIHENFOLGE]. **2.** (*senkrecht*) normal, perpendicular: *normale Gerade* normal (or perpendicular) (line)[*cf.* SENKRECHT]. **3.** (*Zahlenkörper*) normal (number field): *normaler* (*oder galoisscher*) *Körper* normal field

Normal·ansicht f (*descr.*) normal view

Normal·beschleunigung f (*mech.*) normal acceleration

Normal·darstellung f (*alg.*) normal form (or representation)

Normale f **1.** (*Senkrechte*) normal (line), perpendicular (line) [*cf.* ERRICHTEN; FÄLLEN; FUSSPUNKT; LOT]. **2.** (*Normalenlänge in einem Punkt einer Kurve*) (length of) normal (at a point of a curve)

Normal·ebene f normal (or perpendicular) plane

Normalen·länge f (*in einem Kurvenpunkt*) length of normal (at a point of a curve) [*cf.* NORMALE]

Normal·form f **1.** (*einer Gleichung*) normal (or standard) form (of an

equation): *N. der Gleichung einer Geraden* normal form of the equation of a straight line; *N. der Gleichung einer Ellipse* standard form of the equation of an ellipse [*cf.* AUSGEZEICHNET; PRÄNEX; ZURÜCKFÜHRUNG]. **2.** (*der Häufigkeitskurve*) mesokurtosis (of the frequency curve)

Normal·gleichung f normal (or standard) equation

Normalisator m (*alg.*) (*eines Gruppenelements*) normalizer (of a group element)

Normal·körper m (*alg.*) normal field [*cf.* ZUGEHÖRIG]

Normal·kurve f (*statist.*) (*der Verteilung*) normal curve (of distribution) [*cf.* NORMAL]

Normal·reihe f (*alg.*) normal series [*cf.* LÄNGE; VERFEINERUNG]

Normal·schnitt m normal (or right) section

Normal·teiler m (*alg.*) (*einer Gruppe*) normal divisor, self-conjugate (or invariant) subgroup (of a group)

normen *v.t.* standarize; (*ein Meßgerät*) calibrate (a measuring device)

normieren *v.t.* norm, normalize, standardize: *normiertes Polynom* normed polynomial; *normiertes Orthogonalsystem von Vektoren* orthonormal (or: normed orthogonal) system of vectors

Normierung f, **Normung** f standardization; (*eines Meßgeräts*) calibration (of a measuring device)

Note f (*comm.*) note

Noten·bank f (*fin.*) bank of issue,

(note-)issuing bank [*cf.* GOLD-AUSGLEICHSFONDS]

Noten·umlauf *m* (*fin.*) [= BANK-NOTENUMLAUF]

Notierung *f* (*comm.,fin.*) (*an der Börse*) quotation (at the stock exchange) [*cf.* LAUFEN]

not·wendig *adj.* necessary: [*cf* BEDINGUNG; BESTIMMUNGS-STÜCK]

Null *f* zero, naught, cipher: *Faktorielle N.* factorial zero (*symb.* 0 !); *die Funktion hat den Grenzwert N. für x = a* the function has the limit zero (or: is null) at *x = a*; *der N. unbegrenzt sich nähernd* null, tending to zero [*cf.* ALEPH; ANHÄNGEN; DIVISION; EINBEGREIFEN; EXPO-NENT; GRENZWERT; GRÖSSEN-ORDNUNG; SETZEN; WERTGEBEND; ZAHLENREIHE]

Null·ablesung *f* zero reading

Null·darstellung *f* (*alg.*) null representation

null·dimensional *adj.* zero-dimensional

Null·element *n* (*alg.*) (*einer Gruppe*) null (or zero) element (of a group)

Nullen·zirkel *m* spring bow compass, spring bows

Null·folge *f* null sequence

Null·ideal *n* (*alg.*) null ideal

Null·kreis *m* null circle

Null·matrix *f* null matrix

Null·meridian *m* (*geog.*) zero (or first, or prime, or principal, or zone) meridian

Null·punkt *m* zero (point): *absoluter N. der Temperatur* absolute zero of temperature

Null·ring *m* (*alg.*) null ring

Null·schnitt *m* null cut

Null·stelle *f* (*einer Funktion*) zero (of a function): *allgemeine* (*spezielle*) *N.* eines Primideals generic (particular) zero of a prime ideal

Nullstellen·körper *m* (*alg.*) Null-stellenkörper, zero field

Nullstellen·mannigfaltigkeit *f* (*alg.*) zero manifold

Nullstellen·satz *m* (*alg.*) Nullstellensatz: *Weierstraßscher N.* Weierstrass' Nullstellensatz

Null·stellung *f* (*z.B. eines Zeigers*) zero position (e.g. of a pointer)

Null·strich *m* (*einer Skala*) zero mark (in a scale)

Null·teiler *m* (*alg.*) zero divisor, divisor of zero

Null·vektor *m* null vector

Null·winkel *m* zero angle

Numerale *n* (*pl. Numeralia*) (*Lat.*) numeral

numerieren *v.t.* number

Numerierung *f* numbering, numeration [*cf.* FORTLAUFEND]

numerisch *adj.* numerical: *numerische Gleichung* numerical equation; *numerischer Wert* numerical value [*cf.* EXZENTRIZITÄT]

Numerus *m* (*pl. Numeri*) (*Lat.*) antilogarithm, inverse logarithm

Nummer *f* number [*cf.* LAUFEN; SEITENZAHL]

Nutation *f* (*astr.*) nutation

Nutz·effekt *m* (*phys., engin.*) efficiency

Nutzen *m* (*comm.*) profit, proceeds

Nutz·last *f* (*comm., engin.*) net load

Ny *n* (*griechischer Buchstabe* Greek letter N, ν) nu

O

oben *adv.* above, up [*cf.* ABRUNDEN; BESCHRÄNKT; HOCH]

ober *adj.* superior, upper [*cf,* GRENZE; HÄUFUNGSGRENZE; INDEX; LIMES; SCHRANKE; ZEIGER]

Ober·durchschnitt *m* (*statist.*) average of averages

Ober·fläche *f* surface: *O. eines Körpers* surface (or periphery) of a solid; *O. einer Fläche* surface area [*cf.* NETZ]

Oberflächen·inhalt *m* surface area [*cf.* KUGELOBERFLÄCHE]

Oberflächen·ladung *f* (*elec.*) surface charge

Oberflächen·spannung *f* (*phys.*) surface tension

Ober·gruppe *f* (*statist.*) class of classes, larger class

Obergruppen·bildung *f* (*statist.*) formation of larger classes; *Ausgleichung durch O.* smoothing by forming larger classes

Obergruppen·lage *f* (*statist.*) position of class limits of larger classes

oberhalb *adv., prep.* (*gen.*) above

Ober·klasse *f* extension class; (*eines Schnitts*) upper class (of a cut)

Ober·körper *m* (*alg.*) extension field

Ober·menge *f* (*zweier Mengen*) set including (or comprehending) (two) subsets [*cf.* ECHT]

Ober·ring *m* (*alg.*) extension ring

Ober·satz *m* (*log.*) major (premise)

Ober·schwingung *f* (*phys.*) harmonic oscillation

Ober·seite *f* upper (or top) side

oberst *adj.* (*sup. von* **ober**) topmost, supreme

Ober·ton *m* (*acoust.*) overtone

Ober·welle *f* (*phys.*) harmonic (wave)

Objekt *n* object: *Objekte einer Transformation* objects of a transformation

Obligation *f* (*comm.*) bond, debenture (bond) [*cf.* AUSGABE]

Obligo *n* responsibility, liability; (*Zahlungsverpflichtung*) obligation to pay; *ohne O.* without recourse

Obligo·buch *n* (*comm.*) acceptance ledger

oblong *adj.* oblong

offen *adj.* open: *offene Punktmenge* open point set [*cf.* FLÜGEL-GRUPPE; INTERVALL; RESERVE]

Ohm *m* N. [*cf.* GESETZ]

Ohm *n* (*elec. meas.*) ohm

Okta·eder *n* octahedron [= ACHT-FLACH; ACHTFLÄCHNER]

okta·edrisch *adj.* octahedral

Okta·gon *n* octagon [= ACHTECK]

okta·gonal *adj.* octagonal [= ACHTECKIG]

Oktant *m* octant

Oktillion *f* (10^{48}) *Am.* quindecillion; *Br.* octillion

O·mega *n* (*griechischer Buchstabe* Greek letter Ω, ω) omega

O·mikron *n* (*griechischer Buchstabe* Greek letter O, o) omikron

Operation *f* operation: *inverse* (*oder umgekehrte*) *O.* inverse (of an) operation [*cf.* DREI-GLIEDRIGKEIT; EINGLIEDRIG;

EINGLIEDRIGKEIT; ELEMENTAR; INVERS; ITERIERT; UMGEKEHRTES; ZWEIGLIEDRIGKEIT]

Operations·symbol *n*, **Operationszeichen** *n* operative sign, operator [*cf.* ZEICHEN]

Operator *m* operator [*cf.* NABLA]

Operatoren·bereich *m* (*alg.*) domain of operators, operator domain

operator·homomorph *adj.* (*alg.*) operator-homomorphic

Operator·homomorphismus *m* (*alg.*) operator homomorphism

operator·isomorph *adj.* (*alg.*) operator-isomorphic

Operator·isomorphismus *m* (*alg.*) operator, isomorphism

operieren *v.i.* operate

Opposition *f* (*astr.*, *log.*) opposition

Optik *f* optics

Option *f* **Options·recht** *n* (*comm.*, *fin.*) (*z.B. bei einer Aktienausgabe*) option, subscription privilege (e.g. for an issue of stock)

optisch *adj.* optical

ordentlich *adj.* ordinary, orderly, proper [*cf.* STRAHL; UNTER]

Ordinal·zahl *f* ordinal number

Ordinate *f* ordinate

Ordinaten·achse *f* axis of ordinates [*cf.* EINTEILUNG]

Ordinaten·differenz *f* (*zweier Punkte*) rise (between two points)

ordnen *v.t.* order, arrange: *ein Polynom nach steigenden* (*fallenden*) *Potenzen o.* arrange a polynomial in ascending (descending) powers [*cf.* GEORDNET]

Ordnung *f* order, ordering, arrangement: *in richtiger O*, in normal order; *in umgekehrter*

O. in inverted (or inverse) order; *Ableitungen höherer O.* derivatives of higher order; *Differenzen erster, zweiter O.* differences of first, second order; *O. einer algebraischen Kurve, Fläche* order of an algebraic curve, surface; *Determinanten von höherer O.* determinants of higher order, higher-order determinants; *Berührung erster O.* contact of first order; *O. einer Gruppe* order of a group; *die beiden unendlich kleinen Größen sind von derselben O.* (*oder Größenordnung*) the two infinitesimals are of the same order (of magnitude); *unendlich von der n-ten O.* of *n*-th order of infinity [*cf.* BERÜHRUNG; DRITT; FÜNFT; GLIEDERUNG; LEXIKOGRAPHISCH; SECHST; VIERT; ZWEIT]

Ordnungs·axiom *n* ordering axiom

Ordnungs·beziehung *f* order(ing) relation

Ordnungs·prinzip *n* order principle

Ordnungs·zahl *f* ordinal number

orientier·bar *adj.* orientable

Orientierbar·keit *f* orientability

orientieren 1. *v.t.* orient, direct. 2. *v.r.*: **sich** *o.* orient oneself, get one's bearings [*cf.* ORIENTIERT]

orientiert *adj.* oriented, directed: *positiv* (*negativ*) *orientierter Winkel* positively (negatively) oriented angle

Orientierung *f* orientation, sense, bearing

Ort *m* 1. (*Lage*) position: *O. eines Punktes zu einer gegebenen Zeit* position of a point at a given time [*cf.* HIMMELSGEGEND]. **2.**

(*Gebilde, das Bedingungen erfüllt* geometric element satisfying conditions) locus: (*geometrischer*) *O. aller Punkte, welche von zwei Parallelen gleich weit abstehen* locus of a point equidistant (or: equally distant) from two parallel lines [*cf.* GEOMETRISCH; MITTEL-LINIE]

orten *v.t.*, *v.i.* (*nav.*, *av.*) fix the position, navigate; (*peilen*) find the direction

Ortho·achse *f* (*cryst.*) orthoaxis, orthodiagonal axis

ortho·diagonal *adj.* (*cryst.*) orthodiagonal

Ortho·diagonale *f* (*cryst.*) orthoaxis, orthodiagonal (axis) [= ORTHOACHSE]

Ortho·doma *n* (*pl. Orthodomen*) (*cryst.*) orthodome

ortho·gonal *adj.* orthogonal; (*Projektion, auch*) orthographic: *orthogonale Basis eines Vektorraums* orthogonal basis of a vector space [*cf.* DREIFACH; PROJEKTION; TRAJEKTORIE; TRANSFORMATION]

Orthogonalität *f* orthogonality

Orthogonal·projektion *f* orthogonal (or orthographic) projection

Orthogonal·system *n* orthogonal system [*cf.* NORMIEREN]

ortho·graphisch *adj.* (*Projektion*) orthographic (projection)

Ortho·pinakoid *n* (*cryst.*) orthopinacoid, orthopinakoid

Ortho·prisma *n* (*crsyt.*) orthoprism

Ortho·pyramide *f* (*cryst.*) orthopyramid

örtlich *adj.* local; (*lagemäßig*)

positional, topological; (*geographisch*) geographic [*cf.* REIHE]

Orts·beziehung *f* topological relation, topology [*cf.* TOPOLOGIE]

orts·fest *adj.* stationary

Orts·funktion *f* position function

Orts·gleichung *f* equation of a locus

Orts·vektor *m* position vector, radius vector [*cf.* FAHRSTRAHL; LEITSTRAHL]

orts·veränderlich *adj.* mobile, movable

Orts·zeit *f* local time

Ortung *f* (*nav.*, *av.*) position fixing, navigation; (*Peilung*) direction finding

Oskulation *f* osculation (in contact of *usu.* at least third, sometimes second order)

Oskulations·ebene *f* (*einer Raumkurve in einem Punkt*) osculating plane (of a space curve at a point)

Oskulations·kreis *m* osculating circle (with contact of *usu.* at least third, sometimes second order)

Oskulations·kugel *f* (*einer Raumkurve in einem Punkt*) osculating sphere (of a space curve at a point)

oskulieren *v.t.* osculate (in contact of *usu.* at least third, sometimes second order): *oskulierender Kreis* [= OSKULATIONSKREIS]; *oskulierende Ebene* (*Kugel*) *einer Raumkurve in einem Punkt* osculating plane (sphere) of a space curve at a point

Ost *m*, **Osten** *m* east

östlich *adj.* eastern, easterly

Ost·punkt *m* east point

Oszillation *f* (*phys.*) oscillation
Oszillator *m* (*phys.*) oscillator
oszillieren *v.i.* oscillate: *oszil-*

lierende Reihe oscillating series
oval *adj.* oval
Oval *n* oval [*cf.* CARTESISCH]

P

Paar *n* pair, couple
paaren *v.t.* pair: *wir p. die
Resultate der beiden Würfel* we
pair the results of the two dice
paar·weise *adj.* mutual; (*adv.*)
pairwise, mutually: *p. gleiche
Seiten* pairwise (or mutually)
equal sides [*cf.* PARALLEL]
p-adisch *adj.* p-adic: *p-adische
Zahl* p-adic number [*cf.* GANZ]
Panto·graph *m* pantograph
Papier *n* paper [*cf.* BEGEBBAR;
QUADRILLIERT]
Papier·maß *n* paper measure
Parabel *f* parabola: *kubische*
(*semikubische*) *P.* cubical (semicubical) parabola [*cf.* CARTE-
SICH; KUBISCH; TRIDENS]
Parabel·bogen *m* parabolic arc
Parabel·gleichung *f* equation of a
parabola
Parabel·segment *n* parabolic segment
parabolisch *adj.* parabolic: *parabolische Kurve, Spirale* parabolic
curve, spiral; *parabolischer Zylinder* parabolic cylinder; *parabolischer Punkt auf einer Fläche*
parabolic point on a surface
[*cf.* GEOMETRIE]
Paraboloid *n* paraboloid [*cf.*
ELLIPTISCH; HYPERBOLISCH]
paradox *adj.* paradoxical

Paradoxie *f*, **Paradoxon** *n* paradox
parallaktisch *adj.* (*astr.*) parallactic
Parallaxe *f* (*astr.*) parallax
parallel *adj.* parallel: *p. laufen mit*
run parallel with; *p. verschieben*
translate; *Gegenwinkel* (*Wechselwinkel*) *mit paarweise parallelen
Schenkeln sind gleich* corresponding (alternate) angles with pairwise
parallel sides are equal; *Anwinkel
mit paarweise parallelen Schenkeln
sind supplementär* angles with
one pair of corresponding sides
parallel in the same direction,
the other pair parallel in opposite
directions, are supplementary
angles; *parallele Lage* parallelism
[*cf.* GERADE]
Parallel *m* (*geog.*) parallel (circle):
auf dem 56. Parallel on the 56th
parallel
Parallele *f* parallel (line) [*cf.* ORT]
Parallel·ebene *f* parallel plane
Parallelen·axiom *n* parallel axiom
Parallelen·postulat *n* parallel postulate
Parallel·epiped *n*, **Parallel·epipedon**
n parallelepiped: *schiefes P.*
oblique parallelepied [*cf.* RECHT-
WINKLIG]
Parallel·flach *n* parallelepiped
Parallel·fläche *f* parallel surface
Parallelismus *m* parallelism:

(*statist.*) *P. der Korrelation* positive correlation

Parallelität *f* parallelism

Parallel·koordinaten *f pl.* parallel coordinates

Parallel·kreis *m* parallel circle

Parallel·kurve *f* parallel curve

Parallelo·gramm *n* parallelogram

Parallel·perspektive *f* parallel perspective

Parallel·projektion *f* parallel projection

Parallel·schnitt *m* parallel section

Parallel·strahl *m* parallel line (or ray)

Parallel·strahlenbündel *n* bundle (or sheaf) of parallel lines

Parallel·strahlenbüschel *n* pencil of parallel lines

Parallel·strömung *f* parallel flow

Parallel·verschiebung *f* parallel shift, translation

Parameter *m* **1.** (*einer Funktion*) parameter (of a function) [*cf.* HILFSVARIABLE; ÜBERZÄHLIG]. **2.** (*eines Kegelschnitts*) latus rectum, focal chord (of a conic); *halber P. eines Kegelschnitts* semifocal chord of a conic. **3.** (*cryst.*) parameter

Parameter·darstellung *f* parametric representation

Parameter·gleichung *f* parametric equation

parametrisch *adj.* parametric: *parametrische Kurven auf einer Fläche* parametric curves on a surface; *parametrische·Gleichung* parametric equation [*cf.* DARSTELLUNG]

Pari *n*, **pari** *adv.* (*fin.*) par: *über p.* above par, at a premium; *unter p.*

below par, at a discount; (*auf*) *p. stehen* be at par

Partial·bruch *m* partial fraction

Partialbruch·zerlegung *f* decomposition of a fraction into partial fractions

Partial·schwingung *f* partial oscillation

partiell *adj.* partial; *partielle Integration* integration by parts [*cf.* ABLEITUNG; DIFFERENTIAL; DIFFERENTIALQUOTIENT]

Partikel *f* particle, mass point, point mass, differential mass

partikular *adj.* (*log.*) (*Urteil*) particular (judgment)

partikulär *adj.* (*Urteil, Integral*) particular (judgment, integral)

Pascal *m* N. [*cf.* DREIECK; SCHNECKE]

passen *v.i.* fit, suit

passend *adj.* suitable, fitting: *p. gewählte Werte* suitably chosen values

passieren *v.t., v.i.* (*astr.*) pass, transit: (*durch*) *den Meridian p.* pass (or transit) (through) the meridian

Passiv·posten *m* (*comm.*) liability

Passivum *n* (*pl. Passiven, Passiva*) (*comm.*) liability [*ant.:* AKTIVUM]

Pauschal·summe *f* (*comm.*) lump sum

pausen *v.t., v.i.* trace

p.c. (*abbr.*) *pro centum* per cent, (*abbr.*) p.c., (*symb.:* %)

Peano *m.* N. [*cf.* AXIOM]

Peck *n* (*meas.*) peck

Pegel *m* water gauge

Pegel·stand *m* water level

Peil·apparat *m* (*nav., av.*) direction finder

peilen *v.t.*, *v.i.* (*nav.*, *av.*) take the bearings, find one's direction [*cf.* ORTEN]

Peil·feld (*nav.*, *av.*) bearing field

Peil·gerät *n* (*nav.*, *av.*) direction finding set, (*abbr.*) DF set

Peil·linie *f* (*nav.*, *av.*) bearing line

Peil·lot *n* (*nav.*) sounding lead

Peil·reichweite *f* (*nav.*, *av.*) DF range

Peilung *f* (*nav.*, *av.*) bearing(s) [*cf.* ORTUNG]

Peilungs·richtung *f* (*nav.*, *av.*) bearing direction

Pendel *n* (*phys.*) pendulum: *mathematisches P.* mathematical (or simple) pendulum; *physisches* (*oder physikalisches*) *P.* physical (or compound) pendulum [*cf.* AUSSCHLAG]

Pendel·ausschlag *m* (*phys.*) pendulum deflection; (*Amplitude*) pendulum swing (or amplitude)

Pendel·bewegung *f* (*phys.*) pendulum motion

Pendel·länge *f* (*phys.*) pendulum length

pendeln *v.i.* (*phys.*) oscillate, swing

Pendel·schwingung *f* (*phys.*) pendulum swing, oscillation

Pendel·uhr *f* pendulum clock

Pendel·versuch *m* (*phys.*) pendulum test (or experiment, or demonstration): *Foucaultscher P.* Foucault's pendulum experiment

Pent·ade *f* pentad

Penta·gon *n* pentagon [= FÜNFECK]

penta·gonal *adj.* pentagonal [= FÜNFECKIG]

Pentagonal·zahl *f* pentagonal number

Pentagon·dodekaeder *n* pentagon dodecahedron, pentadodecahedron

Penta·gramm *n* pentagram

per *prep.* per: *5 Meter per Sekunde* 5 meters per second [*cf.* ENERGIE]

per·fekt *adj.* (*alg.*) perfect: *perfekter Körper* perfect field; *perfekte Erweiterung eines Körpers* perfect extension of a field; *perfekte Menge* perfect set

Peri·gäum . *n* (*astr.*) perigee [= ERDNÄHE]

Peri·hel *n*, **Peri·helium** *n* (*astr.*) perihelion [= SONNENNÄHE]

Perioden·zahl *f* number of periods (or cycles), frequency

Periode *f* period; (*eines Dezimalbruchs*) repetend (of a circulating decimal

periodisch *adj.* periodic(al), recurring, repeating: *periodischer Kettenbruch* periodic (or recurring) continued fraction; *p. wiederkehrend* recurring, periodic; *periodische Wiederkehr* (*oder Wiederholung*) periodicity [*cf.* DEZIMALBRUCH]

Periodizität *f* periodicity

Periodo·gramm *n* (*statist.*) periodogram

Periodogramm·analyse *f* (*statist.*) periodogram analysis

Peri·pherie *f* periphery, circumference

Peripherie·winkel *m* (*eines Kreises*) inscribed angle (of a circle)

Perl·kurve *f* pearls of Sluze

per·manent *adj.* permanent

Per·manenz *f* permanence: *Prinzip der P. der formalen Rechengesetze* principle of permanence of the formal laws of operation (or: formal calculating rules)

Permanenz·prinzip *n* principle of permanence

Permutation *f* permutation: *gerade* (*ungerade*) *P.* even (odd) permutation [*cf.* TRANSPONIEREN; ZYKLISCH]

Permutations·gruppe *f* permutation group

per·mutieren *v.t., v.i.* permute

Perpetuum mobile *n* (*Lat.*) machine with perpetual motion, perpetuum mobile

per·spektiv *adj.* perspective: *perspektive Lage* perspective position

Per·spektive *f* perspective

per·spektivisch *adj.* perspective: *perspektivisches Bild* perspective picture [*cf.* ÄHNLICH; ÄHNLICH-KEITSTRANSFORMATION; VER-KÜRZEN; VERKÜRZUNG]

Per·spektivität *f* perspectivity

Perspektivitäts·achse *f* axis of perspectivity (or perspective, or homology)

Perspektivitäts·zentrum *n* center of perspectivity (or homology)

Perspektiv·projektion *f* perspective projection

Perspektiv·zeichnung *f* perspective drawing

Per·turbation *f* (*astr.*) perturbation

Per·zent *n* per cent, percent (*symb.:* %) [= PROZENT; P.C.] [*cf.* GENAU; WAHRSCHEINLICH-KEIT]

. . . perzentig *suf. adj.* per cent [*cf.* HUNDERTPERZENTIG]

Perzent·satz *m* percentage

Perzentil *n* (*statist.*) percentile

perzentual, perzentuell *adj.* [= PROZENTUAL, PROZENTUELL]

Pfand *m* (*comm.*) pledge, pawn, security

Pfand·brief *m* (*fin.*) mortgage bond

Pfd. (*abbr.*) *Pfund* pound, (*abbr.*) (*Gewicht*) lb., *pl.* lbs.; (*Geld*) £

Pferde·fessel *f* (*Kurve*) horse fetter, hippopede [= HIPPOPEDE]

Pferde·kraft *f*, **Pferde·stärke** *f* (*mech.*) horsepower [*cf.* PS]

Pfund *n* (*Gewicht* weight; *Geld* money) pound [*cf.* PFD.]

Phase *f* phase [*cf.* WIEDERKEHREN]

phasen·abhängig *adj.* phase-dependent

Phasen·konstante *f* phase constant

Phasen·nacheilung *f* phase lag

Phasen·raum *m* phase space

Phasen·regel *f* (*phys.*) phase rule

phasen·synchron *adj.* phase-synchronous

Phasen·unterschied *m* phase difference

Phasen·verschiebung *f* phase shift

Phasen·verzögerung *f* phase lag

Phasen·voreilung *f* phase lead

Phasen·wahrscheinlichkeit *f* probability of phase

Phasen·welle *f* (*phys.*) phase (or de Broglie) wave

Phasen·winkel *m* phase angle

phasisch *adj.* phasic

Phi *n* (*griechischer Buchstabe* Greek letter Φ, ϕ) phi

Phon *n* (*acoust. meas.*) phon

photo·elektrisch *adj.* photoelectric

Photo·elektrizität *f* photoelectricity

Photo·meter *n* (*opt.*) photometer

Photon *n* (*phys.*) photon

Physik *f* physics

physikalisch *adj.* physical [*cf.*
PENDEL] .
Physiker *m* physicist
physisch *adj.* physical [*cf.* PENDEL]
Pi *n* (*griechischer Buchstabe* Greek
letter $\Pi\ \pi$) pi
Piezo·elektrizität *f* piezoelectricity
Pinakoid *n* (*cryst.*) pinacoid, pina-
koid [*cf.* BASISCH]
Pinte *f* (*meas.*) pint
Plan *m* plan; (*Karte einer Stadt*)
map (of a city)
Planck *m* N. (*phys.*) Plancksches
(*oder elementares*) *Wirkungs-*
. *quantum* Planck's constant, ele-
mentary quantum of action
Planet *m* (*astr.*) planet [*cf.*
ÄUSSER; INNER; LAUF; RECHT-
LÄUFIGKEIT; RÜCKLÄUFIGKEIT;
VERDUNKELN; VERDUNKLUNG;
VERFINSTERN; VERFINSTERUNG]
planetarisch *adj.* (*astr.*) planetary
Planeten·bewegung *f* (*astr.*) motion
of planets, planetary motion
Planetoid *m* (*astr.*) planetoid,
asteroid [= ASTEROID]
Plani·glob *m*, *n* (*usu. pl. Planigloben*)
planisphere [= PLANISPHÄRE]
Plani·meter *m* planimeter
Plani·metrie *f* planimetry, plane
geometry
Plani·sphäre *f* planisphere [=
PLANIGLOB]
Plan·schnitt *m* plane section
Plan·spiegel *m* plane mirror
Plan·symmetrie *f* plane symmetry
plan·symmetrisch *adj.* plane-sym-
metric
plastisch *adj.* plastic
Plastizität *f* plasticity
Platz·wechsel **1.** (*Platzänderung*)
change of place. **2.** (*comm.*)

(*hiesiger Wechsel*) local bill (of
exchange)
Plural *m* plural
plus *adv.* plus; (*in der Addition* in
addition, also) and: *a Quadrat
plus b Quadrat ist gleich c
Quadrat a* square plus *b* square
equals *c* square (*symb.:* $a^2 + b^2 =
c^2$) [*cf.* MAL]
Plus·zeichen *n* plus (or positive)
sign; (*in der Addition* in addition,
also) addition sign
p. m. (*abbr.*) *pro mille* per mille
Pol *m* pole: *P. eines Koordinatensystems* pole of a system of coordinates; *P. einer Funktion* pole
of a function [*cf.* KEGELSCHNITT]
polar *adj.* polar [*cf.* REZIPROK;
REZIPROZITÄT]
Polar·abstand *m* polar distance
[= POLDISTANZ]
Polar·achse *f* polar axis
Polar·distanz *f* (*astr.*) [= POL-
DISTANZ]
Polar·dreieck *n* **1.** (*eines sphäri-
schen Dreiecks*) polar triangle
(of a spherical triangle). **2.** (*eines
Kegelschnitts*) self-polar triangle
(of a conic)
Polare *f* **1.** (*einer Kurve, Fläche
zweiter Ordnung*) polar (line)
(of a quadric). **2.** (*Krümmungs-
achse*) axis of curvature [*cf.*
KEGELSCHNITT]
Polar·ebene *f* polar plane
Polar·ecke *f* polar solid angle
Polaren·theorie *f* polar theory
Polar·form *f* polar form
Polar·gleichung *f* polar equation
Polarisation *f* (*phys.*) polarization
Polarisations·ebene *f* (*phys.*)
polarization plane

Polarisations·winkel *m* (*phys.*) polarization angle

polarisieren *v.t.* (*phys.*) polarize

Polar·kegelschnitt *m* polar conic

Polar·koordinaten *f pl.* polar co-ordinates [*cf.* EXTREMPUNKT; RADIUSVEKTOR]

Polar·kreis *m* (*geog.*) arctic circle

Polar·kurve *f* (*geom.*) polar curve; (*statist.*) polar diagram

Polar·normale *f* polar normal

Polar·planimeter *m* polar plani-meter

Polar·stern *m* (*astr.*) pole star

Polar·subnormale *f* polar sub-normal

Polar·subtangente *f* polar sub-tangent

Polar·tangente *f* polar tangent

Polar·tetraeder *n* (*einer Fläche zweiter Ordnung*) self-polar tetrahedron (of a quadric surface)

Polar·winkel *m* polar (or vectorial) angle, amplitude, anomaly, argu-ment, azimuth [*cf.* AMPLITUDE; ANOMALIE; ARGUMENT; AZIMUT]

Pol·distanz *f* (*astr.*)(*eines Himmels-punkts*) polar ˙ distance, codec-lination (of a celestial point) [*cf.* POLARDISTANZ]

Pol·einheit *f* (*mag.*) unit pole

Pol·höhe *f* (*geog., astr.*) (*eines Punktes auf der Erde*) latitude (of a point on the earth)

Polizze *f* (*ins.*) policy [*cf.* ABLÖSEN; BELEIHUNGSWERT; ERSATZWERT; RÜCKKAUF; UMWANDLUNG]

Pol·stärke *f* (*phys.*) pole strength

Poly·eder *n* polyhedron: *reguläres* (*oder regelmäßiges*) *P.* regular polyhedron [*cf.* BEGRENZUNGS-FLÄCHE; FLÄCHE; FLÄCHENZAHL;

KANTENZAHL; SEITE 2.; SEITEN-FLÄCHE; SEITENZAHL]

poly·edrisch *adj.* polyhedral

Poly·gon *n* polygon [= VIELECK]: *Umkreisradius* (*Inkreisradius*) *eines regulären Polygons* long (short) radius of a regular poly-gon [*cf.* AUSSPRINGEND; ECKEN-ZAHL; ... GON; SEITENZAHL; UMFANG]

poly·gonal *adj.* polygonal

Polygonal·zahl *f* polygonal (or figurate) number

poly·konisch *adj.* (*Projektion*) polyconic (projection)

Poly·nom *n* polynomial [*cf.* AN-FANGSKOEFFIZIENT; AUSGEHEN; GEWICHT; GRAD; HOMOGEN; INHALT; IRREDUZIBEL; NOR-MIEREN; ORDNEN; PRIMITIV; STEIGEN; UNZERLEGBAR]

Polynom·bereich *m* (*alg.*) [= POLYNOMRING]

Polynom·ideal *n* (*alg.*) polynomial ideal

poly·nomisch *adj.* polynomial

Polynom·ring *m* (*alg.*) polynomial ring

Porto *n* (*comm.*) postage

porto·frei (*comm.*) **1.** (*für den Absender*) exempt from postage (for the sender). **2.** (*für den Empfänger*) prepaid (for the consignee)

Porto·spesen *pl.* (*comm.*) (expenses for) postage: *P. vom Absender bezahlt* prepaid

Position *f* position

positiv *adj.* positive [*cf.* DEFINIT; NEIGUNGSWINKEL; ORIENTIEREN; RICHTUNGSWINKEL; VORZEICHEN; WINKEL; WURZEL]

Positron *n* (*phys.*) positron
Possibilität *f* (*statist.*) possibility, likelihood: *Methode der maximalen P.* method of maximum likelihood
Post·anweisung *f* (*comm.*) postal note, money order
Posten *m* (*Einzelgegenstand*) item: (*Summand*) summand, addend [*cf.* AUFRECHNEN; AUSGLEICHEN; VERRECHNEN]
Postulat *n* postulate [*cf.* FORDERUNG]
postulieren *v.t.* postulate [*cf.* FORDERN]
Potential *n* (*phys.*) potential
Potential·differenz *f* (*phys.*) potential difference
Potential·funktion *f* (*phys.*) potential function
Potential·gefälle *n* (*phys.*) potential gradient
Potential·gleichung *f* (*phys.*) potential equation
Potential·strömung *f* (*phys.*) potential flow
Potential·theorie *f* (*phys.*) potential theory
potentiell *adj.* potential [*cf.* ENERGIE]
Potenz *f* power: *dritte P.* third power, cube [*cf.* KUBIEREN]; *eine Zahl zur zweiten P. erheben* square a number [*cf.* QUADRIEREN]; *steigende* (*oder aufsteigende*) *Potenzen* ascending powers; *fallende* (*oder absteigende*) *Potenzen* descending powers; *P. eines Punktes in bezug auf einen Kreis* (*eine Kugel*) power of a point with reference to a circle (a sphere) [*cf.* BASIS; ERHEBEN;

ERHEBUNG; ERST; GLEICH; GRUNDZAHL; HERAUSFALLEN; HOCH; KUBUS; ORDNEN; STEIGEN]
Potenz·ebene *f* (*zweier Kugeln*) radical plane (of two spheres)
Potenz·exponent *m* power exponent
Potenz·funktion *f* power function
potenzieren *v.t.* raise to a power
Potenzieren *n* [= POTENZIERUNG] [*cf.* FREMD]
Potenzierung *f* raising to a power, involution
Potenz·linie *f* (*zweier Kreise*) radical axis (of two circles) [= CHORDALE; RADIKALACHSE]
Potenz·mittelpunkt *m*, **Potenz·punkt** *m* (*von drei Kreisen, vier Kugeln*) radical center (of three circles, four spheres) [= POTENZZENTRUM; RADIKALZENTRUM]
Potenz·reihe *f* power series: *steigende* (*oder aufsteigende*) *P.* ascending power series; *fallende* (*oder absteigende*) *P.* descending power series [*cf.* KONVERGENT; KONVERGENZRADIUS]
Potenz·rest *m* (*alg.*) power remainder
Potenz·summe *f* sum of powers
Potenz·zentrum *n* [= POTENZPUNKT]
prädikabel *adj.* (*log.*) predicable
Prädikat *n* (*log.*) predicate: *P. der ersten, zweiten Stufe* predicate of first, second level [*cf.* DREIGLIEDRIG; INDIVIDUELL; PRÄDIKATSBEGRIFF]
Prädikaten·begriff *m* (*log.*) concept of predicate [= PRÄDIKATSBEGRIFF 1.]
Prädikaten·kalkül *m* (*log.*) predi-

cate calculus: *der engere P.* the restricted predicate calculus [*cf.* IDENTISCH; REDUKTIONSSÄTZE]; *erweiterter P.* extended predicate calculus [*cf.* ELIMINATIONSPROBLEM]; [*cf.* EINSTELLIG]

Prädikaten·prädikat *n* (*log.*) predicate of predicates, predicate of second level, second-level predicate: *individuelles P.* predicate constant of second level, second-level predicate constant

Prädikaten·variable *f* (*log.*) predicate variable

prädikativ *adj.* predicative [*cf.* INDIVIDUENPRÄDIKAT]

Prädikats·begriff *m* (*log.*) **1.** (*Begriff des Prädikats*) concept of predicate [*cf.* PRÄDIKATENBEGRIFF]. **2.** (*in der Aussage*) predicate (term) (in a sentence)

Prädikat·zeichen *n* (*log.*) predicate symbol

Prä·fix *n* (*log.*) (*einer Aussagenformel*) prefix (of a sentential formula)

Prämie *f* (*comm., fin.*) premium, bonus

Prämien·geschäft *n* (*comm.*) option, optional bargain, option (or future) business

Prämien·satz *m* (*ins.*) (premium) rate

Prä·misse *f* (*log.*) premise

prä·nex *adj.* prenex: *pränexe Normalform des Aussagenkalküls* prenex normal form of the predicate calculus

Prä·zession *f* (*astr.*) precession

Präzisions·maß *n* precision measure

Preis *m* (*comm.*) price: *im Preise fallen* (*oder herabsinken*) depreci-

ate in price [*cf.* ABSCHLAG; ABSCHLAGEN; ANZIEHEN; AUFSCHLAG; AUFSCHLAGEN; FIX; ZUSCHLAGEN]

Preis·entwicklung *f* (*comm.*) trend of prices

Preis·index *m*, **Preis·meßzahl** *f* (*statist.*) price index

Preis·nachlaß *m* (*comm.*) deduction (from the price), rebate; (*Diskont*) discount

prim *adj.* prime: *relativ p.* relatively prime, prime to each other

Prima·nota *f* (*comm.*) ledger abstract

primär *adj.* primary: (*alg.*) *stark* (*schwach*) *primäres Ideal* strongly (weakly) primary ideal

Primär·ideal *n* (*alg.*) primary ideal

Primär·komponente *f* (*alg.*) primary component: *isolierte P.* isolated primary component

Primär·statistik *f* collection of statistical data for statistical purposes [*ant.:* SEKUNDÄRSTATISTIK]

Prima·wechsel *m* (*comm.*) first of exchange

Prim·element *n* (*alg.*) prime element

Prim·faktor *m* prime factor

Prim·faktor(en)zerlegung *f* prime factorization

Prim·ideal *n* (*alg.*) prime ideal: *höheres* (*niederes*) *P.* higher (lower) prime ideal; *teilerloses P.* maximal prime ideal [*cf.* NULLSTELLE; UNVERKÜRZBAR]

primitiv *adj.* primitive: *primitive Einheitswurzel* primitive root of unity; (*alg.*) *primitives Polynom* primitive polynomial [*cf.* EINHEITSFORM]

Prim·körper *m* (*alg.*) prime field [*cf.* CHARAKTERISTIK]

Prim·zahl *f* prime number: *relative Primzahlen* relatively prime numbers, numbers prime to each other

Primzahl·grad *m* (*alg.*) prime degree: *metazyklische Gleichung von P.* metacyclic equation of prime degree

Primzahl·potenz *f* power of a prime number, prime power

Primzahlpotenz·gruppe *f* prime-power group

Prinzip *n* principle [*cf.* AKTION; GRUNDSATZ; PERMANENZ]

Prioritäten *pl.* (*fin.*) preference bonds

Prioritäts·obligation *f* (*fin.*) preference bond

Prisma *n* prism: *gerades, schiefes P.* right, oblique prism; *vierseitiges P.* quadrangular prism; *gerades vierseitiges P.* right quadrangular prism, rectangular solid [*cf.* ACHTSEITIG; DARSTELLEN; DITRIGONAL; DREISEITIG; FÜNF-SEITIG; GRUNDFLÄCHE; SÄULE; SECHSSEITIG; SEITENFLÄCHE; SIEBENSEITIG; VIELSEITIG]

prismatisch *adj.* prismatic

Prismatoid *n*, **Prismoid** *n* prisma-toid, prismoid [*cf.* MITTEL-SCHNITT]

Privatwirtschafts·statistik *f* business statistics (of the firm)

pro *prep.* per: *Kilogramm p. Quadratzentimeter* kilograms per square centimeter; *p. centum* per cent [*cf.* P.C.; PROZENT]; *p. mille*

per mille [*cf.* P.M.; PROMILLE]

Probabilismus *m* (*phys.*) proba-bilism

probabilistisch *adj.* (*phys.*) proba-bilistic

Probe *f* **1.** (*Prüfung* examination) test; *auf eine Regel die P. machen* test a rule. **2.** (*Nachprüfung* re-examination) check: *P. auf die (Richtigkeit der) Lösung einer Gleichung* check on (the correct-ness of) a solution of an equation; *die P. auf eine Rechnung machen* check a computation

Probe·bilanz *f* (*comm.*) trial balance

Problem *n* problem [*cf.* AUFGEBEN; DELISCH; ENTSTEHEN]

problematisch *adj.* problematic(al)

Problem·stellung *f* posing (or formulation) of a problem

Pro·dukt *n* product: *äußeres (oder vektorielles) P. zweier Vektoren* cross (or vector, or outer) product of two vectors) [= VEKTORPRODUKT]; *inneres P. zweier Vektoren* inner (or dot) product of two vectors [= SKALARPRODUKT]; [*cf.* DIREKT; FAKTOR; LOGISCH; UNENDLICH; VERSCHRÄNKT; ZUSAMMENGE-SETZT]

Produkten·börse *f* (*comm.*) produce exchange

Profil *n* profile: *im P.* (in) profile

Pro·fit *m* (*comm., fin.*) profit

Pro·gression *f* progression [*cf.* ARITHMETISCH; GEOMETRISCH; HARMONISCH; REIHE]

Pro-jektion *f* (*descr.*) projection, view: *orthogonale (oder recht-winklige) P.* orthogonal (or orthographic) projection; *erste (oder horizontale) P.* horizontal projection, top view [= GRUNDRISS]; *zweite (oder vertikale) P.* vertical projection, front view [= AUFRISS]; *dritte (oder seitliche) P.* side view [= SEITENRISS] [*cf.* ABBILDUNG; ANISOMETRISCH; AXONOMETRISCH; DARSTELLEN 2.; DARSTELLUNG 2.; DIMETRISCH; GNOMONISCH; ISOMETRISCH; KOTIERT; ORTHOGONAL; ORTHOGRAPHISCH; STEREOGRAPHISCH; TRIMETRISCH; VERMITTELND]

Projektions·achse *f* (*descr.*) reference line of projection [*cf.* ACHSE]

Projektions·apparat *n* projection apparatus, projector

Projektions·ebene *f* (*descr.*) projection plane: *erste (oder horizontale) P.* horizontal (projection) plane, ground plane [= GRUNDRISSEBENE]; *zweite (oder vertikale) P.* vertical (projection) plane [= AUFRISSEBENE]; *dritte (oder seitliche) P.* profile plane [= KREUZRISSEBENE; SEITENRISSEBENE] [*cf.* BILDEBENE; QUADRAT; SPUR; TAFEL 2.]

Projektions·lehre *f* (*descr.*) theory of projection, descriptive geometry

Projektions·strahl *m* (*descr.*) ray of projection, projector

Projektions·tafel *f* (*descr.*) [= PROJEKTIONSEBENE; TAFEL 2.]

Projektions·zentrum *n* (*descr.*) center of projection, ray center

pro·jektiv *adj.* projective: *projektive Beziehung, Ebene* projective relation, plane [*cf.* GEOMETRIE]

Pro-jektivität *f* projectivity

Projektivitäts·achse *f* (*zweier Punktreihen*) cross axis (of projectivity) (of two ranges of points)

pro·jizieren *v.t., v.r.:* sich *p.* (*descr.*) project: *projizierender Zylinder* projecting cylinder; *projizierende Ebene* projecting plane, plane projector; *projizierender Strahl* projecting ray, projector [*cf.* ABBILDEN]

Pro·messe *f* (*fin.*) promissory note

Pro·mille *n* per mille, per mil, per thousand

Pro·portion *f* proportion [*cf.* AUSSENGLIED; ÄUSSER; FORTLAUFEND; GLIED; INNENGLIED; INNER; STETIG; VERHÄLTNIS; ZUSAMMENGESETZT]

pro·portional *adj.* proportional: *umgekehrt (oder invers) p.* inversely proportional [*cf.* DIREKT; VERHÄLTNISMÄSSIG]

Pro·portionale *f* proportional: *vierte P.* fourth proportional; *dritte stetige P.* third proportional [*cf.* MITTEL]

Pro·portionalität *f* proportionality

Proportionalitäts·faktor *m* factor of proportionality

Proton *n* (*phys.*) proton

Proto·prisma *n* (*cryst.*) protoprism, prism of the first order, unit prism [*cf.* GRUNDPRISMA]

Proto·pyramide *f* (*cryst.*) protopyramid, pyramid of the first order, unit pyramid [*cf.* GRUNDPYRAMIDE]

Provision *f* (*comm.*) (*des Geschäftsvermittlers*) commission (of the broker)

provisorisch *adj.* (*zeitweilig*) provisional, temporary; (*versuchsweise*) tentative; (*hilfsweise*) auxiliary [*cf.* MITTELWERT]
Pro·zent *n* per cent, percent [*cf.* ZINS]
. . . **prozentig** *suf. adj.* per cent [*cf.* HUNDERTPROZENTIG]
Prozent·satz *m* percentage [*cf.* VERHÄLTNISZAHL]
pro·zentual, pro·zentuell *adj.* per cent, percentage of: *der prozentuelle Anteil* the percentage of share
Pro·zeß *m* process [*cf.* VORGANG]
PS (*abbr.*) *Pferdestärke* horsepower, (*abbr.*) HP
Pseudo·sphäre *f* pseudosphere
pseudo·sphärisch *adj.* pseudospherical: *pseudosphärische Fläche* pseudospherical surface
Psi *n* (*griechischer Buchstabe* Greek letter Ψ, ψ) psi
ptolemäisch *adj.* Ptolemaic, Ptolemy's: *ptolemäisches System* (*oder Weltsystem*) Ptolemaic (cosmic) system; *ptolemäischer Lehrsatz* Ptolemy's theorem [*cf.* GEGENSEHNENSATZ]
Ptolemäus *m* N. Ptolemy [*cf.* PTOLEMÄISCH]
Punkt *m* **1.** (*geom.*) point: *Entfernung* (*oder Abstand oder Distanz*) *zweier Punkte* distance between two points; *durch denselben Punkt* (*gehend*) concurrent, copunctal; *Linien, Ebenen durch einen P.* concurrent (or copunctal) lines, planes [*cf.* ABSTAND; ABSTEHEN; ABSZISSENDIFFERENZ; ALLGEMEIN; ANPASSUNG; ANSCHMIEGEN; ANSCHMIEGUNG; AUSGEHEN;

ÄUSSER; AUSZEICHNEN; BILD; DOPPELVERHÄLTNIS; DREHUNG; DURCHSTOSSEN; EINPASSEN; EINTRAGEN; EINZEICHNEN; ELLIPTISCH; FÄLLEN; FEST; GEBILDE; GEHEN; GELTEN; GERADE; GEWÖHNLICH; GROSS; HARMONISCH; HÖHENDIFFERENZ;HYPERBOLISCH; INNER; INVERS; INVERSION; ISOLIERT; KONJUGIERT; KRAFTMOMENT; LAGE; LEGEN; MASSENMITTELPUNKT; MATERIELL; MEHRFACH; MOMENT^2; NACHBARSCHAFT; ORDINATENDIFFERENZ; ORT 1.,2.; PARABOLISCH; POTENZ; REIHE; REZIPROK; SCHEINBAR; SINGULÄR; SPHÄRISCH; STETIG; TAFELABSTAND; TANGENTE; TREFFEN; UMGEBUNG; UNEIGENTLICH; UNENDLICH; ZUORDNEN; ZUSAMMENSTELLUNG]. **2.** (*Tüpfelchen*) dot. **3.** (*Interpunktion* punctuation) *Am.* period, *Br.* full stop
Punkte·paar *n* [= PUNKT·PAAR]
Punkt·feld *n* (*ebenes*) (plane) field of points
punkt·förmig *adj.* punctiform, point-shaped
punktieren *v.t.* dot: *punktierte Linie* dotted line
Punkt·koordinate *f* point coordinate
Punkt·ladung *f* (*phys.*) point charge
Punkt·masse *f* **1.** (*phys.*) point mass [= MASSENPUNKT]. **2.** (*statist.*) statistical universe or time series of point (or cumulative) data [*ant.:* STRECKENMASSE] [*cf.* BEWEGUNGSMASSE; EREIGNISMASSE; STRECKENMASSE]
Punkt·menge *f* point set, set of points [*cf.* ÄUSSER; DISKRET;

DURCHMESSER; HÄUFUNGSPUNKT; INNER; INNERES; ISOLIERT; OFFEN; MASS; MAJORANTE; MINORANTE]
Punkt·paar *n* pair of points, point pair [*cf.* HARMONISCH]
Punkt·quelle *f* (*phys.*) point source
Punkt·reihe *f* range (or row, or series, or pencil) of points [*cf.* FUNDAMENTALPUNKT; INEINANDERLIEGEN; PROJEKTIVITÄTSACHSE; TRÄGER 2.; WURF]
punkt·weise *adj., adv.* point by point [*cf.* BESTIMMEN]
Punkt·wolke *f* (*statist.*) point cloud, bi-variate point distribution
pyramidal *adj.* pyramidal
Pyramide *f* (*geom.*) pyramid; (*cryst.: Doppelpyramide*) pyramid, bipyramid: *abgestumpfte* (*oder abgestutzte*) *P.* frustum of a pyramid, truncated pyramid

[*cf.* ACHTSEITIG; FÜNFSEITIG; GRUNDFLÄCHE; MANTEL; NETZ; SECHSSEITIG; SEITENFLÄCHE; SEITENHÖHE; SIEBENSEITIG; SPITZE; VIELSEITIG; VIERSEITIG]
Pyramiden·fläche *f* pyramidal surface
pyramiden·förmig *adj.* pyramidal
Pyramiden·oktaeder *n* (*cryst.*) triakisoctahedron [=TRIAKISOKTAEDER]
Pyramiden·stumpf *m*, **Pyramidenstutz** *m* frustum of a pyramid
Pyramiden·würfel *m* tetrahexahedron, tetrakishexahedron [= TETRAKISHEXAEDER]
pythagoräisch *adj.* Pythagorean, Pythagoras': *pythagoräische Zahlen* Pythagorean numbers; *pythagoräischer Lehrsatz* Pythagorean (or Pythagoras') theorem

Q

q.e.d. (*abbr.*) *quod erat demonstrandum* (*Lat.*) (*was zu beweisen war* which was to be demonstrated) (*abbr.*) Q.E.D.
Quader *m* right parallelepiped, rectangular solid, cuboid
Quadrant *m* quadrant: *erster* (*zweiter*) *Q.* first (second) quadrant; *Winkel im ersten Quadranten* first quadrant angle; *die beiden Projektionsebenen teilen den Raum in vier Quadranten* the two projection planes divide the space into four quadrants (or angles)

Quadrat *n* (*math., geom.*) square: *magisches Q.* magic square [*cf.* ABWEICHUNG; ERGÄNZEN; ERGÄNZUNG; KLEINST; PLUS; VERVOLLSTÄNDIGEN; VIERECK; VOLLSTÄNDIG]
Quadrat·dezimeter *n* (*abbr.* qdm, dm^2) square decimeter (or decimetre), (*abbr.* sq. dm.)
Quadrat·fuß *m* square foot, (*abbr.* sq. ft.)
quadratisch *adj.* quadratic, quadric, square: *quadratische Gleichung* quadratic (equation), quadric [*cf.* ABWEICHUNG; FEH-

LER; FORM; MATRIX; MITTEL; SCHEMA; VIERECKIG]

Quadrat·kilometer *n* (*abbr.* qkm, km²) square kilometer (or kilometre), (*abbr.* sq. km.)

Quadrat·meile *f* square mile

Quadrat·meter *n* (*abbr.* qm, m²) square meter (or metre), (*abbr.* sq. m.)

Quadrat·millimeter *n* (*abbr.* qmm, mm²) square millimeter (or millimetre), (*abbr.* sq. mm.)

Quadrat·myriameter *n* (*abbr.* qμm, μm²) square myriameter

Quadratrix *f* (*Kurve*) quadratrix

Quadrat·rute *f* square rod

Quadrat·schein *m* (*astr.*) [= GEVIERTSCHEIN]

Quadrat·summe *f* sum of squares

Quadratur *f* **1.** (*einer Fläche*) quadrature, squaring (of a surface): *Q. des Kreises* (*oder Zirkels*) quadrature of a circle, squaring the circle [*cf.* MECHANISCH]. **2.** (*astr.*) [= GEVIERTSCHEIN]

Quadrat·wurzel *f* square root [*cf.* WURZEL]

Quadrat·yard *n* square yard (*abbr.* sq. yd.)

Quadrat·zahl *f* square number

Quadrat·zentimeter *n* (*abbr.* qcm, cm²) square centimeter (or centimetre), (*abbr.* sq. cm.) [*cf.* PRO]

Quadrat·zoll *m* square inch (*abbr.* sq. inch)

quadrierbar *adj.* **1.** (*Fläche*) squarable (surface), (surface) whose area can be determined; (*integrierbar*) integrable (surface) [*cf.* INTEGRIERBAR]. **2.** (*Zahl, Ausdruck*) squarable (number, expression), (number, expression) whose

square can be determined

quadrieren *v.t.* **1.** (*zur zweiten Potenz erheben*) square, raise to the second power. **2.** (*eine Fläche*) square, determine the area of (a surface)

Quadrierung *f* **1.** (*einer Zahl*) squaring (of a number), raising (a number) to the second power. **2.** (*einer Fläche*) squaring, quadrature (of a surface)

Quadri·folium *n* (*Kurve*) quadrifolium [= VIERBLATT]

quadrilliert *adj.* quadrillé, ruled in squares: *quadrilliertes Papier* graph (or coordinate, or cross-section, or ruled, or squared, or quadrillé) paper [*cf.* MILLIMETERPAPIER]

Quadrillion *f* (= 10²⁴) *Am.* septillion; *Br.* quadrillion

Quadrupel *n* quadruple

Qualität *f* quality

qualitativ *adj.* qualitative [*cf.* KONKURRIEREND]

Quant *n* (*phys.*) quantum

quanteln *v.t.* (*phys.*) quantize

Quantelung *f* (*phys.*) quantization

Quanten·bahn *f* (*phys.*) quantum orbit (or path)

Quanten·mechanik *f* (*phys.*) quantum mechanics

quanten·mechanisch *adj.* (*phys.*) quantum-mechanical

Quanten·theorie *f* (*phys.*) quantum theory

Quanten·zahl *f* (*phys.*) quantum number

Quanti·fikation *f* quantification

quanti·fizieren *v.t.* quantify

Quantität *f* quantity [*cf.* MENGE; UNENDLICH]

quantitativ *adj* quantitative [*cf.* KONKURRIEREND]

Quantum *n* (*pl. Quanten*) quantum

Quart *n* (*meas.*) quart

Quartal *n* (*eines Jahres*) quarter (of a year) [*cf.* LAUFEN]

Quartil *n* (*statist.*) quartile

Quartils·abstand *m* (*statist.*): (*mittlerer*) *Q.* quartile deviation, semi-interquartile range

quasi·gleich *adj.* (*alg.*) quasi-equal

Quasi·gleichheit *f* (*alg.*) quasi-equality

Quasi·teiler *m* (*alg.*) quasi-divisor

Quasi·vielfache(s) *n* (*alg.*) quasi-multiple

quaternär *adj.* quaternary

Quaternion *f* quaternion

Quaternionen·gruppe *f* quaternion group

Quaternionen·körper *m* (*alg.*) quaternion field, algebra of quaternions

Quaternionen·ring *m* (*alg.*) quaternion ring

quer *adj.* cross, transversal, transverse; *adv.* across

Quer·achse *f* transversal (or cross) axis

Quer·doma *n* (*pl. Querdomen*) (*cryst.*) macrodome

Quer·profil *n* cross profile

Quer·schnitt *m* cross (or transverse) section [*cf.*DURCHSCHNITT; UMFANG]

Quer·schwingung *f* (*phys.*) transversal oscillation (or vibration)

Quer·strich *m* cross bar

Quer·welle *f* (*phys.*) transversal wave

Quintillion *f* (10^{30}) *Am.* nonillion, *Br.* quintillion

Quintupel *n* quintuple

quittieren *v.t.* (*comm.*) (*eine Rechnung*) receipt (a bill)

Quittung *f* (*comm.*) receipt

quod erat demonstrandum [*cf.* Q.E.D.]

Quote *f* quota

Quotient *m* quotient

Quotienten·gruppe *f* (*alg.*) quotient group

Quotienten·körper *m* (*alg.*) field of quotients, quotient field

Quotienten·ring *m* (*alg.*) quotient ring

R

Rabatt *m* discount; (*für Wiederverkäufer*) trade discount (for retailer)

radial *adj.* radial

Radiale *f* radial (curve)

Radial·komponente *f* radial component

Radian *m*, **Radiant** *m* radian

[= *Einheit im* BOGENMASS]

radiär *adj.* radial

Radiär·komponente *f* radial component

Radikal *n* radical

Radikal·achse *f* [= POTENZLINIE]

Radikal·zentrum *n* [= POTENZPUNKT]

Radikand *m* radicand
radio·aktiv *adj.* (*phys.*) radioactive
[*cf.* HALBWERTSZEIT]
Radius *m* (*pl. Radien*) (*eines Kreises, einer Kugel*) radius (of a circle, a sphere) [*cf.* EIN-SCHLIESSEN; REZIPROK]
Radius·vektor *m* **1.** (*in Polar-koordinaten* in polar coordinates) radius vector, polar radius [*cf.* ANFANGSRICHTUNG]. **2.** (*eines Kegelschnittpunkts*) focal radius (or distance) (of a point of a conic). **3.** (*Ortsvektor*) position vector
radizieren *v.t.* extract a root
Radizierung *f* extraction of a root, evolution
Rad·kurve *f*, **Rad·linie** *f* cycloid [= ZYKLOIDE]
Rahmen *m* frame, framework
Rand *m* (*eines Bereichs, einer Menge*) boundary, frontier (of a domain, a set)
Rand·bedingung *f* boundary condition
rändern *v.t.* (*eine Determinante*) border (a determinant)
Rand·integral *n* boundary integral
Rand·punkt *m* (*eines Intervalls, einer Menge*) boundary point (of an interval, of a set) [*cf.* ABGE-SCHLOSSEN]
Rand·wert *m* boundary value
Randwert·aufgabe *f*, **Randwert-problem** *n* boundary value problem
Rang *m* rank: *R. einer Matrix* rank of a matrix
Rate *f* (*comm.*) installment [*cf.* ABSCHLAG; ABZAHLUNG; TEIL-ZAHLUNG; TILGEN]

Raten·geschäft *n* [= ABZAHLUNGS-GESCHÄFT]
Raten·zahlung *f* installment payment
rational *adj.* rational: *rationale Zahl* rational number; *rationale Kurve* rational curve, unicursal (curve); *r. machen* rationalize [*cf.* GANZ; WURZELAUSDRUCK]
Rationalität *f* rationality
Rationalitäts·bereich *m* domain of rationality, (commutative) field
Rational·machung *f* rationalization
Rational·zahl *f* rational number
rational·zahlig *adj.* rational; (*mit rationalen Koeffizienten*) with rational coefficients [*cf.* UNZER-LEGBAR]
Raum *m* space [*cf.* AUFSPANNEN; AUSGEDEHNT; DIMENSION; EU-KLIDISCH; GEKRÜMMT; LEER; LI-NEAR; METRISCH; QUADRANT; SENKRECHT; TOPOLOGISCH; VIER-DIMENSIONAL]
Raum·abmessung *f* (spatial) dimension
raum·artig *adj.* (*phys.*) (*Intervall*) space-like (interval)
Raum·ausdehnung *f* **1.** (*Erwei-terung*) volume (or spatial, or cubical) expansion. **2.** (*Di-mension*) spatial dimension
Raum·bild *n* stereopicture, three-dimensional view; (*Stereo-skopbild*) stereoscopic image
Raum·dimension *f* space dimension
Raum·geometrie *f* solid (or space) geometry, stereometry
Raum·gerade *f* line of space
Raum·gewicht *n* specific weight, weight per unit volume

Raum·gitter *n* space lattice (or grating)

Raum·inhalt *m* volume, solid space [= VOLUMEN]

Rauminhalts·element *n* element of volume

Raum·integral *n* space integral

Raum·koordinate *f* space co-ordinate.

Raum·kurve *f* space curve: *mehrfach* (*oder doppelt*) *gekrümmte R.* skew (or tortuous, or twisted) curve [*cf.* DREIBEIN; HAUPT-NORMALE; KRÜMMUNG; KRÜM-MUNGSACHSE; OSKULATIONS-EBENE; OSKULATIONSKUGEL; OSKULIEREN; REKTIFIZIEREN; SCHMIEGUNGSEBENE; SCHMIE-GUNGSKUGEL; TANGENTEN-FLÄCHE; TORSION; TORSIONS-RADIUS; TORSIONSWINKEL; WIN-DUNG; WINDUNGSWINKEL]

räum·lich *adj.* spatial, cubical: *räumliche Ausdehnung* **a.** (*Erweiterung*) cubical (or volume, or spatial) expansion; **b.** (*Dimension*) spatial dimension

Räumlich·keit *f* spatiality

Raum·maß *n* cubic measure

Raum·meter *n* [= KUBIKMETER]

Raum·punkt *m* point of space, spatial point

Raum·winkel *m* solid angle, dihedral (angle)

Raumwinkel·maß *n* steradian measure; *Einheit im R.* steradian

Raum·zeit *f* (*phys.*) space-time

Raumzeit·kontinuum *n* space-time continuum

Raute *f*, **Rauten·fläche** *f* rhomb, rhombus, lozenge, diamond

rauten·flächig *adj.* rhombohedral

rauten·förmig *adj.* rhombic, diamond-shaped

reagibel *adj.* (*statist.*) sensitive: *reagibler Index* index of sensitive prices

reagieren *v.i.* react

Reaktion *f* reaction [*cf.* AKTION]

Real·besitz *m* real estate [*cf.* BELEIHUNGSWERT]

Rechen·blatt *n* (*statist.*) nomogram, nomograph, alignment chart

Rechen·brett *n* abacus, counting frame [= ABAKUS] [*cf.* RECHEN-TAFEL]

Rechen·fehler *m* **1.** (*Fehler beim Rechnen*) computational mistake (or error). **2.** (*Fehler durch Abrundung*) rounding error

Rechen·formular *n* computational worksheet

Rechen·gesetz *n* rule (or law) of operation, operation of arithmetic, calculating rule [*cf.* PER-MANENZ]

Rechen·maschine *f* calculating (or computing) machine, calculator; (*Abakus*) abacus [*cf.* EINSTELL-WERK; SCHAULOCH; SCHLITTEN; ZÄHLWERK]

Rechen·operation *f* operation of arithmetic, arithmetical operation (or performance), counting operation

Rechen·regel *f* calculating (or computing) rule, rule of calculation (or: of arithmetic), algorithm

Rechen·schieber *m* slide rule [*cf.* LÄUFER; RECHENSTAB; ZUNGE]

Rechen·stab *m* (*des Rechenschiebers*) rule (of slide rule)

Rechen·tafel *f* **1.** (*Rechenbrett*) abacus. **2.** (*Nomogramm*) nomograph, nomogram, alignment chart. **3.** (*Schreibtafel*) blackboard

Rechen·tisch *m* abacus

Rechen·vorteil *m* short method (or cut) (in an arithmetical operation)

rechnen *v.t.*, *v.i.* calculate, compute, reckon; *v.t.* figure (out)

Rechnen *n* **1.** (*Verfahren* method) arithmetic: *kaufmännisches R.* business (or commercial, or mercantile) arithmetic. **2.** (*Ausführung* operation) computation, calculation, figuring, reckoning [*cf.* RECHENFEHLER]

Rechner *m* computer, calculator

rechnerisch *adj.* computational; *rechnerische Behandlung logischer Ausdrücke* way of calculating with logical expressions

Rechnung *f* **1.** (*mathematische Operation* mathematical operation) calculation, computation, reckoning [*cf.* PROBE; RECHNUNGSMÄSSIG; STIMMEN]. **2.** (*comm.*) (*zu zahlende*) bill, invoice (to be paid) [*cf.* ABRECHNUNG; QUITTIEREN]

Rechnungs·abschluß *m* (*comm.*) balance of accounts

Rechnungs·art *f* operation of arithmetic, algorithm: *die vier Rechnungsarten* the four fundamental (or basic) operations of arithmetic [= *die vier* SPEZIES]

Rechnungs·auszug *m* [= KONTOAUSZUG]

Rechnungs·jahr *n* (*comm.*) fiscal year

Rechnungs·kontrolle *f* computational check

rechnungs·mäßig *adj.* **1.** (*durch Rechnung*) by calculation, numerical: *r. feststellen* determine by calculation (or numerically). **2.** (*comm.*) (*Konto betreffend*) concerning accounts: *rechnungsmäßige Differenzen* differences in accounts [*cf.* AUSGLEICHEN]

recht 1. (*Richtung, Seite* direction, side) right, right-hand [*cf.* SEITE 3., 4.]. **2.** (*Winkel*) right (angle) (= 90°) [*cf.* DREI; WINKEL]

Rechte *f* right (hand): *zur Rechten* on (or to) the right

Recht·eck *n* rectangle, oblong [*cf.* LÄNGE; INHALT]

Rechteck·diagramm *n* (*statist.*) bar graph (or chart)

recht·eckig *adj.* rectangular, oblong

Rechte(r) *m* right angle

recht·läufig *adj.* (*astr.*) (*Bewegung*) direct (motion)

Rechtläufig·keit *f* (*astr.*) (*eines Planeten*) direct motion (of a planet); (*der Bewegung*) direct sense (of motion)

rechts *adv.* on (or to) the right

Rechts·ansicht *f* right-side view

Rechts·drall *m* right-handed twist

rechts·drehend *adj.* (*phys.*) dextrorotatory

rechts·gängig *adj.* (*Kurve*) right-handed, dextrorse (curve) [*cf.* KURVE]

rechts·gelegen *adj.* right, right-hand

rechts·gerichtet *adj.* right-handed

Rechts·gewinde *n* (*einer Schraube*) right-handed thread (of a screw)

rechts·gewunden *adj.* right-handed, dextrorse [*cf.* KURVE]

Rechts·ideal *n* (*alg.*) right ideal

Rechts·inverse *f*, **Rechts·inverse(s)** *n* right inverse

rechts-links *adj.* right-to-left: *r.-l. verlaufende Achse* right-to-left axis

Rechts·modul *m* (*alg.*) right module

Rechtsmultiplikatoren·bereich *m* right multiplicative domain

rechts·schief *adj.* (*statist.*) (*Häufigkeitskurve*) skew to the left, negatively skew (frequency curve) [= RECHTSSTEIL]

rechts·seitig *adj.* right, right-hand, on the right [*cf.* ASYMMETRISCH; GRENZWERT; IDEAL; NEBENKLASSE; STETIG]

rechts·steil *adj.* [= RECHTSSCHIEF]

Rechts·vielfache(s) *n* right multiple

rechts·wendig *adj.* (*z.B. Schraubenlinie*) right-handed, dextrorse (e.g. helix) [*cf.* KURVE]

recht·wink(e)lig *adj.* orthogonal, rectangular; (*Dreieck*) right, right-angled (triangle): *rechtwinkliges* (*sphärisches*) *Dreieck* right (or right-angled) (spherical) triangle; *die Seiten mancher rechtwinkligen Dreiecke verhalten sich wie rationale Zahlen* some right triangles have their sides in the ratio of rational numbers; *im gleichschenklig rechtwinkligen Dreieck ist das Verhältnis der Hypotenuse zu jeder Kathete irrational* in an isosceles right triangle the ratio of the hypotenuse to either of the (other) sides (or of the legs) is irrational; *rechtwinkliges Parallelepiped* [=

QUADER] right parallelepiped, rectangular solid, cuboid [*cf.* GERADE; KATHETE; KOORDINATE; PROJEKTION; TRAJEKTORIE]

Rechtwink(e)lig·keit *f* rectangularity, orthogonality

Re·duktion *f* reduction

Reduktions·formel *f* (*der Integration, der Trigonometrie*) reduction formula (in integration, in trigonometry)

Reduktions·sätze *m pl.* (*log.*) (*des engeren Prädikatenkalküls*) reduction theorems (of the restricted predicate calculus)

Reduktions·zirkel *m* proportional compass

reduzibel *adj.* reducible

Reduzibilitäts·kriterium *n* reducibility criterion

reduzier·bar *adj.* reducible

Reduzierbar·keit *f* reducibility

re·duzieren *v.t.* (*auf*) reduce (to); (*eine benannte Zahl*) change (a denominate number) by reduction ascending [*ant.* RESOLVIEREN]: *reduzierte Norm, Spur* reduced norm, trace; *reduzierter Grad eines Körpers* reduced degree of a field [*cf.* BRINGEN]

reell *adj.* real: *reelle Zahl* real (number)[*cf.* ACHSE; HALBACHSE; HYPERBEL]

reell-abgeschlossen *adj.* (*alg.*) (*Körper*) real closed (field)

Reelle *f* real (number)

Reellität *f* reality

re·flektieren *v.t.* (*opt.*) reflect

Re·flexion *f* (*opt.*) reflection

re·flexiv *adj.* (*Beziehung*) reflexive (relation)

Reflexivität *f* reflexivity

Re·fraktion *f* (*opt.*) refraction

Refraktions·winkel *m* (*opt.*) angle of refraction

Regel *f* rule: *Simpsonsche R.* Simpson's rule, prismoidal formula [*cf.* EMPIRISCH]

Regel·de·tri *f* rule of three

Regel·fläche *f* ruled surface [*cf.* EINSCHARIG; ERZEUGENDE; WINDSCHIEF; ZWEISCHARIG]

regel·los *adj.* random; *adv.* at random

Regellosig·keit *f* randomness

regel·mäßig *adj.* regular: *regelmäßige Wiederkehr* regular recurrence, periodicity; *r. wiederkehren* recur periodically (or at regular intervals); *r. wiederkehrend* periodic [*cf.* GESETZLICH; POLYEDER; SEITENHÖHE; UMKREISRADIUS; VIELECK; VIERECK]

Regelmäßig·keit *f* regularity [*cf.* GESETZLICHKEIT]

Regel·schar *f* (*einer windschiefen Fläche*) regulus, generation (of a warped surface)[*cf.* ERZEUGENDE]

Regie *f* (*usu. pl. Regien*) overhead expenses (or charges), overheads [*cf.* AB; VERHÄLTNISMÄSSIG]

Regie·auslagen *f pl.*, **Regie·kosten** *pl.* [= REGIEN] [*cf.* REGIE]

Register·tonne *f* register ton

Registrier·apparat *m* recording mechanism (or instrument), recorder

registrieren *v.t.* register, record [*cf.* AUFZEICHNEN]

Registrierung *f* registering, recording [*cf.* AUFZEICHNUNG]

Re·gression *f* regression

Regressions·koeffizient *m* (*statist.*) coefficient of regression

Regula falsi *f* regula falsi, rule (or method) of false position

regulär *adj.* regular; (*cryst.*) regular, isometric [*cf.* HEXAEDER; POLYEDER; POLYGON; VIELECK]

Reibung *f* (*phys.*) friction: *rollende* (*gleitende*) *R.* rolling (sliding) friction

Reibungs·koeffizient *m* (*phys.*) coefficient of friction

Reibungs·widerstand *m* (*phys.*) frictional resistance

Reibungs·winkel *m* (*phys.*) angle of friction

Reich·weite *f* range

Reihe *f* 1. (*Summe von Gliedern einer Folge* sum of terms of a sequence) series: *Fouriersche, Maclaurinsche, Taylorsche R.* Fourier, Maclaurin's, Taylor's series [*cf.* ALLGEMEIN; ALTERNIEREN; BEDINGT; BINOMISCH; DIVERGENT; DIVERGENZ; ENTWICKLUNG; GRENZWERT; HYPERGEOMETRISCH; KRITERIUM; LOGARITHMISCH; MONOTON; OSZILLIEREN; UMGRUPPIEREN; UNBEDINGT; UNENDLICH; ZUNEHMEN]. 2. (*Progression*) progression [*cf.* ARITHMETISCH; GEOMETRISCH; HARMONISCH]. 3. (*in einem Schema; ant.: Kolonne*) (in an array; *ant.:* column) row [*cf.* ANORDNUNG; DETERMINANTE; ENTHALTEN; VERTAUSCHEN]. 4. (*Folge*) sequence, series; (*Menge*) set: *eine R. von Zahlen, Punkten* a sequence (a set) of numbers, points; *eine R. von Beobachtungen* a sequence (or series) of observations; *statistische R.* statistical series (or universe, or distribution) [*cf.* AUSSCHLAG; WESENSFORM; WESENSSTREUUNG; ZUFALLSFORM; ZUFALLSSTREU-UNG]; (*statist.*) *örtliche R.* geographic (or local) distribution; (*statist.*) *zeitliche R.* time series; (*statist.*) *sachliche R.* qualitative distribution [*cf.* ANPASSUNG; EINZEICHNEN; VERTEILUNG]

Reihen·entwicklung *f* expansion in(to) a series: *R. einer Funktion* expansion of a function in a series

Reihen·folge *f* (order of) sequence, order (of succession), ordering, ordinal succession: *in richtiger* (*oder normaler*) *R.* in normal order (or sequence); *in umgekehrter R.* in inverted (or inverse, or reverse) order [*cf.* UMGEKEHRT]

Reihen·gestalt *f* (*statist.*) form of a statistical distribution

Reihen·index *m* row index

Reihen·umfang *m* (*statist.*) size of a distribution

. . . reihig *adj. suf.* -row(ed) [*cf.* ZWEIREIHIG]

rein *adj.* pure; (*verbessert*) corrected, refined: *reine Gleichung* pure equation; (*alg.*) *r. transzendente Erweiterung* pure transzendental extension; (*statist.*) *reine Ziffer* corrected (or refined) rate (or ratio) [*cf.* IMAGINÄR; MATHEMATIK; WURZELAUSDRUCK]

Reiseunfall·versicherung *f* traveler's accident insurance

Reiß·brett *n* drawing board

Reiß·dreieck *n* triangle, set square

[=ZEICHENDREIECK] [*cf.* WINKEL]

Reiß·feder *f* ruling (or drawing) pen

Reiß·schiene *f* T-square [*cf.* KOPF; SCHIENE]

Reiß·zeug *n* drawing (or drafting) instrument set

Rekt·aszension *f* (*astr.*) right ascension

Rektaszensions·kreis *m* (*astr.*) circle of right ascension

Rekta·wechsel *m* (*comm.*) nonnegotiable acceptance

Rekti·fikation *f* rectification

rektifizier·bar *adj.* rectifiable [*cf.* INTEGRIERBAR]

Rektifizierbar·keit *f* rectifiability

rekti·fizieren *v.t.* rectify: *eine Kurve r., die Länge eines Kurvenbogens bestimmen* rectify a curve, determine the arc length of a curve; *rektifizierende Ebene einer Raumkurve* rectifying plane of a space curve

Rekti·fizierung *f* rectification

re·kurrent *adj.* recurrent

re·kurrierend *adj.* recursive: *rekurrierende Definition* recursive (or recursion) definition

Re·kursion *f* recursion, recurrence

Rekursions·formel *f* recurrence formula

re·kursiv *adj.* recursive; *rekursive Bestimmungsrelation* recursion relation

Re·lation *f* relation

relativ *adj.* relative: *relative Geschwindigkeit* relative velocity; (*alg.*) *relativer Isomorphismus* relative isomorphism; *relative Häufigkeit* relative frequency, rate of frequency [*cf.* HÄUFIG-

KEITSKOEFFIZIENT]. [*cf.* ALGEBRA-
ISCH; FEHLER; MASSSTAB; PRIM;
PRIMZAHL; VERHÄLTNISMÄSSIG;
ZAHL]
Relativ·geschwindigkeit *f* (*gerich-
tete* directed) relative velocity;
(*ungerichtete* scalar) relative speed
relativistisch *adj.* relativistic
Relativität *f* relativity
Relativitäts·theorie *f* (*phys.*) relativity theory, theory of relativity
Rendite *f* (*fin.*) net yield (of
securities)
Rente *f* (*ins.*) annuity, rent [*cf.*
BARWERT; ENDWERT; EWIG;
LEBENSLÄNGLICH]
Renten·anleihe *f* (*comm.*, *fin.*)
perpetual bond
Rentner *m* (*ins.*) annuitant
Repräsentant *m* (*alg.*, *statist.*)
(*einer Klasse*) representative (of
a class)
repräsentativ *adj.* (*statist.*) representative: *repräsentative Erfas-
sung* (*oder Darstellung*) *statistischer Gegebenheiten* sampling
method of collecting statistical
data
Reserve *f* (*fin.*, *comm.*) reserve
(fund) [= RESERVEFONDS]: *stille*
(*offene*) *Reserven* hidden (dis-
closed) reserves
Residuum *n* residue: *R. einer
analytischen Funktion* residue of
an analytical function
Re·solvente *f* resolvent [*cf.*
GALOISSCH; KUBISCH]
re·solvieren *v.t.* (*eine benannte
Zahl*) change (a denominate
number) by reduction descending
[*ant.* REDUZIEREN]
re·sonant *adj.* (*phys.*) resonant

Re·sonanz *f* (*phys.*) resonance
Resonanz·spektrum *n* (*phys.*) reso-
nance spectrum
re·sonieren *v.i.* (*phys.*) resonate
Respekt·tag *m* (*comm.*) day of
grace
Rest *m* difference, remainder; (*in
Zahlenklassen* in number classes)
residue [*cf.* AUFGEHEN; ENT-
HALTEN]
Rest·charakter *m* (*alg.*) (*einer
Zahl modulo n*) residue character
(of a number modulo *n*)
Rest·glied *n* (*einer Reihe*) re-
mainder (of a series)
Rest·kaufpreis *m*, **Rest·kauf-
schilling** *m* (*comm.*) balance of
purchase price
Rest·klasse *f* (*alg.*) residue class
(or system)
Restklassen·folge *f* (*alg.*) residue
class sequence
Restklassen·modul *m* (*alg.*) residue
class module
Restklassen·ring *m* (*alg.*) residue
class ring
Rest·satz *m* (*alg.*) residue theorem
Rest·schwankung *f* (*statist.*) resid-
ual fluctuation
Resultante *f* (*eines Systems von
Gleichungen*) resultant (or elimi-
nant) of a set of equations; (*von
Kräften*) resultant (of forces)
Resultanten·system *n* resultant
system
Resultat *n* result [*cf.* ANGENÄHERT;
BEILÄUFIG; ERHALTEN; VERFEI-
NERN]
resultieren *v.i.* result
resultierend *adj.* resultant
Resultierende *f* resultant
re·tardieren *v.t.* retard

re·versibel *adj.* reversible

Re·versibilität *f* reversibility

Re·volution *f* (*astr.*) revolution

reziprok *adj.* reciprocal, inverse *reziproker Wert* (*einer Zahl*) reciprocal (or inverse) value, reciprocal, inverse (of a number); *Abbildung eines Punktes durch reziproke Radien* inversion of a point with respect to a circle, reciprocal (or inverse) mapping of a point; *reziproker Wert des Verhältnisses zweier Zahlen* reciprocal ratio of two numbers; *polar reziproke Elemente* polar reciprocals [*cf.* LOGARITHMUS; VERHÄLTNIS]

Reziproke(s) *n* reciprocal

Reziprozität *f* reciprocity, reciprocation: *polare R.* polar reciprocation

Rho *n* (*griechischer Buchstabe* Greek letter P, ρ) rho

Rhomben·dodekaeder *n* rhombic dodecahedron

rhombisch *adj.* rhombic; (*cryst.*) rhombic, orthorhombic

Rhombo·eder *n* rhombohedron

rhombo·edrisch *adj.* rhombohedral, rhombohedric

Rhomboid *n* rhomboid

rhomboidisch *adj.* rhomboid(al)

Rhombus *m* rhomb, rhombus, lozenge, diamond

Rhumb·linie *f* [= LOXODROME]

richtig *adj.* correct, right; (*regelrecht*) normal; (*wahr*) true: *eine richtige Aussage* a true sentence [*cf.* ANORDNUNG; IMMER; ORDNUNG; REIHENFOLGE; VERHÄLTNIS]

Richtig·keit *f* correctness; (*Wahr-*

heit) truth [*cf.* PROBE]

Richtung *f* direction, sense; (*eines Strebens* of a tendency) trend: *die geometrische R. in der Algebra* the geometrical trend in algebra [*cf.* AUSGEDEHNT; GERADE; SCHIEF; STREICHEN; STREICHUNG; STRICH; TANGENTE; UHRZEIGER]

Richtungs·koeffizient *m* (*einer Geraden*) slope (of a straight line): *R. der Tangente einer Kurve in einem Punkt* slope of a curve at a point

Richtungs·kosinus *m* direction cosine

Richtungs·sinn *m* directional sense, orientation

Richtungs·unterschied *m* difference in direction [*cf.* WINKEL]

Richtungs·winkel *m* 1. (*Winkel einer Geraden mit einer Koordinatenachse* angle of a line with a coordinate axis) direction angle; *R. einer Geraden mit der positiven x-Achse* angle of inclination (or slope angle) of a straight line. 2. (*ball.*) angle of elevation

Riemann *m* N. [*cf.* FLÄCHE; GEOMETRIE; KRÜMMUNG]

Ries *n* (*Papiermaß* paper measure) (*altes*) ream (= 480 or 500 sheets); (*Neuries*) 1000 sheets

Ring *m* (*geom., alg.*) ring; (*Kreisring*) (circular) ring, annulus; (*Ringfläche*) ring surface, anchor ring, torus (ring): (*alg.*) *euklidischer R.* Euclidean ring [*cf.* DARSTELLEN; GAUSSSCH]

Ring·fläche *f* ring surface, torus (ring), anchor ring [= TORUS, WULST] [*cf.* RING]

Riß *m* projection, view [*cf.* AUF-
RISS; GRUNDRISS; SEITENRISS]
roh *adj.* crude, rough: (*statist.*)
rohe Ziffer crude rate (or ratio)
[*cf.* ANNÄHERUNG]
Roh·bilanz *f* (*comm.*) trial balance
Roh·einnahme(n) *f* (*pl.*) (*comm.*)
gross receipts *pl.*
Roh·gewinn *m* (*comm.*) gross profit
Roh·last *f* (*comm.*) gross (or total)
load
Röhre *f* tube; (*rad.: Verstärker-
röhre*) *Am.* tube, *Br.* valve
röhren·förmig *adj.* tubular
Roll·bewegung *f* rolling motion
Rolle *f* (*mech.*) pulley [*cf.* BEWEG-
LICH]
rollen *v.i.* roll [*cf.* REIBUNG]
Roll·kurve *f* roulette[= ROULETTE]
römisch *adj.* Roman [*cf.* ZAHL-
ZEICHEN]
Rosen·kurve *f* rhodonea
Rost·pendel *n* (*phys.*) gridiron
pendulum
Rotation *f* revolution, rotation
Rotations·achse *f* rotational axis,
axis of revolution (or rotation)
Rotations·ellipsoid *n* ellipsoid of
revolution, spheroid: *abgeplat-
tetes* (*verlängertes*) *R.* oblate
(prolate) spheroid
Rotations·fläche *f* surface of revolution
Rotations·hyperboloid *n* hyperboloid of revolution
rotations·invariant *adj.* rotation-
invariant
Rotations·kegel *m* cone of revolution; *schiefer Stumpf* (*oder
Stutz*) *eines Rotationskegels*
ungula of a cone [*cf.* ER-
ZEUGENDE]

Rotations·körper *m* solid of revolution; *schiefer Stumpf* (*oder
Stutz*) *eines Rotationskörpers*
ungula [*cf.* HUF]
Rotations·paraboloid *n* paraboloid
of revolution
Rotations·sinn *m* sense (or direc-
tion) of rotation (or revolution)
Rotations·zylinder *m* cylinder of
revolution; *schiefer Stumpf* (*oder
Stutz*) *eines Rotationszylinders*
ungula of a cylinder
rotieren *v.i.* (*um*) revolve (about,
around)
Rotor *m* curl [= WIRBEL 1.]
Roulette *f* roulette [= ROLLKURVE]
Rubrik *f* (*statist.*) blank, box
Rück·ansicht *f* rear view
rück·bezüglich *adj.* reflexive
Rückbezüglich·keit *f* reflexivity
Rück·kauf *m* (*comm.*) redemption,
repurchase [*cf.* ABLÖSUNG]
rück·kaufen *v.t.* (*comm.*) redeem,
repurchase [*cf.* ABLÖSEN]
Rückkaufs·preis *m* (*comm.*) repurchase price
Rückkaufs·wert *m* (*comm.*) repurchase value; (*einer Polizze*)
(cash) surrender (or non-for-
feiture) value (of a policy)
Rück·kehr *f* regression
Rückkehr·kante *f* edge of regression, cuspidal edge
Rückkehr·punkt *m* cuspidal (or
stationary) point, cusp, spinode
[*cf.* HYPOZYKLOIDE]
Rück·lage *f* (*fin.*) **1.** (*Reserve*)
reserve (fund). **2.** (*usu. pl.*)
(*Ersparnisse*) savings *pl.*
rück·läufig *adj.* (*astr.*) retrograde
Rückläufig·keit *f* (*astr.*) (*eines
Planeten*) retrograde motion (of

a planet); (*der Bewegung*) retrograde sense (of motion)
Rück·seité *f* rear, back
Rückstrahl·ortung *f* (*nav.*, *av.*) radar
Rück·strahlung *f* reflection
Rück·versicherung *f* (*ins.*) reinsurance
Rück·zahlung *f* (*comm.*) (*einer Schuld, Hypothek*) repayment (of a debt, mortgage); (*von Kapital*) return (of capital); (*geleisteter Zahlung*) refund, reimbursement (of payment made); (*Einlösung*

von Anleihen) redemption (of loans) [*cf.* ABLÖSUNGSFONDS; EINLÖSEN]
Ruhe *f* rest: *Körper in R.* bodies at rest
Ruhe·lage *f* equilibrium position [*cf.* SCHWANKEN; SCHWANKUNG]
ruhend *adj.* stationary; (*statisch*) static
Ruh·masse *f* (*phys.*) rest mass
rund *adj.* round [*cf.* EINKLAMMERN; KLAMMER]
Rundung *f* roundness
Rute *f* (*meas.*) rod

S

Sach·konto *n* (*comm.*) nominal account
sachlich *adj.* (*artmäßig*) qualitative; (*tatsächlich*) factual; (*objektiv*) matter-of-fact, objective [*cf.* REIHE 4.]
Sach·verhalt *m* (*log.*) relation, condition
Sach·versicherung *f* property insurance
Sägezahn·kurve *f* (*statist.*) saw tooth curve
Saison *f* (*Fr.*) (*comm.*) season
Saison·ausschlag *m* (*statist.*) seasonal deviation
Saison·bereinigung *f* (*statist.*) adjustment for seasonal variation
Saison·index *m* seasonal index: *beweglicher* (*starrer*) *S.* moving (stable) seasonal index [*cf.* SAISONVERÄNDERUNGSZAHLEN]
Saison·schwankungen *f pl.* seasonal

fluctuations (or variation, *sing.*): *bewegliche* (*starre*) *S.* changing (stable) seasonal variation
Saisonveränderungs·zahlen *f pl.* (*statist.*) **1.** (*beweglicher Saisonindex*) moving seasonal index. **2.** (*monatliche Unterschiede*) average differences between months
Saison·ziffer *f* seasonal index
säkular, säkulär *adj.* secular: (*astr.*) *säkulare* (*oder säkuläre*) *Störungen* secular perturbations
Säkular·bewegung *f* (*statist.*) secular trend; *sekundäre S.* secondary trend; (*comm.*) long waves (of business)
Säkular·gleichung *f* (*astr.*, *alg.*) secular equation
Säkulum *n* (*p. Säkula*) (*Lat.*) century
Saldo *m* (*comm.*) balance: *einen S. aufweisen* (*oder ausweisen*)

show a balance; *den S. ziehen*
strike the balance; *einen S.*
vortragen carry over a balance
[*cf.* GUTHABEN]
sammeln *v.t.* collect, gather [*cf.*
ERFASSEN; ERHEBEN]
Sammlung *f* collection [*cf.* ERFAS-
SUNG; ERHEBUNG]
Sand·rechnung *f* sand reckoning
Sand·uhr *f* sand clock, sandglass
Satellit *m* (*astr.*) satellite
Sattel·fläche *f* saddle surface;
(*hyperbolisches Paraboloid*)hyper-
bolic paraboloid
Satz *m* (*Aussage*) sentence, pro-
position; (*Lehrsatz*) proposition,
theorem, thesis, law, lemma:
Fermatscher, Taylorscher S.
Fermat's, Taylor's theorem [*cf.*
BINOMISCH; DRITT; DUAL; ERWEI-
TERN; MOIVRE; SCHNEIDEN;
WIDERSPRUCH]
Säule *f* **1.** (*arch.*) culumn. **2.**
(*geom.: Prisma*) prism. **3.**
(*statist.*) bar [*cf.* SÄULEN-
DIAGRAMM]
Säulen·diagramm *n* (*statist.*) bar
chart (or graph)
schachbrett·artig *adj.* chessboard,
checkerboard, checkered; *sch.*
gewürfelt (*oder gemustert*) checkered
Schachbrett·muster *n* checkerboard pattern
schachteln *v.t.* nest: *einen Würfel*
in den andern sch. nest one cube
into the other; *in einander sch.*
[= INEINANDERSCHACHTELN]
Schachtelung *f* nest(ing)
Schale *f* **1.** (*einer Fläche*) sheet,
nappe (of a surface): *Sch. eines*
Hyperboloids sheet of a hyper-

boloid. **2.** (*phys.*) (*Elekronen-*
schale) (electron) shell
Schall *m* (*acoust.*) sound: *Lehre*
vom Sch. theory of sound,
acoustics
Schall·geschwindigkeit *f* (*acoust.*)
velocity of sound
Schalter·geschäft *n* (*comm.*) (*in*
Effekten) over-the-counter trade
(in securities)
Schalt·jahr *n* leap year
Schar *f* family, system [*cf.*
ERZEUGENDE]
Schatten *m* (*opt., descr.*) (*Eigen-*
schatten) shade; (*Schlagschatten*)
shadow
Schatten·grenze *f* (*des Eigen-*
schattens) shade line; (*des Schlag-*
schattens) shadow boundary
Schatten·kegel *m* shadow cone
schattieren *v.t.* shade; (*schraffieren*)
hatch
Schattierung *f* shading; (*Schraf-*
fierung) hatching
schätzen *v.t.* estimate, appraise;
(*nach dem Steuerwert*) assess (for
taxable value)
Schätzung *f* estimate, appraisal;
assessment [*cf.* SCHÄTZEN]
schätzungs·weise *adj.* approximate
Schätzungs·wert *m*, **Schätz·wert** *m*
(*comm.*) estimated (or appraised)
value; (*Steuerwert* taxable value)
assessed value
Schau·bild *n* diagram, graph,
chart
Schau·loch *n* (*einer Rechen-*
maschine) dial (of a computing
machine)
Scheck *m* (*comm.*) *Am.* check,
Br. cheque
Scheffel *m* (*meas.*) bushel

Scheide·münze *f* (*fin.*) fractional currency

Schein *m m* (*comm.*) note; (*Bestätigung* acknowledgment) voucher

schein·bar *adj.* apparent: *scheinbarer Abstand zweier Punkte* apparent distance of two points [*cf.* Sonnenbahn]

Schein·korrelation *f* (*statist.*) spurious (or nonsense) correlation

Schein·periodizität *f* (*statist.*) spurious periodicity

Scheitel *m*, **Scheitel·punkt** *m* **1.** (*eines Winkels, Kegels*) vertex (of an angle, a cone); (*einer Kurve, z.B. eines Kegelschnitts*) vertex (of a curve, e.g. a conic); (*der Häufigkeitskurve*) mode (of the frequency curve); (*Extrempunkt einer Kurve in Polarkoordinaten*) apse (of a curve). **2.** (*des Horizonts*) zenith (of the horizon) [= Zenit]

Scheitel·tangente *f* vertex tangent

Scheitel·wert *m* (*statist.*) (*der Häufigkeitsfunktion*) mode (of the frequency function)

Scheitel·winkel *m* vertical (or vertically opposite) angle [*cf.* pairs of angles: A, B′; B, A′; C, D′; D, C′ in *Fig.* to Transversale]

Schema *n* **1.** (*regelmäßige Anordnung* regular arrangement) array, schema, scheme: *das quadratische Sch. einer Determinante* the square array of a determinant [*cf.* Reihe 3.; Stellung]. **2.** (*Diagramm*) diagram, schema, scheme. **3.** (*Muster*) pattern:

nach demselben Sch. after the same pattern

schematisch *adj.* schematic(al)

schematisieren *v.t.* schematize

Schematisierung *f* schematization

Schematismus *m* schematism

Schenkel *m* **1.** (*eines Winkels*) side, arm, leg (of an angle) [*cf.* parallel]. **2.** (*eines gleichschenkeligen Dreiecks, Trapezes*)lateral side (of an isosceles triangle, trapezoid). **3.** (*eines Zirkels*) leg (of a compass)

scheren *v.t.* (*mech.*) shear

Scher·festigkeit *f* (*mech.*) shearing strength

Scherung *f* (*mech.*) shear

Schicht·linie *f* (*cart.*) level (or contour) line [= Höhenlinie; Isohypse]

schief *adj.* (*schräg*) oblique, bevel, slant(ing), slantwise; (*unsymmetrisch*) skew, lopsided; (*Häufigkeitskurve, auch*) allokurtic (frequency curve): *schiefer Winkel* oblique angle; *unter schiefem Winkel sich schneidende Gerade* oblique lines; *schiefer Schnitt* oblique section; *sich in schiefer Richtung bewegen* move slantwise [*cf.* Abschneiden; Aufsteigung; einseitig 3.; Kegel; Kreiskegel; Kreiszylinder; Parallelepiped; Rotationskegel; Rotationskörper; Rotationszylinder; Strich]

Schiefe *f* obliquity; (*Unsymmetrie*) skewness; (*der Häufigkeitskurve, auch*) allokurtosis (of the frequency curve): (*astr.*) *Sch. der Ekliptik* obliquity of the ecliptic

Schief·endfläche *f* (*cryst.*: *Basis*

im monoklinen und triklinen System) basal pinacoid in the monoclinic and triclinic systems

Schief·körper *m* (*alg.*) skew field [*cf.* CHARAKTERISTIK]

schief·symmetrisch *adj.* (*z.B. Matrix, Tensor*) antisymmetric, skew-symmetric (e.g. matrix, tensor) [*cf.* DETERMINANTE]

schief·wink(e)lig *adj.* oblique: *schiefwinkliges Dreieck* oblique triangle [*cf.* KOORDINATE]

Schiene *f* (*der Reißschiene*) blade (of a T-square)

schlagen *v.t.* (*einen Kreis*) strike (off), describe (a circle) [*cf.* ZIRKEL]

Schlag·schatten *m* (cast) shadow [*ant.:* EIGENSCHATTEN] [*cf.* SCHATTEN; SCHATTENGRENZE]

Schlagschatten·grenze *f* boundary of the (cast) shadow, shadow boundary

schlängeln *v.r.:* **sich** *sch.* wind, meander

Schlangen·kurve *f*, **Schlangen·linie** *f* serpentine

Schleife *f* (*einer Kurve*) loop (of a curve)

Schleif·schnitt *m* (*zweier gezeichneter Linien*) (inaccurate) intersection (of two drawn lines) at a very small angle

schließen *v.t.* **1.** (*zumachen*) close; (*einschließen*) enclose: *eine Klammer sch.* close a parenthesis (a bracket) [*cf.* KLAMMER]; *Klammer geschlossen* parentheses (brackets) closed, end of parentheses (brackets); *in eine Klammer* (*oder in Klammern*) *sch.* enclose in parentheses (in brackets); *in*

sich sch. include, involve, imply [*cf.* EINBEGREIFEN]. **2.** (*log.*) conclude, infer, gather [*cf.* INHALTLICH]

Schlinge *f* (*einer Kurve*) loop (of a curve)

Schlitten *m* (*der Rechenmaschine*) carriage (of a computing machine)

Schluß *m* **1.** (*Ende*) end, conclusion, termination: *Sch. der Klammer* end of parenthesis, parentheses (brackets) closed. **2.** (*log.*) (*Schlußfigur*) syllogism; (*Folgerung*) deduction, inference, conclusion [*cf.* ABLEITUNG FOLGERUNG; MITTELBEGRIFF]

Schluß·art *f* (*log.*) (kind of) syllogism

Schluß·dividende *f* (*fin.*) final dividend

schlüsseln *v.t.* (*statist.*) code [*cf.* AUSZEICHNEN; SIGNIEREN]

Schlüsselung *f* (*statist.*) coding [*cf.* AUSZEICHNUNG; SIGNIERUNG]

Schlüssel·zahl *f* code number [*cf.* KENNZIFFER]

Schluß·figur *f* (*log.*) figure of inference, syllogism [*cf.* SCHLUSS]

Schluß·kurs *m*, **Schluß·notierung** *f* (*fin.*) (*an der Börse*) closing (or final) quotation (at the stock exchange)

Schluß·satz *m* (*log.*) (*eines Syllogismus*) conclusion (of a syllogism)

Schluß·schema *n* (*log.*) rule of implication

Schluß·weise *f* (*log.*) (kind of) syllogism

schmal *adj.* narrow [*cf.* ZWICKEL]

Schmal·heit *f* narrowness

Schmal·seite *f* (*Kante*) edge; (*Ende*) end

Schmalseiten·ansicht *f* (*Kantenansicht*) edge view; (*Ansicht vom Ende her*) end view

schmiegen 1. *v.t.* fit tightly to: *wir sch. einen Kreis an die Kurve* we fit a circle closely to the curve, we draw a circle osculating the curve. **2.** *v.r.:* **sich** *sch.* (*an*) hug, osculate (*dir. obj.*)

schmieg·sam *adj.* (*bildsam*) plastic; (*biegsam*) flexible

Schmiegsam·keit *f* (*Bildsamkeit*) plasticity; (*Biegsamkeit*) flexibility

Schmiegungs·ebene *f* (*einer Raumkurve in einem Punkt*) osculating plane (of a space curve at a point)

Schmiegungs·kreis *f* (*einer ebenen Kurve*) osculating circle (of a plane curve) (of at least third order of contact)

Schmiegungs·kugel *f* (*einer Raumkurve in einem Punkt*) osculating sphere (of a space curve at a point)

Schnabel *m* (*einer Kurve*) cusp (of a curve) of second kind

Schnabel·punkt *m* cusp of the second kind

Schnecke *f* [= SCHNECKENLINIE]: *Pascalsche Sch.* Pascal's limaçon [= KREISKONCHOIDE]

Schneckenhaus·linie *f* cochleoid[= KOCHLEOIDE, SCHRAUBENKURVE]

Schnecken·linie *f* (*Spirale*) spiral; (*Schraubenlinie*) helix

schneiden 1. *v.t.* cut, intersect, cross; *Schneiden und Verbinden* (*oder Projizieren*) *geometrischer Grundgebilde* incidence of basic geometrical elements; *duale Sätze über Schneiden und Verbinden* dual propositions of incidence. **2.** *v.recip., v.r.* **sich** *sch.* intersect, cross [*cf.* ERZEUGENDE; INEINANDERLIEGEN; SCHIEF; SEKANTE; ÜBERSCHNEIDEN]

schneidend *adj.* secant, intersecting

Schnitt *m* **1.** (*zweier Gebilde*) intersection (of two geometrical elements): *Sch. zweier Flächen* intersection of two surfaces. **2.** (*Schnittfläche* surface of intersection) cut, section: *gerader* (*oder senkrechter*) *Sch. eines Zylinders* right section of a cylinder [*cf.* ACHSENSCHNITT; EBEN; SCHIEF]. **3.** (*Zahlenklasse* number class) cut, separation: *Dedekindscher Sch.* Dedekind cut [*cf.* OBERKLASSE; UNTERKLASSE]. **4.** (*Teilung*) division, section: *goldener Sch.* golden section, (division in) extreme and mean ratio

Schnitt·ebene *f* intersecting (or cutting, or secant) plane

Schnitt·eigenschaft *f* property of cuts

Schnitt·fläche *f* section, cut, surface of intersection [*cf.* SCHNITT 2.]

Schnitt·gerade *f* line of intersection

Schnitt·kurve *f* curve of (inter-)section

Schnitt·linie *f* (line of) intersection

Schnitt·punkt *m* intersection (point) [*cf.* HÖHE; MITTELLINIE]

Schnitt·winkel *m* angle of intersection

Schock *n* (= 60 Stück) threescore (= 60 pieces)

schraffieren *·v.t.* shade, hatch, hachure: *die schraffierte Fläche* the shaded (or hatched) area

Schraffierung *f* shading, hatching

schräg *adj.* oblique, bevel, slant(ing) [*cf.* STROPHOIDE]

Schräg·ansicht *f*, **Schräg·bild** *n* (*descr.*) oblique view

schräge *adj.* [=SCHRÄG]

schräg·gestellt *adj.* tilted, oblique

Schräg·perspektive *f* oblique perspective

Schräg·schnitt *m* oblique (or bevel) section (or cut)

Schräg·stellung *f* tilt(ing), inclination

Schranke *f* bound: *obere* (*untere*) *Sch.* upper (lower) bound

Schraube *f* screw [*cf.* ARCHIMEDISCH; ENDE; ENDLOS; GANG; GANGHÖHE; LINKSGEWINDE; RECHTSGEWINDE; UMGANG; WINDUNG]

schrauben *v.t.*, *v.r.*: *sich sch.* screw

Schrauben·bewegung *f* screwing motion

Schrauben·fläche *f* helicoid, screw surface: *abwickelbare Sch.* developable helicoid, (helical) convolute

schrauben·förmig *adj.* (*Linie*) helical (line); (*Fläche*) helicoidal (surface)

Schrauben·gang *m* convolution, turn, flight (of a screw, a helix)

Schrauben·kurve *f* cochleoid [= KOCHLEOIDE, SCHNECKENHAUSLINIE]

Schrauben·linie *f* helix: *gewöhnliche Sch.* circular helix; *zylindrische* (*konische*) *Sch.* cylindrical (conical) helix [*cf.* GANG; GANG-

HÖHE; RECHTSWENDIG; SCHNEKKENLINIE; STEIGUNGSWINKEL; UMGANG; WINDUNG]

Schrauben·winkel *m* helix angle

schraubig *adj.* helical, screwed, twisted [*cf.* DREHEN]

Schraubung *f* screw(ing motion)

schreiben *v.t.*, *v.i.* write [*cf.* BESCHREIBEN; TABELLIERMASCHINE; UNTER]

Schreib·tafel *f* blackboard [*cf.* RECHENTAFEL]

Schreibung *f* notation, way of writing: *abgekürzte Sch.* abridged notation [*cf.* DETERMINANTE; ENTWICKELT]

Schreib·weise *f* notation, way of writing [*cf.* ENTWICKLUNG]

Schrift *f* writing [*cf.* KOPF]

Schrift·zeichen *n* character, notation, symbol [*cf.* BEZEICHNUNG]

Schritt *m* step [*cf.* ABBRECHEN]

schritt·weise *adj.* step by step

schrumpfen *v.i.* shrink

Schrumpfung *f* shrinking, shrinkage

Schub *m* (*mech.*) thrust

Schuld *f* (*comm.*, *fin.*) debt; *Schulden eines kaufmännischen Betriebs* accounts payable of a business establishment [*cf.* A CONTO; RÜCKZAHLUNG; TILGEN; TILGUNG; ZURÜCKZAHLEN]

Schuld·brief *m* (*fin.*) (*einer Körperschaft*) debenture (of a corporation)

schulden *v.t.* owe; (*comm.*) *was sch. Sie?* what are your accounts payable?

schulden·frei *adj.* (*comm.*, *fin.*) (*Person*) (person) free from debt; (*Hausbesitz*) unencumbered (real estate)

Schulden·last *f* (*comm.*, *fin.*) (*Verbindlichkeiten*) liabilities, bills (or accounts) payable; (*schwere*) (heavy) burden (or load) of debt; (*auf Grundstücken*) encumbrance (on real estate)

Schuldner *m* (*comm.*, *fin.*) debtor

Schuld·schein *m* (*comm.*, *fin.*) **1.** (*schriftliche Anerkennung einer Schuld*) IOU (= I owe you); (*mit Zahlungsverpflichtung*) promissory note. **2.** (*Schuldverschreibung*) (*einer Körperschaft*) debenture (of a corporation)

Schuld·umwandlung *f* (*fin.*) (*comm.*) conversion of debts

Schuld·verschreibung *f* (*fin.*) bond, debenture [*cf.* SCHULDSCHEIN]

schummern *v.t.* (*cart.*) shade [= SCHATTIEREN]

Schummerung *f* (*cart.*) shading [= SCHATTIERUNG]

Schuß·bahn *f* (*ball.*) trajectory, ballistic curve

schwach *adj.* weak [*cf.* AUSSAGENVERBINDUNG; NEIGUNG; PRIMÄR]

schwanken *v.i.* (*fluktuieren*) fluctuate, oscillate; (*um eine Ruhelage*) librate (about an equilibrium position)

Schwankung *f* (*Fluktuation*) fluctuation, oscillation, variation; (*um eine Ruhelage*) libration (about an equilibrium position)

Schwankungs·maß *n* (*statist.*) **1.** (*Streuungsmaß*) measure of dispersion (or variation). **2.** (*mittlere Abweichung*) standard deviation [*cf.* FUNKTION]

Schwebung *f* (*acoust.*) beat

Schwebungs·frequenz *f* (*acoust.*) beat frequency

schwer *adj.* (*phys.*) subject to gravity, having weight, heavy: *ein schwerer Körper* a body subject to gravity; *schweres Wasser* heavy water [*cf.* SCHWERPUNKT]

Schwere *f* (*phys.*) gravitation, gravity [*cf.* ANZIEHUNG]

Schwere·anziehung *f* (*phys.*) gravitational attraction, attraction (or pull) of gravity

Schwere·beschleunigung *f* (*phys.*) acceleration of gravity, gravity acceleration

Schwere·feld *n* (*phys.*) gravitational (or gravity) field

Schwere·konstante *f* (*phys.*) constant of gravity

Schwer·kraft *f* (*phys.*) gravity [*cf.* ANZIEHUNG]

Schwer·punkt *m* (*einer Figur*) centroid (or center of gravity) (of a figure); (*Massenmittelpunkt*) centroid (or center) of mass; (*eines schweren Körpers*) center of gravity (of a body)

schwingen *v.i.* oscillate, vibrate, swing

Schwingung *f* oscillation, vibration, swing: (*phys.*) *gedämpfte Sch.* damped oscillation; (*phys.*) *gekoppelte Sch.* coupled oscillation; 20.000 *Schwingungen pro Sekunde*, 20.000 *Hertz* 20,000 cycles (per second), 20 kilocycles [*cf.* DÄMPFEN; DAUER; DEKREMENT; ERZWUNGEN; FREI]

Schwingungs·bauch *m* (*phys.*) vibration antinode

Schwingungs·dauer *f* (*phys.*) vibration period

Schwingungs·gleichung *f* equation

of oscillation

Schwingungs·knoten *m* (*phys.*) vibration node

Schwingungs·kreis *m* (*phys.*) oscillation circuit

Schwingungs·weite *f* (*phys.*) amplitude [*cf.* AMPLITUDE]

Schwingungs·zahl *f* (*phys.*) frequency (number) (of oscillation or vibration)

secans *m* (*von* α) (*symb.:* sec α) [= SEKANS, SEKANTE]

secans hyperbolicus *m* (*eines Winkels* α) (*symb.:* sec h α) hyperbolic secant (of an angle α) (*symb.:* sech α)

sechs *card. num.* six

Sechs *f* (*Zahl, Ziffer*) (number, figure) six [*cf.* SEITE]

Sechs·eck *n* hexagon [= HEXAGON] [*cf.* . . . ECK]

sechs·eckig *adj.* hexagonal [= HEXAGONAL]

Sechser *m* (figure) six

sechs·fach *adj.* sixfold, sextuple

sechs·hundert *card. num.* six hundred

sechs·mal *num.* six times

sechs·malig *adj.* (done) six times [*cf.* DREIMALIG]

sechs·seitig *adj.* six-sided; (*Prisma, Pyramide*) hexagonal (prism, pyramid)

Sechs·stern *m* hexagram [= HEXAGRAMM]

sechst *ord. num.* sixth; *vom sechsten Grade, von der sechsten Ordnung* sextic [*cf.* VIERT]

Sechstel *n* sixth (part)

sechstens *adv.* sixthly, in the sixth place

sechs·zählig *adj.* sixfold, sextuple;

(*Symmetrie, auch*) hexagonal (symmetry)

sech·zehn *card. num.* sixteen

sech·zig *card. num.* sixty

sech·zigst *ord. num.* sixtieth [*cf.* MINUTE]

See·höhe *f* sea level

See·karte *f* (*cart.*) marine map, chart [*cf.* LANDKARTE]

See·meile *f* (*meas.*) nautical (or sea) mile

Segment *n* segment

Seh·linie *f* line of sight

Sehne *f* chord [*cf.* TANGENTE]

Sehnen·sechseck *n* (*eines Kegelschnitts*) hexagon inscribed (in a conic)

Sehnen·viereck *n* (*eines Kreises*) quadrilateral inscribed (in a circle)

Seh·strahl *m* line of sight (or direction), principal visual ray, direct radial

Seh·winkel *m* visual (or sight) angle

Seil·eck *n*, **Seil·polygon** *n* funicular (or link) polygon

sein *v.i.* be: *der Neigungswinkel einer Geraden sei* 30° let the inclination of a line be 30°, given that the inclination of a line is 30° [*cf.* IST; SIND]

Seins·zeichen *n* (*log.*) existential quantifier

Seite *f* **1.** (*eines ebenen Dreiecks, Vielecks*) side (of a plane triangle, polygon); (*eines sphärischen Dreiecks*) side, face angle (of a spherical triangle) [*cf.* ANLIEGEND; EINSCHLIESSEN; GEGENÜBERLIEGEND; RECHTWINKLIG]. **2.** (*Begrenzungsfläche eines Gegen-*

stands) side (of an object); (*Seitenfläche eines Polyeders*) side, face (of a polyhedron): *der Würfel hat sechs Seiten* a cube has six faces (or sides) [*cf.* EINSEITIG 1.]. **3.** (*einer Gleichung, Ungleichung*) member, side (of an equation, inequality); *linke S. einer Gleichung* left (or first) member of an equation; *rechte S. einer Gleichung* right (or second) member of an equation [*cf.* FREMD; TRANSPONIEREN]. **4.** (*auf einen Gegenstand bezogene Lage* position relative to an object) side: *zur* (*oder: auf der*) *rechten S. der y-Achse* on the right side of the *y*-axis [*cf.* EINSEITIG 2.]

Seiten·ansicht *f* (*Projektion*) side view (or elevation); (*Profil*) profile

Seiten·anzahl *f* **1.** (*eines Polygons*) number of sides (of a polygon); (*eines Polyeders*) number of sides (or faces) (of a polyhedron) [= SEITENZAHL 1., 2.]. **2.** (*eines Buches*) number of pages (of a book) [*cf.* SEITENZAHL 3.]

Seiten·ecke *f* lateral corner

Seiten·fläche *f* **1.** (*seitliche Fläche*) lateral area (or surface, or face): *S. eines Prismas, einer Pyramide* lateral face of a prism, a pyramid. **2.** (*Seite eines Polyeders*) face, side (of a polyhedron) [*cf.* BEGRENZUNGSFLÄCHE; FLÄCHE; SEITE]

Seiten·höhe *f* (*einer regelmäßigen Pyramide*) slant height (of a regular pyramid)

Seiten·kante *f* lateral edge

Seiten·linie *f* (*eines Zylinders,*

Kegels) [= MANTELLINIE]

Seiten·projektion *f* [= SEITENRISS]

Seitenprojektions·ebene *f* (*descr.*) profile plane [= SEITENRISSEBENE]

Seiten·riß *m* (*descr.*) side view (or elevation), profile [= KREUZRISS] [*cf.* PROJEKTION]

Seitenriß·ebene *f* (*descr.*) profile plane [= KREUZRISSEBENE] [*cf.* PROJEKTIONSEBENE]

seiten·verkehrt *adj.* (*Bild*) laterally transposed, side-inverted (picture)

Seiten·zahl *f* **1.** (*geom.*) (*eines Polygons*) number of sides (of a polygon); (*eines Polyeders*) number of faces (or sides) (of a polyhedron) [= FLÄCHENZAHL]. **2.** (*im Buch*) (*Nummer der Seite*) page (or folio) number; (*Seitenanzahl*) number of pages [*cf.* SEITENANZAHL]

seitlich *adj.* lateral, side [*cf.* PROJEKTION; PROJEKTIONSFLÄCHE; SEITENFLÄCHE]

Sekans *m* (*von* α) (*symb.:* sec α) [= SEKANTE, SECANS]

Sekante *f* **1.** (*schneidende Gerade*) secant, intersecting line. **2.** (*eines Winkels* α) secant (of an angle α) (*symb.:* sec α) [*cf.* SECANS; SEKANS]

Sekanten·linie *f* secant curve

Sektor *m* sector

sekundär *adj.* secondary

Sekundär·statistik *f* collection of statistical data for nonstatistical purposes [*ant.:* PRIMÄRSTATISTIK]

Sekunda·wechsel *m* (*comm.*) second of exchange

Sekunde *f* (*Zeit, Winkel* time, angle) second [*cf.* PER; SCHWINGUNG]

Sekunden·pendel n (*phys.*) seconds pendulum

Sekunden·zeiger m (*einer Uhr*) second hand (of a clock)

Selbstberührungs·punkt m (*einer Kurve*) tacnode, double cusp, point of osculation (of a curve)

Selbst·kosten pl. (*comm.*) first (or prime) cost; (*Einkaufspreis*) purchase (or cost) price

Selbstkosten·preis m (*comm.*) purchase (or cost) price

Selbst·schatten m shade [= EIGEN-SCHATTEN]

Selbstschatten·grenze f shade line

Selbst·zählung f (*statist.*) self-enumeration (method of census) [*ant.:* ZÄHLERZÄHLUNG]

Semantik f (*log.*) semantics

semantisch adj. (*log.*) semantical

semi·definit adj. (*alg.*) semidefinite

semi·invariant adj. seminvariant

semi·konvergent adj. semiconvergent

semi·kubisch adj. semicubical [*cf.* PARABEL]

senken 1. v.t. drop. 2. v.r. sich s.: (*fallen*) drop; (*sich neigen*) slope, slant (away)

senk·recht adj. 1. (*normal*) normal, perpendicular, right: *senkrechte Ebene* normal plane; *die beiden Geraden stehen auf einander s.* (*oder normal*) the two lines are perpendicular to each other (or: are mutually perpendicular); *auf einander senkrechte* (*oder: senkrecht stehende*) *Achsen* rectangular axes; *zu einem Vektor senkrechter Raum* space perpendicular to a vector [*cf.* GERADE; NORMAL; SCHNITT]. 2. (*lotrecht*)

perpendicular, vertical [*cf.* GE-RADE; STRICH]

Senk·rechte f normal (line), perpendicular (line) [*cf.* FÄLLEN; NORMALE]

Senkrecht·stehen n perpendicularity

Senkung f (*Fall*) drop; (*Neigung*) inclination, slope

separabel adj. separable

Separabilität f separability

Separation f separation

Separat·konto n (*comm.*) special account

separieren v.t. separate

Septillion f ($= 10^{42}$) *Am.* tredecillion; *Br.* septillion

Serie f (*statist.*) series, sequence: *Gesetz der S.* law of sequence [*cf.* DURCHSCHNITTSLAUFZEIT]

Serien·anleihe f, **Serienanleihe-stücke** n pl. (*fin.*) serial bonds pl.

Serpentine f serpentine; (*einzelne Windung, auch*) hairpin bend (or curve)

setzen v.t. set: *wir setzen a* $= b$ we set $a = b$; *gleich Null s.* equate (or: set equal) to zero [*cf.* FALSCH]

sexa·gesimal adj. sexagesimal

Sexagesimal·system n sexagesimal system

Sextant m sextant

Sextillion f ($= 10^{36}$) *Am.* undecillion; *Br.* sextillion

Sextil·schein m (*astr.*) [= GE-SECHSTSCHEIN]

Sextupel n sextuple

sicher adj. certain

Sicherheit f 1. (*Gewißheit*) certainty. 2. (*comm.: Kaution*) security [*cf.* BÜRGSCHAFT; KAUTION]

Sicherheits·summe f (*fin.*) 1.

(*Kaution*) security. **2.** (*Einschuß bei Börsenaufträgen*) margin (for buying orders at the stock exchange)

Sicherstellung *f* (*comm.*) security: *doppelte S.* collateral security

Sicht·akzept *n* [= SICHTWECHSEL]

sicht·bar *adj.* visible: *wir ziehen die sichtbaren Kanten des Tetraeders aus und stricheln die unsichtbaren* we mark the visible edges of the tetrahedron by full lines, the invisible ones by broken lines

Sichtbar·keit *f* visibility

Sicht·wechsel *m* (*comm.*) draft (or note) payable at sight, demand draft (or note)

siderisch *adj.* (*astr.*) sidereal

Sieb *n* sieve: *S. des Eratosthenes* sieve of Eratosthenes

sieben *card. num.* seven

Sieben *f* (*Zahl, Ziffer*) (number, figure) seven

Sieben·eck *n* heptagon [= HEPTAGON]

sieben·eckig *adj.* heptagonal [= HEPTAGONAL]

Siebener *m* (figure) seven

sieben·hundert *card. num.* seven hundred

sieben·mal *num.* seven times [*cf.* IN]

sieben·malig *adj.* (done) seven times [*cf.* DREIMALIG]

sieben·seitig *adj.* seven-sided; (*Prisma, Pyramide*) heptagonal (prism, pyramid)

siebent *ord. num.* seventh

Siebentel *n* seventh (part)

siebentens *adv.* seventhly, in the seventh place

sieben·zählig *adj.* sevenfold, septuple; (*Symmetrie, auch*) heptagonal (symmetry)

sieb·zehn *card. num.* seventeen

Siebzehn·eck *n* polygon of seventeen sides

sieb·zig *card. num.* seventy

sieb·zigst *ord. num.* seventieth

Siede·punkt *m* (*phys.*) boiling point

Sigma *n* (*griechischer Buchstabe* Greek letter Σ, σ, ς) sigma

signieren *v.t.* (*statist.*) code [= SCHLÜSSELN]

Signierung *f* (*statist.*) coding [= SCHLÜSSELUNG]

simultan *adj.* simultaneous [*cf.* MATRIX]

Simultan·gleichungen *f pl.* simultaneous equations

sind (*3rd pers. pl. pres. of sein* be) [*cf.* UND]

Singular *m* singular

singulär *adj.* singular: *singuläre Lösung einer Differentialgleichung* singular solution of a differential equation; *singulärer Punkt einer Kurve* singular (or critical) point of a curve

Singularität *f* singularity

sinken *v.i.* drop, fall

Sinn *m* **1.** (*Richtung*) sense, direction [*cf.* UHRZEIGER; UNGLEICHUNG]. **2.** (*Bedeutung*) meaning, sense, significance [*cf.* BEILEGEN]

sinn·los *adj.* (*bedeutungslos*) meaningless; (*unsinnig*) absurd [*cf.* BEDEUTUNGSLOS]

Sinnlosig·keit *f* (*Bedeutungslosigkeit*) meaninglessness; (*Unsinnigkeit*) absurdity [*cf.* BEDEUTUNGSLOSIGKEIT]

sinn·voll *adj.* meaningful

sinus *m* (*von* α) (*symb.:* sin α) [= SINUS] [*cf.* VERSUS]

Sinus *m* (*eines Winkels* α) sine (of an angle α) (*symb.:* sin α) [*cf.* LOGARITHMUS; SINUS; VERSUS]

sinus hyperbolicus *m* (*eines Winkels* α) (*symb.:* sin h α) hyperbolic sine (of an angle α) (*symb.:* sinh α)

Sinus·linie *f* sine curve, sinusoid

Sinuslinien·projektion *f* (*cart.*) sinusoidal projection

sinus·linig *adj.* sinusoidal: *sinuslinige Erdkartenprojektion* sinusoidal map projection

Sinusoide *f* [= SINUSLINIE]

Sinus·reihe *f* sine series

Sinus·satz *m* law of sines [*cf.* ZURÜCKFÜHRBAR]

Sinus·schwingung *f* (*phys.*) sinusoidal oscillation

Sinus·spirale *f* sinusoidal spiral

Sinus·tafel *f* table of (natural) sines

sinus versus (*von* α) (*symb.:* vers α) [= SINUSVERSUS]

Sinusversus *m* (*eines Winkels* α) versed sine, versine (of an angle α) (*symb.:* vers α ≡ 1 — cos α); *halber S. eines Winkels* α haversine of an angle α (*symb.:* hav α $=\frac{1-\cos\ \alpha}{2}$) [*cf.* SINUS VERSUS; VERSUS]

Sinus·welle *f* sine wave

Situations·kalkül *m* [= ANALYSIS SITUS]

Skala *f* scale, graduation [*cf.* HUNDERTTEILIG; GLEITEN; LOGARITHMISCH; LEITER; NULLSTRICH]

skalar *adj.* scalar: *skalare Größe* scalar quantity [*cf.* FELD; GE-

SCHWINDIGKEIT; MULTIPLIKATION]

Skalar *m* scalar

Skalar·feld *n* scalar field

Skalar·größe *f* scalar quantity

Skalar·multiplikation *f* (*zweier Vektoren*) scalar multiplication (of two vectors)

Skalar·produkt *n* (*zweier Vektoren u und v*) scalar (or dot, or inner, or direct) product (of two vectors *u* and *v*) (*symb.:* *u · v*) [*cf.* PRODUKT: *inneres Produkt*]

Skalen·ablesung *f* scale reading

Skaleno·eder *n* (*cryst.*) scalenohedron

Skizze *f* sketch

skizzieren *v.t.* sketch: *den Beweis s.* sketch the proof

Skrupel *m* (*Gewicht* weight) scruple

Sola·wechsel *m* (*comm.*) **1.** (*Eigenwechsel*) promissory note. **2.** (*einziger Wechsel*) sole of exchange

Solidar·schuld *f*, **Solidar·verpflichtung** *f* (*comm.*) joint and several obligation (or liability)

Soll *n* (*comm.*) debit (side), liability [*cf.* BELASTEN]

Soll·bestand *m* (*comm.*) balance as shown by books or records [*ant.:* ISTBESTAND]

Solstitium *n* (*astr.*) solstice [= SONNENWENDE]

Sommer·solstitium *n*, **Sommersonnenwende** *f* (*astr.*) summer solstice

Sonder·konto *n* [= SEPARATKONTO]

Sonne *f* sun [*cf.* BAHN; HÖHE; LAUF; NACHTBOGEN; TAGBOGEN; VERFINSTERN; VERFINSTERUNG]

Sonnen·aufgang *m* sunrise

Sonnen·bahn *f* (*astr.*) orbit (or track, or path) of the sun; (*scheinbare*) ecliptic

Sonnen·ferne *f* (*astr.*) aphelion [= APHEL(IUM)]

Sonnen·finsternis *f* (*astr.*) solar eclipse

Sonnen·nähe *f* (*astr.*) perihelion [= PERIHEL(IUM)]

Sonnen·tag *m* (*astr.*) solar day

Sonnen·uhr *f* sundial

Sonnen·untergang *m* sunset

Sonnen·wende *f* (*astr.*) solstice [= SOLSTITIUM] [*cf.* WENDEPUNKT]

Sonnen·zeit *f* (*astr.*) solar time: *wahre S.* apparent solar time; *mittlere S.* mean solar time

Sortier·maschine *f* (*statist.*) electrical sorter

Sozial·statistik *f* 1. (*Gesellschaftsstatistik*) social statistics. 2. (*Fürsorgestatistik*) welfare statistics

Spann·breite *f* span

Spanne *f* 1. (*Längenmaß* linear measure) span. 2. (*Intervall*) range, interval

spannen *v.t.* 1. (*strecken*) stretch: *gespannte Feder* stretched spring. 2. (*aufspannen*) span: *die Fläche ist in die Kurve gespannt* the surface is spanned in the curve

Spannung *f* (*phys.*) tension; (*elec., in Volt*) voltage

Spann·weite *f* 1. (*einer Brücke usw.*) span (of a bridge, etc.). 2. (*Intervall*) interval; (*Bereich*) range

Spar·einlage *f* (*fin.*) savings deposit [*cf.* ABHEBUNG]

Spar·genossenschaft *f* (*comm.*) (*auf Gegenseitigkeit*) mutual savings

(or loan) association (or society)

Spar·kasse *f* savings bank: *S. auf genossenschaftlicher Grundlage* mutual savings bank

Spar·konto *n* (*fin.*) savings account

Spat *m* (*cryst.*) parallelepiped

spektral *adj.* (*phys.*) spectral

Spektral·analyse *f* (*phys.*) spectral analysis

Spektro·meter *n* (*phys.*) spectrometer

Spektro·skop *n* (*phys.*) spectroscope

Spektrum *n* (*pl. Spektra*) (*phys.*) spectrum

Spesen *pl.* (*comm.*) expenses, charges [*cf.* ABGEHEN; ABZÜGLICH; AUFRECHNEN; VERRECHNEN]

Spezial·fall *m* special case

Spezial·konto *n* [= SEPARATKONTO]

speziell *adj.* special, proper, particular: *spezieller Fall* special case; *spezielle Zahl* proper number; *spezieller Wert* particular value [*cf.* NULLSTELLE]

Spezies *f* fundamental operation of arithmetic [*cf.* RECHNUNGSART; VIER]

spezifisch *adj.* specific: *spezifisches Gewicht* specific gravity; *spezifische Wärme* specific heat

Sphäre *f* sphere

sphärisch *adj.* spherical: *sphärische Koordinaten* spherical coordinates; *sphärisches Bild eines Punktes auf einer Fläche* spherical image of a point on a surface; *sphärisches Dreieck* spherical triangle, trihedral angle [*cf.* DREIFACH-RECHTWINKLIG; POLAR-

DREIECK; SEITE; WINKEL];
sphärische Trigonometrie spherical trigonometry [*cf.* EXZESS;
GRAD; HALBWINKELSÄTZE;
KETTENLINIE; RECHTWINKLIG;
WINKEL; ZWEIECK]

Sphäroid *n* oblate spheroid

sphäroidal, sphäroidisch *adj.*
oblately spheroidal

Spiegel *m* mirror

Spiegel·bild *n* mirror image, reflection

spiegel·gleich *adj.* mirror-symmetric

Spiegelgleich·heit *f* mirror symmetry

spiegeln 1. *v.t.* reflect, mirror.
2. *v.r.:* **sich** *s.* be reflected

Spieg(e)lung *f* reflection, mirroring: *S. an* (*oder in*) *einer
Achse* reflection in an axis

spiegel·verkehrt *adj.* (*Bild*) mirror-inverted (image)

Spiel *n* (*statist.*) (*mit Würfeln usw.*)
game (at dice, etc.) [*cf.* WÜRFEL]

Spiel·raum *m* margin, latitude,
(free) play; (*Fehlerspielraum*)
margin (of error), allowance;
(*mach.*) tolerance [*cf.* EINENGEN]

Spielraum·theorie *f* (*statist.*) theory
of free ranges

Spin *m* (*phys.*) spin

Spinn·linie *f* clothoid [=
KLOTHOIDE]

Spirale *f* spiral: *archimedische Sp.*
spiral of Archimedes: *hyperbolische Sp.* hyperbolic (or reciprocal) spiral; *logarithmische
Sp.* logarithmic (or equiangular,
or logistic) spiral [*cf.* ASYMPTOTISCH; PARABOLISCH; SCHNECKENLINIE]

spiralig *adj.* spiral

spitz *adj.* acute: [*cf.* WINKEL]

Spitze *f* **1.** (*eines Dreiecks, einer
Pyramide, eines Kegels*) vertex,
apex (of a triangle, a pyramid, a
cone) : *Winkel an der Sp.* vertex
(or apex) angle, vertical (or
apical) angle. **2.** (*einer Kurve*)
cusp, cuspidal (or stationary)
point, spinode (of a curve):
Sp. erster Art cusp of first kind,
simple cusp; *Sp. zweiter Art* cusp
of·second kind. **3.** (*z.B. eines
Zirkels*) (needle) point (e.g. of a
compass)

Spitzen·zirkel *m·* dividers *pl.*

spitzig *adj.* pointed

spitz·wink(e)lig *adj.* acute: *spitzwinkeliges Dreieck* acute triangle

Sprech·weise *f* (*log.*) parlance,
way of speaking

Sprung *m* jump, discontinuity

sprung·haft *adj.* discontinuous,
discrete [*cf.* FUNKTION]

Sprunghaftig·keit *f* discontinuity

Sprung·stelle *f* (point of) discontinuity

Sprung·weite *f* jump, amount of
discontinuity

Spur *f* (*descr., alg.*) trace: *Sp.
einer Ebene in einer Projektionsebene* trace of a plane on a
projection plane; *Sp. in der
horizontalen* (*vertikalen*) *Projektionsebene* horizontal (vertical)
trace; (*alg.*) *Sp. einer Matrix*
trace of a matrix [*cf.* DARSTELLEN
2.; REDUZIEREN]

Spur·linie *f* (*descr.*) (*einer Ebene*)
trace (of a plane)

Spur·punkt *m* (*descr.*) (*einer
Geraden im Raum*) trace, piercing

point (of a line in space)

Staats·renten *f pl.* (*fin.*) government annuities (or bonds)

Stäbchen·diagramm *n,* **Stab·diagramm** *n* (*statist.*) bar chart (or graph)

stabil *adj.* (*phys.*) stable [*cf.* GLEICHGEWICHT; UNVERÄNDERLICH]

Stabilität *f* (*phys.*) stability [*cf.* UNVERÄNDERLICHKEIT]

Staffel *f* scale

Staffel·bild *n* **Staffel·diagramm** *n* (*statist.*) [= TREPPENPOLYGON]

Staffel·zins(en) *m pl.* (*fin.*) interest according to equated calculation

Staffelzins·rechnung *f* (*fin.*) equated calculation of interest

Stamm·aktie *f* (*comm.*) common share (or stock)

Stamm·aktienkapital *n* (*comm.*) common (or capital) stock

Stamm·bruch *m* unit fraction

Stamm·kapital *n* (*comm.*) (*Gründungskapital*) nominal capital (or stock); (*Aktienkapital*) capital stock

Standard·abweichung *f* (*statist.*) standard deviation

Standard·ziffer *f* (*statist.*) standard (or corrected) rate

stand·fest *adj.* (*phys.*) stable

Standfestig·keit *f* (*phys.*) stability

Stangen·zirkel *m* beam compass

stark *adj.* strong, intense, intensive [*cf.* ABFALLEN; AUSSAGENVERBINDUNG; NEIGUNG; PRIMÄR]

Stärke *f* strength, intensity

starr *adj.* (*unbiegsam*) rigid, inflexible; (*unveränderlich*) stable; (*fest*) solid: *starrer Körper* rigid body; *im starren Zustand* in the

solid state [*cf.* FEST; SAISONINDEX; SAISONSCHWANKUNGEN]

Starre *f* (*Unbiegsamkeit*) rigidity; (*Festheit*) solidity

Starr·heit *f* (*Unbiegsamkeit*) rigidity, inflexibility, (*Unveränderlichkeit*) stability

Statik *f* (*phys.*) statics

stationär *adj.* stationary

statisch *adj.* (*phys.*) static: [*cf.* MOMENT^2; RUHEND; UNBESTIMMT]

Statistik *f* statistics

Statistiker *m* statistician

statistisch *adj.* statistical: *statistische Einheit* **a.** (*als Maß* as measure) statistical unit; **b.** (*als Einzelstück einer Gesamtmasse*) item in a statistical universe; *statistische Kurve* **a.** (*Häufigkeitskurve*) (frequency) curve; **b.** (*Bild der Zeitreihe*) line chart (of time series) [*cf.* AUFARBEITUNG; AUFGLIEDERN; AUSGLEICHUNGSRECHNUNG; BILD; ERHEBUNG; MASSE; NACHWEISUNG; REIHE; REPRÄSENTATIV; VERDICHTUNG; WAHRSCHEINLICHKEIT]

Stech·zirkel *m* dividers [*cf.* ZIRKEL]

stehen *v.i.* stand, be upright, be [*cf.* SENKRECHT; VERHALTEN]

stehend *adj.* standing, stationary: *stehende Welle* stationary wave [*cf.* KNOTENLINIE; STEHEN]

steigen *v.i.* rise, increase, ascend; (*Preise*) rise, go up: *steigende Potenzen einer Veränderlichen in einem Polynom* ascending powers of a variable in a polynomial; *nach steigenden Potenzen geordnet* ascending, arranged by ascending powers [*cf.* ANZIEHEN; ORDNEN; POTENZ; POTENZREIHE; TENDENZ]

Steigung *f* ascent, grade, gradient, slope

Steigungs·winkel *m* angle of elevation; (*einer Schraubenlinie*) helix angle

steil *adj.* steep [*cf.* ABFALLEN]

Steil·heit *f* steepness; (*der Häufigkeitskurve*) kurtosis (of the frequency curve) [*cf.* EXZESS]

Steiner *m* N.: *Steinersche Kurve* tricuspid [*cf.* HYPOZYKLOIDE]

Stelle *f* place, spot, point; (*Stellenwert*) place; (*Stellenziffer*) (place) digit: *alle Stellen der Zahl sind Vierer* all digits of the number are fours [*cf.* ABBRECHEN; HUNDERTER; TREIBEN; VERSCHIEBEN]

Stellen·wert *m* place (or local) value [*cf.* EINER; STELLE; ZEHNER]

Stellen(wert)ziffer *f* (place) digit [*cf.* STELLE]

. . . stellig *adj. suf.* (*ganze Zahl*) -figure, -digit (integer); (*Dezimalzahl*) -figure, -place (decimal); (*log.: mit . . Leerstellen*) -place, -adic [*cf.* DREISTELLIG; EINSTELLIG; FÜNFSTELLIG; VIELSTELLIG; VIERSTELLIG; ZWEISTELLIG]

Stellung *f* position: *St. einer Zahl in einem Schema* position of a number in an array

Ster *m* (*meas.*) stere

Sterbe·tafel *f* (*ins., statist.*) mortality table

Sterblich·keit *f* (*ins., statist.*) mortality

Sterblichkeits·tabelle *f* (*ins., statist.*) mortality (or life) table

Sterblichkeits·ziffer *f* (*ins., statist.*) mortality (or death) rate

Stereo·chemie *f* stereochemistry

stereo·graphisch *adj.* (*cart.*) (*Projektion*) stereographic (projection)

Stereo·metrie *f* solid geometry, stereometry

stereo·metrisch *adj.* stereometric(al)

Stereo·skop *n* (*opt.*) stereoscope

Stereoskop·bild *n* stereograph, stereoscopic image [*cf.* RAUMBILD]

stereo-skopisch *adj.* stereoscopic

Stereoskop·zeichnung *f* stereograph

Stern *m* star [*cf.* FÜNFSTRAHLIG; GESTIRN; GRÖSSE; MERIDIANDURCHGANG; VERDUNKELN; VERDUNKLUNG; VERFINSTERN; VERFINSTERUNG]

Stern·bedeckung *f* (*astr.*) occultation of a star

Stern·jahr *n* (*astr.*) sidereal year [*cf.* GESTIRN]

Stern·figur *n* star-shaped (or starlike) figure, star polygon

Stern·flächner *m* star polyhedron

Stern·karte *f* (*astr.*) star map (or chart)

Stern·körper *m* star-shaped (or starlike) solid, star polyhedron

Stern·kurve *f* [= ASTEROIDE]

Stern·polyeder *n* star polyhedron

Stern·polygon *n* star polygon

Stern·tag *m* (*astr.*) sidereal day

Stern·verdunklung *f*, **Stern·verfinsterung** *f* (*astr.*) occultation of a star

Stern·vieleck *n* star polygon

Stern·vielflach *n*, **Stern·vielflächner** *m* star polyhedron

Stern·zeit *f* (*astr.*) sidereal time

stetig *adj.* (*kontinuierlich*) continuous, continued; (*topologisch*) topological: *stetige Proportion* **a.** (*fortlaufende Proportion*) continued proporuon; **b.** (*zwischen drei Größen* between three quantities) proportion with equal means, proportion by extreme and mean ratio; *stetige Abbildung von Punkten* continuous mapping (or correspondence) of points; *stetige Transformation* continuous transformation; *linksseitig* (*rechtsseitig*) *st.* continuous on the left (right); *st. in einem Gebiet* continuous in a region; *stetige Funktion* continuous function; (*alg.*) *st. isomorph* topologically isomorphic [*cf.* FAST; GLEICHGRADIG; PROPORTIONALE; VERLAUFEN]

Stetig·keit *f* (*z.B. einer Funktion*) continuity (e.g. of a function) [*cf.* GLEICHMÄSSIG]

Stetigkeits·axiom *n* axiom of continuity

Stetigkeits·bedingung *f* condition for continuity

Stetigkeits·prinzip *n* principle of continuity

Steuer *f* (*fin.*) duty, tax: *direkte* (*indirekte*) *St.* direct [indirect] tax [*cf.* AUFSCHLAG]

Steuer·aufschlag *m* (*fin.*) surtax

steuer·frei *adj.* (*fin.*) tax-exempt, nontaxable

Steuer·jahr *n* (*fin.*) fiscal year

Steuer·wert *m* (*fin.*) taxable (or assessed) value [*cf.* ABSCHÄTZEN; SCHÄTZEN]

Steuer·zuschlag *m* (*fin.*) surtax

Stich·probe *f* spot test; (*statist.*) random sample

Stichproben·erhebung *f* (*statist.*)

sampling: *kontrollierte St.* controlled (or stratified) sampling; *wahllose St.* random sampling [*cf.* GRUPPENWEISE]

Stich·zeit *f* (*statist.*) (*Zeitpunkt*) critical date; (*Zeitraum*) critical period

Stiftung *f* (*fin.*) foundation, endowment fund

Stiftungs·fonds *m*, **Stiftungs·vermögen** *n* (*fin.*) endowment fund

stimmen *v.i.* **1.** (*richtig sein*) come out right (or even), add up, check: *die Ziffern st.* the figures check; *die Rechnung stimmt* the computation comes out right. **2.** (*statist.*) (*abstimmen*) vote

Stimmenzähl·apparat *m* (*statist.*) voting machine

Stochastik *f* (*statist.*) stochastics

stochastisch *adj.* (*statist.*) stochastic: *stochastische Grenze* stochastic limit

Storch·schnabel *m* pantograph

stören *v.t.* (*phys.*) disturb, interfere; (*astr.*) perturb

Störung *f* (*phys.*) disturbance, interference; (*astr.*) perturbation [*cf.* SÄKULAR]

Störungs·rechnung *f* (*astr.*) (*allgemeine*) theory of perturbations; (*einzelne*) calculation of a perturbation

Stoß *m* (*phys.*) impact, thrust, push, percussion; (*Zusammenstoß*) collision

stoßen (*phys.*) *v.t.* push, thrust, impinge

Stoß·kraft *f* (*phys.*) momentum, impact [*cf.* WUCHT]

Stoß·welle *f* (*phys.*) shock (or percussion) wave

Stoß·zahl *f* (*phys.*) number of collisions

Strahl *m* **1.** (*geom.*) (straight) line, unlimited line, ray. **2.** (*phys.*) ray, beam: *ordentlicher* (*außerordentlicher*)*St.*ordinary(extraordinary) ray [*cf.* BEUGEN; EINFALL; EINFALLEN; EMITTIEREN; GERICHTET; PROJIZIEREN]

strahlen *v.i.* (*phys.*) radiate

Strahlen·brechung *f* (*phys.*) refraction

Strahlen·bündel *n* (*geom.*) bundle (or sheaf, or star) of lines; (*opt.*) bundle (or beam) of rays

Strahlen·büschel *n* (*geom.*) pencil of lines; (*opt.*) pencil of rays [*cf.* INEINANDERLIEGEN; WURF]

Strahlen·feld *n* (*ebenes*) (plane) net of lines

Strahlen·kegel *m* ray cone

... **strahlig** *adj. suf.* -rayed, -pronged [*cf.* FÜNFSTRAHLIG]

Strahlung *f* (*phys.*) radiation [*cf.* AUSSENDEN]

Strahlungs·energie *f* (*phys.*) radiant energy

Strahlungs·gesetz *n* (*phys.*) law of radiation

Strecke *f* line (segment), straight segment, distance, interval [*cf.* ABTRAGUNG; AUFTRAGEN; ÄUSSER; GERICHTET; HALBIEREN; HALBIERUNGSLINIE; HALBIERUNGSPUNKT; HARMONISCH; LÄNGE; MITTELLINIE; MITTELPUNKT; MITTELSENKRECHTE; TEILEN; TEILUNG; VERLÄNGERN; VERLÄNGERUNG; ZURÜCKLEGEN]

strecken *v.t.* stretch [*cf.* SPANNEN]

Strecken·masse *f* (*statist.*) statistical universe (or time series) of

period (or noncumulative) data [*ant.* PUNKTMASSE] [*cf.* BESTANDESMASSE; BESTANDSMASSE; PUNKTMASSE]

Streckung *f* (*z.B. einer Feder*) stretching (e.g. of a spring)

streichen I. *v.t.* **1.** (*ausstreichen*) strike out, cross out, cancel, delete [*cf.* ABSCHREIBEN]. **2.** (*phys.*) (*z.B. mit dem Magnet*) stroke (e.g. with a magnet). **II.** *v.i.* **3.** (*geol., geog.*)(*in einer Richtung*) bear, strike (in a direction) [*cf.* STREICHUNG; STRICH]

Streich·richtung *f* (*geol., geog.*) (direction of) strike, trend

Streichung *f* (*Ausstreichung*) cancellation, deletion; (*geol., geog.*) (*Streichen in einer Richtung*) strike [*cf.* ABSCHREIBUNG]

Streichungs·richtung *f* [= STREICHRICHTUNG]

Streif *m*, **Streifen** *m* strip

streng *adj.* exact, rigorous, rigid: *die strengen Wissenschaften* the exact sciences; *strenge Ableitung* rigorous derivation

Strenge *f* exactness, exactitude, rigor

streuen 1. *v.t.* spread, disperse. **2.** *v.i.* be spread, be dispersed

Streuung *f* (*statist.*) (*Variation*) dispersion, variation; (*Quadrat der mittleren quadratischen Abweichung*) variance [*cf.* VERTEILUNG]

Streuungs·bild *n* (*statist.*) scatter (or dot, or dispersion) diagram, bivariate frequency chart

Streuungs·maß *n* (*statist.*) measure of dispersion (or variation) [*cf.*

SCHWANKUNGSMASS; VARIABILI-
TÄTSINDEX]

Strich *m* **1.** (*mit dem Bleistift, der
Feder*) stroke (with the pencil,
pen); (*einer gestrichelten Linie*)
dash: *ein kurzer St.* a short
stroke. **2.** (*geradliniges Zeichen*)
bar, line, dash [*cf.* BRUCHSTRICH;
ÜBERSTREICHUNG;   UNTER-
STREICHUNG]; (*verbindende Über-
streichung*) vinculum; (*Binde-
strich*)   hyphen;   (*Trennungs-
zeichen*) separation (or division)
sign: *wagrechter, senkrechter,
schiefer St.* horizontal, vertical,
slanting bar (or line). **3.** (*Index
superscript*) prime, accent: *a
Strich hat einen Strich* a prime is
marked by one accent, (*symb.:
a′*); *y zwei Strich y* double prime,
(*symb.: y″*); *f Strich x* [= *erste*
ABLEITUNG *von x*] *f* prime of *x*,
(*symb.: f′(x)*). **4.** (*geol., geog.*)
(*Streichen in einer Richtung*)
(direction of) strike, trend. **5.**
(*des Kompasses*) point (of the
compass)

stricheln *v.t.* mark by a broken (or
dotted) line (or: by a series of
dashes), dot [*cf.* GESTRICHELT;
SICHTBAR]

Strichel(ungs)·verfahren *n* (*statist.*)
tallysheet method

strich·punktiert *adj.* (*Linie*) dot-
dash (line)

Strich·richtung *f* (*geol., geog.*)
strike

Striktion *f* striction

Striktions·linie *f* (*eines einschaligen
Hyperboloids*) line of striction
(or: of the gorge) of an unparted
hyperboloid

Strom *m* (*phys.*) stream, flow;
(*elec.*) current

Strom·dichte *f* (*phys.*) current
density

strömen *v.i.* (*phys.*) flow

Strom·faden *m*, **Strom·linie** *f*
(*phys.*) streamline

strom·linig *adj.* (*phys.*) streamlined

Strom·stärke *f* (*elec.*) current
intensity

Strophoide *f* strophoid: *gerade
(schräge) St.* right (oblique)
strophoid

Struktur *f* structure

strukturell *adj.* structural

Struktur·formel *f* (*chem.*) structural formula

Stück *n* piece

stückeln *v.t.* divide into pieces,
cut to pieces

Stückelung *f* division into pieces;
St. von Aktien division into shares

Stück·zinsen *m pl.* (*fin.*) (*von
Aktien*) accrued interest (from
shares)

Stufe *f* step; (*Niveau*) level [*cf.*
PRÄDIKAT]

Stufen·funktion *f* step function

Stufen·kalkül *m* (*log.*) calculus of
order ω

Stufen·leiter *f* scale

Stumpf *m* frustum [*cf.* ROTATIONS-
KEGEL;   ROTATIONSKÖRPER;
ROTATIONSZYLINDER]

stumpf *adj.* obtuse [*cf.* WINKEL]

stumpf·wink(e)lig *adj.* obtuse

Stunde *f* hour [*cf.* GESCHWINDIG-
KEIT; MINUTE]

Stunden·glas *n* hour glass

Stunden·kreis *m* (*astr.*) (*eines Him-
melspunkts*) hour circle (of a
celestial point)

Stunden·winkel *m* (*astr.*) (*eines Punkts am Himmel*) hour angle (of a celestial point)

Stunden·zeiger *m* (*einer Uhr*) hour hand (of a clock or watch)

stündlich *adj.* hourly, per hour

Sturm *m N.* [*cf.* FUNKTION; KETTE; THEOREM]

Stutz *m* frustum [*cf.* ROTATIONS-KEGEL; ROTATIONSKÖRPER; ROTATIONSZYLINDER]

Stütz·punkt *m* (*mech.*) (*eines Hebels*) fulcrum (of a lever)

Sub·determinante *f* (*eines Elements einer Determinante*) subdeterminant, minor (determinant) (of an element in a determinant) [= MINOR; UNTERDETERMINANTE]

Sub·jekt *n* (*log.*) subject [*cf.* SUBJEKTSBEGRIFF]

Subjekts·begriff *m* (*log.*) **1.** (*Begriff des Subjekts*) concept of subject. **2.** (*in der Aussage*) subject (term) (in a sentence)

sub·konträr *adj.* (*log.*) (*Urteil*) subcontrary (judgment)

Sub·normale *f* subnormal

sub·stituieren *v.t.* substitute

Sub·stitution *f* substitution [*cf.* INVERS]

Substitutions·gruppe *f* (*alg.*) substitution group

sub·sumieren *v.t.* (*log.*) subsume

Sub·sumtion *f* (*log.*) subsumption

Sub·tangente *f* subtangent

Sub·trahend *m* subtrahend

sub·trahieren *v.t.* subtract, deduct [*cf.* BORGEN]

Sub·traktion *f* subtraction [*cf.* MINUS]

Subtraktions·zeichen *n* subtraction sign, sign of subtraction

Sub·vention *f* (*fin.*) subsidy

sub·ventionieren *v.t.* (*fin.*) subsidize

suchen *v.t.* seek, look for, find, require: *die Quadratwurzel s.* find the square root; *gesucht sind* required are

Süd *m*, **Süden** *m* south

südlich *adj.* southern, southerly

Süd·pol *m* south pole [*cf.* VERBINDEN]

Süd·punkt *m* south point

Suggestiv·frage *f* (*statist.*) biased (or loaded) question

Suk·zession *f* succession

suk·zessive *adj.* successive

Summand *m* summand, addend [= ADDEND] [*cf.* POSTEN]

Summation *f* summation

Summations·zeichen *n* summation sign

Summe *f* sum: *algebraische S.* algebraic sum [*cf.* ARITHMETISCH; GAUSSSCH; GEOMETRISCH; LOGISCH; REIHE; WURZELAUSDRUCK]

Summen·index *m* **1.** (*math.*) sum index (or subscript). **2.** (*statist.*) aggregative type index number

Summen·kurve *f* (*statist.*) ogive, summation curve, cumulative frequency curve

Summen·polygon *n* [= SUMMEN-KURVE]

Summen·tafel *f* (*statist.*) cumulative table

summier·bar *adj.* summable

Summierbar·keit *f* summability

summieren 1. *v.t.* sum (up), add. **2.** *v.r. sich s.* accumulate: *der Fehler summiert sich* the error accumulates

Summierung *f* summation

Summierungs·kurve f [= SUMMEN-
KURVE]
superior *adj.* (*Lat.*) superior [*cf.*
LIMES]
super·ponieren *v.t.* superpose,
superimpose
Super·position f superposition,
superimposition
Supplement n (*eines Winkels*) sup-
plement (of an angle)
supplementär *adj.* supplementary
[*cf.* PARALLEL]
Supplementär·winkel m supplementary angle
Syl·logismus m (*log.*) syllogism
[*cf.* SCHLUSSSATZ]
syl·logistisch *adj.* (*log.*) syllogis-
tic(al)
Sym·bol n symbol: *Christoffelsches
S.* Christoffel symbol
Sym·bolik f symbolism
sym·bolisch *adj.* symbolic: (*alg.*)
symbolische Adjunktion symbolic
adjunction [*cf.* LOGIK]
Sym·metrie f symmetry; (*der
Häufigkeitskurve*) isokurtosis (of
the frequency curve): *n-fache
(oder n-zählige) S.* n-fold ·sym-
metry [*cf.* ACHTZÄHLIG; DREI-
ZÄHLIG; FÜNFZÄHLIG; SECHS-
ZÄHLIG; SIEBENZÄHLIG; VIER-
ZÄHLIG; ZENTRISCH]
Symmetrie·achse f axis of
symmetry: *S. einer Kurve* axis
(of symmetry) of a curve
Symmetrie·ebene f symmetry (or
principal) plane

Symmetrie·zentrum n center of
symmetry
sym·metrisch *adj.* symmetric(al);
(*Häufigkeitskurve*) isokurtic (frequency curve): *symmetrische
Beziehung, Funktion, Gruppe* symmetric relation, function, group;
symmetrischer Tensor symmetri-
cal tensor [*cf.* DETERMINANTE;
HERMITE; MATRIX]
syn·chron *adj.* synchronous
Syn·chronisation f synchronization
syn·chronisieren *v.t.* synchronize
Syn·chronisierung f synchronization
syn·klastisch *adj.* (*Krümmung*)
synclastic (curvature)
Syn·these f, **Syn·thesis** f synthesis
syn·thetisch *adj.* synthetic [*cf.*
GEOMETRIE]
Syn·traktrix f (*Kurve*) syntractrix
Sy·stem n system, set: *ein S.
gerader Linien* a system (or set)
of straight lines [*cf.* ALGEBRA 2.;
DREIFACH-RECHTWINKLIG; FREI-
HEITSGRAD; GERADENDFLÄCHE;
KOMPOSITION; MASSENMITTEL-
PUNKT; MATRIX; METRISCH;
PTOLEMÄISCH; RESULTANTE;
SCHIEFENDFLÄCHE]
sy·stematisch *adj.* systematic(al)
[*cf.* FEHLER]
sy·stematisieren *v.t.* systematize
Sy·stematisierung f systematiza-
tion
Syzygie f, **Syzygium** n (*pl. Syzygien*)
(*astr.*) syzygy

T

tabellarisch *adj.* tabular

tabellarisieren *v.t.* tabulate

Tabelle *f* table, tablet, chart; *in Tabellen bringen* tabulate [*cf.* TAFEL; ZEILE]

Tabellen·form *f* tabular form

Tabellen·kopf *m* caption (in a table); (*Rubrik*) boxhead

Tabellen·spalte *f* table column

Tabellen·verarbeitung *f* (*statist.*) condensation of primary table

Tabellen·zeile *f* table row (or line)

Tabellier·maschine *f* (*nur sortierend*) electrical sorter; (*schreibend*) electrical tabulator

Tafel *f* **1.** (*Tabelle*) table, tablet [*cf.* AUFARBEITEN; AUFARBEITUNG]. **2.** (*descr.*) (*Projektionsebene*) projection plane: *erste, zweite, dritte T.* horizontal, vertical, profile (projection) plane. **3.** (*Schreibtafel*) blackboard [*cf.* ANSCHREIBEN]

Tafel·abstand *m* (*descr.*) (*eines Punktes*) distance (of a point) from the projection plane: *erster, zweiter, dritter T.* distance from the horizontal, vertical, profile (projection) plane

Tafel·differenz *f* (*in einer Logarithmentafel*) tabular difference, proportional part (in a table of logarithms)

Tafel·methode *f* (*in der Versicherungsstatistik*) actuarial method, table method (in actuarial statistics)

Tafel·ziffer *f* (*in der Versicherungsstatistik*) actuarial rate, corrected (or standardized) rate (in actuarial statistics)

Tag *m* day [*cf.* GENAU; VIERZEHN]

Tag·bogen *m* (*astr.*) (*der Sonne*) diurnal arc (of the sun)

Tages·kurs *m*, **Tages·preis** *m* (*comm.*) current exchange (or price)

täglich *adj.* daily, diurnal; (*comm.*) *tägliches Geld* demand deposit (or money)

Tag·und·nacht·gleiche *f* (*astr.*) equinox [= ÄQUINOKTIUM, NACHTGLEICHE] [*cf.* FORTSCHREITEN; VORRÜCKEN]

Tangens, tangens *m* (*von* α) (*symb.*: tang α, tg α) [= TANGENTE 3.]

tangens hyperbolicus *m* (*eines Winkels* α) (*symb.*: tg h α, tang h α) hyperbolic tangent (of an angle α), (*symb.*: tanh α)

Tangens·linie *f* [= TANGENTEN-LINIE]

Tangente *f* **1.** (*einer Kurve*) (line) tangent (to a curve), tangent line (of a curve): *Winkel einer T. mit einer Sehne durch den Berührungspunkt* angle of chord and tangent at point of tangency, tan-chord angle; *T. in einem Punkt, und Berührungspunkt* point-tangent; (*phys.*) *in der Richtung der T. wegfliegen* fly off at a tangent [*cf.* MEHRFACH]. **2.** (*Länge der T.* length of tangent) tangent [= TANGENTENLÄNGE]. **3.** (*eines Winkels* α) (*symb.*: tg α, tang α) tangent (of an angle α), (*symb.*: tan α) [*cf.* TANGENS; TANGENS]

Tangenten·fläche *f* (*einer Raum-kurve*) tangent surface (of a space curve)

Tangenten·formel *f* tangent formula

Tangenten·kurve *f* [= TANGENTEN-LINIE]

Tangenten·länge *f* (*in einem Kurvenpunkt*) length of tangent (at a point of a curve) [*cf.* TANGENTE 2.]

Tangenten·linie *f* tangent curve

Tangenten·satz *m* (*der Trigonometrie*) law of tangents, tangent law (in trigonometry)

Tangenten·sechseck *n* (*eines Kegelschnitts*) hexagon circumscribing (a conic)

Tangenten·viereck *n* (*eines Kreises*) quadrilateral circumscribing (a circle)

Tangential·beschleunigung *f* (*phys.*) tangential acceleration

Tangential·ebene *f* tangent plane; *T. eines Kegels* plane tangent to a cone

Tangential·geschwindigkeit *f* (*phys.*) tangential velocity

Tangential·kegel *m* tangent cone

Tangential·komponente *f* tangential component

Tara *f* (*comm.*) tare

Tarif *m* (*comm., fin.*) tariff

Taster·zirkel *m* caliper

Tau *n* (*griechischer Buchstabe* Greek letter T, τ) tau

tausend *card. num.* one (or a) thousand

Tausend *n* thousand: *viele Tausend(e)* many thousands; *vom Tausend*, (*abbr.*) *v.T.* per mille, per thousand [*cf.* v.T.]

Tausendel *n* thousandth (part)

Tausender *m* thousand

Tausender·stelle *f* thousand's (or thousands) place

Tausend·satz *m* permillage

tausendst *ord. num.* thousandth

Tausendstel *n* thousandth (part)

Tauto·chrone *f* tautochrone

Tauto·logie *f* (*log.*) tautology

tauto·logisch *adj.* (*log.*) tautologic(al)

taxieren *v.t.* (*comm.*) value, assess

Taxierung *f* (*comm.*) valuation, assessment

Taylor *m* *N.* [*cf.* FORMEL; REIHE; SATZ]

technisch *adj.* technical, technological: *technisches Zeichnen* technical drawing

Teil *m* part, portion [*cf.* ACHT; ALIQUOT; AUSZIEHEN; DOPPEL-KEGEL; DRITT; KREISTEILUNG; ÜBRIG; UMRANDEN; VERHÄLTNIS; VIER]

Teil·aussage *f* (*log.*) component sentence

teil·bar *adj.* divisible [*cf.* GERADE]

Teilbar·keit *f* divisibility

Teil·bereich *m* subdomain

Teilchen *n* particle

Teil·disjunktion *f* (*log.*) [= DISJUNKTIONSGLIED]

teilen *v.t.* divide; (*einteilen*) graduate, calibrate: *eine Strecke in die Hälfte t.* divide a line segment in half; *zwanzig durch fünf t.* (*oder dividieren*) divide twenty by five [*cf.* ABTEILEN; DIVIDEND; QUADRANT; VIER; ZWICKEL]

Teiler *m* divisor, factor [*cf.* ECHT; GEMEINSAM; MASS]

teiler·fremd *adj.* relatively prime, prime to each other

Teil·erhebung *f* (*statist.*) partial enumeration, sampling

Teiler·induktion *f* (*alg.*) divisor induction

Teiler·kette *f* (*alg.*) divisor chain

Teilerketten·satz *m* (*alg.*) divisor chain condition

teiler·los *adj.* (*alg.*) (*Ideal*) maximal (ideal) [*cf.* PRIMIDEAL]

Teil·folge *f* subsequence, partial sequence

Teil·intervall *n* subinterval

Teil·konjunktion *f* (*log.*) [= KON-JUNKTIONSGLIED]

Teil·korrelation *f* partial correlation

Teil·mannigfaltigkeit *f* submanifold

Teil·masse *f* (*statist.*) class, group

Teil·menge *f* subset, subclass

Teil·produkt *n* partial product

Teil·punkt *m* point of division

Teil·quotient *m* partial quotient

Teil·resultante *f* subresultant

Teil·strich *m* mark, division (or graduation) mark; *mit Teilstrichen versehen* graduate [*cf.* EIN-TEILEN; EINTEILUNG; TEILUNG; UNTERTEILEN; UNTERTEILUNG]

Teil·summe *f* partial sum, subtotal

Teil·system *n* subsystem

Teilung *f* division; (*durch Teilstriche*) scale, graduation (by marks): *T. einer Strecke* division of a line (segment) [*cf.* HARMO-NISCH; LOGARITHMENPAPIER; LOGARITHMISCH]

Teilungs·problem *n* (*in der Wahrscheinlichkeitsrechnung*) problem of points (in theory of probability)

Teilungs·punkt *m* point of division

Teilungs·verhältnis *n* division ratio, ratio of division [*cf.* INNER]

teil·weise *adj.* partial, by parts: *t. Integration* integration by parts

Teil·zahlung *f* (*comm.*) partial payment; (*Rate*) installment (payment) [*cf.* ABZAHLUNG]

Teil·zirkel *m* bow compass

Tele·skop *n* (*opt.*) telescope

tele·skopisch *adj.* (*opt.*) telescopic(al)

Temperatur *f* (*phys.*) temperature [*cf.* KRITISCH; NULLPUNKT]

Tendenz *f* tendency; (*comm., statist.*) trend: *fallende* (*steigende*) *T.* (*oder Entwicklung*) downward (upward) trend

tendieren *v.i.* tend

Tensor *m* tensor: *kontravarianter* (*kovarianter*) *T.* contravariant (covariant) tensor [*cf.* SCHIEF-SYMMETRISCH; SYMMETRISCH]

Tensor·analysis *f* tensor analysis

Tensor·feld *n* tensor field

Tensor·kalkül *m*, **Tensor·rechnung** *f* tensor calculus

Termin *m* (*comm., fin.*) term, appointed day (or time); *auf T. kaufen* (*verkaufen*) purchase (sell) for future delivery [FRIST; ZAHLUNGSFRIST]

Termin·geschäft *n* option (or future) business; (*pl.*) *Termingeschäfte* forward operations, futures [*cf.* TERMINKAUF]

Termin·handel *m* (*comm.*) forward operations *pl.*, futures *pl.*

Termin·kauf *m* (*Kauf auf Kredit*) purchase on credit; (*Termingeschäft*) forward buying, business

in (or: buying of) futures
Termin·käufer *m* forward-buyer
Termino·logie *f* terminology
termino·logisch *adj.* terminological
Terminus *m* (*Lat.*) term, expression: *T. technicus* technical term
ternär *adj.* ternary
Tertia·wechsel *m* (*comm.*) third of exchange
Tetarto·eder *n* (*cryst.*) tetartohedron
Tetarto·pyramide *f* (*cryst.*) tetartopyramid
Tetrade *f* tetrad
Tetra·eder *n* tetrahedron [= VIERFLACH; VIERFLÄCHNER] [*cf.* SICHTBAR]
tetra·edrisch *adj.* tetrahedral
Tetra·gon *n* tetragon [= VIERECK]
tetra·gonal *adj.* (*cryst.*) tetragonal [*cf.* GERADENDFLÄCHE]
Tetrakis·hexaeder *n* tetrahexahedron, tetrakishexahedron [= PYRAMIDENWÜRFEL]
Teuerungs·zulage *f* (*comm.*) cost-of-living bonus
Teufels·kurve *f* devil's curve
Theodolit *m* theodolite
Theorem *n* theorem: *Sturmsches Th.* Sturm's theorem
theoretisch *adj.* theoretical [*cf.* LOGIK]
Theorie *f* theory: *Th. der Gleichungen* theory of equations [*cf.* GALOISSCH; LEHRE[1]]
thermisch *adj.* (*phys.*) thermal
Thermo·dynamik *f* thermodynamics: *der erste Hauptsatz der Th.* the first law of thermodynamics]*cf.* WÄRMELEHRE]

Thermo·meter *n* (*phys.*) thermometer [*cf.* HUNDERTTEILIG]
Thermo·statik *f* (*phys.*) thermostatics
These *f* thesis
Theta *n* (*griechischer Buchstabe* Greek letter Θ, θ) theta
Theta·funktion *f* theta function
tief *adj.* deep
Tiefe *f* depth
Tiefen·dimension *f* dimension of depth, extension in depth
Tiefen·stufe *f* gradient [*cf.* GEOTHERMISCH]
Tiefst·preis *m* (*comm.*) rock bottom price
Tier·kreis *m* (*astr.*) zodiac [= ZODIAK]
tilgen *v.t.* (*eine Schuld*) pay off, extinguish; (*in planmäßigen Raten*) amortize (a debt) [*cf.* AMORTISIEREN; EINLÖSEN]
Tilgung *f* (*comm.*) (*einer Schuld*) extinction, repayment, amortization (of a debt) [*cf.* AMORTISIERUNG; TILGEN]
Tilgungs·fonds *m* (*fin.*) sinking fund
Tilgungs·rate *f* (*fin.*) amortization rate
titrieren *v.t.*, *v.i.* (*chem.*) titrate
Titrierung *f* (*chem.*) titration
Ton *m* (*acoust.*) tone, sound
Ton·art *f* (*acoust.*) key [*cf.* GRUNDTON]
Tonnage *f* tonnage [= TONNENGEHALT]
Tonne *f* (*meas.*) ton: *metrische T.* metric ton
Tonnen·gehalt *m* tonnage [= TONNAGE]
Topo·logie *f* (*Ortsbeziehungen*)

topology; (*Geometrie der Lage*) topology, analysis situs

topo·logisch *adj.* topological: *topologischer Raum* topological space; *topologische Transformation* topological transformation, homeomorphism; *topologische Geometrie* topological geometry [*cf.* STETIG]

Torse *f* developable (surface) [= DEVELOPPABLE]

Torsion *f* (*einer Raumkurve*) torsion, second curvature (of a space curve) [*cf.* KRÜMMUNG]

Torsions·pendel *n* (*phys.*) torsion pendulum

Torsions·radius *m* (*einer Raumkurve*) radius of torsion (of a space curve)

Torsions·waage *f*, **Torsions·wage** *f* (*phys.*) torsion balance

Torsions·winkel *m* (*einer Raumkurve*) angle of torsion (of a space curve) [= WINDUNGS-WINKEL]

Torus *m* torus (ring), anchor ring, ring surface [= RINGFLÄCHE, WULST]

total *adj.* total: *totales Differential* total (or exact) differential; *totale Differentialgleichung* total (or exact) differential equation [*cf.* ABLEITUNG 2.; DIFFERENTIAL; DIFFERENTIALQUOTIENT; EINFACH; TOTAL-POSITIV]

Total·betrag *m* total amount

total-positiv *adj.* (*in einem Zahlkörper*) totally positive (in a number field)

Touren·zahl *f* (*in der Minute*) (number of) revolutions (per minute), (*abbr.*) rpm

Trabant *m* (*astr.*) satellite

träg(e) *adj.* inert: *träge Masse* inert mass

Träger *m* **1.** (*der, die, das Tragende*) carrier. **2.** (*geom.*) (*einer Punktreihe*) base (of a range of points); (*Mittelpunkt eines Bündels, Büschels*) center, vertex (of a sheaf, a pencil); (*Achse eines Büschels*) axis (of a pencil). **3.** (*Balken*) girder, beam [*cf.* BALKEN]

Träg·heit *f* (*phys.*) inertia

Trägheits·achse *f* (*phys.*) axis of inertia

Trägheits·ellipsoid *n* (*phys.*) inertia ellipsoid

Trägheits·form *f* (*alg.*) inertia form: *die Trägheitsformen bilden ein Ideal* the inertia forms form an ideal

Trägheits·gesetz *n* (*phys.*) law of inertia

Trägheits·hauptachse *f* (*phys.*) principal axis of inertia

Trägheits·index *m* (*alg.*) index of inertia

trägheits·los *adj.* (*phys.*) inertialess, inertiafree

Trägheits·moment *n* (*phys.*) moment of inertia, second moment

Trajektorie *f* (*geom., ball.*) trajectory: *rechtwinklige* (*oder orthogonale*) *Trajektorie* orthogonal trajectory

Traktorie *f* tractory, tractrix [= TRAKTRIX]

Traktrix *f* tractrix, tractory, equitangential curve [= TRAKTORIE; ZUGLINIE]

trans·finit *adj.* transfinite

Trans·formation *f* transformation: *affine, kollineare, kongruente, homogene, lineare, orthogonale T.* affine, collineatory, congruent, homogeneous, linear, orthogonal transformation [*cf.* IDENTISCH; INVERS; OBJEKT; STETIG; TOPOLOGISCH; UNITÄR; WINKELTREU]

Transformations·gruppe *f* transformation group

trans·formieren *v.t.* transform

Trans·formierte *f* transform

transitiv *adj.* (*Beziehung*) transitive (relation)

Transitivität *f* transitivity

Transitivitäts·gebiet *n* domain of transitivity; (*einer Menge*) transitivity set (of a set)

Trans·lation *f* translation

translations·invariant *adj.* translation-invariant

Translativ·bewegung *f* translatory motion

trans·latorisch *adj.* translatory

trans·ponieren *v.t.* transpose: *ein Glied einer Gleichung auf die andere Seite t.* (*oder bringen oder hinüberschaffen*) transpose a term from one side of an equation to another; *Elemente einer Komplexion durch Permutation t.* (*oder vertauschen*) transpose elements of an arrangement by permutation; *eine Matrix t.* transpose a matrix; *transponierte Matrix* transpose of a matrix

Trans·porteur *m* protractor [= WINKELMESSER]

Transport·versicherung *f* transport (or conveyance) insurance

Trans·position *f* transposition

trans·versal *adj.* transversal

Trans·versale *f* transversal

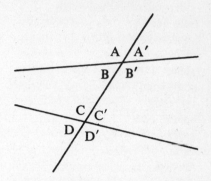

Fig.: Winkel zweier Geraden mit einer T. angles between two lines and a transversal:

A, A'	⎤ Nebenwinkel
A, B	⎦
A, B'	Scheitelwinkel
A, C	Gegenwinkel
A, D	Anwinkel, entgegengesetzte Winkel
A, C'	konjugierte Winkel
A, D'	Wechselwinkel

[*cf.* ANWINKEL; GEGENWINKEL; KONJUGIERT; KORRESPONDIEREN; NEBENWINKEL; SCHEITELWINKEL; WECHSELWINKEL]

Trans·versalität *f* transversality

Transversal·schwingung *f* (*phys.*) transversal oscillation (or vibration)

Transversal·welle *f* (*phys.*) transversal wave

trans·zendent *adj.* transcendental: *transzendente Funktion* (*Zahl*) transcendental function (number); (*alg.*) *transzendente Erweiterung eines Körpers* transcendental extension of a field [*cf.* REIN]

Trans·zendente *f* transcendental

(number): (*alg.*) *unabhängige T.* independent transcendental

Trans·zendenz *f* transcendence

Transzendenz·grad *m* (*alg.*) degree of transcendence

Trapez *n* trapezoid [*cf.* GLEICH-SCHENKLIG; GRUNDLINIE; MIT-TELLINIE]

Trapezo·eder *n* trapezohedron

Trapezoid *n* trapezium

Tratte *f* (*comm.*) draft [*cf.* ANNAHME; ANNEHMEN; WECHSEL]

treffen *v.t.* meet, strike: *die Höhe trifft die Gegenseite im Punkt P.* the altitude meets (or strikes) the side opposite in the point *P*

Treffer *m* (*statist.*) success, hit

Treff·punkt *m* meeting point

treiben *v.t.* carry: *wir t.* (*oder führen*) *die Division* (*weiter*) *bis zu* 7 *Stellen* we carry the division to 7 places

Trend *m* trend

Trend·abweichung *f* (*statist.*) deviation from trend

Trend·bereinigung *f* (*statist.*) adjustment for trend

Trend·wert *m* (*statist.*) trend ordinate

trenn·bar *adj.* separable

Trennbar·keit *f* separability

trennen *v.t.* (*z.B. die Variablen*) separate (e.g. the variables) [*cf.* HARMONISCH]

Trennung *f* (*z.B. von Variablen*) separation (e.g. of variables)

Trennungs·zeichen *n* separation sign [*cf.* STRICH]

Treppen·funktion *f* step function

Treppen·polygon *n* (*statist.*) staircase (or stepped) polygon, staircase curve, histogram

treu *adj.* faithful [*cf.* DARSTELLUNG]

Triade *f* triad

Triakis·oktaeder *n* triakisocta-hedron, trigonal trisoctahedron [= PYRAMIDENOKTAEDER]

Triakis·tetraeder *n* triakistetra-hedron

Triangular·zahl *f* triangular number

Triangulation *f* triangulation

triangulieren *v.t., v.i.* triangulate

Triangulierung *f* triangulation

Tridens *n* trident: *Newtons T.* trident of Newton, parabola of Descartes [= CARTESISCHE PARA-BEL] [*cf.* CARTESISCH]

Tri·eder *n* trihedron

tri·gonal *adj.* (*cryst.*) trigonal

Trigonal·schein *m* (*astr.*) trigon, trine

Trigonal·zahl *f* triangular number

Trigono·metrie *f* trigonometry [*cf.* ADDITIONSTHEOREME; ELEMENT; HALBSEITENSÄTZE; REDUKTIONS-FORMEL; SPHÄRISCH; TANGENTEN-SATZ]

trigono·metrisch *adj.* trigono-metric: *trigonometrische Funktion* (*Kofunktion*) trigonometric function (cofunction)

tri·klin, tri·klinisch *adj.* (*cryst.*) triclinic, triclinate, anorthic [*cf.* SCHIEFENDFLÄCHE]

tri·linear *adj.* trilinear

Trillion *f* *Am.* quintillion; *Br.* trillion

tri·metrisch *adj.* (*Projektion*) tri-metric (projection)

Tri·nom *n* trinomial

tri·nomisch *adj.* trinomial

Tripel *n* triplet, triple

Tri·sektion *f* (*eines Winkels*) tri-

section (of an angle)
Tri·sektrix *f* (*Kurve*) trisectrix
Trito·prisma *n* (*cryst.*) prism of the third order
Trito·pyramide *f* (*cryst.*) pyramid of the third order
tri·vial *adj.* trivial: *triviale Lösung* trivial solution
Tri·vialität *f* triviality
Trochoide *f* trochoid: *gestreckte* (*oder geschweifte*) *T.* curtate trochoid (or cycloid); *verschlungene T.* prolate trochoid
Trocken·hohlmaß *n*, **Trocken·maß**

n dry measure
tropisch *adj.* tropical [*cf.* JAHR]
Troy·gewicht *n* troy weight
Trug·schluß *m* (*log.*) fallacy, paralogism
... tupel *n suf.* ... tuple: *k-tupel* k-tuple
Typ *m* (*log.*) type
Typen·lehre *f*, **Typen·theorie** *f* (*log.*) theory of types: *einfache* (*verzweigte*) *T.* simple (ramified) theory of types
typisch *adj.* typical [*cf.* EINZELFALL]
Typus *m* (*log.*) type

U

über *prep.* (*dat., acc.*) over, above: *Integral ü. eine Fläche* integral over a surface
über·all *adv.* everywhere [*cf.* DICHT; FAST]
übereinander·lagern (*sep.*) **1.** *v.t.* (*z.B. Wellen*) superpose, superimpose (e.g. waves). **2.** *v.i., v.r.:* sich *ü.* be superposed, be superimposed
Übereinander·lagerung *f* superposition, superimposition
übereinander·legen (*sep.*) *v.t.* superpose, superimpose
Übereinander·legung *f* superposition, superimposition
überein·stimmen (*sep.*) *v.i.* (*mit*) agree (with). check (against), coincide: *die beiden Reihen stimmen bis auf Glieder vom Grade* $\geq$ *n überein* the two series coincide except for terms of

degree $\geq$ *n*
über·fließend *adj.* (*Zahl*) redundant, abundant (number)
über·führen (*sep.*) *v.t.* **1.** (*hinüberführen*) carry (over): *in die nächste Kolonne ü.* carry (over) to the next column. **2.** (*umformen*) transform, take, carry: *diese Zuordnung führt Produkte wieder in Produkte über* this correspondence takes products into products
Über·gang *m* transition, passing: *Ü. zum Grenzwert* transition (or passing) to the limit
über·gehen (*sep.*) *v.i.* **1.** (*sich verwandeln* be transformed) (*in*) go (over) (into): *die Gleichung* (1) *geht in die Gleichung* (2) *über* the equation (1) goes over into the equation (2); *Summen gehen bei dieser Abbildung wieder in*

Summen über in this mapping sums go again into sums. **2.** (*fortschreiten* proceed) pass: *zum Grenzwert ü.* pass to the limit

über·greifen (*sep.*) *v.i.* (*ineinander*) overlap [*cf.* ÜBERSCHNEIDEN]

über·höht *adj.* excessive; (*Häufigkeitskurve*) leptokurtic (frequency curve)

Über·höhung *f* excess; (*der Häufigkeitskurve*) leptokurtosis (of the frequency curve)

über·mäßig *adj.* excessive, redundant

über·schießend *adj.* (*Zahl*) redundant, abundant (number)

Über·schlag *m* estimate, rough calculation

über·schla'gen *adj.* (*Polygon*) (polygon) with sides cutting each other; (*Polyeder*) (polyhedron) with faces cutting each other; *überschlagenes Polygon* star polygon; *überschlagenes Polyeder* star polyhedron

Überschlags·rechnung *f* (rough) estimate (or calculation)

über·schnei'den *v.t.*, *v.recip.*, *v.r.*: sich (*oder* einander) *ü.* (*schneiden*) cut, intersect; (*übergreifen*) overlap

über·schrei'ten *v.t.* exceed, transcend, go beyond: *die Grenze ü.* **a.** (*die Begrenzung*) go beyond the boundary; **b.** (*das Maß*) exceed the limit

Über·schuß *m* excess; (*über eine Summe*) excess sum [*cf.* EXZESS; ÜBERTRAGEN; ÜBRIGBLEIBENDES]

über·steigen *v.t.* exceed

über·strei'chen *v.t.* overline

Über·strei'chung *f* overlining, bar (over an expression), vinculum

(*symb.:* ‾‾‾, e.g. $\overline{a+b}$) [*cf.* STRICH; VERBINDUNGSZEICHEN]

über·stumpf *adj.* (*Winkel*) convex (angle)

Über·trag *m* carry-over [= FÜRTRAG; VORTRAG]

übertra'g·bar *adj.* (*Größen*) transferable (quantities); (*phys., engin.*) (*Kräfte*) transmissible (forces); (*fin.*) (*Wertpapiere*) negotiable (papers)

Übertra'gbar·keit *f* (*von Größen*) transferability (of quantities); (*von Kräften*) transmissibility (of forces); (*von Wertpapieren*) negotiability (of papers)

über·tra'gen *v.t.* **1.** (*Größen*) transfer, carry (over) (quantities): (*beim Addieren*) *den Überschuß* (*oder das Übrigbleibende*) *von einer Kolonne zur anderen ü.* carry the excess sum of one column to the next (in addition). **2.** (*phys., engin.*) (*Kräfte*) transmit (forces). **3.** (*comm., fin.*) (*Wechsel, Wertpapiere*) negotiate, give; (*mittels Indossaments*) endorse (bills of exchange, papers)

Über·tra'gung *f* (*von Größen*) transfer, carrying (over) (of quantities); (*phys., engin.*) (*von Kräften*) transmission (of forces); (*comm., fin.*) (*von Wertpapieren*) negotiation; (*mittels Indossaments*) endorsement (of papers)

ü'ber·zählig *adj.* excess, supernumerary, surplus, redundant, superfluous, extra: *überzählige Parameter* superfluous parameters

übrig *adj.* remaining, left: *die übrigen Teile des Dreiecks* the remaining parts of the triangle

übrig·bleiben (*sep.*) *v.i.* remain

Übrig·bleibende(s) *n* remainder; (*Überschuß*) excess (sum) [*cf.* ÜBERTRAGEN]

Übungs·aufgabe *f* exercise

Uhr *f* clock; (*Taschenuhr*) watch [*cf.* GLEICHLAUF; GLEICHLAUFEN; GLEICHLAUFEND; SEKUNDENZEIGER; STUNDENZEIGER; VORGEHEN]

Uhr·zeiger *m* hand of a clock or watch; *im Sinne* (*oder: in der Richtung*) *des Uhrzeigers* clockwise; *entgegengesetzt dem Sinn* (*oder: der Richtung*) *des Uhrzeigers, im entgegengesetzten Sinn des Uhrzeigers* counterclockwise

Ultra·kurzwelle *f* (*phys.*) ultrashort wave

ultra·real *adj.* (*Zahl*) ultrareal (number)

Ultra·schallwelle *f* (*acoust.*) ultrasonic (or supersonic) wave

Umbenennungs·regel *f* (*log.*) (*für gebundene Variable*) rule for rewriting (bound variables)

um·deuten (*sep.*) *v.t.* reinterpret

Um·deutung *f* reinterpretation

Um·drehung *f* revolution, rotation [*cf.* DREHUNG; UMLAUF]

Umdrehungs·achse *f* axis of revolution (or rotation)

Umdrehungs·ellipsoid *n* ellipsoid of revolution

Umdrehungs·fläche *f* surface of revolution

Umdrehungs·hyperboloid *n* hyperboloid of revolution

Umdrehungs·körper *m* solid of revolution

Umdrehungs·paraboloid *n* paraboloid of revolution

Umdrehungs·zylinder *m* cylinder of revolution

Um·fang *m* 1. (*eines Polygons, einer Kurve*) circumference, perimeter, periphery, boundary (of a polygon, a curve): *U. eines Dreiecks* perimeter of a triangle; *von* (*oder mit*) *gleichem U.* isoperimetric [*cf.* HALB; UMKREIS]. 2. (*eines Körpers von konstantem Querschnitt*) girth (of a solid with equal cross sections). 3. (*eines Begriffs*) extent, extension (of a concept)

um·fassen *v.t.* comprise, comprehend

um·fassend *adj.* comprehensive, comprehending: *umfassende Menge* set comprehending a subset [= OBERMENGE] [*cf.* GANZ]

um·formen (*sep.*) *v.t.* transform

Um·formung *f* transformation

Um·gang *m* (*einer Schraubenlinie, Schraube*) turn, thread (of a helix, screw)

Um·gebung *f* surrounding, environments, neighborhood: *in der Umgebung eines Punktes* in the neighborhood of a point [*cf.* UMKREIS]

um·gekehrt *adj.* inverse, inverted, reverse, converse; *adv.* inversely, conversely, vice versa: *umgekehrte Reihenfolge* inverse (or inverted) order, inversion [*cf.* ANORDNUNG; OPERATION; ORDNUNG; PROPORTIONAL; REIHENFOLGE; VERHÄLTNIS]

Umgekehrte(s) *n* inverse: *das Umgekehrte einer Operation* the inverse of an operation

um·geschrieben past participle of

[U'MSCHREIBEN]

Um·grenzung *f* boundary

um·gruppieren (*sep.*) *v.t.* (*Glieder eines Ausdrucks, einer Reihe*) group, regroup, rearrange (terms of an expression, a series) [*cf.* U'MSCHREIBEN]

Um·gruppierung *f* rearrangement

um·hü'llen *v.t.* envelop [= EINHÜLLEN]

Um·hüllende *f* envelope [= EINHÜLLENDE]

umkehr·bar *adj.* reversible; *nicht u.* nonreversible, irreversible

Umkehrbar·keit *f* reversibility

um·kehren (*sep.*) *v.t.* reverse, invert [*cf.* UNGLEICHUNG]

Um·kehrung, *f* inversion, reversion, converse, conversion

um·klappen (*sep.*) *v.t.* (*um eine Achse in eine Ebene*) turn, revolve, rotate (about an axis into a plane) [= UMLEGEN]

Um·klappung *f* turn(ing), revolving, rotation [= UMLEGUNG] [*cf.* UMKLAPPEN]

Um·kreis *m* **1.** (*umschriebener Kreis*) circumscribed circle, circumcircle; *Mittelpunkt des Umkreises* circumcenter. **2.** (*Umgebung*) compass, range, scope, surroundings: *in einem U. von fünf Kilometern* within a compass (or range) of five kilometers, for five kilometers round; *im ganzen U.* all around. **3.** (*Umfang*) circumference: *der Platz mißt 500 Meter im U.* the square measures 500 meters in circumference

Umkreis·mittelpunkt *m* center of circumscribed circle, circumcenter

Umkreis·radius *m* radius of the circumscribed circle; (*eines regelmäßigen Vielecks, auch*) long radius (of a regular polygon) [*cf.* POLYGON]

Um·lauf *m* (*Umdrehung*) revolution; (*Kreislauf*) circulation [*cf.* BANKNOTENUMLAUF]

um·laufen (*sep.*) *v.i.* revolve; (*im Kreislauf*) circulate

Umlaufs·geschwindigkeit *m* (*eines Planeten*) velocity of revolution (of a planet); (*des Geldes*) velocity of (money) circulation

Umlaufs·kapital *n,* **Umlaufs·vermögen** *n* (*fin.*) circulating capital

Umlaufs·zeit *f* (*astr.*) period (or time) of revolution

um·legen (*sep.*) *v.t.* turn (down) [= UMKLAPPEN]

Um·legung *f* turning (down) [= UMKLAPPUNG]

um·ra'nden *v.t.* border, bound: *umrandeter Teil einer Fläche* (bounded) piece of a surface, surface patch, disk [*cf.* AUSSCHNITT]

Um·ra'ndung *f* border, boundary

um·rechnen (*sep.*) *v.t.* convert: *Bogenmaß in Winkelmaß u.* convert radians to degrees

Um·rechnung *f* **1.** (*in andere Maßeinheit*) conversion (to another unit of measurement): *U. von Zoll in Zentimeter* conversion from inches to centimeters. **2.** (*statist.: durch Ausschaltung von Nebenfaktoren*) adjustment (for secondary factors): *U. auf Einheitsmonate* adjustment for calendar variation

Umrechnungs·kurs *m* (*fin.*) (*von*

Devisen) rate of exchange

Umrechnungs·tabelle *f* conversion table

um·rei'ßen *v.t.* outline

U'm·riß *m* contour, outline

Umriß·linie *f* contour line, outline

Um·satz *m* (*comm.*) turnover

Umsatz·steuer *f* (*comm.*) sales tax

um·schrei'ben *v.t.* circumscribe: *umschriebener* (*oder: umgeschriebener*) *Kreis eines Dreiecks, der einem Dreieck umschriebene* (*oder: umgeschriebene*) *Kreis* circumcircle (or: circumscribed circle) of a triangle, circle circumscribing (or: circumscribed to) a triangle [*cf.* UMKREIS]; *Mittelpunkt des umschriebenen Kreises* center of the circumscribed circle, circumcenter; *umschriebener Kegel* circumscribed cone, circumcone [*cf.* U'M·SCHREIBEN 2.]

u'm·schreiben (*sep.*) *v.t.* **1.** (*umgruppieren*) group, rearrange. **2.** [= UMSCHREI'BEN] [*cf.* LIEGEN]

um·schrie'ben past participle of [UMSCHREI'BEN]

Um·schuldung *f* (*comm.*) conversion of debts

um·wandeln (*sep.*) *v.t.* (*in*) transform (into), reduce (to), commute (into), convert (into)

Um·wandlung *f* conversion, reduction, change, commutation: *U. einer benannten Zahl in höhere* (*niedrigere*) *Einheiten* reduction ascending (descending) of a denominate number; (*ins.*) *U. einer Polizze in eine andere* conversion (or commutation) of one policy into another

um·werten (*sep.*) *v.t.* revalue

Um·wertung *f* revaluation

un·abgekürzt *adj.* unabridged, long, longhand: *unabgekürzte Division, Multiplikation* long division, multiplication; *u. multiplizieren* multiply longhand

un·abgeschlossen *adj.* non-closed

Un·abgeschlossenheit *f* non-closure

un·abhängig *adj.* independent [*cf.* LINEAR; TRANSZENDENTE; VARIABLE]

Unabhängig·keit *f* independence

un·bedingt *adj.* unconditional, absolute: *unbedingte Ungleichung* unconditional inequality; *u. divergente Reihe* properly divergent series [*cf.* KONVERGENT]

un·begrenzt *adj.* unlimited, limitless, unbounded, boundless [*cf.* NULL]

Unbegrenzt·heit *f* unlimitedness, boundlessness

un·bekannt *adj.* unknown [*cf.* GRÖSSE]

Un·bekannte *f* unknown [*cf.* BESEITIGUNG; ELIMINIEREN]

un·benannt *adj.* (*Zahl*) absolute, abstract (number) [*cf.* ABSOLUT; ABSTRAKT]

un·beschränkt *adj.* unbounded

Unbeschränkt·heit *f* unboundedness

un·bestimmt *adj.* indefinite, indetermined, undetermined, indeterminate: *unbestimmte Gleichung* indeterminate equation; *unbestimmte Form* indeterminate form (e.g. $\frac{0}{0}$); *Methode der unbestimmten Koeffizienten* method of undetermined coefficients; (*mech.*) *statisch u.*

statically indeterminate [*cf.* INTEGRAL]

Un·bestimmte *f* indeterminate

Unbestimmt·heit *f* indeterminacy, indeterminedness, indefiniteness

un·beweglich *adj.* immobile, immovable: (*comm.*) *unbeweglicher Besitz, unbewegliches Vermögen* immovable property, immovables *pl.*, real (or landed estate)

Unbeweglich·keit *f* immobility

unbeweis·bar *adj.* unprovable

Unbeweisbar·keit *f* unprovability

un·bewiesen *adj* unproved

un·bezeichnet *adj.* (*Zahl*) unsigned (number)

un·biegsam *adj.* inflexible, rigid [*cf.* STARR]

Unbiegsam·keit *f* inflexibility, rigidity [*cf.* STARRE; STARRHEIT]

und *cj.* and; (*in der Addition* in addition, also) plus: *sieben und fünf ist* (*oder sind*) *zwölf* seven and (or plus) five is (or are) twelve

un·definierbar *adj.* indefinable

Undefinierbar·keit *f* indefinability

un·definiert *adj.* undefined

Undulation *f* undulation

undulatorisch *adj.* undulatory: (*statist.*) *undulatorische Komponente* cyclical (or periodical) component

un·echt *adj.* improper [*cf.* BRUCH]

un·eigentlich *adj.* improper; (*unendlich fern*) ideal: *uneigentliches Integral* improper integral; *die uneigentliche Zahl* ∞ the improper number ∞; *uneigentlicher* (*oder: unendlich ferner*) *Punkt* ideal point, point at infinity; *uneigentliche* (*oder: unendlich ferne*)

Gerade, Ebene ideal line, plane; line, plane at infinity [*cf.* HYPEREBENE]

un·elastisch *adj.* inelastic

un·endlich *adj.* infinite, nonterminating, unending, never-ending: *u. groß* infinite, infinitely great; *u. groß werden* approach infinity; *u. ferner Punkt* infinite (or: infinitely distant, or ideal) point, point at infinity; *unendliches Integral* infinite integral; *unendliches Produkt* infinite (or continued) product; *unendliche· Folge, Reihe* infinite sequence, series; *unendliche* (*oder u. große*) *Menge* **a.** (*Quantität*) infinite (or: infinitely great) quantity; **b.** (*von Elementen*) infinite set (of elements); *u. klein* infinitely small, infinitesimal; *u. kleine Größe* infinitely small quantity, infinitesimal (quantity) [*cf.* ORDNUNG]; *unendliche Ferne* infinite distance, infinity; *unendliche Anzahl* infinite number, infinitude; *unendlicher Dezimalbruch* nonterminating (or infinite, or unending, or never-ending) decimal [*cf.* ABZÄHLBAR; GRUPPE; ORDNUNG; UNEIGENTLICH]

Un·endlich *n* infinity: *sich* (*dem Grenzwert*) *U. nähern* approach infinity

Un·endliche(s) *n* infinite, infinity: *ins Unendliche* (*an*)*wachsen* approach infinity; *bis ins Unendliche* ad infinitum, to infinity; *der Begriff des Unendlichen* the concept of the infinite (or: of infinity)

Unendlich·keit *f* infinity, infinitude

un·entbehrlich *adj.* indispensable
Unentbehrlich·keit *f* indispensability
Unfall·versicherung *f* accident insurance
un·geändert *adj.* unaltered, unchanged
un·gefähr *adv.* about, approximately [*cf.* ABPLATTUNG]
un·gemischt *adj.* (*z.B.* (*alg.*) *Ideal*) unmixed (e.g. ideal)
un·genau *adj.* inexact, inaccurate
Ungenauig·keit *f* inaccuracy
un·geordnet *adj.* irregular, disarranged; (*zufällig*) random
un·gerad(e) *adj.* (*Zahl*) odd (number); (*Linie*) not straight, unstraight (line) [*cf.* HERAUSFALLEN; PERMUTATION; UNPAARIG]
Ungerad·heit *f* (*einer Zahl*) oddness (of a number); (*einer Linie*) unstraightness (of a line)
un·geradlinig *adj.* not rectilinear [*cf.* GERADLINIG]
Ungeradlinig·keit *adj.* lack of rectilinearity
ungerad·zahlig *adj.* odd-numbered
un·gerichtet *adj.* undirected, scalar [*cf* GESCHWINDIGKEIT; RELATIVGESCHWINDIGKEIT]
Ungerichtet·heit *f* undirectedness
un·gleich *adj.* unequal, unlike: *Brüche mit ungleichen Nennern* unlike fractions
un·gleichförmig *adj.* 1. (*veränderlich*) nonuniform, inconstant, variable: *ungleichförmige Bewegung, Beschleunigung, Geschwindigkeit* nonuniform motion, acceleration, velocity. 2. (*inhomogen*) inhomogeneous
Ungleichförmig·keit *f* 1. (*Veränder-*

lichkeit) inconstancy, variability. 2. (*Inhomogeneität*) inhomogeneity
Ungleich·heit *f* inequality (e.g. $a \neq b$) [*cf.* UNGLEICHUNG]
un·gleichmäßig *adj.* (*Konvergenz*) nonuniform (convergence)
Ungleichmäßig·keit *f* nonuniformity
un·gleichnamig *adj.* unlike, dissimilar: *ungleichnamige Zahlen, Brüche* unlike numbers, fractions
Ungleichnamig·keit *f* property of being unlike (or dissimilar)
ungleich·seitig *adj.* (*Dreieck*) scalene (triangle)
Ungleichseitig·keit *f* (property of) being scalene
Un·gleichung *f* inequality, inequation (e.g. $a < b$) [*cf.* UNGLEICHHEIT]: *der Sinn der U. kehrt sich um* the sense of the inequality is reversed [*cf.* UNBEDINGT]
ungrad(e) [= UNGERADE]
Ungrad·heit *f* [= UNGERADHEIT]
un·gradlinig *adj.* [= UNGERADLINIG]
Ungradlinig·keit *f* [= UNGERADLINIGKEIT]
un·günstig *adj.* (*statist.*) unfavorable, unsuccessful: *ungünstiger Fall* failure
uni·formisieren *v.t.* uniformalize: *uniformisierte Funktion* uniform(alized) function
Uni·formisierung *f* (*einer Funktion*) uniformalization (of a function)
uni·kursal *adj.* unicursal
Unikursal·kurve *f* unicursal curve
uni·modular *adj.* (*Matrix*) unimodular (matrix)
unitär *adj.* (*Transformation*) unitary (transformation)

uni·versal *adj.* universal
Uni·versalität *f* universality
uni·versell *adj.* universal [*cf.*
ALLGEMEIN]
Uni·versum *n* (*astr.*) universe
un·korreliert *adj.* (*statist.*) uncorrelated [*cf.* UNVERBUNDEN]
Un·kosten *pl.* (*comm.*) expenses:
allgemeine U. overhead expenses
[*cf.* AUSLAGE]
un·kürzbar *adj.* (*Bruch*) (fraction)
in its lowest terms
un·lösbar *adj.* unsolvable
Unlösbar·keit *f* unsolvability
un·meßbar *adj.* immeasurable, not
measurable
Unmeßbar·keit *f* immeasurability
un·mittelbar *adj.* immediate, direct
Unmittelbar·keit *f* directness,
immediacy
un·nachgiebig *adj.* rigid
Unnachgiebig·keit *f* rigidity
un·negiert *adj.* (*log.*) unnegated
un·orientiert *adj.* unoriented
un·paarig *adj.* unpaired; (*ungerade*)
odd
un·sicher *adj.* uncertain
Unsicher·heit *f* uncertainty [*cf.*
EINENGEN]
Unsicherheits·prinzip *n* uncertainty
principle
Unsicherheits·relation *f* uncertainty
relation
un·sichtbar *adj.* invisible [*cf.*
SICHTBAR]
Unsichtbar·keit *f* invisibility
Un·sinn *m* nonsense
un·sinnig *adv.* absurd [*cf.* SINNLOS]
Unsinnig·keit *f* absurdity [*cf.*
SINNLOSIGKEIT]
un·stetig *adj.* discontinuous:
unstetige Funktion discontinuous

function [*cf.* FUNKTION; VER-
HALTEN]
Unstetig·keit *f* discontinuity [*cf.*
BEHEBEN; ENDLICHES; NICHT]
Unstetigkeits·punkt *m* point of
discontinuity
Un·symmetrie *f* asymmetry; (*Ver-
teilung, auch*) skewness (of
distribution)
un·symmetrisch *adj.* asymmetric;
(*Verteilung, auch*) skew (distribution)
unten *adv.* below, down [*cf.*
BESCHRÄNKT]
unter *adj.* lower, inferior [*cf.*
GRENZE; HÄUFUNGSGRENZE;
INDEX; LIMES; SCHRANKE;
ZEIGER]
unter *prep.* (*dat., acc.*) below,
underneath: *Ziffern ordentlich
u. einander schreiben* align figures
properly (in a column)
Unter·abteilung *f* subdivision
Unter·bereich *m* subregion, subdomain
Unter·determinante *f* (*eines
Elements einer Determinante*)
subdeterminant, minor (determinant) (of an element in a
determinant) [= MINOR; SUB-
DETERMINANTE]
Unter·einheit *f* subunit
unter·gehen (*sep.*) *v.i.* (*astr.*) set
Unter·gruppe *f* subgroup, subclass:
ausgezeichnete (*oder invariante*)
U. self-conjugate (or invariant)
subgroup, normal divisor [*cf.*
CHARAKTERISTISCH; DIREKT;
INDEX; KONJUGIERT; ZULÄSSIG]
Untergruppen·bildung *f* (*statist.*)
subclassification; (*in der Diffe-
renzenmethode*) revealing a con-

cealed classification [*cf.* Diffe-
renzenmethode 2.]
unter·halb *adv., prep.* (*gen.*) below
Unter·ideal *n* (*alg.*) subideal
Unterklasse *f* subclass; (*eines
Schnitts*) lower class (of a cut)
Unter·körper *m* (*alg.*) subfield
Unter·menge *f* subset, subclass
[*cf.* echt]
Unter·modul *m* (*alg.*) submodule
Unter·raum *m* subspace
Unter·ring *m* (*alg.*) subring
Unter·satz *m* (*log.*) minor (premise)
Unter·schied *m* difference [*cf.*
Längenunterschied; Saison-
veränderungszahlen]
Unter·seite *f* underside, lower side
unter·strei'chen *v.t.* underline,
underscore
Unter·strei'chung *f* underlining,
underscoring, bar (underneath an
expression) [*cf.* Strich]
unter·tei'len *v.t.* (sub)divide;
(*durch Teilstriche*) graduate (by
marks) [*cf.* einteilen]
Unter·tei'lung *f* (sub)division;
(*durch Teilstriche*) graduation (by
marks) [*cf.* Einteilung]
un·trennbar *adj.* inseparable
Untrennbar·keit *f* inseparability
un·treu *adj.* unfaithful [*cf.* Dar-
stellung]
un·umkehrbar *adj.* irreversible
Unumkehrbar·keit *f* irreversibility
un·veränderlich *adj.* invariable,
constant; (*stabil*) stable [*cf.*
anallagmatisch; starr; Wert]
Unveränderlich·keit *f* invariability,
constancy; (*Stabilität*) stability
[*cf.* Starrheit]
un·verbunden *adj.* unconnected;

(*unkorreliert*) uncorrelated; (*ohne
Beziehung*) unrelated
Unverbunden·heit *f* unconnected-
ness; lack of correlation; un-
relatedness [*cf.* unverbunden]
un·vereinbar *adj.* incompatible,
inconsistent
Unvereinbar·keit *f* incompatibility,
inconsistency
un·verkürzbar *adj.* (*alg.*)
irreducible, irredundant: *unver-
kürzbarer Durchschnitt von Prim-
idealen* irredundant intersection
of prime ideals
un·verneint *adj.* (*log.*) unnegated
un·verträglich *adj.* incompatible,
inconsistent
Unverträglich·keit *f* incompatibility, inconsistency
un·verzinslich *adj.* non-interest-
bearing
un·vollkommen *adj.* imperfect:
unvollkommene Zahl imperfect
number [*cf.* Körper 3]
un·vollständig *adj.* incomplete: *un-
vollständige Induktion* incomplete
induction
Unvollständig·keit *f* incomplete-
ness
un·zählbar *adj.* innumerable
Unzählbar·keit *f* innumerability
un·zählig *adj.* innumerable,
countless
Unzählig·keit *f* innumerability
Unze *f* (*Gewicht* weight) ounce
un·zerlegbar *adj.* irreducible, indecomposable; (*in Faktoren*) non-
factorable: *ganzzahlig* (*rationalzahlig*) *unzerlegbares Polynom*
polynomial indecomposable into
factors with integral (rational)
coefficients [*cf.* direkt]

Unzerlegbar·keit *f* indecomposability

un·zusammenhängend *adj.* unconnected, uncoherent

un·zweideutig *adj.* unambiguous

Unzweideutig·keit *f* unambiguity, unambiguousness

Uran·batterie *f* (*phys.*) uranium pile

Ur·bild *n* inverse image, preimage, antecedent [*ant.:* ABBILD]

Ur·liste *f* (*statist.*) list (of items of a statistical series)

Ur·sache *f* cause [*cf.* KRAFT; WIRKUNG]

ur·sächlich *adj.* causal

Ur·sprung *m* origin: *U. eines Koordinatensystems* origin of a coordinate system (or: of coordinates) [*cf.* ASYMPTOTISCH; VEKTOR]

Ur·tabelle *f* (*statist.*) primary (or: general reference) table

Ur·teil *n* (*log.*) judgment [*cf.* ALLGEMEIN; ASSERTORISCH; BESONDER; PARTIKULAR; PARTIKULÄR; SUBKONTRÄR]

ur·teilen *v.i.* (*log.*) judge

Urteils·lehre *f* (*log.*) theory of judgment

V

Vakuum *n* (*phys.*) vacuum

Valenz *f* (*chem.*) valence

Valuta *m* (*pl. Valuten*) (*comm., fin.*) **1.** (*Devisen, usu. pl.*) foreign exchange. **2.** (*Währung*) currency, monetary standard: *welche V. hat Frankreich?* what is the monetary standard of France?; *eine gute V.* a sound currency. **3.** (*fälliger Wert*) value (payable): *V. heute* value as per today, (value) payable today. **4.** (*Gegenwert*) equivalent, consideration: *als V. für seine Leistungen* as an equivalent for (or in consideration of) his services

variabel *adj.* variable

Variabilität *f* variability

Variabilitäts·index *m* (*statist.*) **1.** (*Streuungsmaß*) measure of dispersion. **2.** (*mittlere Abweichung*) standard deviation

Variable *f* variable: *abhängige* (*unabhängige*) *V.* dependent (independent) variable; (*log.*) *gebundene* (*freie*) *V.* bound (free) variable [*cf.* UMBENENNUNGSREGEL]. [*cf.* AUSDRÜCKEN; BEREICH; FUNKTION; TRENNEN; TRENNUNG]

Variation *f* variation; (*statist.:* *Streuung*) dispersion [*cf.* FUNKTION; STREUUNG]

Variations·breite *f* range of variation

Variations·rechnung *f* calculus of variations

variieren *v.t., v.i.* vary.

Vektor *m* vector: *V. aus dem Ursprung* localized (or radius, or coordinate) vector [*cf.* MULTIPLIKATION; NORMIEREN; PRODUKT; SENKRECHT; SKALARPRODUKT; VEKTORMULTIPLIKA-

TION; VEKTORPRODUKT; ZUSAM-
MENSETZUNG]

Vektor·addition f vector addition

Vektor·algebra f vector algebra

Vektor·analysis f vector analysis

Vektor·division f vector division

Vektor·feld n vector field

Vektor·funktion f vector function
[cf. DIVERGENZ; WIRBEL]

vektoriell adj. vectorial, vector [cf.
MULTIPLIKATION; PRODUKT]

Vektor·kalkül m vector calculus

Vektor·komponente f vector component

Vektor·multiplikation f (zweier
Vektoren) vector multiplication
(of two vectors)

Vektor·produkt n (zweier Vektoren
u und v) vector (or cross, or
outer) product (of two vectors
u and v) (symb.: u × v) [cf.
PRODUKT: äußeres Produkt]

Vektor·raum m vector (or linear)
space [cf. ORTHOGONAL]

Vektor·rechnung f vector analysis
(or calculus)

Vektor·subtraktion f vector subtraction

ver·allgemeinern v.t. generalize:
verallgemeinerter Mittelwertsatz
generalized mean value theorem

Ver·allgemeinerung f generalization

ver·änderlich adj. variable: v. sein
vary [cf. MERKMAL; UNGLEICH-
FÖRMIG]

Ver·änderliche f variable [cf. ELI-
MINIEREN; STEIGEN; ZUFÄLLIG;
ZULÄSSIG]

Veränderlich·keit f variability [cf.
UNGLEICHFÖRMIGKEIT]

ver·ändern 1. v.t. change, alter,

vary. 2. v.r. sich v. change, vary,
fluctuate

Ver·änderung f change, alteration,
variation, fluctuation [cf. AUS-
MASS; FUNKTION; KONKURRIE-
REND; MASS]

ver·anschaulichen v.t. represent (or
illustrate) graphically; (in einem
Diagramm) trace (in a graph);
sich etwas (innerlich) v. visualize
something (mentally)

Ver·anschaulichung f graphic representation (or illustration);
(innere) visualization

ver·ästeln v.r.: sich v. ramify,
branch

ver·ästelt adj. ramified, branched

Ver·ästelung f ramification

ver·bessern v.t. correct; (verfeinern) refine [cf. BEREINIGEN; REIN]

Ver·besserung f correction; (Verfeinerung) refinement [cf. BE-
REINIGUNG]

ver·biegen v.t. deform: eine Fläche
in eine andere v. deform one
surface into another

Ver·biegung f deformation

ver·binden v.t. connect, combine,
join die Meridiane v. den Nord-
und Südpol the meridians connect
(or join) the north and south
poles [cf. SCHNEIDEN; STRICH 2.]

Verbindlich·keit f obligation;
(comm.) (pl.) Verbindlichkeiten
liabilities, bills (or accounts)
payable; Nichterfüllung einer V.
default (of payment) [cf. SCHUL-
DENLAST]

Ver·bindung f connection, combination

Verbindungs·gerade f connecting
line

Verbindungs·zeichen *n* connection (or connective) sign; (*Über-streichung*) vinculum

ver·bunden *adj.* connected, combined; (*zusammenhängend*) coherent

Verbunden·heit *f* connectedness; (*Zusammenhang*) coherence

ver·dichten *v.t.* condense, compress [*cf.* VERDICHTUNG]

Ver·dichtung *f* **1.** (*Zusammen-drückung*) compression. **2.** (*Ver-flüssigung* liquefaction) condensation. **3.** (*statist.*) (*statistischer Daten*) reduction (of statistical data)

ver·dicken *v.t.* thicken

Ver·dickung *f* thickening

Verdienst·spanne *f* (*comm.*) margin of profit

ver·doppeln *v.t., v.r.:* **sich** *v.* double, duplicate

Ver·dopplung *f* duplication [*cf.* WÜRFEL]

ver·drängen *v.t.* (*z.B. Wasser*) displace (e.g. water)

Ver·drängung *f* (*z.B. von Wasser*) displacement (e.g. of water)

ver·drehen *v.t.* contort, distort, twist; (*Flächen, auch*) warp (surfaces) [*cf.* FLÄCHE; GEWORFEN]

Ver·drehung *f* contortion, distortion, twist, torsion

ver·dreifachen *v.t., v.r.:* **sich** *v.* treble, triple, triplicate

Ver·dreifachung *f* triplication

ver·dunkeln *v.t.* (*astr.*) (*einen Stern, Planeten*) occult (a star, planet)

Ver·dunklung *f* (*astr.*) (*eines Sterns, Planeten*) occultation (of a star, planet)

ver·dünnen *v.t.* thin; (*eine Lösung*) dilute (a solution); (*ein Gas*) rarefy (a gas)

Ver·dünnung *f* thinning; (*einer Lösung*) dilution (of a solution); (*eines Gases*) rarefaction (of a gas)

ver·einfachen *v.t.* simplify, reduce [*cf.* KÜRZEN]

Ver·einfachung *f* simplification, reduction: *V. eines Ausdrucks, einer Gleichung* reduction of an expression, an equation

ver·einigen *v.t., v.r.:* **sich** *v.* join, combine, unite

Ver·einigung *f* (*von Mengen, Klassen*) join, union (of sets, classes) [*ant.:* DURCHSCHNITT 1.]

Vereinigungs·klasse *f* union (or join) of classes

Vereinigungs·menge *f* (set) union, join of sets

ver·engen *v.t.* narrow, constrict

Ver·engung *f* constriction

ver·fahren *v.i.* proceed [*cf.* VORGEHEN]

Ver·fahren *n* procedure, process, method [*cf.* ABGEKÜRZT; ABKÜRZEN; AUSGLEICHUNGSRECHNUNG; DEZIMALRECHNUNG; RECHNEN]

ver·feinern *v.t.* (*z.B. ein Resultat*) refine (e.g. a result) [*cf.* BEREINIGEN]

Ver·feinerung *f* refinement: (*alg.*) *V. einer Normalreihe* refinement of a normal series [*cf.* BEREINIGUNG; VERBESSERUNG]

Verfeinerungs·satz *m* (*alg.*) refinement theorem

ver·finstern *v.t.* (*astr.*) (*die Sonne, den Mond*) eclipse (the sun, the moon); (*einen Planeten, Stern*) occult (a planet, star)

Ver·finsterung *f* (*astr.*) (*der Sonne, des Mondes*) (solar, lunar) eclipse; (*eines Planeten, Sterns*) occultation (of a planet, star)
Ver·flüssigung *f* (*phys.*) liquefaction, condensation [*cf.* VERDICHTUNG]
Verfolgungs·kurve *f* curve of pursuit [= HUNDEKURVE]
ver·fünffachen *v.t.* quintuple
Ver·fünffachung *f* quintuplication
ver·gleichen *v.t.* compare
Ver·gleichung *f* comparison
ver·größern *v.t.* increase, enlarge, magnify: *den Wert v.* increase the value [*cf.* MASSSTAB]
Ver·größerung *f* enlargement, magnification; (*Zunahme*) increase
ver·halten *v.r.:* -sich *v.* **1.** (*sich betragen*) behave: *die Funktion verhält sich unstetig in der Nähe des Ursprungs* the function behaves discontinuously in the neighborhood of the origin. **2.** (*im Verhältnis stehen*) (*zu*) be (to): 16 *verhält sich zu* 32 *wie* 1 *zu* 2 16 is to 32 in the ratio of 1 to 2, 16 is to 32 as 1 is to 2 [*cf.* RECHTWINKLIG]
Ver·halten *n* (*z.B. einer Funktion*) behavior (e.g. of a function) [*cf.* VERLAUF]
Ver·hältnis *n* **1.** (*zweier Größen*) ratio, rate (of two quantities): *umgekehrtes* (*oder inverses oder reziprokes*) *Verhältnis* inverse (or reciprocal) ratio; *äußeres* (*inneres*) *V.* external (internal) ratio; *aufeinanderfolgende Glieder einer geometrischen Progression wachsen in konstantem Verhältnis*

consecutive terms of a geometrical progression increase by a constant rate (or ratio) [*cf.* ÄUSSER; GRENZE; HINTERGLIED; INNER; MASS; RECHTWINKLIG; REZIPROK; VERHALTEN; VERHÄLTNISMÄSSIG; VORDERGLIED]. **2.** (*der Teile zum Ganzen*) proportion (of the parts relative to the whole): *die richtigen Verhältnisse* (*oder Proportionen*) the right proportions
verhältnis·gleich *adj.* proportional
Verhältnis·gleichheit *f* proportionality
verhältnis·mäßig *adj.* (*relativ*) relative; (*proportional*) proportional, proportionate; (*comm., auch*) pro rata: *v. groß* relatively large; *verhältnismäßiger Maßstab* proportional scale; (*comm.*) *verhältnismäßiger Anteil* proportionate share, quota, contingent; (*comm.*) *die Regien wurden v.* (*oder: im Verhältnis*) *geteilt* expenses (or overheads) were divided pro rata
Verhältnis·zahl *f* rate, ratio; (*statist., auch*) relative (number); (*Prozentsatz*) percentage
Veri·fikation *f* verification
veri·fizieren *v.t.* verify
ver·jähren *v.i.* (*comm.*) be barred by the statute of limitation; *verjährte Forderung* statute-barred claim, claim barred by limitation
Ver·jährung *f* (*comm.*) statutory limitation
ver·jüngen *v.t.* reduce, scale down: *in verjüngtem Maßstab* at a reduced scale

Ver·jüngung *f* (*des Maßstabs*) reduction (of scale)

Ver·kauf *m* (*comm.*) sale [*cf.* BANKABRECHNUNG]

ver·kaufen *v.t.* (*comm.*) sell [*cf.* FREIHÄNDIG; TERMIN]

Ver·käufer *m* (*comm.*) seller

ver·kehrt *adj.* reverse, inverse, inverted: *ein verkehrtes Bild* an inverted image

ver·ketten *v.t.* link, chain; (*korrelieren*) correlate; (*statist.*) *verkettete Ereignisse* linked events

Ver·kettung *f* linkage, chaining; (*Korrelation*) correlation [*cf.* KETTENZAHL].

ver·kleinern 1. *v.t.* diminish, decrease, reduce: *im Maßstab v.* reduce in scale. 2. *v.r.:* **sich** *v.* diminish, decrease, be reduced [*cf.* MASSSTAB; MASSSTÄBLICH]

Ver·kleinerung *f* diminution, decrease, reduction: *V. des Maßstabs* reduction of scale

ver·knüpfen *v.t.* (*z.B. Aussagen*) connect (or combine) (e.g. sentences)

Ver·knüpfung *f* connective, connection, combination [*cf.* GLIED]

ver·kürzen *v.t.* shorten; (*perspektivisch*) foreshorten

Ver·kürzung *f* shortening; (*perspektivische*) foreshortening

ver·längern *v.t.* lengthen, elongate, extend, protract, produce, prolong, continue: *eine Linie v.* extend a line; *eine Strecke um ihre eigene Länge verlängern* extend a line segment its own length [*cf.* VERLÄNGERT]

ver·längert *adj.* prolate, elongated: *verlängertes* (*oder gestrecktes*)

Ellipsoid prolate ellipsoid [*cf.* ROTATIONSELLIPSOID; VERLÄNGERN]

Ver·längerung *f* lengthening, extension, elongation, protraction, prolongation, continuation: *V. einer Strecke* extension of a line

ver·langsamen *v.t.* retard, slow (down), decelerate

Ver·langsamung *f* deceleration, slowdown, retardation

Ver·lauf *m* (*einer Kurve, Funktion, der Zeit, eines Prozesses*) course (of a curve, a function, of time, of a process); (*Gestalt, z.B. einer Kurve*) shape (e.g. of a curve); (*Verhalten, z.B. einer Funktion*) behavior (e.g. of a function)

ver·laufen *v.i.* run (along), go (on); (*Kurve, Funktion*) behave, take (or follow) a course; (*Zeit*) pass, elapse; (*Prozeß*) go (on), run: *die Kurve verläuft stetig* the curve runs along continuously [*cf.* RECHTS-LINKS; VORN-HINTEN]

ver·mehren 1. *v.t.* increase, augment. 2. *v.r.:* **sich** *v.* increase, grow

Ver·mehrung *f* increase

ver·messen *v.t.* survey

Ver·messer *m* surveyor

Ver·messung *f* surveying

ver·mindern *v.t.*, *v.r.:* **sich** *v.* (*um*) diminish, reduce, decrease (by) [*cf.* WERT]

Ver·minderung *f* diminution, reduction, decrease, decrement

ver·mittelnd *v.t.* intermediate, compromise: (*Landkarte*) *vermittelnde Projektion* compromise projection (in a map)

Ver·mögen *n* (*fin.*) (*Besitz*) prop-

erty; (*Kapital*) capital; (*Aktiva*)
assets [*cf.* UNBEWEGLICH]

Vermögens·anlage *f* (*fin.*) capital
investment; *feste* (*oder fixe*)
Vermögensanlagen (*oder Aktiven*)
fixed assets

ver·nachlässigen *v.t.* neglect: *die
Glieder zweiter und höherer
Ordnung v.* neglect the terms of
second and higher degrees; *zu
vernachlässigen*(*d*) negligible; *zu
vernachlässigende Größe* negligible quantity

Ver·nachlässigung *f* neglect(ing)

ver·neinen *v.t.* deny, answer in the
negative, negate

Ver·neinung *f* negation, negative
[*cf.* GEGENTEIL]

ver-n-fachen *v.t.* form the n-th
multiple of

Vernier *m* vernier

ver·pfänden *v.t.* (*comm.*) pledge,
pawn; (*Immobilien*) mortgage [*cf.*
BELASTEN]

Ver·pfändung *f* pledging, pawning;
(*von Immobilien*) mortgaging [*cf.*
BELASTUNG]

ver·rechnen **I.** *v.t.* (*comm.*) **1.**
(*nachweisen*) put to account,
itemize: *er muß jeden Posten v.*
he has to put to account every
single item, he has to itemize his
statement. **2.** (*begleichen, z.B.
Spesen*) settle (e.g. expenses).
II. *v.i.* (*comm.*) **3.** (*abrechnen*)
settle (or balance) accounts. **III.**
v.r. **3. sich** *v.* miscalculate

ver·ringern **1.** *v.t.* diminish,
decrease, reduce. **2.** *v.r.:* **sich**
v. diminish, decrease

Ver·ringerung *f* diminution, decrease, reduction

ver·rücken *v.t.*, *v.r.:* **sich** *v.* [=
VERSCHIEBEN]

Ver·rückung *f* [= VERSCHIEBUNG]
[*cf.* VIRTUELL]

ver·schieben *v.t.*, *v.r.:* **sich** *v.* move,
shift, displace: *den Dezimalpunkt
um zwei Stellen v.* move the
decimal point two places [*cf.*
PARALLEL]

Ver·schiebung *f* shift, displacement
[*cf.* VIRTUELL]

ver·schieden *adj.* different, distinct
[*cf.* EINSEITIG 2.]

Verschieden·heit *f* difference,
distinctness

ver·schlingen **1.** *v.t.* intertwine,
interlace. **2.** *v.r.:* **sich** *v.* (*sich
verflechten*) interlace, intertwine,
be interlaced, be intertwined;
(*sich verwickeln*) become involved
(or complicated, or entangled)

Ver·schlingung *f* (*Verflechtung*)
interlacing, intertwining; (*Ver-
wicklung*) involvement, compli-
cation, entanglement

ver·schlungen *adj.* (*gewunden*)
winding, tortuous, twisted; (*ver-
flochten*) interlaced, intertwined;
(*verwickelt*) entangled, intricate,
involved, complicated [*cf.*
TROCHOIDE]

Verschlungen·heit *f* (*Gewunden-
heit*) tortuousness; (*Verwickelt-
heit*) intricacy, complexity

ver·schlüsseln *v.t.* (*statist.*) code

Ver·schlüsselung *f* (*statist.*) coding

ver·schneiden *v.t.; v.recip., v.r.:*
sich *v.* intersect: *die beiden
Flächen v. sich in einer Kurve
vierten Grades* the two surfaces
intersect in a quartic

Ver·schneidung *f* (*von Flächen,*

Körpern) intersection (of surfaces, solids)

ver·schränkt *adj.* (*alg.*) cross: *verschränktes Produkt eines Körpers mit seiner Galoisschen Gruppe zu einem Faktorensystem* cross product of a field with its Galois group pertaining to a factor set

Ver·schuldung *f* (*comm.*, *fin.*) indebtedness

ver·schwinden *v.i.* vanish, disappear: *die Determinante verschwindet* the determinant vanishes

Verschwindungs·punkt *m* vanishing point

ver·sechsfachen *v.t.* sextuple

ver·sehen *y.t.* (*mit*) equip, supply (with), assign: *jedes Element ist mit zwei Indizes versehen* each element is assigned two indices [*cf.* BESCHREIBEN; BUCHSTABE; LINIE; TEILSTRICH; VORZEICHEN; ZAHL]

ver·sichern *v.t.* (*ins.*) insure; *sich v. lassen* take out an insurance policy, buy insurance [*cf.* DIVIDENDE]

Ver·sicherte(r) *m* (*ins.*) insured person [= VERSICHERUNGSNEHMER]

Ver·sicherung *f* insurance, (*Br.*, also) assurance: *V.* (*oder Lebensversicherung*) *auf den Todesfall* straight (or ordinary, or [*Am.*] whole) life insurance [= ABLEBENSVERSICHERUNG]; *V.* (*oder Lebensversicherung*) *auf den Erlebensfall, gemischte V.* endowment life insurance; *V. auf Gegenseitigkeit, gegenseitige V.* mutual insurance

Versicherungs·leistung *f* (*ins.*) insurance benefit

Versicherungs·mathematik *f* (*ins.*) insurance mathematics, actuarial theory

Versicherungs·mathematiker *m* (*ins.*) actuary

Versicherungs·nehmer [= VERSICHERTE(R)]

Versicherungs·polizze *f* (*ins.*) insurance policy

Versicherungs·prämie *f* (*ins.*) insurance premium

Versicherungs·statistik *f* (*ins.*, *statist.*) insurance (or actuarial) statistics [*cf.* TAFELMETHODE; TAFELZIFFER]

Versicherungs·statistiker *m* (*ins.*, *statist.*) actuary

Versicherungs·träger *m* (*ins.*) insurance carrier, insurer

Versiera *f* [= AGNESISCHE KURVE]

ver·stärken *v.t.* strengthen, intensify, amplify, reinforce

Ver·stärker *m* (*phys.*) amplifier

Verstärker·röhre *f* (*rad.*) *Am.* amplifying tube, *Br.* amplifier valve [*cf.* RÖHRE]

Ver·stärkung *f* strengthening, intensification, amplification, reinforcement

versus *adj.* (*Lat.*) versed: *sinus versus* versed sine [*cf.* SINUSVERSUS]; *cosinus versus* versed cosine [*cf.* KOSINUSVERSUS]

vertausch·bar *adj.* exchangeable, interchangeable, permutable; (*kommutativ*) commutable, commutative

Vertauschbar·keit *f* exchangeability, interchangeability, permutability; (*Kommutativität*)

commutability, commutativity
ver·tauschen′ *v.t.* exchange, interchange, transpose, invert, permute, commute: *Reihen und Kolonnen in einer Matrix v.* interchange (or transpose) rows and columns in a matrix [*cf.* TRANSPONIEREN]
Ver·tauschung *f* exchange, interchange, transposition, inversion, permutation, commutation [*cf.* INVERSION]
Vertauschungs·formel *f* (*log.*) transposition formula
ver·teilen 1. *v.t.* distribute, spread. **2.** *v.r.:* **sich** *v.* (be) spread, be distributed; (*statist.: streuen*) be dispersed [*cf.* GLIEDERN]
Ver·teilung *f* distribution, spread; (*statist.*) (*Reihe*) distribution, series; (*statist.*) (*Streuung*) dispersion, variation [*cf.* ASYMMETRIE; ASYMMETRISCH; CHARAKTERISTIKUM; GLIEDERUNG]
Verteilungs·funktion *f* (*statist.*) distribution function
Verteilungs·kurve *f* (*statist.*) distribution curve [= FEHLERKURVE; HÄUFIGKEITSKURVE] [*cf.* NORMAL; WAHRSCHEINLICHKEITSKURVE]
Verteilungs·maß *n* (*statist.*) measure of dispersion (or variation)
Verteilungs·tafel *f* (*statist.*) frequency table; *primäre V.* array of data; *reduzierte V.* condensed table
vertikal *adj.* vertical [*cf.* GERADE; PROJEKTION; PROJEKTIONSEBENE; SPUR]
Vertikal *m* (*astr.*) vertical (circle)
Vertikal·achse *f* vertical axis
Vertikale *f* vertical (line)

Vertikal·ebene *f* vertical plane
Vertikalität *f* verticality
Vertikal·komponente *f* vertical component
Vertikal·kreis *m* (*astr., geog.*) vertical circle
Vertikal·linie *f* vertical line
Vertikal·projektion *f* (*descr.*) vertical (or orthographic) projection
Vertikal·schnitt *m* vertical section
verträg·lich *adj.* compatible, consistent
Verträglich·keit *f* (*von Axiomen, Gleichungen*) compatibility, consistency (of axioms, equations)
Verträglichkeits·bedingung *f* compatibility condition
ver·vielfachen *v.t., v.r.:* **sich** *v.* multiply, form a multiple (of)
Ver·vielfachung *f* multiplication, formation of a multiple
ver·vierfachen *v.t. v.r.:* **sich** *v.* quadruple, quadruplicate
Ver·vierfachung *f* quadruplication
ver·vollständigen *v.t.* complete: *zu einem Quadrat v.* complete the square [*cf.* ERGÄNZEN]
Ver·vollständigung *f* completion
ver·wandeln 1. *v.t.* (*in*) change (to), reduce (to), transform (into): *einen gemeinen Bruch in einen Dezimalbruch v.* reduce a common fraction to a decimal; *eine Zahl in Brüche v.* transform a figure into fractions; *eine Figur in eine flächengleiche v.* change a geometric figure into another equal to it. **2.** *v.r.:* **sich** *v.* change (to), be reduced (to), be transformed (into): *das Vorzeichen verwandelt sich* the sign changes

Ver·wandlung *f* change, transformation, reduction: *V. des Vorzeichens* change of sign; *V. eines gemeinen Bruchs in einen Dezimalbruch* change of a common fraction into a decimal fraction; *V. einer Figur in eine flächengleiche* changing (or change of) one figure into another equal to it

ver·weisen *v.t.* (*auf*) refer (to)

Ver·weisung *f* (cross) reference

ver·zerren *v.t.* deform

Ver·zerrung *f* deformation

verzerrungs·frei *adj.* free from distortion

Verzerrungs·freiheit *f* freedom from distortion

ver·zinsen (*fin.*) **1.** *v.t.* (*z.B. ein Darlehen*) pay interest on (a loan). **2.** *v.r.:* **sich** *v.* yield (or bear) interest

verzins·lich *adj.* (*fin.*) interest-bearing

Ver·zinsung *f* (*fin.*) yield of interest [*cf.* EFFEKTIV]

Verzugs·zinsen *m pl.* (*comm., fin.*) interest for delay

ver·zweigen *v.r.:* **sich** *v.* ramify, branch

ver·zweigt *adj.* ramified, branched [*cf.* TYPENTHEORIE]

Ver·zweigung *f* ramification

Verzweigungs·punkt *m* (*einer Riemannschen Fläche*) branch point (of a Riemann surface)

v.H. (*abbr.*) *vom Hundert* per cent, (*abbr.*) p.c. [*cf.* HUNDERT]

v.H.-Satz *m* (*abbr.*) *Vomhundertsatz* percentage

Vibration *f* (*phys.*) vibration

vibrieren *v.i.* (*comm.*) vibrate

viel *adj.* (*sing.*) much, (*pl.*) many: *gleich v. Flächenraum* just as much (or: the equal amount of, or: the same) area; *gleich viele Größen* equally many quantities [*cf.* ENDLICH]

viel·deutig *adj.* having many meanings; (*vielwertig*) multiple-valued

Vieldeutig·keit *f* multiplicity; (*Vielwertigkeit, auch*) multiple-valued character

Viel·eck *n* polygon [= POLYGON]: *regelmäßiges* (*oder reguläres*) *V.* regular polygon [*cf.* ECKE; ECKPUNKT; INKREISRADIUS; LIEGEN; UMKREISRADIUS]

viel·eckig *adj.* polygonal

Vielecks·zahl *f* polygonal (or figurate) number

viel·fach *adj.* multiple [*cf.* MANNIGFALTIG; VIELFÄLTIG]

Vielfache(s) *n* multiple [*cf.* FESTLEGEN; GEMEINSAM]

Vielfach·heit *f* (*einer Wurzel, Nullstelle*) multiplicity (of a root, zero) [*cf.* MANNIGFALTIGKEIT]

viel·fältig *adj.* (*vielfach*) multiple; (*mannigfaltig*) varied [*cf.* MANNIGFALTIG]

Vielfältig·keit *f* multiplicity [*cf.* MANNIGFALTIGKEIT]

Viel·flach *n* polyhedron [= POLYEDER; VIELFLÄCHNER]

viel·flächig *adj.* polyhedral

Viel·flächner *m* polyhedron [= POLYEDER, VIELFLACH]

Viel·heit *f* multiplicity, manyness

Viel·kant *n* polyhedral (angle)

viel·phasig *adj.* (*phys.*) polyphase

viel·seitig *adj.* manysided; (*Prisma,*

Pyramide) polygonal (prism, pyramid)

viel·stellig *adj.* **1.** (*ganze Zahl*) (integer) of many digits. **2.** (*Dezimalzahl*) (decimal) of many places. **3.** (*log.: mit vielen Leerstellen*) with many argument places

viel·wertig *adj.* many-valued, multiple-valued [*cf.* VIELDEUTIG]

Vielwertig·keit *f* multiplicity, multiple-valued character [*cf.* VIELDEUTIGKEIT]

vier *card. num.* four: *die v. Grundrechnungsarten* (*oder Grundrechnungsoperationen oder Spezies*) the four fundamental operations of arithmetic; *in v. Teile teilen* divide into four parts, quarter [*cf.* HARMONISCH; HYPOZYKLOIDE; VIERSTELLIG]

Vier *f* (*Zahl, Ziffer*) (number, figure) four

Vier·blatt *n* (*Kurve*) quadrifolium [= QUADRIFOLIUM]

vier·dimensional *adj.* four-dimensional: *vierdimensionaler Raum* four-dimensional space

Vier·dimensionalität *f* four-dimensionalness, four-dimensionality

Vier·eck *n* quadrangle, quadrilateral: *vollständiges* (*einfaches*) *V.* complete (simple) quadrangle [*cf.* NEBENECKE]; *regelmäßiges V.* regular quadrangle (or quadrilateral), square [= QUADRAT]; [*cf.* TETRAGON]

vier·eckig *adj.* quadrangular; (*quadratisch*) square

Vierecks·zahl *f* square number

Vierer *m* (figure) four [*cf.* STELLE]

Vierer·gruppe *f* four(s)-group:

Kleinsche V. Klein's four(s)-group, axial (or quadratic) group

vier·fach *adj.* fourfold, quadruple, quadruplicate

Vierfarben·problem *n* four-color problem

Vier·flach *n* tetrahedron [= TETRAEDER]

vier·flächig *adj.* tetrahedral

Vier·flächner *m* tetrahedron [= TETRAEDER]

vier·gliedrig *adj.* four-termed, quadrinomial; (*log.*) four-place, tetradic; (*statist.*) tetrachoric

vier·hundert *card. num.* four hundred

Vier·kant *n* tetrahedral (angle)

vier·mal *num.* four times

vier·malig *adj.* done (four times)

Vier·seit *n* quadrilateral: *vollständiges* (*einfaches*) *V.* complete (simple) quadrilateral [*cf.* NEBENSEITE]

vier·seitig *adj.* four-sided, quadrangular, quadrilateral: *vierseitige Pyramide* quadrangular pyramid [*cf.* PRISMA]

vier·spitzig *adj.* tetracuspid [*cf.* HYPOZYKLOIDE]

vier·stellig *adj.* (*ganze Zahl*) four-figure, four-digit (integer); (*Dezimalzahl*) four-figure, four-place (decimal); (*log.: mit vier Leerstellen*) four-place, tetradic [*cf.* FÜNFSTELLIG]

vier·strahlig *adj.* four-rayed, tetraradiate

viert *ord. num.* fourth: *das vierte Glied* the fourth term; *der vierte Teil* the fourth part; *Ausdruck, Gleichung vierten Grades* expression, equation of fourth degree, quartic (expression, equation); *Kurve (Fläche) vierter Ordnung* curve (surface) of fourth order, quartic (curve, surface) [*cf.* AUFLÖSUNG; PROPORTIONALE]

Viertel *n* quarter, fourth (part); *erstes (letztes) V. des Mondes* first (last) quarter of the moon

Viertel·kreis *m* quadrant (of a circle), quarter circle

Viertel·pyramide *f* (*cryst.*) tetartopyramid

viertels·flächig *adj.* (*cryst.*) tetartohedral

Viertels·flächner *m* (*cryst.*) tetartohedron

Viertels·wert *m* (*statist.*) quartile

Viertelswert·abstand *m* (*statist.*) quartile deviation

viertens *adv.* fourthly, in the fourth place

vier·wertig *adj.* (*math.*) fourvalued; (*chem.*) quadrivalent, tetravalent

Vierwertig·keit *f* (*math.*) fourvaluedness, quadruplicity;(*chem.*) quadrivalence, tetravalence

vier·zählig *adj.* fourfold, quadruple; (*Symmetrie, auch*) tetragonal (symmetry)

vier·zehn *card. num.* fourteen: *alle v. Tage* every two weeks, biweekly

vier·zig *card. num.* forty

vier·zigst *ord. num.* fortieth

virtuell *adj.* virtual: (*mech.*) *virtuelle Verschiebung* (*oder Verrückung*) virtual displacement; (*opt.*) *virtuelles Bild* virtual image

Viviani *m N.: Vivianische Kurve* Viviani's curve (or windows *pl.*)

Vogel·perspektive *f* bird's-eye perspective [*ant.:* FROSCHPER-

SPEKTIVE]

Vogel·schau *f* bird's-eye view

Volks·zählung *f* (*statist.*) census [*cf.* ZÄHLER 2.]

voll *adj.* full, complete, total: *voller Matrizenring* full (or complete) matrix ring [*cf.* AUSSCHLAG]

voll·ausgezogen *adj.* (*Linie*) full (or unbroken) line

voll·flächig *adj.* (*cryst.*) holohedral

Voll·flächner *m* (*cryst.*) holohedron

voll·kommen *adj.* perfect: *vollkommene Zahl* perfect number [*cf.* KÖRPER 3.]

Voll·kreis *m* full circle

Voll·schwingung *f* (*phys.*) cycle (of oscillation)

Voll·spiegel *m* convex mirror

voll·ständig *adj.* complete, perfect: *vollständiges Quadrat* perfect square [*cf.* ERGÄNZEN; ERGÄNZUNG; INDUKTION; VIERECK; VIERSEIT]

Vollständig·keit *f* completeness

Voll·winkel *m* round angle, perigon (angle) ($=360°$)

Volt *n* (*elec. meas.*) volt [*cf.* SPANNUNG]

Volt·meter *n* (*elec.*) voltmeter

Volum·ausdehnung *f* volume expansion

Volum·differential *n* differential of volume

Volum·einheit *f* unit (of) volume

Volum·element *n* element of volume

Volumen *n* volume [= RAUMINHALT] [*cf.* LADUNGSFÄHIGKEIT]

volumetrisch *adj.* volumetric

Volum·prozent *n* volume per cent, per cent by volume

Vomhundert·satz *m* percentage

von *prep.* (*dat.*) from, of: *fünf v. acht, bleibt drei* five from eight leaves three

vor *prep.* (*dat.*, *acc.*) before, in front of, ahead of

voran·gehen (*sep.*) *v.i.* precede (*dir. obj.*)

voraus·gehen (*sep.*) *v.i.* precede (*dir. obj.*)

voraus·setzen (*sep.*) *v.t.* assume, (pre)suppose [*cf.* ANNEHMEN]

Voraus·setzung *f* assumption, hypothesis, (pre)supposition, premise, antecedent [*cf.* ERFÜLLEN; GRUND]

Vor·bilanz *f* (*comm.*) trial balance

vorder *adj.* front, head, preceding, leading

Vorder·ansicht *f* front(al) view

Vorder·ecke *f* front corner

Vorder·fläche *f* front face

Vorder·glied *n* (*ant.:* *Hinterglied*) **1.** (*math.*) (*eines Verhältnisses*) antecedent (of a ratio). **2.** (*log.*) (*einer Konjunktion, Disjunktion usw.*) first component (of a conjunction, disjunction, etc.)

Vorder·kante *f* front(al) edge

Vorder·satz *m* (*log.*) antecedent (sentence)

Vorder·seite *f* front (side), face

vorderst *adj.* (*sup.* of *vorder*) foremost

Vor·gang *m* event, occurrence; (*Prozeß*) process

Vor·gänger *m* predecessor [*cf.* ZAHLENREIHE]

Vorgangs·masse *f* (*statist.*) [= EREIGNISMASSE, PUNKTMASSE 2.]

vor·gehen (*sep.*) *v.i.* **1.** (*verfahren*) proceed. **2.** (*Uhr* clock) run (or be) fast. **3.** (*vorhergehen*) precede.

4. (*sich ereignen*) happen, go on

vor·kommen (*sep.*) *v.i.* occur, happen, appear [*cf.* MEHRFACH]

vor·läufig *adj.* provisional

vor·letzt *adj.* last but one, next to last

vorn·hinten *adj.* front-to-back: *v.-h. verlaufende Achse* front-to-back axis

vor·rücken (*sep.*) *v.i.* advance

Vor·rücken *n* advance: (*astr.*) *V. der Tagundnachtgleichen* (*oder Äquinoktien*) precession of the equinoxes

vor·schießen *v.t.* (*fin.*) (*Geld*) advance (money)

Vor·schuß *m* (*fin.*) advance (of money)

Vor·spalte *f* (*statist.*) stub

vor·springend *adj.* salient, projecting: *vorspringender Winkel* salient angle

vor·stellen (*sep.*) *v.t.* represent: *sich etwas v.* imagine, visualize (something)

Vor·stellung *f* mental image, idea

Vor·trag *m* (*comm.*) carry-over [= FÜRTRAG]

vor·tragen (*sep.*) *v.t.* (*comm.*) carry (over) [*cf.* SALDO]

vor·vorletzt *adj.* last but two

Vor·zahl *f* coefficient

Vor·zeichen *n* (algebraic) sign: *positives, negatives V.* positive, negative sign; *mit V. versehen* sign(ed); *ohne V.* unsigned [*cf.* ÄNDERN; VERWANDELN; VERWANDLUNG; WECHSEL; ZAHL]

vorzeichen·los *adj.* unsigned

Vorzeichen·regel *f* rule (or law) of signs

Vorzeichen·wechsel *m* change (or

variation) in (or of) sign
Vorzugs·aktien *f pl. (fin.) Am.*
preferred stock (or shares), *Br.*

preference stock (or shares)
v.T. *(abbr.) vom Tausend* per
mille, per thousand

W

Waage *f* scale(s), balance
waag·recht *adj.* horizontal
Waag·schale *f* scale (of a balance)
wachsen *v.i.* grow, increase [*cf.*
GRENZE; VERHÄLTNIS]
Wachs·tum *n* growth, increase
Wachstums·kurve *f* (*statist.*)
growth curve
Wage *f* [= WAAGE]
wägen *v.t.* weigh, weight [*cf.*
GEWOGEN]
wag·recht *adj.* [= WAAGRECHT] [*cf.*
STRICH]
Wag·schale *f* [= WAAGSCHALE]
Wahl *f* choice, selection; (*zwischen
zwei Möglichkeiten*) alternative
(between two possibilities)
wählen *v.t.* choose, select [*cf.*
GRUNDFORM]
wahl·los *adj.* random; (*adv.*) at
random [*cf.* STICHPROBENER-
HEBUNG]
wahr *adj.* true: *wahre Länge,
Gestalt* true length, shape [*cf.*
ANOMALIE; RICHTIG; SONNENZEIT
Wahr·heit *f* truth [*cf.* RICHTIGKEIT]
Wahrheits·funktion *f* (*log.*) truth
function
Wahrheits·gehalt *m* (*log.*) truth
content
wahrheits·gleich *adj.* (*log.*) having
the same truth value
Wahrheits·wert *m* (*log.*) truth value

wahr·scheinlich *adj.* probable, likely [*cf.* HÄUFIGKEITSKOEFFIZIENT]
Wahrscheinlich·keit *f* (*statist.*)
probability, likelihood, odds,
chance: *die W. ist fünfzig Perzent*
the chances (or odds) are fifty-
fifty; *mathematische (statistische)
W.* mathematical (statistical)
probability [*cf.* EMPIRISCH;
HÄUFIGKEITSKOEFFIZIENT]
Wahrscheinlichkeits·dichte *f* (*statist.*) probability density
Wahrscheinlichkeits·funktion *f*
(*statist.*) probability function
Wahrscheinlichkeits·kurve *f* (*statist.*) probability curve [= *normale Fehler- oder Häufigkeits-
oder Verteilungskurve; cf.* NOR-
MAL]
Wahrscheinlichkeits·rechnung *f*
calculus (or theory) of proba-
bilities, probability calculus [*cf.*
TEILUNGSPROBLEM]
Währung *f* (*fin.*) currency, monetary standard [*cf.* AUSGLEICHS-
FONDS; VALUTA]
Währungs·einheit *f,* **Währungs-
standard** *m* monetary standard
Walze *f* (*Zylinder*) cylinder; (*Werk-
zeug*) roller
walzen·förmig *adj.* cylindrical
Waren·börse *f* (*comm.*) commodity
exchange

Waren·kredit *m* commercial credit

Waren·umsatzsteuer *f* (*comm.*) sales tax

Wärme *f* (*phys.*) heat [*cf.* LEITEN; SPEZIFISCH]

Wärme·äquivalent *n* (*phys.*) equivalent of heat [*cf.* JOULE *m*]

Wärme·ausdehnung *f* (*phys.*) thermal expansion [*cf.* AUFRECHNEN]

Wärme·einheit *f* (*phys.*) thermal unit

Wärme·energie *f* (*phys.*) thermal (or heat) energy

Wärme·grad *m* (*phys.*) degree of heat (or temperature)

Wärme·kapazität *f* (*phys.*) caloric (or thermal) capacity

Wärme·lehre *f* (*phys.*) theory of heat; (*Thermodynamik*) thermodynamics

Wärme·leiter *m* (*phys.*) heat conductor

Wärmeleit·fähigkeit *f* (*phys.*) heat conductivity

Wärme·menge (*phys.*) quantity of heat

Wärme·schwankung *f* (*phys.*) thermal fluctuation

Wärme·strahlung *f* (*phys.*) heat (or thermal) radiation

Wärme·strom *m* (*phys.*) heat flow

Wärme·tod *m* (*phys.*) heat death

Wasser·libelle *f* water level

Wasser·uhr *f* water clock

Wasser·waage *f* water level

Watt *n* (*phys. meas.*) watt

Watt·stunde *f* (*phys. meas.*) watt-hour

Wechsel *m* 1. (*Änderung*) change, variation: *W. des Vorzeichens* change of sign. 2. (*comm.*) bill of exchange, draft: *eigener W.* promissory note; *gezogener W.* draft [= TRATTE] [*cf.* DISKONTERLÖS; EINLÖSEN; GIRIEREN; LAUFEN; LAUFZEIT; SOLAWECHSEL; ÜBERTRAGEN; ZIEHEN]

Wechsel·bestand *m* (*comm.*) notes receivable

Wechsel·beziehung *f* correlation; *in W. stehend* correlative

Wechsel·diskont *m* (*comm.*) discount on a note

Wechsel·forderungen *f pl.* [= WECHSELBESTAND]

Wechsel·punkt *m* (*statist.*) exact class limit

wechsel·seitig *adj.* mutual, reciprocal [*cf.* ABHÄNGIGKEIT]

Wechsel·strom *m* (*elec.*) alternating current

Wechsel·verpflichtungen *f pl.* (*comm.*) notes payable

Wechsel·winkel *m* (*zweier Geraden und einer Transversalen*) one of a pair of alternate angles (both on different sides of two lines and on different sides of a transversal) [*cf.* pairs of angles: A, D′; A′, D; B, C′; B′, C in *Fig.* to TRANSVERSALE] [*cf.* PARALLEL]

Wechsel·wirkung *f* interaction

Weg *m* path, way, track; (*zurückgelegter*) distance (covered) [*cf.* MÖGLICHKEIT]

Weg·fall *m*, **Weg·fallen** *n* (*eines Ausdrucks*) cancellation (of an expression)

weg·fallen (*sep.*) *v.i.* cancel (out): *die letzten Glieder fallen weg* the last terms cancel out

weg·heben (*sep.*) *v.r.:* *sich w.* cancel (out): *dieses Glied hebt sich weg* this term cancels

Weg·kurve *f* (*phys.*) hodograph

weg·kürzen (*sep.*) *v.t.*, *v.r.*: **sich** *w.* cancel (out)

Weg·länge *f* distance (covered), length of path

weg·nehmen (*sep.*) *v.t.* deduct, subtract, take away

Weg·nahme *f* deduction, subtraction, taking away

weg·schaffen (*sep.*) *v.t.* eliminate, cancel, remove: *die Brüche in* (*oder aus*) *einer Gleichung wegschaffen* remove (or eliminate) the fractions in (or from) an equation [*cf.* ELIMINIEREN]

Weg·schaffung *f* elimination, cancellation, removal [*cf.* BESEITIGUNG]

weg·streichen (*sep.*) *v.t.* strike out, cross out, discard, reject [*cf.* ABSTREICHEN]

Weierstraß *m* N. [*cf.* NULLSTELLENSATZ]

weisen *v.t.* point: *der Zeiger weist nach Norden* the sighter points (or is pointed) to the north

weit *adj.* (*breit*) wide, broad; (*entfernt*) far (distant) [*cf.* ABSTEHEN; ORT]

Weite *f* (*Breite*) width, breadth; (*Ferne*)(*long*) distance [*cf.* BREITE; LICHT]

weiter·führen (*sep.*) *v.t.* (*fortsetzen*) continue, carry (on); (*extrapolieren*) extrapolate [*cf.* TREIBEN]

Weiter·führung *f* (*Fortsetzung*) continuation; (*Extrapolation*) extrapolation [*cf.* TREIBEN]

Welle *f* (*phys.*) wave [*cf.* FORTSCHREITEND; HERTZ; KNOTENLINIE; STEHEND; ÜBEREINANDERLEGEN]

Wellen·berg *m* (*phys.*) crest of a wave

Wellen·bewegung *f* (*phys.*) undulatory (or wave) motion, undulation

Wellen·eigenschaft *f* (*phys.*) wave (or undulatory) character

Wellen·fortpflanzung *f* (*phys.*) wave transmission, propagation of waves

Wellen·gleichung *f* wave equation

Wellen·linie *f* wave curve

Wellen·länge *f* (*phys.*) wave length

Wellen·lehre *f* (*phys.*) wave (or undulatory) theory

Wellen·mechanik *f* (*phys.*) wave mechanics

Wellen·natur *f* wave (or undulatory) character

Wellen·paket *n* (*phys.*) wave pack

Wellen·tal *n* (*phys.*) trough of a wave

Wellen·theorie *f* (*phys.*) wave (or undulatory) theory

Wellen·zug *m* (*phys.*) wave train

wellig *adj.* wavy, sinuous [*cf.* GESCHWEIFT]

Welt *f* world, universe

Welt·achse *f* (*astr.*) celestial axis [= HIMMELSACHSE]

Welt·karte *f* (*cart.*) world map

Welt·körper *m* (*astr.*) celestial body

Welt·linie *f* (*phys.*) world line

Welt·raum *m* universal (or cosmic) space

Welt·system *n* (*astr.*) cosmic system [*cf.* PTOLEMÄISCH]

Wende·kreis *m* (*geog.*) tropic

Wendel *f* spiral, helix

Wendel·fläche *f* (*common*) helicoid, screw surface

wenden *v.t.*, *v.r.*: **sich** *w.* turn

Wende·punkt *m* **1.** (*einer Kurve*) point of inflection (or: of con-. trary flexure), flex (point) (of a curve). **2.** (*astr.*) (*Punkt der Sonnenwende*) solstitial point

Wende·tangente *f* (*einer Kurve*) inflectional (or stationary, or flex) tangent (to a curve)

Wendung *f* (*einer Kurve*) (*Biegung*) turn, flection, flexion; (*an einem Wendepunkt*) inflection, contrary flexure [*cf.* DREHUNG]

wenig *adj.* (*sing.*) little; (*pl.*) few [*cf.* WENIGER; WENIGST]

weniger *adj.* (*comp.* of **wenig**) less, fewer; (*minus*) minus, less: *w. Punkte* less points; *fünf weniger* (*oder minus*) *drei* five less (or minus) three

wenigst *adj.* (*sup.* of **wenig**) least

werfen 1. *v.t.* cast, throw. **2.** *v.r.:* **sich** *w.* become warped [*cf.* GEWORFEN]

Wert *m* worth, value: *konstanter* (*oder beständiger oder unveränderlicher*) *Wert* constant value; *größter* (*oder höchster oder maximaler*) *W.* maximal (or maximum) value; *den W. herabsetzen* (*oder vermindern*) depreciate the value; (*statist.*) *dichtester* (*oder häufigster*) *W.* mode [*cf.* ABSOLUT; ANNÄHERUNG; ANNEHMEN; ARBITRÄR; BERECHNEN; BESTIMMT; EFFEKTIV; EINZIG; EXTREM; FEST; FIGUR; GEHEN; GRÖSST; HERABSETZEN; HERABSETZUNG; HERAUSKOMMEN; KLEINST; KOMPLEX; LINEAR; MITTEL; NIEDRIG; NUMERISCH; PASSEN; REZIPROK; SPEZIELL; VALUTA; ZULÄSSIG; ZU-

RÜCKKEHREN]

Werte·vorrat *m* (*einer Funktion*) range of values (of a function)

wert·gebend *adj.* significant: *die Nullen nach dem Dezimalpunkt in 0.005 haben wertgebende Bedeutung* (*oder: sind w.*) the zeros after the decimal point in 0.005 are significant

. . . wertig *adj. suf.* (*math.*) -valued (*chem.*) . . . valent [*cf.* DREIWERTIG; EINWERTIG; MEHRWERTIG; VIELWERTIG; ZWEIWERTIG]

Wertig·keit *f* (*chem.*) valence

. . . wertigkeit *f suf. noun* (*math.*) -valuedness; (*chem.*) . . . valence [*cf.* DREIWERTIGKEIT; EINWERTIGKEIT; MEHRWERTIGKEIT; VIELWERTIGKEIT; ZWEIWERTIGKEIT]

Wert·maß *n*, **Wert·maßstab** *m*, **Wert·messer** *m* standard of value

Wert·papiere *n pl.* (*fin.*) securities; (*Aktien und Anlagewerte*) stocks and bonds. [=EFFEKTEN] [*cf.* A 1; AUSGEBEN; BELASTEN 2.; BELEHNEN; EINLÖSEN; MÜNDELSICHER; ÜBERTRAGBAR; ÜBERTRAGBARKEIT; ÜBERTRAGEN; ÜBERTRAGUNG]

Wert·sache *n* (*comm., fin.*) valuable thing (or item); (*pl.*) valuables

Wert·verlust *m* (*comm., fin.*) depreciation

Wert·verminderung *f* (*comm., fin.*) depreciation [*cf.* ABSCHREIBUNG]

Wert·zoll *m* (*comm.*) ad valorem duty

Wesens·form *f* (*statist.*) (*einer statistischen Reihe*) form (of a statistical series) due to probability function (of a statistical universe) [*ant.:* ZUFALLSFORM]

Wesens·streuung *f* (*statist.*) (*einer statistischen Reihe*) dispersion of the probability distribution (of a statistical universe) [*ant.:* ZUFALLSSTREUUNG]

West *m*, **Westen** *m* west

westlich *adj.:* western, westerly [*cf.* GENAU]

West·punkt *m* west point

Wider·sinn *m* absurdity

wider·sinnig *adj.* absurd

wider·sprechen *v.i.* (*dat.*) contradict (*dir. obj.*): *einander widersprechend* contradictory, incompatible, inconsistent

Wider·spruch *m* contradiction: *Satz vom W.* principle of contradiction

wider·sprüchlich *adj.* (self-)contradictory, incompatible, inconsistent

Widersprüchlich·keit *f* (self-)contradictoriness, inconsistency, incompatibility

widerspruchs·frei *adj.* free from contradiction, compatible, consistent

Widerspruchs·freiheit *f* (*von Axiomen, Gleichungen*) freedom from contradiction, compatibility, consistency (of axioms, equations)

Wider·stand *m* (*elec.*) resistance [*cf.* KETTENLINIE]

Wiederbeschaffungs·kosten *pl.* (*comm.*) replacement costs

wieder·holen 1. *v.t.* repeat, iterate. **2.** *v.r.:* sich *w.* recur, repeat (oneself)

wieder·holt *adj.* repeated

Wieder·holung *f* repetition [*cf.*

KOMBINATION; PERIODISCH]

Wiederholungs·reihe *f* (*statist.*) time series with periodic variation

Wieder·kehr *f* recurrence, return [*cf.* PERIODISCH; REGELMÄSSIG]

wieder·kehren (*sep.*) *v.i.* recur, repeat: *die wiederkehrenden Phasen des Mondes* the recurring phases of the moon [*cf.* PERIODISCH; REGELMÄSSIG]

Wieder·verkauf *m* (*comm.*) resale; (*Einzelverkauf*) sale at retail, retail selling

wieder·verkaufen *v.t.* (*comm.*) resell; (*im Einzelverkauf*) sell at retail

Wieder·verkäufer *m* (*comm.*) reseller; (*Einzelverkäufer*) retailer

Wiederverkäufer·preis *m* (*comm.*) trade (or wholesale) price

wiegen 1. *v.t.* weigh, weight. **2.** *v.i.* weigh [*cf.* GEWOGEN]

Will·kür *f* arbitrariness: *W. in der Wahl der Konstanten* arbitrariness in the choice of the constant

willkür·lich *adj.* arbitrary: *willkürliche Konstante* arbitrary constant

Willkürlich·keit *f* arbitrariness

winden *v.t.*, *v.r.:* sich *w.* wind, twist

Wind·rose *f* compass chart (or card), wind (or compass) rose [*cf.* HAUPTPUNKT; HAUPTRICHTUNG]

wind·schief *adj.* skew; (*Fläche, auch*) warped, twisted: *windschiefe Gerade* skew lines; *windschiefe Regelfläche* skew ruled surface, warped (or twisted) surface [*cf.* DREHEN; HYPERBOLISCH; LEITEBENE; LEITKEGEL]

Wind·schiefe *f* skewness

wind·schnittig *adj.* streamlined

Windung *f* (*einer ebenen Kurve*) turn (of a plane curve); (*einer Raumkurve*) torsion (or: second curvature) (of a space curve); (*einer Schraubenlinie, Schraube*) turn, thread (of a helix, screw); (*einer Fläche*) convolution (of a surface) [*cf.* DREHUNG; KRÜM-MUNG; SERPENTINE]

Windungs·winkel *m* (*einer Raumkurve*) angle of torsion (of a space curve) [= TORSIONSWINKEL]

Winkel *m* **1.** (*Richtungsunterschied* difference in direction) angle: *gestreckter W.* flat angle (= 180°); *spitzer* (*stumpfer*) *W.* acute (obtuse) angle; *rechter W.* right angle [*cf.* ABSTECKEN]; *mit zwei rechten Winkeln* birectangular; *positiver* (*oder: positiv gerichteter*) *W.* positive (or: positively directed) angle; *negativer* (*oder: negativ gerichteter*) *W.* negative (or: negatively oriented) angle; *ebener* (*sphärischer*) *W.* plane (spherical) angle; *W. einer Geraden mit der positiven x-Achse* slope angle of a straight line; *W. zwischen zwei Ebenen* dihedral angle; *W. eines sphärischen Dreiecks* (dihedral) angle of a spherical triangle [*cf.* ABTRAGUNG; ANLIEGEND; ANSTOSSEND; ARCUS COTANGENS HYPERBOLICUS; ARCUS TANGENS HYPERBOLICUS; ARKUS; ARKUSKOSEKANS; ARKUSKOSINUS; ARKUSKOTANGENS; ARKUS-SEKANS; ARKUSSINUS; ARKUS-TANGENS; AUSSPRINGEND; BILDEN; COSINUS HYPERBOLICUS; DRE-HUNG; DREI; EINSCHLIESSEN; EIN-SPRINGEND; ENTGEGENGESETZT; ERGÄNZEN; ERGÄNZUNG; ER-HABEN; ERHALTEN 2.; GEGENÜBER-LIEGEND; GESTRECKT; GERICHTET; GLEICH; GRAD; HALBIERUNGS-EBENE; HALBIERUNGSLINIE; KO-FUNKTION; KOMPLEMENT; KON-JUGIERT; KÖRPERLICH; KORRE-SPONDIEREN; KOSEKANTE; KO-SINUS; KOSINUSVERSUS; KOTAN-GENS; KOTANGENTE; ORIENTIEREN; QUADRANT; RECHT; SCHEITEL; SCHEITELPUNKT; SCHENKEL; SCHIEF; SEKANS; SEKANTE; SE-KUNDE; SINUS; SINUS HYPERBOLI-CUS; SINUSVERSUS; SPITZE; SUP-PLEMENT; TANGENS; TANGENTE; TRANSVERSALE; TRISEKTION; ÜBERSTUMPF; VORSPRINGEND]. **2.** (*Reißdreieck*) triangle, set square

Winkel·abstand *m* angular distance

Winkel·beschleunigung *f* (*phys.*) angular acceleration

Winkel·einheit *f* unit of angle, angular unit

Winkel·funktion *f* trigonometric function

Winkel·geschwindigkeit *f* (*phys.*) (*skalare* scalar) angular speed; (*gerichtete* directed) angular velocity

Winkel·grad *m* angular degree, degree of angle

Winkel·halbierende *f* bisector, bisectrix (of an angle)

Winkel·maß *n* angular measure(ment) [*cf.* GRAD; UMRECHNEN]

Winkel·messer *m* protractor [= TRANSPORTEUR]

Winkel·messung *f* goniometry

Winkel·minute *f* angular minute, minute of angle

Winkel·sekunde *f* angular second,

second of angle

Winkel·summe *f* angular sum

Winkel·tabelle *f* table of angles

winkel·treu *adj.* (*Abbildung, Transformation*) equiangular, isogonal, conformal, angle-preserving (mapping, transformation) [= KONFORM]

Winkel·treue *f* (*einer Abbildung*) preservation of angles, isogonality (of a map)

Winter·solstitium *n*, **Wintersonnenwende** *f* (*astr.*) winter solstice

Wirbel *m* **1.** (*einer Vektorfunktion F*) curl (of a vector function *F*) (*symb.:* $\nabla \times F \equiv$ rot $F \equiv$ curl *F*) [*cf.* ROTOR]. **2.** (*phys.*) (*Hydrodynamik* hydrodynamics) vortex

Wirkung *f* (*Folge einer Ursache*) effect (of a cause); (*phys.*) (*Effekt*) action, power [*cf.* EFFEKT; FOLGE]

Wirkungs·bereich *m* (*eines logischen Zeichens*) scope (of a logical symbol)

Wirkungs·grad *m* (*mach.*) efficiency, effectiveness

Wirkungs·quantum *n* (*phys.*) quantum of action [*cf.* PLANCK]

Wirt·schaft *f* (*comm., fin.*) economy

Wirtschafts·index *m* (*comm.*) index of business activity, business index [*cf.* GENERALINDEX]

Wirtschafts·statistik *f* (*comm., statist.*) economic (or business) statistics

Wirtschafts·zyklus *m* (*comm., statist.*) (*von Hochkonjunktur und Depression*) business cycle (of prosperity and depression)

Wissen·schaft *f* science [*cf.* EMPIRISCH; EXAKT; STRENG]

Woche *f* week

wöchentlich *adj.* weekly

wohl·geordnet *adj.* well-ordered: *wohlgeordnete Menge* well-ordered set

wohl·ordnen *v.t.* make (or render) well-ordered [*cf.* WOHLGEORDNET]

Wohl·ordnung *f* well-ordering

wölben 1. *v.t.* make convex; (*eine Linie, auch*) form an arch (of a line) (*eine Fläche, auch*) form a vault (of a surface). **2.** *v.r.:* sich *w.* be convex; (*Linie* line, *auch*) be arched, form an arch, (*Fläche* surface, *auch*) be vaulted, form a vault

Wölbung *f* convexity; (*einer Linie, auch*) arch (formed by a line); (*einer Fläche, auch*) vault (formed by a surface)

Wucher·zinsen *m pl.* excessive (or usurious) interest

Wucht *f* (*phys.*) (*Stoßkraft*) momentum, impact; (*kinetische Energie*) kinetic energy

Wulst *m* torus (ring), anchor ring, ring surface [= RINGFLÄCHE, TORUS]

Wurf *m* **1.** (*Werfen*) cast, throw. **2.** (*einer Punktreihe*) anharmonic range (of points); (*eines Strahlenbüschels*) anharmonic pencil (of rays)

Wurf·bahn *f* trajectory

Würfel *m* **1.** (*Hexaeder*) cube, regular hexahedron: *Verdopplung des Würfels* duplication of the cube [*cf.* NETZ; KUBUS; SEITE]. **2.** (*statist.*) (*im Spiel*) die, *pl.* dice (in games) [*cf.* AUGE; INHALT;

SCHACHTELN; SPIEL]

würfeln (*statist.*) *v.i.* cast (or throw, or play at) dice [*cf.* AUGENZAHL]

Wurzel *f* **1.** (*aus einer Zahl*) root, radix, radical (of a number); (*Quadratwurzel*) square root: *dritte W.* third root, cube root; *n-te W. einer Zahl* n-th root of a number; *W. aus fünf* square root of five; *wir nehmen das positive Zeichen der W.* we take the positive sign of the radical [*cf.* AUSZIEHEN; AUSZIEHUNG; ZIEHEN; ZIEHUNG]. **2.** (*einer Gleichung*) root (of an equation) [*cf.* ALGEBRAISCH; EINFACH; FREMD; MEHRFACH]

Wurzel·ausdruck *m* radical, surd: *reiner W.* (*ohne rationale Glieder oder Faktoren*) entire surd (with-out rational terms or factors); *gemischter W.* (*mit rationalen Gliedern oder Faktoren*) mixed surd (with rational terms or factors); *Summe irrationaler Wurzelausdrücke* sum of ir-rational radicals, surd

Wurzel·ausziehen *n*, **Wurzel·ausziehung** *f* extraction of a root, evolution

Wurzel·exponent *m* index (or order) of a root (or radical)

Wurzel·größe *f* (*alg.*) (*eines Ringes*) root element (of a ring)

Wurzel·körper *m* (*alg.*) root field

Wurzel·zeichen *n* radical (or root) sign; *Zahl unter dem Wurzelzeichen* radicand

Wurzel·ziehen *n*, **Wurzel·ziehung** *f* extraction of a root, evolution

X

x-Achse *f* x-axis [*cf.* ABSCHNITT; AUFTRAGEN; BILDEN; FALLEN; NEIGUNGSWINKEL; RICHTUNGS-WINKEL] [= ABSZISSENACHSE]

Xi *n* (*griechischer Buchstabe* Greek letter Ξ, ξ) xi

Y

y-Achse *f* y-axis [*cf.* GRAPHISCH; MASSGRÖSSE; SEITE 4.] [= ORDI-NATENACHSE]

Yard *n* yard, (*abbr.*) yd.

Ypsilon *n* (*griechischer Buchstabe* Greek letter Y, υ) upsilon

Z

z-Achse *f* z-axis
Zacke *f* jag
Zahl *f* number, figure; (*einstellige, auch*) digit: *relative* (*oder: mit Vorzeichen versehene oder: algebraische*) *Z.* relative (or signed, or algebraic) number; *mangelhafte* (*oder defiziente*) *Z.* defective (or deficient) number; (*statist.*) *Gesetz der großen Zahl(en)* law of large numbers; (*statist.*) *Gesetz der kleinen Zahlen* law of small numbers, Bortkiewicz's law [*cf.* ABRUNDEN; ABRUNDUNG; ABSOLUT; ABSTRAKT; ABUNDANT; ACHT; ALGEBRA; ALGEBRAISCH; ALLGEMEIN; BELIEBIG; BENANNT; BENENNUNG; BERNOULLI; BETRAG; BEZEICHNET; BUCHSTABE; DIVIDEND; DREI; DREISTELLIG; EINHEIT; EINS; EINSETZEN; EINSTELLIG; ENDLICH; FIGURIERT; FÜNF; FÜNFSTELLIG; GANZ; GAUSSSCH; GEMISCHT; GERADE; GERADHEIT; GERICHTET; GLEICHNAMIG; HOCHGESTELLT; IDEAL; IMAGINÄR; IRRATIONAL; KOMPLEX; KONGRUENZ; KONJUGIERT; KONKURS; KÜRZUNG; LOGARITHMIEREN; NATÜRLICH; NEGATIV; NEUN; NIEDRIG; P-ADISCH; POTENZ; PYTHAGORÄISCH; RATIONAL; REELL; REIHE; RESTCHARAKTER; REZIPROK; SECHS; SIEBEN; SPEZIELL; STELLE; STELLUNG; TRANSZENDENT; ÜBERFLIESSEND; ÜBERSCHIESSEND; UMWANDLUNG; UNBENANNT; UNBEZEICHNET; UNEIGENTLICH; UNGERADE; UNGERADHEIT; UNGLEICHNAMIG; UNVOLLKOMMEN; VERWANDELN; VIELSTELLIG; VIER; VOLLKOMMEN; WURZEL; WURZELZEICHEN; ZAHLENLINIE; ZAHLENREIHE; ZEHN; ZEHNERZAHL; ZERLEGBAR; ZUSAMMENGESETZT; ZWEI; ZWEISTELLIG]

zahl·bar *adj.* (*comm.*) payable; (*fällig*) due
Zahl·begriff *m* number concept, concept of number
Zähl·bezirk *m* (*statist.*) census (or registration) district
Zähl·blatt *n* (*statist.*) (census) card; (*Lochkarte*) punch card
Zähl·einheit *f* unit of counting [*cf.* BENENNUNG]
zahlen *v.i.* (*comm.*) pay [*cf.* RECHNUNG]
zählen *v.t. v.i.* count, number
Zählen *n* numeration, counting
Zahlen·beispiel *n* numerical example
Zahlen·dreieck *n* number triangle
Zahlen·ebene *f* number plane, plane of complex numbers: *Gaußsche Z.* Gauss (or complex) (number) plane [*cf.* KOMPLEX]
Zahlen·folge *f* sequence (of numbers) [*cf.* BESCHRÄNKTHEIT; ZAHLENREIHE]
Zahlen·gleichung *f* numerical equation
Zahlen·klasse *f* number class [*cf.* REST; SCHNITT]
Zahlen·kongruenz *f* congruence of numbers

Zahlen·kontinuum *n* continuum of numbers

Zahlen·körper *m* (*alg.*) number field (or domain) [= ZAHL-KÖRPER] [*cf.* ÄHNLICH-ISOMORPH; ALGEBRAISCH; ANGEORDNET; BASIS; BEWERTUNG; ENTSTEHEN; ERWEITERUNG; NORMAL]

Zahlen·lehre *f* theory of numbers

Zahlen·linie *f* number scale (or axis): *Z. der natürlichen Zahlen* natural scale [*cf.* EINHEITSPUNKT; ZAHLENREIHE]

zahlen·mäßig *adj.* numerical, quantitative [*cf.* ABHÄNGIGKEIT]

Zahlen·menge *f* set (or assemblage) of numbers, number set [*cf.* GLEICHMÄCHTIG; GLEICHMÄCH-TIGKEIT; HÄUFUNGSWERT; MÄCH-TIGKEIT]

Zahlen·modul *m* (*alg.*) number module

Zahlen·paar *n* pair of numbers, number couple

Zahlen·polygon *n* number polygon

Zahlen·quadrat *n* number square

Zahlen·reihe *f* number series; (*Zahlenfolge*) number sequence; (*Zahlenlinie*) number scale [= ZAHLREIHE]: *in der natürlichen Z. hat jede Zahl einen Nachfolger und jede, bis auf die Null, einen Vorgänger* in the natural scale every number has a successor (or consequent), and every one, except zero, a predecessor [*cf.* ABSCHNITT]

Zahlen·ring *m* (*alg.*) number ring [= ZAHLRING]

Zahlen·sprache *f* number language

Zahlen·stock *m* tally stick

Zahlen·symbolik *f* number sym-bolism (or lore)

Zahlen·system *n* number system [*cf.* BASIS; DEKADISCH; DYA-DISCH]

zahlen·theoretisch *adj.* number-theoretic

Zahlen·theorie *f* number theory, theory of numbers

Zahlen·tripel *n* number triplet (or triple)

Zahlen·vieleck *n* number polygon

Zahlen·viereck *n* number square

Zahlen·wert *m* numerical value

Zähler *m* 1. (*eines Bruches*) numer-ator (of a fraction) [*cf.* KLEINST; KÜRZEN; KÜRZUNG]. 2. (*statist.*) (*bei der Volkszählung*) census enumerator (or taker). 3. (*Messer*) meter, counter: *elek-trischer Z.* electric meter

Zähler·determinante *f* numerator determinant

Zähler·zählung *f* (*statist.*) inter-view (enumerator) method of census [*ant.:* SELBSTZÄHLUNG]

. . . **zählig** *adj. suf. . . .* fold; (*Sym-metrie, auch*) *. . .* gonal [*cf.* ACHTZÄHLIG; DREIZÄHLIG; FÜNF-ZÄHLIG; SECHSZÄHLIG; SIEBEN-ZÄHLIG; SYMMETRIE; VIERZÄHLIG; ZWEIZÄHLIG]

Zähl·karte *f* [= ZÄHLBLATT]

Zahl·körper *m* (*alg.*) number field (or domain) [= ZAHLENKÖRPER] [*cf.* GAUSSSCH; TOTAL-POSITIV]

Zahl·reihe *f* [= ZAHLENREIHE]

Zahl·ring *m* [= ZAHLENRING]

Zähl·rohr *n* (*phys.*) counter: *Geigersches Z.* Geiger counter

Zahlung *f* (*comm., fin.*) payment [*cf.* A CONTO; DURCHSCHNITTS-LAUFZEIT; LEISTEN; LEISTUNG;

RÜCKZAHLUNG; ZURÜCKZAH-
LUNG]

Zählung *f* numeration, count(ing);
(*statist.*) (*z.B. einer Bevölkerung*)
census (e.g. of a population)

Zahlungs·empfänger *m* (*comm.*,
fin.) payee

zahlungs·fähig *adj.* (*comm.*)
solvent

Zahlungs·fähigkeit *f* (*comm.*)
solvency

Zahlungs·frist *f* (*comm.*) (*Termin*)
term (or time) of payment;
(*Aufschub*) respite

zahlungs·unfähig *adj.* (*comm.*) in-
solvent

Zahlungs·unfähigkeit *f* (*comm.*)
insolvency

Zahlungs·verpflichtung *f* (*comm.*)
obligation to pay, financial obligation [*cf.* OBLIGO]

Zahlungs·verzögerung *f*, **Zahlungs-
verzug** *m* (*comm.*) default of payment

Zähl·werk *n* (*einer Rechenmaschine*) counter (in a computing machine)

Zahl·wort *n* numeral, number
word

Zahl·zeichen *n* numeral, number
symbol: *arabische* (*römische*) *Z.*
(*oder Ziffern*) Arabic (Roman)
numerals [*cf.* ZIFFER]

zehn *card. num.* ten: *zu. z.* by tens

Zehn *f* (*Zahl, Ziffer*) (number,
figure) ten

Zehn·eck *n* decagon

zehn·eckig *adj.* decagonal

Zehner *m* 1. (*Ziffer*) (figure) ten.
2. (*Stellenwert* place value) ten:
fünf Einer, drei Z. five units,
three tens. 3. (*Banknote* bank

note) ten-. . . note (or bill); (*z.B·
Zehnmarkschein*) ten-mark note

Zehner·basis *f* decadic base, base
ten

Zehner·bruch *m* decimal fraction

Zehner·gruppe *f* decade

Zehner·kolonne *f* column of tens
[*cf.* HINÜBERFÜHREN]

Zehner·logarithmus *m* logarithm
to the base ten, common logarithm [= *dekadischer* LOGA-
RITHMUS]

Zehner·stelle *f* ten's (or tens) place

Zehner·system *n* decadic (or decimal) system

Zehner·zahl *f* 1. (*Zahl an der
Zehnerstelle*) number (or figure)
in the tens place. 2. (*dekadische
Zahl*) decadic number

Zehn·flach *n* decahedron

zehn·flächig *adj.* decahedral

Zehn·flächner *m* decahedron

zehn·mal *num.* ten times

zehn·malig *adj.* (done) ten times
[*cf.* DREIMALIG]

zehnt *ord. num.* tenth: *der zehnte
Teil* the tenth part

zehn·tausend *card. num.* ten
thousand; *Zehntausende* tens of
thousands

zehn·teilen *v.t.* divide in ten (parts)

zehn·teilig *adj.* in (or composed of)
ten parts

Zehntel *n* tenth (part) [*cf.* GENAU]

zehntel *adj.* (*inv.*) tenth (of): *ein z.
Millimeter* a tenth of a millimeter
(= *ein* ZEHNTELMILLIMETER)

Zehntel·grad *m* tenth of a degree

Zehntel·meter *n* decimeter, decimetre

Zehntel·millimeter *n* tenth of a
millimeter (or millimetre)

227

Zehntel·sekunde *f* tenth of a second

zehntens *adv.* tenthly, in the tenth place

Zeichen *n* sign, mark, symbol; (*Operationszeichen*) operator [*cf.* BEZEICHNEN; WIRKUNGSBEREICH; WURZEL]

Zeichen·dreieck *n* (drawing) triangle, set square [= REISS-DREIECK]

Zeichen·fläche *f* drawing surface

Zeichen·regel *f* rule of signs

Zeichen·werkzeug *n* drawing (or drafting) instrument [*cf.* ZIRKEL]

zeichnen *v.t., v.i.* draw, draft, trace, plot: *maßstabgetreu z.* draw to scale; *eine Kurve z.* trace (or draw, or plot) a curve [*cf.* AUGENMASS; AUFZEICHNEN; BESCHREIBEN; DARSTELLEN; FREI; FREIHAND; FREIHÄNDIG; SCHLEIF-SCHNITT]

Zeichnen *n* drawing, drafting [*cf.* TECHNISCH]

Zeichner *m* draftsman

zeichnerisch *adj.* graphic(al) [*cf.* AUSGLEICHUNG; DARSTELLEN]

Zeichnung *f* drawing, graph, diagram [*cf.* AUFZEICHNUNG; MASS-STAB; MASSSTABGETREU]

Zeiger *m* 1. (*Index*) index; (*oberer* upper) superscript; (*unterer* lower) subscript. 2. (*an einer Einteilung*) pointer, sighter, indicator (on a scale) [*cf.* AUSSCHLAG; NULLSTELLUNG; WEISEN]

Zeiger·ablesung *f* pointer (or indicator) reading

Zeile *f* (*einer Determinante*) row (of a determinant)

Zeilen·mittel *n* (*statist.*) row

average

Zeit *f* time: *Differentialquotient nach der Z.* differential quotient with respect to time [*cf.* ENERGIE; ORT; SEKUNDE; VERLAUF; VER-LAUFEN]

Zeit·abschnitt *m* period (of time), time interval

zeit·artig *adj.* (*phys.*) (*Intervall*) time-like (interval)

Zeit·dauer *f* duration, period

Zeit·dimension *f* time dimension

Zeit·einheit *f* time unit, unit (of) time

Zeit·geschäft *n* (*comm.*) credit business

Zeit·gleichung *f* equation of time

Zeit·intervall *n* time interval

Zeit·koordinate *f* time coordinate

Zeit·kurve *f* time curve

zeitlich *adj.* temporal, time; (*Aufeinanderfolge*) chronological (order); *zeitliche Ableitung* derivative with respect to time [*cf.* REIHE; ZUSAMMENFALLEN]

Zeit·maß *n* measure of time; (*Zeiteinheit*) unit (of) time, time unit

Zeit·messer *m* chronometer, time piece, clock

Zeit·minute *f* minute of time

Zeit·punkt *m* point of time, moment, instant [*cf.* STICHZEIT]

Zeit·raum *m* interval, period [*cf.* STICHZEIT]

Zeit·rechnung *f* chronology; (*Ära*) era

Zeit·reihe *f* (*statist.*) time series [*cf.* STATISTISCH]

Zeit·rente *f* (*comm.*) annuity certain

Zeit·sekunde *f* second of time

Zeit·serie *f* (*statist.*) time series

Zeitumkehr:probe *f* (*statist.*) time reversal test

Zeitweg·kurve *f* time-path curve

Zeit·weiser *m* calendar

Zenit *m* zenith [= SCHEITEL(PUNKT) 2.]

Zenit·distanz *f* (*astr.*) zenith distance, coaltitude

Zenti·grad *m* centigrade

Zenti·gramm *n* (*abbr.* cg) centigram, centigramme, (*abbr.* cg.)

Zenti·liter *n* centiliter, centilitre

Zenti·meter *n* (*abbr.* cm) centimeter, centimetre, (*abbr.* cm.)

Zentimeter-Gramm-Sekunden-System *n* centimeter-gram-second system (of units) [*cf.* C.G.S.-SYSTEM]

Zentner *m* (*Gewicht* weight) centner, hundredweight, quintal

zentral *adj.* central

Zentral·bewegung *f* central motion

Zentrale *f* (*zweier Kreise, Kugeln*) line of (or: joining the) centers (of two circles, spheres)

Zentral·kegelschnitt *m* central conic

Zentral·perspektive *f* central (or linear) perspective

Zentral·projektion *f* central projection

Zentral·punkt *m* central point

Zentral·symmetrie *f* central symmetry

zentral·symmetrisch *adj.* centrally symmetric(al)

Zentral·wert *m* (*statist.*) median

zentrieren *v.t.* center

Zentrierung *f* centering

zentri·fugal *adj.* centrifugal

Zentrifugal·bewegung *f* (*phys.*) centrifugal motion

Zentrifugal·kraft *f* (*phys.*) centrifugal force

zentripetal *adj.* centripetal

Zentripetal·bewegung *f* (*phys.*) centripetal motion

Zentripetal·kraft *f* (*phys.*) centripetal force

zentrisch *adj.* central: *zentrische Symmetrie* central symmetry; *z. symmetrisch* central-symmetrical

zentrisch·symmetrisch *adj.* central-symmetrical

Zentri·winkel *m* central angle

Zentrum *n* (*Mittelpunkt*) center, centre; (*einer Gruppe*) center, centrum, central (of a group): *Z. (oder Mittelpunkt) eines Kreises* center of a circle [*cf.* LAUFEN]

Zer·fall *m* decomposition; (*phys., auch*) decay

zer·fallen *v.i.* decompose, be decomposed, split, be split; (*phys., auch*) decay

zer·fällen *v.t.* decompose, resolve, split

Zer·fällung *f* decomposition, splitting

Zerfällungs·körper *m* (*alg.*) decomposition (or splitting) field

zer·gliedern *v.t.* dissect; (*analysieren*) analyze

Zer·gliederung *f* dissection; (*Analyse*) analysis

zerleg·bar *adj.* decomposable, reducible; (*in Faktoren* into factors) factorable: *in Faktoren zerlegbare Zahl* composite (or factorable) number [*cf.* DIREKT]

zer·legen *v.t.* decompose, split (up); (*in Faktoren*) factor, factorize, split up (into factors); (*analy-*

sieren) analyze [*cf.* FAK**T**OR]

Zer·legung *f* decomposition, splitting (up); (*in Faktoren* into factors) factorization; (*Analyse*) analysis

zerren *v.t.* strain, deform

Zerrung *f* (*in einem Körper*) strain, deformation (in a [*phys.*] body, [*geom.*] solid)

zer·schneiden *v.t.* cut up, dissect

Zer·schneidung *f* dissection

zer·streuen *v.t.* scatter, disperse, spread

Zer·streuung *f* scattering, dispersion, spread

Zeta *n* (*griechischer Buchstabe* Greek letter *Z, ζ*) zeta

Zick·zack *n*, **zick·zack** *adj.* zigzag

Zickzack·linie *f* zigzag (or broken) line

ziehen *v.t.* **1.** (*eine Linie*) trace, draw (a line). **2.** (*eine Wurzel*) extract (a root): *die Wurzel aus einer Zahl z.* extract the root of a number. **3.** (*einen Wechsel*) draw (or make out, or issue) (a bill of exchange) [*cf.* WECHSEL]

Ziehung *f* **1.** (*einer Linie*) drawing (of a line). **2.** (*einer Wurzel*) extraction of a root

Ziel·kauf *m* (*comm.*) purchase on credit

Ziffer *f* **1.** (*Zahl*) figure, digit; (*Verhältnis*) rate, ratio. **2.** (*Zahlzeichen* character) numeral, figure [*cf.* ACHT; DREI; EINS; FÜNF; FÜNFER; NEUN; REIN; ROH; SECHS; SIEBEN; STIMMEN; UNTER; VIER; ZAHLZEICHEN; ZEHN; ZEHNER; ZWEI]

Ziffern·schrift *f* numeral (or number) script

Ziffern·sprache *f* numeral (or number) language

Ziffern·summe *f* sum of digits

Zins *m* (*fin.*) **1.** (*usu. pl.*) (*Interessen*) interest: *Z.* (*oder Zinsen*) *vom Kapital* interest from capital; *fünf Prozent Zinsen* five per cent interest; *die Zinsen sind am ersten des Monats fällig* interest is due on the first day of the month [*cf.* 2.]; *angewachsene* (*oder zugewachsene oder aufgelaufene*) *Zinsen* accrued interest; *Zinsen zum Kapital schlagen* add interest to the capital (or principal) [*cf.* EINFACH; GENAU; LAUFEN]. **2.** (*Miete*) rent: *der Z. ist am ersten des Monats fällig* the rent is due on the first day of the month [*cf.* 1.]

Zinsen·berechnung *f* calculation (or computation) of interest [*cf.* KALENDERJAHR]

Zinsen·rechnung *f* (method of) interest calculation (or computation)

Zinsen·zuwachs *m* accrued interest

Zinses·zins(en) *m* (*pl.*) compound interest

Zinseszins·rechnung *f* (method of) compound interest calculation (or computation)

Zins·fuß *m* interest rate

Zins·rechnung *f* [≈ ZINSEN-RECHNUNG]

Zins·schein *m* [= KUPON]

Zirkel *m* **1.** (*Zeichenwerkzeug* drawing instrument) (*Einsatzzirkel*) compass, (pair of) compasses; (*Stechzirkel*) dividers [*cf.* EINSATZ; EINSATZTEIL; EIN-

SETZEN; KONSTRUKTION; SPITZE].
2. (*Kreis*) circle: *einen Z. schlagen*
describe a circle [*cf.* QUADRATUR].
3. (*log.: Zirkelschluß*) circle:
logischer (*oder falscher*) *Z.* vicious
circle
Zirkel·einsatz *m* **1.** (*Einsatzteil*)
(removable) point of a (drawing)
compass. **2.** (*das Einsetzen*) setting in the (needle point of the)
compass
Zirkel·schluß *m* (*log.*) vicious
circle [*cf.* ZIRKEL]
Zirkel·spitze *f* (needle) point of a
(drawing) compass
Zirkel·zahl *f* circular number
zirkulär *adj.* circular
zirkum·polar *adj.* (*astr.*) circum-
polar
Zirkumpolar·stern *m* (*astr.*) cir-
cumpolar (star)
Zissoide *f* cissoid [= EFEULINIE;
EPHEULINIE; KISSOIDE]
Zodiak *m* (*astr.*) zodiac [= TIER-
KREIS]
Zoll *m* **1.** (*meas.*) inch: *drei Z.*
three inches. **2.** (*comm.*) (*Abgabe*)
custom, duty .
Zoll·stab *m*, **Zoll·stock** *m* foot rule
Zoll·tarif *m* (*fin.*) (customs) tariff
Zone *f* zone
zu *prep.* (*dat.*) to, by, in: *a* (*verhält
sich*) *zu b wie c zu d a* is to *b* as *c*
is to *d; zu* (*je*) *zehn* by (or in) tens
Zu·fall *m* (*statist.*) chance, acci-
• dent, random cause
zu·fällig *adj.* random, accidental,
chance; *adv.* at random, acci-
dentally: *zufälliges Ereignis*
chance event; (*statist.*) *zufällige
Veränderliche* (*oder Variable*)
random variable [*cf.* AUSWAHL;

UNGEORDNET]
Zufalls·apparat *m* (*statist.*)
Galton's board
Zufalls·form *f* (*statist.*) (*einer
statistischen Reihe*) form (of a
statistical series) due to empirical
(or sampling) distribution (of a
statistical series) [*ant.:* WESENS-
FORM]
Zufalls·kurve *f* Galtonian curve
[*cf.* GALTON]
Zufalls·schwankung *f* (*statist.*)
random fluctuation
Zufalls·streuung *f* (*statist.*) (*einer
statistischen Reihe*) empirical (or
sampling) dispersion (of a statistical series) [*ant.:* WESENS-
STREUUNG]
Zufalls·ursache *f* random cause
Zug *m* (*phys.*) pull
zu·gehörig *adj.* belonging to: (*alg.*)
*der einem Erweiterungskörper
zugehörige Normalkörper* the
normal field belonging to an
extension field
zu·geordnet *adj.* corresponding,
conjugate, coordinated, associated: *sich selbst z.* self-corresponding [*cf.* ZUORDNEN]
Zug·festigkeit *f* (*phys.*) tensile
strength
Zug·linie *f* tractrix [= TRAKTRIX]
zu·lässig *adj.* admissible, allow-
able, permissible: *zulässiger Wert
einer Veränderlichen* permissible
value of a variable; *zulässige
Untergruppe* admissible subgroup
Zu·nahme *f* increment, increase:
Z. einer Funktion increase (or
increment) of a function
zu·nehmen (*sep.*) *v.i.* increase,
ascend, grow: *zunehmende Funk-*

tion increasing function; *zu-nehmende Reihe* ascending series [*cf.* MONOTON]; [*cf.* KONKURS]

Zunge *f* (*des Rechenschiebers*) slide (of a slide rule)

zu·ordnen (*sep.*) *v.t.* coordinate, map, associate, assign: *wir ordnen die Elemente zweier Mengen einander zu* we map the elements of two sets on each other; *wir können jedem Polynom ein anderes zuordnen* to every polynomial we can associate (or assign) another polynomial; *jedem Punkt ist eine Koordinate zugeordnet* a co-ordinate is assigned to each point [*cf.* ZUGEORDNET]

Zu·ordnung *f* coordination, cor-respondence [*cf.* ÜBERFÜHREN]

zurück·führbar *adj.* reducible: *auf den Sinussatz z.* reducible to the law of sines

zurück·führen (*sep.*) *v.t.* (*auf*) re-duce (to) [*cf.* BRINGEN]

Zurück·führung *f* (*auf*) reduction (to): *Z. einer Gleichung auf die Normalform* reduction of an equation to the normal form

zurück·kehren (*sep.*) *v.i.* return, revert: *zum selben Wert z.* revert to the same value

zurück·legen (*sep.*) *v.t.* (*eine Strecke*) cover, travel (a distance) [*cf.* BESTECKAUFNAHME]

zurück·werfen (*sep.*) *v.t.* reflect

Zurück·werfung *f* reflection

zurück·zahlen *v.t.* (*comm.*) (*eine Schuld, Hypothek*) repay (a debt, mortgage); (*Kapital*) return (capital); (*geleistete Zahlung*) re-fund, reimburse (payment made); (*Anleihe einlösen*) redeem (a loan)

[*cf.* RÜCKZAHLUNG]

zusammendrück·bar *adj.* (*phys.*) compressible

Zusammendrückbar·keit *f* (*phys.*) compressibility

zusammen·drücken (*sep.*) *v.t.* (*phys.*) compress

Zusammen·drückung *f* (*phys.*) com-pression [*cf.* VERDICHTUNG]

zusammen·fallen (*sep.*) *v.i.* co-incide: *zusammenfallend* co-incident; *zeitlich z.* (*lassen*) syn-chronize

Zusammen·fallen *n* coincidence

zusammen·fassen (*sep.*) *v.t.* **1.** (*zu einem Ganzen*) collect, combine (in a whole): *gleichnamige Glieder z.* collect like terms; *in Klammern z.* parenthesize, collect in paren-theses [*cf.* GRUPPE]. **2.** (*sum-marisch* summarily) sum up, sum-marize: *die Regeln z.* sum up the rules

zusammen·gesetzt *adj.* composite, compound, complex: *zusam-mengesetzte Funktion* composite function; *zusammengesetzter Bruch* compound (or complex) fraction; *zusammengesetztes Pro-dukt* composite product; *zusam-mengesetzte Proportion* com-pound proportion; *zusammenge-setzte Zahl* composite number; *zusammengesetzte benannte Zahl* compound number

Zusammen·hang *m* coherence; (*eines Bereichs*) connectivity (of a region)[*cf.* VERBUNDENHEIT]

zusammen·hängen (*sep.*) *v.i.* be connected, be coherent

zusammenhängend *adj.* connected, coherent: *einfach* (*mehrfach*) *zu-*

sammenhängender Bereich simply (multiply) connected region [*cf.* VERBUNDEN]

zusammen·laufen (*sep.*) *v.i.* converge [*cf.* KONVERGENT]

Zusammen·laufen *n* (*von Linien*) convergence (of lines)

zusammen·laufend *adj.* convergent

Zusammenlegung *f* (*von Aktien*) consolidation (of shares); (*von Banken*) consolidation (or merger) of banks

zusammen·setzen (*sep.*) *v.t.* compose, compound, combine

Zusammen·setzung *f* composition, combination: Z. *von Kräften*, *Vektoren* composition of forces, vectors; Z. (*oder Komposition*) *von Elementen einer Menge* combination (or composition) of elements of a set

Zusammensetzungs·vorschrift *f* rule of combination (or composition)

zusammen·stellen (*sep.*) *v.t.* collect, compile; (*in einer Tabelle*) tabulate

Zusammen·stellung *f* table, compilation; Z. *von Punkten, Linien usw.* configuration (of points, lines, etc.)

Zusammen·stoß *m* collision [*cf.* STOSS]

zusammen·stoßen (*sep.*) *v.i.* collide

zusammen·zählen (*sep.*) *v.t.* add (together)

Zusatz·dividende *f* (*fin.*) additional (or extra) dividend

Zu·schlag *m* [= AUFSCHLAG]

zu·schlagen (*sep.*) *v.t.* (*comm.*) (*zum Preis*) [= AUFSCHLAGEN *zum* (*oder: auf den*) *Preis*]

Zustands·änderung *f* (*phys.*) change of state

Zustands·gleichung *f* (*phys.*) equation of state

zu·streben (*sep.*) *v.i.* (*dat.*) tend (to): *einem Grenzwert z.* tend to a limit

zu·treffen (*sep.*) *v.i.* hold, be valid

Zu·wachs *m* increase, increment

zu·wachsen (*sep.*) *v.i.* accrue [*cf.* ZINS]

Zuwachs·rate *f* (*statist.*) rate of increase

zwan·zig *card. num.* twenty

Zwanzig·flach *n* icosahedron

zwanzig·flächig *adj.* icosahedral

Zwanzig·flächner *m* icosahedron

zwan·zigst *ord. num.* twentieth

zwei *card. num.* two [*cf.* AUSWAHL; GERADE; HARMONISCH; JAHR; MÖGLICHKEIT; MONAT; WAHL; ZWEISTELLIG]

Zwei *f* (*Zahl, Ziffer*) (number, figure) two

zwei·achsig *adj.* biaxial, diaxial

Zwei·blatt *n* double folium [*cf.* BLATTKURVE]

zwei·deutig *adj.* ambiguous, having two meanings; (*zweiwertig*) two-valued

Zweideutig·keit *f* ambiguousness, duplicity; (*Zweiwertigkeit, auch*) two-valuedness

zwei·dimensional *adj.* two-dimensional, bidimensional [*cf.* FLÄCHE]

Zwei·dimensionalität *f* bidimensionality

Zwei·eck *n* lune: *sphärisches Z.* spherical lune [*cf.* KREISZWEIECK]

Zweier *m* (figure) two

Zweier·system *n* dyadic system

zwei·fach *adj.* double, twofold: *zweifacher Index* double subscript (e.g. a_{12}, x_{jk}) [*cf.* INTEGRAL]

Zwei·flach *n* dihedral, dihedron

zwei·flächig *adj.* dihedral, two-sided

Zwei·flächner *m* dihedral, dihedron

Zweig *m* (*einer Kurve*) branch (of a curve)

zwei·gipfelig *adj.* (*Häufigkeitskurve*) bimodal (frequency curve)

zwei·gliedrig *adj.* (*math.*) two-term(ed), binomial; (*log.*) two-place, dyadic [*cf.* EINGLIEDRIG]

Zweigliedrig·keit *f* (*eines Ausdrucks*) binomial character (of an expression); (*einer Operation*) dyadic character (of an operation) [*cf.* ZWEIGLIEDRIG]

Zweihorn·kurve *f* bicorn, cocked hat

zwei·hundert *card. num.* two hundred

zwei·mal *num.* two times, twice [*cf.* JAHR]

zwei·malig *adj.* (done) twice: *durch zweimaliges Quadrieren* by squaring twice; *zweimaliges Integral* iterated integral

Zweiparameter·schar *f* two-parameter family, bundle, sheaf

Zweipunkt·perspektive *f* two-point perspective

zwei·reihig *adj.* two-row(ed): *zweireihige Determinante* two-row(ed) determinant

zwei·schalig *adj.* of two sheets, parted [*cf.* HYPERBOLOID]

zwei·scharig *adj.* (*Regelfläche*) doubly ruled (surface) [*cf.* ERZEUGENDE]

zwei·seitig *adj.* two-sided, bilateral: *zweiseitige Fläche* two-

sided surface; *zweiseitige Symmetrie* bilateral symmetry [*cf.* IDEAL]

Zweiseitig·keit *f* two-sidedness, bilaterality

zweiseitig·symmetrisch *adj.* bilaterally symmetric(al)

zwei·spitzig *adj.* bicuspid

zwei·stellig *adj.* (*ganze Zahl*) two-figure, two-digit (integer); (*Dezimalzahl*) two-figure, two-place (decimal); (*log.: mit zwei Leerstellen*) two-place, dyadic [*cf.* FÜNFSTELLIG]

zweit *ord. num.* second: *zweiten Grades* of second degree, quadric, quadratic; *Kurve zweiten Grades* curve of second degree, quadric (curve), quadratic curve; *Kurve (oder Kegelschnitt) zweiter Ordnung* point conic; *Kurve (oder Kegelschnitt) zweiter Klasse* line conic, conic envelope; *Fläche zweiter Ordnung* surface of second order, quadric (surface), conicoid [*cf.* POLARTETRAEDER]; [*cf.* ABLEITUNG; DIFFERENTIALQUOTIENT; GEOMETRIE; JAHR; KRÜMMUNG; MONAT; POLARE; POTENZ; PROJEKTION; PROJEKTIONSEBENE; QUADRANT; SPITZE; STUFE; TAFELABSTAND]

Zweitafel·projektion *f* (*descr.*) projection on two planes, two-plane projection

Zwei·teilung *f* bisection, division in two

zweitens *adv.* secondly, in the second place

zweit·letzt *adj.* last but one, next to last

zwei·wertig *adj.* (*math.*) two-valued; (*chem.*) bivalent, divalent [*cf.* ZWEIDEUTIG]

Zweiwertig·keit *f* (*math.*) two-valuedness, duplicity; (*chem.*) bivalence, divalence [*cf.* ZWEIDEUTIGKEIT]

zwei·zählig *adj.* (*Symmetrie*) binary, twofold (symmetry)

Zwickel *m* gore: *eine Kugel kann durch Meridianebenen in schmale Z. geteilt werden* a sphere can be divided by meridian planes into narrow gores

zwie·fach *adj.* twofold, double

zwie·fältig *adj.* twofold

Zwilling *m* (*cryst.*) twin

zwischen *prep.* (*dat., acc.*) between [*cf.* LIEGEN; MITTE]

Zwischen·beziehung *f* relation of between(ness)

Zwischen·glied *n* intermediate term

Zwischen·gruppe *f* (*alg.*) intermediate group

Zwischen·körper *m* (*alg.*) intermediate field

Zwischen·raum *m* interval

Zwischen·relation *f* relation of between(ness)

Zwischen·summe *f* (*statist.*) partial sum, subtotal

Zwischen·wert *m* intermediate value

Zwischen·zeit *f* time interval

zwölf *card. num.* twelve

Zwölf·eck *n* dodecagon

zwölf·eckig *adj.* dodecagonal

Zwölfer·system *n* duodecimal system

Zwölf·flach *n* dodecahedron

zwölf·flächig *adj.* dodecahedral

Zwölf·flächner *m* dodecahedron

zwölft *ord. num.* twelfth

Zykel *m* cycle

zyklisch *adj.* cyclic, circular: *zyklische Permutation* cyclic (or circular) permutation, cycle [*cf.* KREISLAUF]

Zykloide *f* cycloid [= RADKURVE, RADLINIE]: *gestreckte* (*oder geschweifte*) *Z.* curtate cycloid (or trochoid) [*cf.* TROCHOIDE]; *verschlungene Z.* prolate cycloid

Zyklo·metrie *f* cyclometry

zyklo·metrisch *adj.* (*Funktion*) inverse trigonometric, antitrigonometric, arc-trigonometric (function) [*cf.* HAUPTWERT]

Zyklus *m* (*pl. Zyklen*) cycle

Zylinder *m* cylinder: [*cf.* ABSCHNEIDEN; ACHSE; ELLIPTISCH; ERZEUGENDE; GRUNDFLÄCHE; HYPERBOLISCH; INNER; MANTEL; MANTELLINIE; MITTELLINIE; PARABOLISCH; PROJIZIEREN; SCHNITT; SEITENLINIE; WALZE]

Zylinder·erzeugende *f* ruling (or element) of a cylinder [*cf.* MANTELLINIE]

Zylinder·funktion *f* cylindrical (or Bessel) function [*cf.* BESSEL]

Zylinder·huf *m* ungula of a cylinder

Zylinder·koordinate *f* cylindrical coordinate

Zylinder·projektion *f* (*card.*) cylindrical projection: *flächentreue Z.* cylindrical equal-area projection

Zylinder·stumpf *m*, **Zylinder·stutz** *m* ungula of a cylinder [*cf.* ABSCHNEIDEN]

zylindrisch *adj.* cylindrical: *zylindrische Koordinaten* cylindrical coordinates [*cf.* SCHRAUBENLINIE]

Zylindroid *n* cylindroid